Rhetoric in Civic Life

Rhetoric in Civic Life

second edition

Catherine Helen Palczewski
University of Northern Iowa

Richard Ice
College of St. Benedict | St. John's University

John Fritch
University of Northern Iowa

Strata Publishing, Inc.
State College, Pennsylvania

9 8 7 6 5 4 3

Rhetoric in Civic Life

Copyright © 2016, 2012 by Strata Publishing, Inc.

Strata Publishing, Inc.
P.O. 1303
State College, PA 16803
USA

Telephone: 814-234-8545

Web site: www.stratapub.com

Printed and bound in the United States by Thomson-Shore.

Photo on front cover: *Pedal Thru (Bikin' in the O-Zone)*
     © 2008 City of Philadelphia Mural Arts Program/Paul Santoleri
     Photo courtesy of the artist. Reprinted by Permission.

     More of Mr. Santoleri's work can be seen on his web site,
     www.paulsantoleri.com

Credits and acknowledgments appear on pages 307–309 and on this page by reference.

The URLs in this book were accurate as of the date cited or the date of publication. Neither the authors nor Strata guarantee the accuracy of information provided in websites listed.

ISBN: 978-1-891136-37-5

to Arnie, Jeanne, and Trudy
our partners in life
who enact with us
the possibility of disagreeing
without being disagreeable

Brief Contents

Preface   xiii

Part I: Introduction   1

   1. Rhetoric as Symbolic Action   3

Part II: Forms of Symbolic Action   39

   2. Language   41

   3. Visual Rhetoric   69

   4. Argument   99

   5. Narrative   129

Part III: Components of Symbolic Action   161

   6. Rhetors   163

   7. Audiences   199

   8. Rhetorical Situations   225

   9. Publics and Counterpublics   265

Credits and Acknowledgments   307

Index   311

About the Authors   319

Contents

Preface xiii

Part I: Introduction   1

1. Rhetoric as Symbolic Action   3

Symbolic Action and Social Reality   6
> *Symbols   6*
> *Symbolic Action   7*
> *Social Reality   12*

Rhetoric as Civic Engagement   13
> *Classical Origins   13*
> *Rhetoric as Addressed   16*
> *Civic Engagement   16*

Constraints on and Resources for Symbolic Action   20
> *Persuasive Continuum   20*
> *Culture   23*
> *Public and Collective Memory   24*
> *Power, Ideology, and Hegemony   27*

Part II: Forms of Symbolic Action   39

2. Language   41

Language and the Construction of Social Reality   42
> *Semiotics   42*
> *Linguistic Relativity   43*

Language as Symbolic Action   45
> *Terministic Screens   45*
> *Public Vocabulary   48*
> *Discursive and Presentational Forms   53*
> *Resignification   56*

The Misuse of Language   58
> *Doublespeak   58*
> *Truncated Passives   60*
> *People, Places, and Topics of Silence   61*

3. Visual Rhetoric   69
   Presence   71
   The Rise of Visual Culture   72
   Analyzing Visual and Material Rhetorics   76
   Types of Visual and Material Rhetoric   77
         Bodies   77
         Photographs   80
         Monuments, Memorials, and Museums   84
         Image Events   88

4. Argument   99
   The Place of Argument in a Civil Society   100
   Classical Conceptions   106
   The Toulmin Model   109
         Parts of Argument₁   109
         Argument Fields   116
   Presumption and Burden of Proof   117
   Spheres of Argument   119

5. Narrative   129
   Form and Function of Narratives   131
         Forming Memory   131
         Creating Culture and Community   135
   Judging Narratives   140
         Aesthetics   141
         Authorial Intent   143
         Empirical Truth   144
         Social Truth   146

Part III: Components of Symbolic Action   161

6. Rhetors   163
   Persona as Performance   165
   Facets of Persona   167
         Ethos   167
         Roles   168
         Identity   169
         Authority   175
         Image   179
   Rhetor Analyzed   181
   Rhetors in a Postmodern World   184

7. Audiences   199
      Adapting Rhetoric to Audiences   201
              Rhetoric as Addressed   201
              Appealing to an Audience   203
      Audience Agency   211
      Adapting Audiences to Rhetoric   212
              Second Persona   213
              Third Persona   214
              Indirectly Addressed Audiences   217

8. Rhetorical Situations   225
      Rhetoric as Situational   226
              Exigence   228
              Audience   229
              Constraints   231
              Fitting Response and Genre   233
              Analysis: The Challenger *Explosion   236*
      Situations as Rhetorical   239
      A Synergistic Understanding of Rhetoric and Situations   240
              Definition of the Situation   241
              Analysis: 9/11 Defined as an "Act of War"   242
              Analysis: 9/11 Redefined   245
              Analysis: 9/11 Redefined, Again   248
      Fitting Responses Reconsidered   250
              Cultural Variations and Historical Context   251
              Responses to Rhetorical Situations   252

9. Publics and Counterpublics   265
      The Public Sphere   268
              Strong and Weak Publics   270
              Hybrid Publics   272
      Publics, Counterpublics, and Transnational Publics   272
              Counterpublics   273
              Transnational Publics and Counterpublics   278
              Publics, Counterpublics, and the Economy   278
              Relationships among Publics   281
      Publics in the Internet Age   281
              "Publics" in a Digital Age   283
              Digital Participation and Access   285
              Networked Publics and the Blogosphere   290
      The Networked Public Screen   294

Credits and Acknowledgments   307

Index   311

About the Authors   319

Preface

Rhetoric in Civic Life is intended for introductory rhetorical theory courses; persuasion courses that adopt a rhetorical approach; courses on rhetoric, civic life, and civic engagement; and rhetorical criticism courses that approach criticism as an inventional practice. It could also be used for advanced rhetorical theory courses, perhaps supplemented with primary texts from core theorists.

The impetus for writing this book came from our desire for a textbook for our own courses that would approach rhetoric from a conceptual perspective, rather than unfolding chronologically or focusing on key theorists. We wanted to provide our students with a sense of the disciplinary evolution of rhetorical concepts, but with an emphasis on the concepts, rather than on who said what and when.

The impetus for the second edition was our desire to update the book to reflect recent theoretical perspectives and issues such as the role of the rhetor in a digital and postmodern world, the emergence of networked public spheres, and the importance of emotion in public life. The new edition continues our commitment to provide examples that make rhetorical theories and concepts come alive. It also continues our commitment to work closely with our peers and colleagues who have used the book, reviewed our ideas for revisions, and recommended changes for the book on the basis of their own classroom needs and experiences. We have sought to incorporate the feedback we have received in ways that would make the book accessible yet thoughtful; timely, yet building on historical as well as contemporary examples; and relevant, while also engaging the timeless concepts of rhetoric.

Our goal with this edition, as with the first, was to help students understand how rhetoric shapes and creates meaning in the full range of civic life, from the instrumental rhetoric of deliberative and electoral politics to the constitutive rhetoric of public memory and identity formation. We wanted a textbook that students would find useful and engaging, and that also presented scholarship clearly and substantively, describing complex theories with the nuance and subtlety they deserve. We reference a range of classical and contemporary theories and theorists, comparing and interweaving ideas from the rise of ancient Greek democracy (Aristotle, Plato, Isocrates, and the Sophists), to twentieth-century theorists (including Kenneth Burke, Susanne K. Langer, Lucie Olbrechts-Tyteca, and Chaïm Perelman), to the most recent cutting-edge research appearing in the discipline's books and journals. We wrote this book from the perspective that rhetoric—whether verbal, visual, argumentative, or narrative—is symbolic action with consequences and, as such, deserves careful study.

We strove for writing that is clear and concise, but not oversimplified, providing extensive documentation through endnotes. We endeavored to define terms and concepts clearly and to provide an abundance of detailed examples that would resonate with students. By including short texts and offering brief analyses that deploy the concepts covered, we attempted to show students how a rhetorical approach offers an enhanced understanding of how social reality is created, maintained, and challenged.

FEATURES OF THE BOOK

Emphasis on civic life: Although the book discusses rhetoric across its many theoretical, cultural, and practical contexts, the central emphasis is on rhetoric in civic life—not only the discourse of people in political power, but also deliberative debates about policy and cultural debates about civic identity. We wanted students to understand that all members of a public have a role to play in civic life, and to understand the range of, and limits on, each person's power. We wanted them to understand that rhetoric has consequences—particularly for identity, power, memory, and ideology—and, thus, shapes social reality.

Conceptual approach: We have attempted to provide a heuristic vocabulary that will help students make sense of rhetoric's forms, functions, and consequences. The textbook explores theories and theorists from an integrated, topical perspective. Thus, the contributions of some theorists appear in multiple chapters. We do not dictate a particular methodological approach, but rather offer a range of concepts that enable more subtle and nuanced analyses of symbolic action. The concepts should be generative; they should enable students to ask smarter questions about the symbolic actions they encounter.

Expansive range of rhetorical theories: The textbook grounds each chapter in traditional rhetorical theories, describing the core concept (rhetor, audience, argument, and so on), then extends the study of that concept by drawing from recent scholarship. For example, in the discussion of rhetors, we cover the classical conceptions of ethos, but also problematize the very notion of the rhetor with a careful consideration of the role of authorial intent in meaning making, the ways rhetors may both invent and be invented by rhetoric, and the possibility of rhetoric without rhetors in an age of algorithms. We also focus on identity as intersectional (rather than essential) and the possibilities of using strategic essentialism as a rhetorical resource. This approach enables the study of rhetorical forms from legislative debates and public address to body argument and visual rhetorics.

Detailed examples: Abundant historical and contemporary examples show how words, images, arguments, and stories have consequences. These examples include presidential speeches in times of crisis, criticisms of NSA surveillance and drone warfare, youth activism on same sex marriage and campus sexual violence, a city council meeting about whether to protect local merchants or permit "big box" stores, abolitionist speakers who caused northerners to think of slaves as suffering human beings, image events and street theatre in political protest, political campaigns, national monuments that celebrate a shared history and reinforce a shared set of values, public debates over issues such as health care and immigration, and events and issues in students' personal and campus lives.

FEATURES OF THE NEW EDITION

In the new edition, the book has been revised in response to our own classroom experiences with the book, as well as feedback from people who have used the first edition. We have also updated the book in several significant respects. The revisions include:

Expanded and clarified explanations of difficult concepts: In particular, we have expanded the discussion of the role of classical rhetoric in Chapter 1, with attention to how more recent theory has been influenced by and developed from its historical roots. We have also enhanced the explanation of power, identification, and agency, with the hope of making these complex ideas clearer to students.

Updated discussions of current theory: The second edition pays particular attention to advances in rhetorical theory over the past few years, especially the implications of posthumanist rhetorical theory of agency and the roles of rhetors (especially in Chapter 3), as well as current theory regarding public emotion (Chapter 7) and networked publics (Chapter 9).

Increased emphasis on digital discourse and social media: Reflecting the increasingly complex nature of public discourse in our mass-mediated and digitally connected world, this edition includes new discussions of networked publics, public screens, networked activism, and slacktivism; numerous examples drawn from Twitter, Facebook and YouTube campaigns; and a heightened focus on how contemporary theoreticians incorporate social media.

Updated examples: Continuing our focus on providing examples that are both timeless and timely, the new edition has numerous new examples drawn from current issues and controversies, recent events, and the manner in which people come to understand their world through rhetoric. Many of the examples that begin chapters are new. Among the new extended examples are those on NSA surveillance, same sex marriage, LeBron James' return to Cleveland, legalization of marijuana, drone warfare, youth activism on campus, and sexual violence.

ORGANIZATION OF THE BOOK

Rhetoric in Civic Life is composed of nine chapters, organized into three parts. The chapters are organized around the central facets of rhetoric's form and function. The organization of chapters is flexible; we believe instructors can teach the chapters in any order they wish, according to their own needs.

Part I, "Introduction," consists of a single chapter.

Chapter 1, "Rhetoric as Symbolic Action," defines rhetoric and explains its historical foundation in democratic traditions. It explains rhetoric as a form of symbolic action; as a central means of enacting civic engagement; and as both a creator and practice of ideology, public memory, and power. In this edition, we have expanded the discussion of the roots of current theory in classical rhetoric, endeavored to develop a keener understanding of agency as it operates in a posthumanist world, and revised the sections on power, identification, and rhetorical agency.

Part II, "Forms of Symbolic Action," includes four chapters.

Chapter 2, "Language," introduces language as symbolic action, a novel idea for many students. Drawing on theories of linguistic relativity, semiotics, and dramatism, the chapter shows that language is not merely a means by which humans transmit information; it also constitutes social reality. The chapter explores the ways that a public vocabulary forms social reality (through characterizations, metaphors, and ideographs), as well as the possibilities of resignification.

Chapter 3, "Visual Rhetoric," encourages students to ask not just "What does an image mean?" but also "What does an image do?" The chapter examines the power of four categories of visual rhetoric: iconic photographs, monuments, bodies, and image events. A new section develops the concept of presence as it relates to visual rhetoric.

Chapter 4, "Argument," describes the role of argument in civic life, the classical concept of logos, and approaches to analyzing an argument. It explores argument as a thing and as an interactional process, drawing on the Toulmin model and on theory about spheres of argument (technical, personal, and public).

Chapter 5, "Narrative," is informed by Walter Fisher's narrative paradigm and by Kenneth Burke's representative anecdote and comic/tragic frames, providing students with a critical approach to understanding narrative.

Part III, "Components of Symbolic Action," includes four chapters.

Chapter 6, "Rhetors," explores the concept of the rhetor as both producing and produced by rhetorical action. The chapter introduces students to the idea of persona and its various facets. It explains identity as a social construction and as intersectional. The second edition explores the complex roles and functions of rhetors in new ways, with particular attention to how rhetors function in a post-modern world. The role of authorial intent in meaning making, how rhetors may both invent and be invented by rhetoric, and the possibility of rhetoric without rhetors in an age of algorithms is explored.

Chapter 7, "Audiences," revisits the basic premise that rhetoric is, at its core, addressed, and that the audience is both the receiver and the product of rhetorical action. The chapter shows how when one audience is created (a second persona), another may be denied existence (a third persona), and yet another may emerge as eavesdropping or silently complicit (a fourth persona). The second edition works to build a better understanding of public emotion and audience agency.

Chapter 8, "Rhetorical Situations," takes a synergistic approach, drawing on Bitzer's discussion of the basic components of the rhetorical situation, on his argument that rhetoric is situational, and on Vatz's argument that situations are rhetorical. The chapter also explores Branham and Pearce's discussion of the various ways that a rhetor may react to a situation. In this edition, we have expanded and clarified the discussion of genre.

Chapter 9, "Publics and Counterpublics," introduces students to current theories of public sphere discourse, beginning with Habermas's basic model and incorporating current theories that recognize the possibility and productivity of multiple publics, as well as ways in which digital technologies have complicated traditional understandings of what constitutes a public and how publics emerge.

The new edition explores networked publics, networked public screens, and digital activism (and slacktivism).

PEDAGOGICAL RESOURCES

Key Concepts: Every chapter opens with a list of key concepts, each of which is highlighted and defined within the chapter. The chapter itself offers definitions of each term, followed by examples.

Discussion Questions: Each chapter ends with a series of questions, updated in this edition, that guide discussion and encourage students to apply concepts to the use of rhetoric in civic life.

Recommended Readings: Every chapter ends with a short list of recommended readings that students can use to explore the foundational literature of the field.

Instructor's Manual: The manual contains a variety of ancillary materials, including sample syllabi, discussion guides, and selected bibliographies for each concept from which additional readings can be assigned. Updated in the new edition, the instructor's manual now also includes case studies for each chapter.

ACKNOWLEDGMENTS

Scholarship is never an isolated endeavor. We are not, and should not be, confined to an ivory tower. Conversations with colleagues, fellow scholars, and friends always enliven our writing and thinking. Many of the examples and felicitous phrasings come from conversations with members of our intellectual family. In particular, we want to thank Robert Asen and Daniel Brouwer for help with all things public and counterpublic; G. Thomas Goodnight for help with all things rhetoric; Donn Parson, Arnie Madsen, and David Williams for help with all things Burke; Bettina Fabos for help with all things visual; Damien Pfister for help with all things networked; Francesca Soans for help with obscure yet perfectly apt examples; Christopher Martin for conversations about current events; Terence Check and Jeanmarie Cook for their conversations about pedagogy; Isaac West for refining our understanding of identification; Bonnie Dow and Roseann Mandziuk for correcting our misrepresentation of Sojourner Truth; Ryan McGeough for help with all things classical; Christian O. Lundberg and Joshua G. Gunn for help with all things posthumanist; Carole Blair for help with all things material and monumental; Brenda J. Allen for help with expanding the diversity of our examples; and Heather Bart for thoughtful examples. The colleagues listed above come from a range of institutions and career locations. But they all share one thing in common: Whenever we sent a message asking for a bibliography on a topic, a review of new content, a conversation about a thorny theoretical issue, a confirmation that we got their research right, or just a word of encouragement, they delivered. Richard thanks the College of St. Benedict and St. John's University for a generous sabbatical leave that enabled him to work on this book's first edition. Richard and John also would like to thank their children (Hannah, Noah, Garrett, and Byron) for being tolerant and supportive throughout this process. We thank the University of Northern Iowa and the Communication Studies department for funding student worker Justus Thompson, who helped map the examples. We also want to recognize three students who introduced us to some of the powerful new examples we used in the second edition: Nicole Brennan, Zoe Russell, and Evan Schares.

The book was transformed throughout the writing process as a result of feedback from numerous reviewers: Lin Allen, University of Northern Colorado; Jennifer Asenas, California State University, Long Beach; Linda Czuba Brigance, State University of New York, Fredonia; Bonnie Dow, Vanderbilt University; Janis L. Edwards, University of Alabama; Pat J. Gehrke, University of South Carolina; Zac Gershberg, Keene State College; Ron Greene, University of Minnesota; Judith Hendry, University of New Mexico; Jim A. Kuypers, Virginia Polytechnic Institute and State University; Lenore Langsdorf, Southern Illinois University; Noemi Marin, Florida Atlantic University; Michael McFarland, Stetson University; Jerry Miller, Ohio University; Emily Plec, Western Oregon University; Lawrence Prelli, University of New Hampshire; Jennifer Reem, Nova Southeastern University; Steven Schwarze, University of Montana; John M. Sloop, Vanderbilt University; Matthew J. Sobnosky, Hofstra University; Stacey K. Sowards, University of Texas at El Paso; Nathan Stormer, University of Maine; Richard Vatz, Towson University; and Dylan Wolfe, Clemson University. Their challenges, corrections, and questions made the book immeasurably better. Any errors that remain are ours, not theirs.

Faculty who used the first edition of the book were extremely helpful in providing feedback through survey responses and conversations about the text. This edition was shaped by their generous sharing of their experiences: Alina Haliliuc, Denison University; Brandon Inabinet, Furman University; Jack Kay, Eastern Michigan University; Ilon Lauer, Western Illinois University; Heather Lettner-Rust, Longwood University; David M. Lucas, Ohio University; Billie Murray, Villanova University; Tony Palmeri, University of Wisconsin–Oshkosh; Emily Plec, Western Oregon University; Kara Shultz, Bloomsburg University; Elizabeth Chiseri Strater, University of North Carolina–Greensboro; and Isaac West, Vanderbilt University.

We would like to extend a special thank you to Jack Kay. Jack passed away in early 2015. His influence on one of the authors, John, began when Jack was John's undergraduate director of forensics. His influence is seen in the textbook in many of the examples and understandings of rhetoric. During his final months, he helped us by providing examples and thoughts about the book and the direction of culture.

We also would like to thank the reviewers of the second edition of the text. Their insights helped shape the text in a number of wants, both in our explanations of large concepts and in our attention to detail in many of the examples: Roger Aden, Ohio University; M. Kelly Carr, University of Baltimore; Alina Haliliuc, Denison University; Janice Hamlet, Northern Illinois University; Christine Harold, University of Washington; Heather Ashley Hayes, Whitman College; Nate Kreuter, Western Carolina University; Heather Lettner-Rust,

Longwood University; Billie Murray, Villanova University; Ross Singer, Saginaw Valley State University; Gordon Stables, University of Southern California; Paul Stob, Vanderbilt University; Bryan C. Taylor, University of Colorado; Isaac West, Vanderbilt University; and Leslie Wolcott, University of Central Florida.

We also thank our editor and publisher, Kathleen Domenig, for her patience and guidance throughout the writing of this book. We are sure that working with an authorial triumvirate is an editorial nightmare. We hope the end result made the hundreds, if not thousands, of e-mails worth it.

I

Introduction

1

KEY CONCEPTS

civic engagement

collective memory

constitutive rhetoric

culture

ethos

hegemony

identification

ideology

logos

pathos

posthumanist theory
    of agency

power

public memory

rhetor

rhetoric

rhetorical agency

social reality

symbol

symbolic action

verbal symbols

visual symbols

Rhetoric as Symbolic Action

Human beings make sense of their inter-actions with the world and with each other through the symbols (words and images) they attach to their experiences. Words (language) and images (icons, pictures, photos, bodies, architectural structures) are not merely a means to transmit information, they are the grounds for the judgments people make about things, events, and other people. Quite simply, symbols matter.

How many people do you know who went home from grade school crying because of something another person said or a mean picture another person drew? Even if some children shouted, "Sticks and stones may break my bones, but words will never hurt me" through tear-stained faces, they recognized the immense power of words and symbols to hurt.

Words posted online are equally powerful. The story of Phoebe Prince, a fifteen-year-old who was cyberbullied and committed suicide in 2010, demonstrates how hurtful words can be.[1] You have probably encountered other stories of people who were cyberbullied on Facebook or other social media sites, and resorted to suicide. But the words on such sites can also be used for good. Facebook posts were used to identify a New Jersey teenager whom police then persuaded not to commit suicide.[2] Employers use Facebook and LinkedIn to examine potential employees. The things people say (and the words they post on the Internet) matter.

Symbols matter. Your professional self-image is influenced by how others describe you. If you have received a positive job review, you know the power of words to make you feel better about yourself. People's symbol

3

use makes a difference in interpersonal relationships, too. If you grew up in the United States and have been in a serious relationship, you know the power of the words "I love you" or the significance of a gold band worn on the ring finger. Most people do not speak the words lightly. The symbolism of a ring extends far beyond the typical meaning of an expensive gift of jewelry.

People's symbol use also makes a difference in public communication. The words of public figures, as well as symbols of citizenship, possess the power to lead, reflect, inspire, praise, unite, confront, provoke, and entertain.

Words led a nation to reflect on the effects of racism when Martin Luther King, Jr., at the 1963 March on Washington, said, "I have a dream that one day on the red hills of Georgia, the sons of former slaves and the sons of former slave owners will be able to sit down together at the table of brotherhood."[3]

Words spoken from a very particular body inspired the world to fight for education when Malala Yousafzai, the youngest Nobel Laureate in history, delivered her Nobel Prize acceptance speech. After the Taliban took over Pakistan's Swat Valley, Yousafzai, then a fifteen-year-old schoolgirl and already an activist for girl's education, was shot in the face by a gunman who boarded her school bus and asked for her by name. In her speech, she described the changes that the Swat Valley had undergone, then the changes she had experienced as a schoolgirl:

> Girls were stopped from going to school. When my world suddenly
> changed, my priorities changed too. I had two options. One was to
> remain silent and wait to be killed. And the second was to speak up
> and then be killed. I chose the second one. I decided to speak up. . . .
> The terrorists tried to stop us and attacked me and my friends . . . on
> our school bus in 2012, but neither their ideas nor their bullets could
> win. We survived. And since that day, our voices have grown louder and
> louder. I tell my story, not because it is unique, but because it is not.
> It is the story of many girls.[4]

Words praised sacrifice and outlined a course for the future when Abraham Lincoln, in his remarks at the Gettysburg battlefield in 1863, said, "But in a larger sense we cannot dedicate, we cannot consecrate, we cannot hallow this ground. The brave men, living and dead, who struggled here, have consecrated it far above our power to add or detract."[5] Theodore Sorensen, speech writer for President John F. Kennedy, described Lincoln's Gettysburg Address as the "greatest example of American public speech."[6]

Words united a nation when President George W. Bush, on September 11, 2001, said, "None of us will ever forget this day, yet we go forward to defend freedom and all that is good and just in our world."[7]

Words confronted a nation when Malcolm X, speaking out against the Senate filibuster of the Civil Rights Act of 1964, said "No, if you never see me another time in your life, if I die in the morning, I'll die saying one thing: the ballot or the bullet, the ballot or the bullet."[8]

Because images matter, too, people debate the appropriateness of visual representations. Visual symbols can enrage and provoke, as when

Andres Serrano placed a crucifix in a jar of urine as a work of art.[9] Images can also misrepresent. After model Paulina Gretzky appeared on the April 2014 cover of *Golf Digest* wearing only a white sports bra and matching yoga pants, members of the Ladies' Professional Golf Association were frustrated. Gretzky is not a professional player; her link to golf is that she is engaged to a professional golfer and is the daughter of hockey great Wayne Gretzky. The two other women who had most recently appeared on the cover were a Golf Channel anchor and a *Sports Illustrated* swimsuit cover model. In total, only eleven women had appeared on the cover since 1969. Stacy Lewis, the top-ranked US female player explained, "It's frustrating for female golfers. . . . Obviously, *Golf Digest* is trying to sell magazines. But at the same time you'd like to see a little respect for the women's game."[10] Another veteran golfer asked, "Who are they trying to sell to?"[11]

What people communicate, and how they communicate it, has real effects on others and their perceptions. People cannot know what things or events mean until they have the symbols to attach meaning to them.

Because symbols have power and those symbols are grounded in ideas, people can use them to induce others to take ethical, as well as unethical, actions. During World War II, Winston Churchill, considered one of the greatest English-speaking orators, delivered speeches to the British people to rally them to defend democracy and to US audiences to encourage them to become involved in the war. In the wake of British Prime Minister Neville Chamberlain's appeasement of Adolf Hitler on September 30, 1938, and German troops' occupation of the Sudetenland on October 15, Churchill, who at that time served no official role in the British government, sought to persuade the United States to defend democracy. On October 16 he warned, "The lights are going out. . . . We need the swift gathering of forces to confront not only military but moral aggression." He appealed to "English-speaking peoples" and "all the nations, great and small, who wish to walk with them. Their faithful and zealous comradeship would almost between night and morning clear the path of progress and banish from all our lives the fear which already darkens the sunlight to hundreds of millions of men."[12] He painted Hitler's forces as a darkness, smothering the lights of freedom; only the help of the United States could guarantee that Europeans would again see the sunlight of living in a free land. Churchill's speeches would help frame understandings of what the war in Europe meant to people living in the United States.

At the same time, Adolph Hitler was deftly persuading the German people to engage in horrific crimes against humanity and to wage total war. Using the metaphor of disease, Hitler explained on April 1, 1939: "Only when this Jewish bacillus infecting the life of peoples has been removed can one hope to establish a cooperation amongst the nations which shall be built up on a lasting understanding."[13] The vileness of this metaphor becomes clear in Hitler's call for an absolute eradication of the "Jewish bacillus" in order to save the German fatherland from disease. Infection can only be stopped when all the infection is removed. His use of language was dastardly as it sought the "perfection" of an Aryan nation. For Hitler, the Aryan race could only be saved if all Jewish people were eradicated.

These examples illustrate why rhetoric is profoundly important to civic society. **Rhetoric** is *the use of symbolic action by human beings to share ideas, enabling them to work together to make decisions about matters of common concern and to construct social reality.* Rhetoric is the means by which people make meaning of and affect the world in which they live. We use the term **rhetor** to mean *any person, group, or institution that uses symbolic action.*

Rhetoric can enlighten and confuse, reveal and hide. Churchill and Hitler both used rhetoric, but for very different purposes. Accordingly, the study of rhetoric involves not only an assessment of its effects (both Churchill and Hitler were effective) but also of its ethics. (Churchill sought to defend freedom; Hitler sought the genocidal destruction of an entire people.)

In this book, we introduce you to concepts that will help you understand rhetoric and civic life. This chapter offers a foundational vocabulary you will need to understand, analyze, and creatively and ethically use rhetoric. We began by defining rhetoric as symbolic action that constructs reality. We will now explore rhetoric as the central means by which you engage in action in civil society, where you participate in public decision-making and culture formation. Finally, we will outline some constraints on and resources for rhetoric.

SYMBOLIC ACTION AND SOCIAL REALITY

In this section, we will look at two of the important elements of the definition of rhetoric: symbols and action. We will then discuss how rhetoric actively constructs social reality.

Symbols

A **symbol** is *an arbitrary representation of something else, a word, an image, or an artifact that represents a thing, thought, or action.* The symbol $ represents the US dollar, although the symbol ∂ could just have easily been used. The US flag represents the nation and its values; a cross, belief in a Christian faith; a Star of David, in Judaism; and a crescent moon, in Islam. Sports teams are often identified by their mascots or symbols. Most of those symbols are arbitrary. The logo of the Alabama Crimson Tide is an elephant![14] Many sports teams have been represented by various logos or symbols over the years. For instance, the Nebraska Cornhuskers were originally the Nebraska Bug Eaters. The logo for the Kansas Jayhawks has changed at least six times over the years.[15] These symbols or logos could have been almost anything. However, fans of the Crimson Tide, the Cornhuskers, or the Jayhawks typically feel strong connections to those symbols.

Symbols can be verbal, visual, or multisensory. **Verbal symbols** are *symbols found in language* (whether spoken or written). Every word is a symbol insofar as it stands for something other than itself. When you use the term "dog," the word stands for an animal in the canine family. Other languages also have words for "dog" (perro/perra, suka, псина, 狗, chien, cane, hund, گس), so symbols are by nature human constructions rather than innate to the things symbolized. Although people often think of symbols as abstractions, they may not think of words as symbolic. Yet, language is inherently a symbol system, with written languages' use of alphabets and spoken languages' use of sounds to form words that name and represent things, ideas, and people. Every word you use is a symbol.

Visual symbols are *symbols such as pictures, images, objects, artifacts, and actions.* Examples include photographs, religious icons, tattoos, statues, flags, bodies, movies, YouTube clips, and even the acts of bowling or saluting. The US flag is a banner of three colors sewn together, yet when people look at it, they often think of it as representing the nation. During the 2008 presidential campaign, Barack Obama was criticized because he did not wear a US flag pin on his lapel.[16] The pin was seen as more than a piece of metal or an ornament; it was seen as representing patriotism and a commitment to the United States.

The key function of any symbol is that it conveys meaning. Although scholars for many years confined the study of rhetoric to the study of verbal symbols, they now recognize the importance of visual symbols.[17]

The meaning of a symbol is not the same for everyone. The fluidity of meaning is clear even when you consider language-based symbols. For example, the word "Apple" can refer to either a fruit or a technology company. If the word is used to refer to the technology company, people will still have quite different responses to it. Some people will stand in line for hours to buy the newest Apple products because they believe the company is innovative, cutting edge, and cool. Some are quite hostile to the company and would never buy an Apple product. Others are indifferent.

Although we describe verbal and visual symbols separately, almost all symbolic action is a mix of verbal and visual symbols. People listen to—and watch—speeches. People read—and look at—magazines and websites. People hear—and gaze at—movies.

Symbolic Action

When people use symbols, they engage in action. Our definition of rhetoric as symbolic action makes clear that humans use symbols to engage in actions with consequences. For example, when people exchange marriage vows and rings in a wedding ceremony, their actions create a new social relationship. The symbolic actions that compose a marriage ceremony (clothing, ring, vows, witnesses) create meaning beyond the wedding license the couple signs.

Things around you engage in motion: trees are moved by the wind, water by the tide, and earth by quakes. What distinguishes human action from these motions is that human action involves some level of intent and can be communicated about and reflected upon.[18] Human beings act on their environment in a variety of ways, such as walking, driving, planting a garden, and eating food. All these actions are instrumental—specific actions taken in order to cause an effect. Human action is almost always more than instrumental, however; it is also expressive and meaning-making.

Symbolic action is *expressive human action, the rhetorical mobilization of symbols to act in the world.* Symbolic actions include, but are not limited to, speeches, silent marches, movies, documentaries, plays, blogs, newspaper articles, advertisements, photographs, sit-ins, personal testimony, monuments, YouTube videos, tweets, Facebook posts, and street theatre. People act in the world through symbol use that induces cooperation, generates identification, produces division, enables persuasion, and constitutes identity. Thus, when people study rhetoric, they need to ask not only what a rhetorical action *means*, but also what it *does*. Because rhetoric is the study of symbolic action, it studies not only symbols and their meaning, but also their consequences.[19]

Rhetoric is constitutive, not just a tool of persuasion. Literary and legal scholar James Boyd White defines **constitutive rhetoric** as *the "art of constituting character, community, and culture in language."*[20] As communication scholar James Jasinski writes, constitutive rhetoric works by inviting an "audience to experience the world in certain ways."[21]

Identity, whether it is the speaker's or the audience's, is rhetorically constructed rather than some unchanging and innate sense of self, group, and nation. Thus, rhetoric scholar Maurice Charland says, students of rhetoric should ask "how those in Athens [or Texas, the United States, or the Ukraine] come to experience themselves as Athenians [or Texans, Americans, or Ukrainians (or Russians)]."[22] In his discussion of constitutive rhetoric, Charland explains that "the very boundary of whom the term [people] includes and excludes is rhetorically constructed."[23] A particular identity may actually exclude some from membership. Sometimes the very identity is based on exclusions, or on what Judith Butler and others refer to as the "constitutive outside."[24] For example, in his 2013 inaugural address, President Robert Mugabe constituted Zimbabweans as people who "follow African values here. We follow our conscience."[25] But perhaps more than their African values, he suggested, what most identified Zimbabweans was that they were not Western. (His speech mentioned "odd Western countries . . . the vile ones whose moral turpitude we must mourn," "America and her illegal sanctions," and "Anglo-Saxons who dare contradict Africa's verdict".) Zimbabweans were more clearly constituted by what they *were not*, according to Mugabe, than by any sense of particular character, or what they *were*. An understanding of symbolic action as constitutive encourages thinking about how rhetoric creates people's understanding of themselves, their relations to each other, and the world. According to Jasinski, it moves the effects of rhetoric "beyond a narrow causal model of influence."[26]

The power of rhetoric to shape people's ideas of themselves, each other, and the world around them inspired rhetorical critic Kenneth Burke, an influential twentieth-century scholar, to define human beings as the "symbol-using (symbol-making, symbol-misusing) animal."[27] Thus, the study of rhetoric provides insights into what it means to be human. For Burke, rhetoric is rooted in *"the use of language as a symbolic means of inducing cooperation in beings that by nature respond to symbols."*[28] Humans use symbols to interact with one another in order to work together to make decisions about matters of common concern.

Identification. For Burke, the primary aspect of rhetoric as symbolic action is **identification,** *a communicative process through which people are unified into a whole on the basis of common interests or characteristics.*[29] To make decisions about matters of common concern, people need to be able to identify what they have in common. According to Burke, once "their interests are joined, A is *identified* with B."[30]

Although attention to "persuasion" long dominated studies of rhetoric, "identification" functions as a key term for what is known as "the new rhetoric."[31] With identification, the focus is less on how one person can "deliberate[ly] design" symbolic action to persuade other people, and more on how symbolic actions "spontaneously, intuitively, and often unconsciously act upon" people to create a sense of collective identity.[32]

Identification does not automatically exist; it is created through symbolic action. For Burke, the creation of identification is an essential characteristic of rhetoric and an integral element of persuasion. He writes: "there is no chance of keeping apart the meaning of persuasion, identification ('consubstantiality') and communication (the nature of rhetoric as 'addressed' [to other people])."[33]

Identification can be created on the basis of identity characteristics over which a person has limited control (sex, race, class, sexual orientation, etc.) or on the basis of common interests (such as improving elementary and secondary education, lowering college tuition, or ending discrimination). Although Burke notes that "in forming ideas of our personal identity, we spontaneously identify ourselves with family, nation, political or cultural cause, church and so on," he also recognizes that rhetors induce listeners to feel identification with them;[34] the rhetor and audience become "consubstantial," or "substantially one."[35]

Burke does not mean that they become identical. Rather, he explains, when identification makes a person "substantially one" with another, "at the same time [the person] remains unique, an individual locus of motives. Thus, [the person] is both joined and separate, at once a distinct substance and consubstantial with another."[36] Identification "does not deny [people's] distinctness."[37] People often assume identification means that people who identify with one another are identical, but in a complex society, such a perspective on collective and collaborative action is doomed to fail. For example, a metaphor often used for the people of the United States is "melting pot," which implies that all the people who come here are blended into an indistinguishable mass. In fact, many different cultures are still evident. As Burke makes clear, identification maintains distinctions even as it creates a sense of unity.

Communication professor Isaac West suggests we can understand how people seek to share identification through citizenship by thinking about "wholeness, as opposed to oneness."[38] Distinct people, when they identify with one another, become a consubstantial *whole*, not an indistinguishable *one*. Thus, he argues, when people seek to identify on the basis of shared citizenship, they do not have to "rely on an either/or logic of assimilation" or radical difference. Instead, they can think of citizenship as "both/and": a person might "desire to be a citizen like everyone else even as an individual wants to preserve his or her difference."[39] Thus, alternative metaphors such as "quilt" or "mosaic" may make more sense than "melting pot" to represent the shared US identity.

People can communicate and persuade most effectively when they induce their audiences to identify with them. For example, nineteenth-century abolitionist Angelina Grimké Weld used identification when she faced mob violence in Philadelphia on May 16, 1838, during her speech to an antislavery convention. Her challenge to the audience was to consider whether they wanted to identify with her and the slaves, or with the angry mob outside. Historian Gerda Lerner reports that while Grimké Weld was being introduced to the audience of three thousand men and women, "bricks crashed through the windows and glass fell to the floor."[40] As she spoke, the mob outside the hall grew increasingly agitated, throwing stones and screaming during her hour-long speech. Although the audience inside the hall was receptive to her message because they already opposed slavery, the mob outside felt threatened by her argument that slavery was not an objective fact, but an immoral choice. Not wanting the mob to weaken her audience's resolve, Grimké Weld artistically turned the mob response into proof that slavery should be abolished. She challenged the audience to use their fear of the mob as a basis for identifying with slaves' fear of violence from their masters:

> What is a mob? What would the breaking of every window be? What would the levelling of this Hall be? Any evidence that we are wrong, or that slavery is a good and wholesome institution? What if the mob should now burst in upon us, break up our meeting and commit violence upon our persons—would this be anything compared with what the slaves endure? No, no: and we do not remember them "as bound with them" [Heb. 13:3], if we shrink in the time of peril, or feel unwilling to sacrifice ourselves, if need be, for their sake. (*Great noise.*) I thank the Lord that there is yet life left enough to feel the truth, even though it rages at it— that conscience is not so completely seared as to be unmoved by the truth of the living God.[41]

By comparing the threat of mob violence to the constant threat of violence under which slaves lived, she used the moment to induce her audience to identify with the slaves.[42] Her argument was not that whites' experience was identical to the slaves', but that all, white and black, free and slave, were part of a larger whole of humanity.

Identification that provides a sense of wholeness can bring people together to address and solve common concerns. Identification based on a sense of oneness, though, can separate people by constructing "us" versus "them" social realities. If being identical is required for identification, then any difference becomes suspect. For instance, Adolf Hitler induced non-Jewish German people to identify themselves as members of a superior race, an Aryan nation, thus dividing them from Jewish German people.

Identification can function for good or ill, unity or division. It can be used to recognize common concerns or disguise them, to solve common concerns or create new concerns.

Agency. Because rhetoric is an action, when you study rhetoric you study how people rhetorically act on each other, as well as how rhetoric acts on people. In other words, you study **rhetorical agency,** which rhetoric scholar Karlyn Kohrs Campbell defines as *"the capacity to act, that is, to have the competence to speak or write [or engage in any form of symbolic action] in a way that will be recognized or heeded by others in one's community."*[43] Individuals are capable of intentional symbolic action, not just unintentional motion, but that action occurs within a larger web of symbolic action that may help or hinder willingness to recognize or heed other people's messages. Being "recognized or heeded" by others in the community is affected by many things, including who is considered to compose the community, previous rhetorical actions, communication technologies, public vocabularies, and shared social values.

For many years, approaches to rhetorical agency came from the humanist tradition, which focuses on an ideal of an autonomous agent engaging in action.[44] In this tradition, people studied individual speakers to see what choices they made and how those choices influenced other choices. More recently, rhetorical scholars have recognized that no human is an island. Because humans are not isolated from one another or from history, rhetorical agency is better understood as existing within a larger system of interactions. As rhetoric scholar Christian O. Lundberg notes, "the human is not the only or even primary agent in the rhetorical situation."[45]

Scholars who begin with such a view operate within the **posthumanist theory of agency,** which, English scholar Sarah Hallenbeck explains, is *a theory that "rejects the human agent as the primary source of change but redeems that agent as a participant in the larger network of which he or she is a part."* She claims that individuals do not make choices that directly influence other humans. Instead, the choices an individual makes are circumscribed by a variety of factors, ranging from socioeconomic conditions, to language constraints, to the people with whom the individuals are interacting. As Hallenbeck explains, "Hence, agency occurs not solely within the realm of human intention or as the direct result of human action but somewhat outside of human control."[46]

Put simply, much is outside the control of rhetors. To understand rhetoric, scholars must account for the factors over which rhetors lack control and also for the factors that control the rhetor. The theories that incorporate these assumptions are called posthumanist, to make clear that rhetorical scholars should move beyond an exclusive focus on the individual human agent and, instead, attend to the multiple forces at play in rhetorical agency. Thinking about agency as a complex interplay of forces means you should study how the rhetor came to be perceived as the rhetor, and how symbolic action circulates through groups of people, structures of language, technology, and other things[47] that constrain, produce, and condition the possibility for the human to be an agent.

The posthumanist nature of rhetoric is readily apparent. During the early stages of the campaign for the 2016 Republican presidential nomination, candidate Ted Cruz repeatedly told a joke about Vice President Joe Biden: "Joe Biden. You know the nice thing? You don't need a punch line." However, when he told the joke in early June 2015, he received a very negative reaction from Twitter users and the press. The situation had changed: Joe Biden's son, Beau, had died of brain cancer days earlier.[48] Cruz's joke illustrates several aspects of a posthumanist view. First, the communicator (Cruz) does not directly control the meaning of his words. Cruz likely intended a harmless joke, but his words were not received that way. Second, audiences only control a portion of the meaning of any given set of words. Various audiences shape and reshape the meaning of the original words. Prior to the death of Biden's son, the words were considered to be a joke rather than offensive. After his death, audiences were less likely to consider the words to be funny. Finally, the context in which the words are uttered and the words themselves control a portion of the meaning. In this instance, the situation changed the meaning of the words for many audiences.

Social Reality

Rhetoric is more than a means to transmit information or persuade. When people engage in symbolic action, they participate in the construction of social reality. Saying that rhetoric "constructs social reality" does not mean that people and things do not exist prior to human symbolic action. Rather, we are saying that the *meaning* people ascribe to the things in their world is not predetermined, but created by symbolic action. Although people may know things exist apart from their symbol systems, they cannot know what those things mean or how to react to them except through the symbol system. Thus, social reality is constructed—it is made and not given. It is created interactively.

Sociologist Peter Berger explains how, through language, humans impose order on reality.[49] People have individual experiences, but they classify those experiences in social terms. For example, a culture might have a sacred tree. The physical reality is that a plant exists, but the sacredness of the tree is socially constructed; members of the society agree that the tree is sacred and, through the use of symbols, communicate the importance of the tree to others in that society. The use of language orders (makes sense of) the physical reality.

Social reality is *reality as understood through the symbols humans use to represent it*. People create social reality as they name objects, actions, and each other. Although a material world exists from which human beings receive sensory data, they do not know how to interact with that world until symbolic action gives meaning to their sense data. People's only access to reality is through symbols.

Communication scholar Barry Brummett argues that "experience is sensation plus meaning" and "reality is meaning."[50] For example, a study in the *Journal of Consumer Research* found that calling a dish *pasta* rather than a *salad* (even though the ingredients are identical) leads dieters (who are motivated to identify "forbidden foods") to "perceive the item to be less healthful and less tasty than do nondieters."[51] Similar effects were found comparing perceptions of the terms "candy chews" and "fruit chews." The researchers found "the effect of food name on perceptions of healthfulness is pervasive; it does not subside with the presentation of pictures of food items and their ingredients, nor does it diminish when consumers have an opportunity to consume the product."[52] The name determines the meaning of the sensations, regardless of sensory input of taste, sight, smell, and touch, and regardless of people's objective knowledge of ingredients.

Visual communication scholar Kevin Michael DeLuca argues that people should understand rhetoric as "discerning [studying] and deploying [using] the available contingent means of constructing, maintaining, and transforming social reality in a particular context."[53] In other words, symbolic action—words, images, and artifacts—construct, maintain, and transform social reality. Imagine if you lived in a world devoid of symbolic action. You could not speak, take photos, upload video on YouTube, draw, pray, or engage in any action with symbolic importance. You also could not read, listen to music, watch videos, or receive others' symbolic actions. This world would not be total sensory deprivation, but it would be deprivation of all stimuli related to communication. Would you still feel human? Would you still possess the characteristics that make you human? Would you know how to act in the world or react to others? Symbolic action is not just an instrumental means to transmit information, it is central to making meaning of, and in, the world.

RHETORIC AS CIVIC ENGAGEMENT

Our definition of rhetoric focuses on the use of symbolic action to identify and solve issues of common concern and to construct social reality. A key aspect of that definition is that rhetoric is a social activity, meaning that it occurs among people. Thus, rhetoric has always been linked to social action and civic engagement.

Classical Origins

The word "rhetoric" comes from the ancient Greek word *rhetor*, which meant "public speaker." Thus, historically the term "rhetoric" referred to the art of public speaking.[54] Classicist George A. Kennedy explains that rhetoric was a civic art in ancient Greece and is a phenomenon of all human societies; and that every communicative act is rhetorical in that it attempts to persuade someone.[55] Expanding on the original Greek definition, as we note earlier in this chapter, we use the term **rhetor** to mean *any person, group, or institution that uses symbolic action.*

The academic study of rhetoric can be traced back to ancient Athens, where many prominent thinkers and educators focused on it because citizens (adult males who were not slaves and whose parents were both Athenian) needed to understand rhetoric to participate in political, economic, social, and legal structures. Athens's political system of direct democracy allowed citizens the right to engage in civic discussion. When the Assembly met to discuss laws or issues of war, every citizen who had completed his military training was a voting member and had the right to speak and vote. All citizens needed to be prepared to speak as members of the legislative body. Economically, business relied on a system of negotiation and bartering. Socially, citizens spent leisurely afternoons at the gymnasium, a facility devoted not only to athletics, but also to discussions of art, poetry, politics, and gossip. They spent evenings at dinner parties called *symposia*, where a man could be selected by lot to serve as the toastmaster for the evening, or be called on to deliver toasts or tell stories.

The legal system of Athens required rhetorical skill because it used juries, usually comprised of 201 to 501 citizens (but sometimes up to 2,001), depending on the importance of the case.[56] The legal system did not include lawyers; if someone was wronged or accused of wrongdoing, he spoke to the jury directly. (If a female of the citizen class was accused of wrongdoing, her closest male relative spoke for her.)[57] All citizens had to be able to speak effectively in front of the court.

The importance of rhetoric in Athens led to the careful study of rhetoric. It also led to disagreements about its role, which continue to the present time: What is the fundamental nature of rhetoric? Is rhetoric good, evil, or indifferent?

One group maintained that rhetoric was for the most part evil. Plato and his teacher Socrates are most commonly associated with this line of thinking. They believed that people used rhetoric to obscure truth and justice, and that one could only come to know the truth through the use of philosophical methods, including Socratic dialogue. According to Socrates, people often used rhetoric to make the weaker case seem the stronger. Socrates and Plato both maintained that rhetoric could be used to avoid a just punishment or lead a democracy to make poor decisions. Partially as a result of his teachings, and partially as a result of the rhetoric used against him in the trial, Socrates was convicted and sentenced to death.[58]

Plato subsequently wrote several dialogues exploring rhetoric. In one of them, *Gorgias,* he recounted a debate between Socrates and Gorgias about the ethics of rhetoric, in which Socrates warned that rhetoric is a form of flattery and that people would misuse rhetoric for selfish or corrupt ends. In this dialogue, Plato argued that rhetoric, as practiced in a democracy, leads to poor decision making. Good ideas, he said, were only known by the wisest of leaders and not through public deliberation. He maintained that rhetoric could be used to deceive the masses in a democracy and failed to teach virtue.

In contrast to Plato and Socrates were the Sophists. The Sophists taught people to be better public speakers and, on occasion, would write speeches for people who needed to give them.[59] They maintained that the study of rhetoric was essential to citizenship in the Athenian democracy. In summarizing the tradition of the Sophists, communication scholar John Poulakos suggests that their definition of rhetoric would be: "Rhetoric is the art which seeks to capture in opportune moments that which is appropriate and attempts to suggest that which is possible."[60] Sophists such as Protagoras and Gorgias believed rhetoric was an art that could both delight and induce belief. The right thing spoken at the right time could entertain, even as it formed people's knowledge.

After Plato and the Sophists, two people influenced the study of rhetoric in late fourth-century BCE Athens: Aristotle and Isocrates. Aristotle, who was Plato's student, developed a different view of rhetoric that was based on some of Plato's thoughts. An extremely influential philosopher and scientist, he is considered one of the founders of Western philosophy. One of the most influential writings on rhetoric in ancient Greece was his fourth-century BCE treatise, *On Rhetoric.*[61]

Because rhetoric had utility, Aristotle systematized it. He defined rhetoric as "an ability in each [particular] case, to see the available means of persuasion."[62]

Notice that the definition says that rhetoric is an *ability to see.* Thus, the use of rhetoric requires analysis of a situation in order to determine how to persuade. For Aristotle, a rhetorical situation "consists of three things: a speaker and a subject on which he [or she] speaks and someone addressed, and the objective of the speech relates to the last."[63] Rhetoric is addressed to particular people, on particular occasions, in particular times and societies, about particular issues. Because rhetoric is specific to each particular situation, it is distinct from philosophy, which studies universals.

Persuasion plays a prominent role in Aristotle's definition insofar as a rhetor uses rhetorical proofs to persuade an audience. Aristotle identified three types of artistic proofs used in persuasion: **ethos**—*that which is "in the character of the speaker"*; **pathos**—*that which leads the audience "to feel emotion"*; and **logos**—*that which relies on "argument itself, by showing or seeming to show something."*[64] Although Aristotle noted the importance of the reasoned appeals of logos, he also made clear the importance of ethos and pathos. He argued that ethos was the most effective form of proof because an audience who trusted the rhetor would be more receptive to the message. Conversely, if an audience did not trust the rhetor, then the rhetor's use of logos and pathos would be ineffective. Aristotle also pointed out that audiences make decisions based on their state of mind, not only on the basis of reasoned appeals. Because emotions play a significant role in the human experience, pathos appeals are an important part of rhetoric. Many decisions people make are based on emotions, taste, and individual preferences. These decisions are not necessarily irrational. A person's favorite color is based on personal preference. All the logical arguments in the world may not change that preference, but that does not make the preference wrong.

Just as Aristotle followed in Plato's footsteps, many scholars see Isocrates as following in the Sophists' footsteps and offering significant corrections to some of their ideas. Like the Sophists, Isocrates taught for money; he believed rhetoric itself was neither moral nor immoral; and he believed that students (rather than teachers) were responsible for the manner in which rhetoric was used.[65] Unlike the Sophists, however, he argued that rhetoric was a practical tool. Rhetoric, when combined with an understanding of history, could be used to assist in making decisions about affairs of state.[66] The goal, for Isocrates, was to educate "pupils to see beyond their own interests and to serve Athens . . . selfishlessly [*sic*]."[67]

The disagreement between the Sophists and Platonists persists in contemporary times. You have probably heard someone refer to an argument as "sophistry" or "mere rhetoric." Presidential rhetoric and Supreme Court decisions have been called "sophistry."[68]

Plato's attacks gave the Sophists gave a bad name, but contemporary understandings of rhetoric are much closer to that of the Sophists and Isocrates than to Plato's. We, the authors, find ourselves closely aligned with the sophistic definition of rhetoric as the art of capturing the right thing to say in the right moment, of determining what is appropriate and possible, and of being able to teach people to use and understand rhetoric better. We are also aligned with Isocrates's notion that rhetoric is a practical tool.

The controversy between the Platonists and the Sophists over the nature of truth also continues today. Some people maintain that an absolute truth exists and simply needs to be discovered. For instance, some people believe the Bible is the inerrant word of God and contains absolute truth by which all people should live. Other people view truth and justice as things that change, based on conditions and time. The notion that divorce is now acceptable to many people, but once was not, is an example of changing ethical standards. Given our earlier discussion of social reality, you will not be surprised that we have difficulty with Plato's notion of fixed and immutable truth.

Plato, Aristotle, the Sophists, and Isocrates do seem to agree that rhetoric is important in a democracy. (This was one reason Plato rejected democracy as the ideal form of government.) History demonstrates that this belief is correct. Where democracy is strong, the study of rhetoric is vibrant. Where non-democratic government prevails, the study of rhetoric either disappears or is taught as merely a form of entertainment.

Rhetoric as Addressed

For Aristotle, the audience determines the objective of rhetoric. For Burke, rhetoric's "nature as addressed" to others is one of its definitive characteristics (in addition to identification).[69] Humans engage in symbolic action in order to communicate with one another. Rhetoric always involves an audience, even if that audience is not immediately present. Thus, the making of meaning is interactive and intersubjective. To construct, maintain, and transform reality requires the existence of others, of audiences.

Given that rhetors and audiences coproduce meaning, agency belongs not only to rhetors, but also to audiences. Agency includes the ability to construct and interpret symbolic actions, and to take action in response to those interpretations. Campbell describes agency as "communal, social, cooperative, and participatory and, simultaneously, constituted and constrained by the material and symbolic elements of context and culture."[70] In other words, people make meaning through a social, and not just individual, process. When you interpret messages or decode images, you do not do so only with resources you alone possess. Instead, you rely on a complex set of contextual and cultural symbols.

Rhetoric is an action that creates meaning, informing human beings about how to understand and react to the world. It is not merely a mechanism of information transmission, but a means by which human beings construct social reality. The political, personal, and meaning-creating functions highlight how rhetoric affects what laws are passed, how people see themselves, and what people think they know. Consequently, rhetoric is essential to a democratic society.

Civic Engagement

Civic engagement is *people's participation in individual or collective action to develop solutions to social, economic, and political challenges in their* *communities, states, nations, and world.* Examples include talking with others about ballot initiatives or pending legislation, using social networking sites for activism, volunteering with community organizations, participating in parades (whether celebratory or protest), working for electoral campaigns, wearing a T-shirt with a political message, signing petitions, voting, writing letters to the editor, engaging in buycotts and boycotts, and posting to blogs. Change (and maintenance) of social, political, and economic structures is accomplished through civic engagement, and civic engagement is accomplished through rhetoric.

Rhetoric scholar Gerard A. Hauser reviewed the scholarly research on why citizens engage in civic action in their communities, and concluded that the absolutely necessary requirement for "a well-functioning civic community is engagement in the . . . rhetoric of civil society."[71] In any democracy, whether it is direct (like Athens) or representative (like the United States), rhetors must understand how to frame ethical and effective appeals, and audiences need to understand how to see through manipulative appeals.

The use of rhetoric is not confined to people campaigning for office, nor are citizens' roles in rhetorical action confined to membership in audiences. Civic engagement helps each person understand who she or he is. Rhetoric scholar Bruce Gronbeck argues that "Civic engagement . . . is as much a matter of understanding the building and maintenance of political identity . . . as it is about getting legislation passed."[72] People use rhetoric as they develop identity (as individuals and citizens) and determine what should be done (by them as individuals and for them through legislation). They use rhetoric as they develop conceptions of themselves as individuals, group members, and citizens, all of whom can make a claim on others and on the government to act legislatively.

Civic engagement was long defined in terms of what people did when participating in civil society. Citizenship was defined narrowly in terms of the specific acts of voting and civic organization membership.[73] Research using this *what* approach tends to see civic engagement as on the decline, as fewer people vote or belong to civic organizations. Rhetoric scholar Robert Asen is not so pessimistic. He advocates a different perspective, arguing that analysis of citizenship should focus on the *how*—not on citizenship as an act, but as a process of action. Thus, the question is: how do people enact citizenship and civic engagement? The answer is: through rhetoric. Civic engagement as a process, a "mode of public engagement," means participation in society has many different forms, all of which involve symbolic action.[74]

Asen argues that rhetoric is central to civic engagement because, in addressing other people in ways that seek identification, it is an act of interacting and engaging with others: "Engagement positions people as rhetorical agents hoping to persuade and/or seek recognition from others of their views, even as it recognizes that others hope to do the same. Commitment thus extends to a commitment to interaction itself."[75] When you engage in rhetoric, you necessarily commit yourself to an interaction. Thus, to understand citizenship, Asen examines the processes by which people engage and interact with each other.

He explores how people come to understand themselves—through rhetoric—as members of groups and as individuals, and how "actions that begin on a small scale may spread across social, cultural, and political sites."[76] For Asen, engagement occurs when human communication generates new areas for discussion, when people are willing to accept the risk of being wrong (and accept correction of their views), when people affirm a commitment to engage one another in discourse, and when creative forms of communication build social connections among individuals.

Rhetorical citizenship in a democratic society is essential to the process of decision making in situations as mundane as a group of people deciding where to eat dinner (at a national chain or at a restaurant that supports local farmers) to situations as serious as determining whether you want to join a national service organization (the armed services, Americorp, or the Peace Corps). Although people's reasons for doing things can be personal, those reasons can be expressed and contested. To truly enter the realm of rhetoric, people must be open to having their minds changed and to providing the reasons for their beliefs. They must be willing to continually provide reasons, listen, and modify their positions. This process of interaction and modification of positions is essential to decision making in an open society.

For example, if members of a campus group disagreed about how to spend a thousand dollars, it would not be productive if each person simply stated: I want the money spent *this* way, period. Instead, for the group to decide collectively what to do, each person would have to articulate the reason the money should be spent as she or he wanted. As people gave their reasons, some shared interests might become clear, at which point each person could see the merits in others' ideas. As the discussion proceeded, agreement might emerge. Or, it might become clear that the group members had totally competing interests, so that agreement could never be reached. At that point, they may find that the disagreement is less about what to do with the money (policy) and more about what it means to be a member of the group (identity).

Unfortunately, modern society increasingly allows people to refuse such interactions. The fragmentation of media enables you to seek out and listen only to those with whom you agree. When exchanges of diverse opinions do occur, it is becoming more common to hear people refuse to participate. You probably have heard comments such as "we'll just have to agree to disagree," or "it works for me," or "I don't have time to get involved," or even just "whatever." These comments are a way of ending discussion about differing opinions and ideas, rather than actually engaging people in discussion. They are antithetical to decision making based on the principles of rhetoric. Agreeing to disagree is not always a viable option. Often, decisions must be made among competing options and ideas.

What differentiates an open and free society from a closed, fascist, and dictatorial society is its willingness to tolerate the open expression of differing ideas and beliefs. In an open society, communication serves personal, epistemological, and political functions. It serves a personal function when it enables people to express themselves, both communicating and developing their sense of self.

It serves an epistemological function when it enables people to test their ideas and to develop knowledge. It serves a political function when it enables people to participate in the processes of governance. President Abraham Lincoln's ideal of a "government of the people, by the people, for the people" cannot be realized if the people do not participate in those processes.[77] Additionally, a free press and its ability to report on public issues fulfills a political function when it serves as a check on government abuses. Your own rhetoric and your ability to listen to the rhetoric of others are essential to an open society.

For these reasons, the United States has a long tradition of protecting open communication, which it codified in the First Amendment to the Constitution. Supreme Court Justice Holmes articulated this trust in freely exchanged ideas in 1919:

> [T]he ultimate good desired is better reached by free trade in ideas — that the best test of truth is the power of the thought to get itself accepted in the competition of the market, and that truth is the only ground upon which their wishes safely can be carried out. That, at any rate, is the theory of our Constitution. It is an experiment, as all life is an experiment. Every year, if not every day, we have to wager our salvation upon some prophecy based upon imperfect knowledge. While that experiment is part of our system, I think that we should be eternally vigilant against attempts to check the expression of opinions that we loathe and believe to be fraught with death, unless they so imminently threaten immediate interference with the lawful and pressing purposes of the law that an immediate check is required to save the country.[78]

The First Amendment also guarantees the right to petition, a right that was facilitated by the petition portal on the Obama White House's web site: "We the People: Your Voice in Our Government."[79] As the website explains, "The idea of petitioning the White House or the government isn't new, but this online platform is."[80]

Time magazine described the role of petitions in democratic societies, and noted that petitions have been around since ancient Mesopotamia. They also appeared in Imperial China, early modern Japan, and ancient Rome.[81] With the introduction of the printing press, "petitions became something else: not just a deferential request to authorities but a tool for amassing and shaping public opinion," as was the case with the US Declaration of Independence. According to *Time*, "The Internet is Gutenberg on steroids, a printing press without ink, overhead or delivery costs."[82] Initially, it only took twenty-five thousand signatures to trigger a White House response. Seeing how easy it was to generate that number of signatures, the White House raised the requirement to one hundred thousand, but, according to *Time*, "It still doesn't matter how silly or challenging the request. All that matters is that it is on a subject federal government can do something about. All that matters is that it motivates multitudes."[83] Digital communication is two-way, however. On business websites using cookies, or government websites on which you leave your contact information, not only can you communicate with the business or government agency, it can also communicate with you.

Open communication is not to be feared. Ideas with which you disagree should not be avoided or suppressed. Instead, all people should develop the critical faculties that enable them to judge which ideas in the marketplace they should "buy," which expressions are worthy of assent, and which ideas should define their characters. People need the right to express their opinions, but also the skills and knowledge with which to do so, as well as a government and society willing to consider and respond to those opinions.

CONSTRAINTS ON AND RESOURCES FOR SYMBOLIC ACTION

When you engage in rhetorical action, you are constrained by social factors. Not every symbolic action will be completely and immediately understood by everyone hearing or seeing it, or accepted even if it is understood. You also possess resources for rhetorical action: stories, images, memories, and cultural values that are generally shared and can be used to communicate your message. In this section, we discuss some of the limits on and resources for rhetoric: (1) the persuasive continuum, (2) culture, (3) public memory, and (4) power, ideology, and hegemony. This list is not exhaustive; other resources and constraints will be discussed throughout the text. However, this list constitutes overarching constraints and resources that influence most aspects of rhetorical engagement in civic life.

Persuasive Continuum

Because of limits on persuasion stemming from an audience, a topic, or even the rhetor, seldom is persuasion absolutely achieved or an argument completely dismissed. An audience is not totally persuaded or completely unconvinced by a single rhetorical action. When people think of persuasion, they often think of it as intentionally trying to change another person's actions or beliefs (sometimes against the other person's will), but not all rhetoric has such goals.

Communication scholar Karlyn Kohrs Campbell describes persuasive purposes in terms of a continuum:[84]

create virtual experience	alter perception	explain	formulate belief	initiate action	maintain action

$\longleftrightarrow$

In many cases, changing a person's mind is not possible. Beliefs can be so deeply ingrained that an audience may not even recognize that alternative beliefs are possible. In such a case, a rhetor's goal may be to create a virtual experience for the audience members, so they come to feel they have experienced something they never thought possible. For example, when African-American activist Mary Church Terrell wrote about the effect of Jim Crow segregation laws in her 1906 magazine essay "What It Means to Be Colored in the Capital of the United States,"[85] she *created a virtual experience.* When writing to a primarily white, Northern audience, she provided example after example of the segregation African Americans faced in what was thought to be the cradle of liberty and equality: Washington, DC. Moving from finding shelter, to finding food, to finding a place to worship, work, and be entertained and educated, her essay created for her white audience the virtual experience of being "colored in the capital of the United States" and enabled them to identify with African Americans.

The virtual experience need not be based in material reality. For example, readers of the Harry Potter novels were transported to places that never actually existed. J. K. Rowling created a virtual experience for her readers through her detailed descriptions of the characters and settings for the stories. For some readers, the characters and locations were defined in their minds even before the Harry Potter movies were produced. One critic wrote, "Disappointingly, some of the clever nuances from the book don't come through in the film. Harry's miserable home life, which was vibrantly written, is forgettable here."[86] For those readers, the movie, with its reliance on the visual, did not produce the same effect as the written word, which created characters and scenes that allowed the audience to experience an imaginary world.

If rhetors can create virtual experiences for audience members, they might be able to *alter their perception,* or at least introduce them to new perspectives. Ida B. Wells, journalist and long-time activist for African-American rights, fought against lynching. In her 1892 essay (also delivered as a speech), "Southern Horrors: Lynch Law in All Its Phases," she attempted to alter audience members' perception that black men were lynched because they were accused of raping white women.[87] She made clear that, as reported by white sources, the real reason that white people lynched black people was economic. White business people resented black people's economic success. She also pointed out that black children and black women had been murdered by white lynch mobs, but no white man had ever been lynched for raping a black woman, or even a black eight-year-old child, showing that the fear of rape was an inadequate explanation for lynching. Although she may not have been able to convince her audience that all lynching was wrong, she at least opened their minds to an alternative perspective on lynching—that it was an economically and racially motivated crime of hate, rather than an act defending fragile white women's honor. Wells sought to create divisions between white people who lynched and those who would oppose lynching, and to foster identification between white people and black people.

If audience members are willing to entertain the possibility of an alternative perception, a speaker can then *explain* reasons behind that perception. Wells explained the reasons for her opposition to lynching, her demand that northerners condemn the act, and her call to African Americans to arm themselves in self-defense. She ended by explaining: "Of the many inhuman outrages of this present year, the only case where the proposed lynching did *not* occur, was where the men armed themselves in Jacksonville, Fla., and Paducah, Ky., and prevented it. The only times an Afro-American who was assaulted got away has been when he had a gun and used it in self-defense."[88]

Another example of explanation can be found in the reporting of Walter Cronkite on the day of the John F. Kennedy assassination. In 1962, Cronkite became the anchor for the CBS Evening News and, for much of the latter half of the twentieth century, would be known as "the most trusted man in America."[89] In 1963, Walter Cronkite interrupted *As the World Turns*, a top soap opera for CBS, to tell viewers that President Kennedy had been shot and wounded. Minutes later, Cronkite returned to the air and uttered these now famous words, "From Dallas, Texas, the flash apparently official, President Kennedy died at 1 a.m. Central Standard Time, 2 o'clock Eastern Standard Time, some 38 minutes ago."[90] Cronkite's announcement came in the form of an explanation. He told what had happened. However, his explanation is one that has been remembered for more than fifty years. His statement was so powerful that many people who were alive at that time can still recall where they were when they heard his statement. The 9/11 attacks have sometimes been referred to as this "generation's equivalent of John F. Kennedy's assassination."[91] But it was Cronkite's explanation of the events that is etched in many people's memories, rather than images or the event.

Once audience members are willing to alter their perception of an issue and listen to an alternative explanation, a rhetor might be able to *formulate beliefs*. As a result of speeches and essays, Ida B. Wells's and other rhetors were able to begin formulating a belief in audience members' minds that lynching was a criminal act that violated black people's rights and that lynchers should face the most severe legal punishments possible. It took time to formulate that belief: a federal antilynching law was not even proposed until 1900 (and then received only three votes), and lynching persisted well into the 1950s. In fact, no federal antilynching law was ever passed, an oversight for which the US Senate apologized in 2005.[92]

Formulating belief is not the only possible goal for a rhetorician. In many cases, audience members seek out speakers in order to reaffirm their own beliefs. For example, people attend religious services to have their beliefs reaffirmed and attend political rallies for candidates they already support in order to maintain (and demonstrate) their belief in a candidate. In such cases, persuasion can maintain belief as well as formulate it.

Having beliefs does not necessarily mean people act on them. People often have good intentions, but fail to act on them. In recent years, social media has been used to *initiate action*. The revolutions during the Arab Spring were facilitated by social media. The revolution in Tunisia was said to have relied heavily on Facebook; the revolution in Egypt relied on Twitter.[93] The use of social media may not have caused the revolutions, but it allowed "unprecedented waves of spread" that allowed the revolutions to evolve more quickly.[94] The use of Twitter and Facebook also raises the possibility of a "leaderless revolution," in which groups of people organize based on spontaneity, homogeneity, and synchronicity of actions, catalyzed by social media.[95] Messages and images on Twitter and Facebook can seek to initiate action by people who share similar beliefs.

When a movement or campaign achieves success, members must be reminded that there is more work to be done. In recent years, for example, six states have done away with the death penalty,[96] and groups that wish to see it abolished entirely hoped to see further successes. In early 2014, three executions by lethal injection did not go as planned. In the third case, it took two hours for a man convicted of a double murder in Arizona to die.[97] Abolitionists quickly took to Twitter, using #DeathPenalty to mark their tweets. Ed Pilkington of *The Guardian* (@Edpilkington) tweeted, "If you care about the #deathpenalty in US u need to pay attention to Arizona right now—the mother of all botched executions is unfolding."[98] ACLU National (@ACLU) tweeted, "#Deathpenalty experimentation is cruel & unusual & has no place in our country."[99]

Culture

Rhetoric and civic engagement occur within particular cultures. According to anthropologist Clifford Geertz, **culture** is the *"historically transmitted pattern of meanings embodied in symbols, a system of inherited conceptions expressed in symbolic forms by means of which men [and women] communicate, perpetuate, and develop their knowledge about and attitudes toward life."*[100] Culture is composed of knowledge, experiences, beliefs, values, attitudes, meanings, hierarchies, religions, conceptions of time, social roles, worldviews, myths, and even the material possessions or artifacts acquired by a group of people, the meanings of which are transmitted through symbols. Your culture frames how you interpret rhetorical messages.

For example, in an individualist culture, appeals to individual rights may carry more weight than in a more communitarian culture that places the concerns of the group ahead of individuals' rights.[101] In their study of the famous image of the man standing in front of the tank during the 1989 Tiananmen Square protests, communication scholars Robert Hariman and John L. Lucaites argue that Western media sources made that image emblematic of the event, rather than images of massive crowds, because the lone individual confronting the power of the state made sense to Western cultures that emphasize liberal individualism.[102]

Geertz uses the metaphor of a spider's web to explain the complex relationship between culture and symbol use: he says that humans are "suspended in webs of significance" they themselves "have spun."[103] For Geertz, symbols do not literally bring something into existence, but locate it within systems of meaning. Patriotism, the love of or devotion to a country, is an example of a cultural system of meaning. In the US patriotic web of signification, key words such as "freedom," "equality," and "liberty;" visual symbols such as the US flag; and icons such as Uncle Sam and the Statue of Liberty have come to symbolize the country. People who are citizens come to understand who they are because of their relationship to the United States, and pledge allegiance to it. Expressions of patriotism (such as Lee Greenwood's 1984 song "God Bless the USA," which played at the Republican National Convention that year, increased in popularity during Operation Desert Storm in 1991, and then regained popularity in the wake of the 9/11 attacks) create a sense of identification among many citizens.

As that sense of belonging develops so, too, does a sense of differentiation and exclusion. Even as one creates identification (a sense of "us"), one also creates division (a sense of "them"). Identification is meant to counteract the feeling of division, but even as it does so it tends to recreate divisions along new lines. Patriotism normalizes the idea that some people deserve rights in a country because they "belong" while others do not because they do not belong. Patriotism also normalizes the idea that a fellow citizen's loss of life counts more than another person's death.[104] Patriotism gives a particular meaning to being a citizen of a country. The words and symbols interweave so that to attack one (freedom) means you have attacked all (attacking freedom means you are attacking all the United States stands for). Sometimes dissent is called unpatriotic because it means one does not support the country unconditionally. Patriotism is a web of significance in which people are suspended and that they, themselves, have spun.

Geertz's definition of culture includes "a system of inherited conceptions expressed in symbolic forms,"[105] which means that the web of significance is learned. Communication scholars Judith N. Martin and Thomas K. Nakayama state that culture is comprised of "learned patterns of behavior and attitudes shared by a group of people."[106] The primary functions of culture are to teach shared meanings, shared views of the world, and a group identity. Through these functions, cultures also help reduce uncertainty and chaos, largely by socializing their members to behave in prescribed ways. Even as you are enmeshed in the web, however, you also help spin it.

Rhetoric is constrained by culture, but also constructs culture. Rhetoric is constrained by culture because people's interpretations of symbolic action depend on the culture in which they participate. What is persuasive to a rural, midwestern, US audience might not be persuasive to an audience in another nation, or even another part of the United States. Yet, rhetoric can be used to change culture. For example, in the United States, women were once considered inferior and thus were systematically denied the right to vote. This state of affairs was considered "normal" in the eighteenth and nineteenth centuries. Yet, in the twenty-first-century United States, if someone advocated denying women the right to vote, you would probably think that person was crazy. Women achieved their current role through rhetoric and civic engagement that altered the culture.

Public and Collective Memory

Geertz points to the link between culture and memory, to the existence of cultural memory that resides in the web of significance, when he refers to historically transmitted meanings. If culture is learned patterns, where does one learn those patterns? A person does not inherit a chest of drawers that contains the culture. Instead, people develop their culture as they inherit symbol systems that contain memories.

Memories are maintained through symbolic actions. Sociologist Barry Schwartz explains, "Recollection of the past is an active, constructive process, not a simple matter of retrieving information. To remember is to place a part of the past in the service of conceptions and needs of the present."[107] Memories do not just exist; instead, to remember requires human symbols to re-present memory. Communication scholar Carole Blair explains: "memory is based on the capacity to *re-present* an event, a place, a person, or an idea that one has already encountered."[108] People engage in the act of remembering, and in doing so develop a sense of collective identity. Remembering requires symbolic action on the part of people.

Memory can exist at the personal level, as when family members recall past experiences with each other. It can also exist at the cultural level, when the members of a culture engage in the memory work that sustains them as a culture. **Collective memory** is *memory that is not simply an individualized process, but a shared and constructed creation of a group.*[109] **Public memory** is *a particular type of collective memory that combines the memories of the dominant culture and fragments of marginalized groups' memories, and enables a public to make sense of the past, present, and future.*[110] Memory is the product of rhetorical action even as it constrains the rhetorical actions of those who would challenge the dominant memory.

Citizens of a nation maintain and construct public memory through the monuments and memorials they choose to erect, and in the process construct an identity for themselves. In the United States, the Lincoln Memorial, Washington Monument, Vietnam Veterans Memorial, National World War II Memorial, and Korean War Veterans Memorial all construct particular memories of the nation's past. Memorials and monuments are examples of shared resources, collective memory made public.

Just as a person may have particular memories and families may have group memories, public memories give identity to a particular society. You personally have no memory of national events such as the American Revolution, but through your education and your participation in Fourth of July celebrations, through national monuments and speeches, you participate in a public memory of the events of the American Revolution, memories the Tea Party movement seeks to revivify. Thus, an individual's memories do not really make sense unless situated within a larger collective. Communication scholar Iwona Irwin-Zarecka writes, "'Collective memory'—as a set of ideas, images, feelings about the past—is best located not in the minds of individuals, but in the resources they share."[111]

However, remembering always involves forgetfulness. Collective memory may be controversial. It can be a point of contestation, in part because collective remembering is always intimately linked to collective forgetfulness. No single version of the past exists, and dominant interpretations of past events can "wip[e] out many of the others."[112] Thus, the subject of rhetoric can be which things to remember and how to remember them.

For example, memorial depictions of Christopher Columbus illustrate both the amount of work done to maintain collective memory and the way memory also always induces forgetfulness. Symbols in the form of statues and images, poems, stories, and named holidays all sought to fix collective memory of Columbus as definitive of the US identity as a nation of explorers. He has been celebrated as an American mythic hero since the genesis of the nation, partly because the revolutionary leaders were reluctant to ascend the pedestal in a country that ostensibly was built on democratic principles.[113] Into this void people placed Columbus. In the years during and immediately after the Revolutionary War, numerous poetic histories and references to Columbus emerged, including Phillis Wheatley's 1775 innovation of the poetic device "Columbia" as a symbol of both Columbus and America.[114] In 1792, the new capitol in Washington was subtitled the District of Columbia. These acts of rhetoric participated in the creation and maintenance of public memory.

The original narrative of Columbus-the-discoverer was woven into and stabilized US public memory without opposition for many years. Regardless of whether he was the first to land in the Americas, his is the day celebrated, his is the image immortalized in the US capitol, and his is the story told in text-books and movies. In other words, all available anchoring devices for collective memory have been used to fix Columbus-the-discoverer in US public memory. However, in the process of commemorating Columbus, much faded in memory.

The Columbian quincentenary in 1992 provided a unique moment to highlight the way collective forgetting was connected to collective remembering. Native American protests against Columbus Day parades offered a way to materialize grievances. Native Americans engaged in rhetorical action in order to challenge collective memory and public memorializing practices. A leading scholar on indigenous peoples of Latin America, José Barreiro, introduced the special issue of the *Northeast Indian Quarterly* that was dedicated to "American Indian Perspectives on the Quincentenary." He explained the rhetorical significance of the quincentenary: "To the degree that the Quincentenary spectacle exalts Columbus as a metaphor for the expansion of Western materialist culture[,] a debate is joined that focuses issues of cultural values survival, environmental ethics and practice and sustainability in economic activity."[115]

The celebration of Columbus's memory provided a focal point through which to reframe the nation's understanding of discovery and settlement. The reframing was not to be achieved by a single protest or a single text. For Native Americans, the issue was not the accurate chronicling of history, although that was a part of it, but the effects of commemorative holidays and parades on memory of what was done to Native Americans as a result of Columbus's land-fall. The point was that Columbus did not "discover" an empty land, but claimed a land populated by many different peoples. The memory of Columbus is rhetorical insofar as it exhorts people in the United States to perceive their identity as explorers. Native Americans countered that rhetorical exhortation by depicting Columbus not as an explorer but as a colonizer.

Memories, even those enshrined in memorials, monuments, parades, and holidays, do not proceed uncontested. Memory can be a site of rhetorical conflict precisely because of the necessary relationship between remembering and forgetting. Those with power tend to shape public memory; those with less power must contest the absence caused by the partial memory of the powerful.

Power, Ideology, and Hegemony

Power, as defined by feminist scholars Cheris Kramarae and Paula A. Triechler, is *"the ability to get things done."*[116] Power to do something is not inherently bad, but when it transforms into power over others, problems arise. Power is a social phenomenon: people have power in relation to others. Class, gender/sex, race, citizenship, political affiliation, education, sexuality, and religion all influence the cultural resources that rhetors may access and thus how much rhetorical power they have.

Communication scholars John L. Lucaites and Celeste M. Condit point out that people who study rhetoric need to consider the "systems of social conditions and their impact on public discourse."[117] Not all people have equal access to the public podium, because rhetorical actions occur in culturally and historically specific contexts in which power is apportioned unequally. Lucaites and Condit posit a refined definition of rhetoric that "portrays significant rhetors as those able to realign material life experiences and cultural symbols through the artful use of the available means of persuasion."[118] This definition of rhetoric highlights the role of people in shaping experiences and symbols. This shaping is an art form. However, not all people have the same experiences nor do all people have access to the same symbols. The means of persuasion available to a US president differ from those available to an unemployed steelworker, or to an immigrant living and working in the United States without documentation. When you are in an audience, it is important to consider these things before judging a speaker to be a failure or success.

Power is also central to the study of rhetoric because rhetoric is, itself, a form of power. Philosopher Michel Foucault, who has written extensively about power, notes that "as history constantly teaches us, discourse is not simply that which translates struggles or systems of domination, but is the thing for which and by which there is struggle, discourse is the power which is to be seized."[119] In other words, rhetoric is both the object of power over which people struggle and the means by which people engage in a struggle for power.

Foucault theorized that some of the most oppressive power is that which people internalize. He examined Jeremy Bentham's panopticon—a jail with prisoners in individual cells arranged around a guard at the center, so that prisoners could not see each other or the guard, but the guard could always see all the prisoners. Because it was always possible that they were being watched, the prisoners acted *as if* they were always being watched; they disciplined themselves. Foucault says the power of the panopticon "makes it possible to perfect the exercise of power" because

> it can reduce the number of those who exercise it, while increasing
> the number of those on whom it is exercised. Because it is possible to

intervene at any moment and because the constant pressure acts even
before the offences, mistakes or crimes have been committed. Because,
in these conditions, its strength is that it never intervenes, it is exercised
spontaneously and without noise, it constitutes a mechanism whose
effects follow from one another. Because, without any physical instrument
other than architecture and geometry, it acts directly on individuals; it
gives "power of mind over mind."[120]

In other words, a guard does not need to stand over you with a gun in order
to generate your compliance: because you believe you are being watched, you
behave. You internalize the rules, accepting them as the way things are, and act
accordingly. You watch yourself.

As an example, think about how, and whether, you choose to talk. Even
though the United States valorizes freedom of expression, people are often reluctant to speak out for fear of what might happen. Someone might be listening
who will discipline them by showing they are wrong, or disagreeing, or judging
them to be weird. In a classroom, students often self-censor for fear of not giving
the answer the professor wants, even when the professor makes clear there are no
wrong answers. In these examples, there is no guard to discipline you; instead,
you have internalized an ideology that induces you to discipline yourself.

Power is not simply something that one entity has over another, or that flows
from those at the top of the hierarchy to those at the bottom. Foucault emphasizes that power neither resides in only one location nor moves in only one direction: "Power is everywhere, not because it embraces everything, but because
it comes from everywhere . . . power is not an institution, and not a structure;
neither is it a certain strength we are endowed with.[121]

Still, the guard in the prison does not possess absolute power over the
inmates. Foucault writes that power is "a mechanism whose effects flow from
one another," meaning power is not located in one place, but in relationships,
and that "in the relations of power, there is necessarily the possibility of resistance."[122] Political scientist Michael Dutton writes, "the prisoner in the cell has
'all the time in the world' to map the cracks in the wall that offer the opportunity
to escape, for . . . even panoptic power must blink."[123]

Power manifests itself rhetorically through the creation of a dominant
ideology, which can be defined as *the ideas, values, beliefs, perceptions, and
understandings that are known to members of a society and that guide their
behaviors.* In *Making Sense of Political Ideology,* communication scholars
Bernard L. Brock, Mark E. Huglen, James F. Klumpp, and Sharon Howell
describe ideology as "typical ways of thinking about the world [that] help shape
human action"[124] because it normalizes "day-to-day social, political, economic,
and cultural structures" by making them appear natural and inevitable.[125]
In short, ideology is a symbol system that explains why society is the way it is.
Geertz identifies ideology as one example of a web of significance, because "the
inherent elusiveness of ideological thought" is "expressed as it is in intricate
symbolic webs as vaguely defined as they are emotionally charged."[126] Ideology
is created and maintained through symbol use, but the ideological content of
symbols is often difficult to track.

Ideology becomes most powerful when humans forget it is socially constructed and give it "the status of objective reality."[127] For example, marriage ceremonies are socially constructed rituals, but people forget these ceremonies are choices and begin to think they must be performed a particular way in order to be real. Cultural ideology about marriage ceremonies explains why the average cost of a US wedding tops $30,000, a hefty sum for a couple starting out, which might be better spent to make a down payment on a house or to pay off debts. You might even hear someone complain at a nontraditional (or less expensive) wedding that it was "not right" or "unnatural." Such comments indicate the existence of cultural ideology.

Burke offers a metaphorical description of how words operate together to constitute an ideology, and how that ideology induces people to act in certain ways: "An 'ideology' is like a spirit taking up its abode in a body: it makes that body hop around in certain ways; and that same body would have hopped around in different ways had a different ideology [or set of terms] happened to inhabit it."[128] In the case of the mob violence targeted at abolitionists, white supremacist ideology made the mob hop in a particularly violent way, legitimating the violence of slavery and the violence targeted at those who would challenge slavery. Ideology is not neutral, but tends to normalize the possession of power by the "haves" and the denial of power to the "have-nots."

British cultural studies scholar Stuart Hall argues that dominant cultural ideology influences how people come to perceive reality.[129] For example, capitalism is not only an economic system, but also a dominant ideology in the United States that undergirds the values and behaviors that support competition, individualism, and consumerism, and that enables money to determine status and power. This does not mean that every person in US culture embraces the ideology unquestioningly, but it does explain the predominant US culture.

Not all ideologies carry equal power. Some become dominant. **Hegemony** is *the dominant ideology of a society, exerting social control over people without the use of force.*[130] Philosopher Rosemary Hennessy explains that hegemony is not a form of power that controls through overt violence; rather, it subtly controls by determining what makes sense: "Hegemony is the process whereby the interests of a ruling group come to dominate by establishing the common sense, that is, those values, beliefs, and knowledges that go without saying."[131]

Hegemony is constructed and maintained by rhetorical actions. Communication scholars draw on Italian political theorist Antonio Gramsci's concept of hegemonic ideology.[132] Gramsci argues that social control is primarily accomplished through the control of ideas. People are encouraged to see an idea as common sense, even if it conflicts with their own experiences. By following the cultural norms that guide behaviors, members of the culture uphold the ideology.

Hegemony reduces one's agency because it limits the choices that make sense to a rhetor or audience. For example, because capitalism is the hegemonic US ideology, most people in the United States believe in free and open markets and in the freedom of consumers to choose where to shop and what to buy. Recently, in a small town where two locally owned restaurants were located next to a park, a multinational fast-food restaurant offered to buy the park land

and pay to relocate the park so it could build a restaurant on that location. The town council held an open meeting to discuss the proposal. Some members of the community opposed the fast-food restaurant, arguing that it would put the locally owned restaurants out of business and destroy the community by taking away a valuable central public meeting place. These community members were accused of being "antidevelopment" and "against the free enterprise system." One council member said, "If you do not like fast food, then don't eat there. The other restaurants need to learn to compete. It's a free country." These statements did not really answer the opponents' arguments, but sought to silence the opposition by making them seem un-American, opposed to competition and freedom.

Because hegemony is embedded within symbolic actions, rhetorical critics need to learn how to read through it. Media scholar Stuart Hall identifies three positions from which audiences can decode a text: dominant or preferred (hegemonic) reading, negotiated reading, and oppositional (counterhegemonic) reading.[133] Different people in any given time have different resources available for oppositional readings, and have to expend more or less effort to construct them. Communication scholar Bonnie Dow observes that it is easy to "acquire the codes necessary for preferred readings" while "the acquisition of codes for negotiated or oppositional readings is more difficult and less common."[134] This text is intended to provide you with the code, or vocabulary, with which to critically and oppositionally understand rhetoric.

CONCLUSION

Rhetoric is the use of symbolic action by human beings to share ideas, enabling them to work together to make decisions about matters of common concern and to construct social reality. What this definition makes clear, and Aristotle's does not, is that rhetoric is much more than a tool of information transmission or persuasion. Through rhetoric, people constitute identity, construct culture, maintain and challenge memory, and develop and sustain ideology; and are able to identify, maintain, and counter hegemonic power.

Our goal in this book is to introduce you to some of the joys and responsibilities of rhetorical action. Democracy is not a spectator sport, nor is life. To be able to participate, you need to understand how rhetoric works, and that it is at work in a variety of places: politics, religion, family, sports, entertainment, small town life, and workplaces. The ability to attach meaning to the world and to make sense of what the world means requires an understanding of rhetoric.

When studying rhetoric, scholars do not really use a single approach or a preset step-by-step method. Instead, they use what communication scholars William L. Nothstine, Carole Blair, and Gary A. Copeland refer to as "conceptual heuristics or vocabularies."[135] Throughout the chapters that follow, we present a vocabulary that describes the forms, components, and functions of rhetoric, and that should enable you to explain rhetoric's power to liberate *and* subordinate. We introduce you to diverse forms of symbolic action, including language, visual rhetoric, argument, and narrative. We show you ways to analyze rhetorical action as composed of rhetors, audiences, and situations that constrain rhetoric even as they, themselves, are rhetorically constructed. We end with a discussion of publics that shows how you can identify yourself as an agent of civic action.

Rhetoric is essential to the functioning of civic culture. Civic engagement in open societies exists so that citizens can challenge the actions of those in power and engage each other in discussions and debates over what is right—for individuals, communities, the nation, and the world. Civic engagement is much more than the act of voting. It necessitates that you engage with other people and participate in symbolic actions that constitute your identity as a person, a group member, and a citizen. An understanding of how culture, memory, power, and ideology are rhetorical is integral to a complete understanding of the full power of rhetoric and of the constraints on rhetorical action.

DISCUSSION QUESTIONS

1. The authors suggest that the study of rhetoric is tied to democratic societies. Think about how the study of rhetoric may have been helpful in the years preceding the rise of Hitler. How might a society with a stronger emphasis on rhetoric have better understood Hitler and the Nazis?
2. What is power? Give examples of how it functions in politics, the law, and your daily life.
3. What is your position on the debate between Socrates and the Sophists? Is rhetoric morally neutral, or is it to blame for human failures?
4. Give examples of ways people are civically engaged outside the traditional electoral process. Explain how rhetoric is involved with these other forms of engagement.
5. What is rhetorical agency? How does a posthumanist theory change our views of agency?

RECOMMENDED READINGS

Aristotle. *On Rhetoric.* Translated by George A. Kennedy. New York: Oxford University Press, 1991.

Blair, Carole. "Communication as Collective Memory." In *Communication as . . . : Perspectives on Theory.* Edited by Gregory J. Shepherd, Jeffrey St. John, and Ted Striphas, 51–59. Thousand Oaks, CA: Sage, 2006.

Asen, Robert. "A Discourse Theory of Citizenship." *Quarterly Journal of Speech* 90, no. 2 (2004): 189–211.

Hauser, Gerard A. "Rhetorical Democracy and Civic Engagement." In *Rhetorical Democracy: Discursive Practices of Civic Engagement.* Edited by Gerard A. Hauser and Amy Grim, 1–16. Mahwah, NJ: Lawrence Erlbaum Associates, 2004.

Kennedy, George A. *A New History of Classical Rhetoric.* Princeton, NJ: Princeton University Press, 1994.

Poulakos, John. "Toward a Sophistic Definition of Rhetoric." *Philosophy and Rhetoric* 16, no. 1 (1983): 35–48.

ENDNOTES

[1] Mary Niederberger, "Taking Bullying by the Horns: Schools Use Awareness, Training, Outreach and Districtwide Rules to Stop Cyberbullies," *Pittsburgh Post-Gazette*, October 14, 2010, LexisNexis.

[2] Thomas Tracy, "'Jumper' Saved by the Net," *New York Daily News*, November 14, 2013, LexisNexis.

[3] Martin Luther King, Jr., "I Have a Dream," August 28, 1963, http://www.american rhetoric.com/speeches/mlkihaveadream.htm.

[4] Malala Yousafzai, "Nobel Lecture," Oslo, December 10, 2014, http://www.nobelprize .org/nobel_prizes/peace/laureates/2014/yousafzai-lecture_en.html.

[5] Garry Wills, *Lincoln at Gettysburg: The Words That Remade America* (New York: Simon and Schuster, 1992), 261.

[6] Theodore C. Sorensen, "Ted Sorensen on Abraham Lincoln: A Man of His Words," Smithsonian.com, http://www.smithsonianmag.com/history/ted-sorensen-on -abraham-lincoln-a-man-of-his-words-12048177/?page=2.

[7] George W. Bush, "The Text of President Bush's Address Tuesday Night, after Terrorist Attacks on New York and Washington," CNN.com, http://edition.cnn.com/2001 /US/09/11/bush.speech.text.

[8] Malcolm X, "The Ballot or the Bullet," April 3, 1964, http://www.edchange.org /multicultural/speeches/malcolm_x_ballot.html.

[9] Joan Bakewell, "Arts under Siege," *Sunday Times* (London), June 10, 1990, LexisNexis.

[10] Karen Crouse, "Golf Digest's Cover Spurs Criticism from L.P.G.A. Pros," *New York Times*, April 3, 2014, http://www.nytimes.com/2014/04/04/sports/golf/female-golfers -rankled-by-magazines-cover.html.

[11] Steve DiMeglio, "LPGA Players Frustrated by 'Golf Digest' Cover of Gretzky," *USA Today*, April 4, 2014, http://www.usatoday.com/story/sports/golf/2014/04/03/paulina -gretzky-golf-digest-lpga-reaction/7276517.

[12] Winston S. Churchill, "The Lights Are Going Out," *Never Give In: The Best of Winston Churchill's Speeches* (New York: Hyperion, 2003), 182–185.

[13] Adolf Hitler, *The Speeches of Adolf Hitler*, vol. 1, ed. N. H. Baynes (Oxford, UK: Oxford University Press, 1942), 743.

[14] "Traditions: The Elephant Story," http://www.rolltide.com/trads/elephant.html (accessed July 14, 2014).

[15] "The Jayhawk," University of Kansas, http://www.ku.edu/about/traditions/jayhawk (accessed July 14, 2014).

[16] Jeff Zeleny, "Obama's Lapel," *New York Times*, October 4, 2007, http://thecaucus .blogs.nytimes.com/2007/10/04/obamas-lapels/?_php=true&_type=blogs&_r=0.

[17] Charles A. Hill and Marguerite Helmers, eds., *Defining Visual Rhetorics* (Mahwah, NJ: Erlbaum, 2004); Diane S. Hope, ed., *Visual Communication: Perception, Rhetoric, and Technology* (Cresskill, NJ: Hampton, 2006); Lawrence J. Prelli, ed., *Rhetorics of Display* (Columbia: University of South Carolina Press, 2006).

[18] Kenneth Burke, "Dramatism," in *International Encyclopedia of the Social Sciences*, vol. 7, ed. David L. Sills, 445–452 (New York: Macmillan and Free Press, 1968), 447.

[19] Carole Blair, "Contemporary U.S. Memorial Sites as Exemplars of Rhetoric's Materiality," in *Rhetorical Bodies*, ed. Jack Selzer and Sharon Crowley (Madison: University of Wisconsin Press, 1999), 16–57, 19.

[20] James Boyd White, *Heracles' Bow: Essays on the Rhetoric and Poetics of Law* (Madison: University of Wisconsin Press, 1989), x.

21 James Jasinski, "A Constitutive Framework for Rhetorical Historiography: Toward an Understanding of the Discursive (Re)Constitution of 'Constitution' in *The Federalist Papers*," in *Doing Rhetorical History: Cases and Concepts*, ed. Kathleen J. Turner (Tuscaloosa: University of Alabama Press, 1998), 74–75.

22 Maurice Charland, "Constitutive Rhetoric: The Case of the *Peuple Québécois*," *Quarterly Journal of Speech* 73, no. 2 (May 1987): 133–150, 134.

23 Charland, "Constitutive," 136.

24 Judith Butler, *Bodies That Matter* (New York: Routledge, 1993), 8.

25 Robert Mugabe, "President Robert Mugabe's Inauguration Speech—22 August 2013" (Video file uploaded by *Zimbabwe Guardian*), http://www.youtube.com/watch?v=2-es1feKZDw, transcribed by Evan Schares. We thank Evan for introducing us to this example.

26 James Jasinski, *Sourcebook on Rhetoric* (Thousand Oaks, CA: Sage, 2001), 106.

27 Kenneth Burke, *Language as Symbolic Action* (Berkeley: University of California Press, 1966), 16. Original is in italics.

28 Kenneth Burke, *A Rhetoric of Motives* (Berkeley: University of California Press, 1969), 43.

29 Burke, *A Rhetoric*, 20.

30 Burke, *A Rhetoric*, 20.

31 Jasinski, *Sourcebook*, 305.

32 Kenneth Burke, *Development and Design* (Worcester, MA: Clark University Press, 1972), 27–28.

33 Burke, *A Rhetoric*, 46.

34 Burke, *Language*, 301.

35 Burke, *A Rhetoric*, 21.

36 Burke, *A Rhetoric*, 21.

37 Burke, *A Rhetoric*, 21.

38 Isaac West, *Transforming Citizenships: Transgender Articulations of the Law* (New York: New York University Press, 2014), 28. See also Danielle Allen, *Talking to Strangers: Anxieties of Citizenship since Brown v. Board of Education* (Chicago: University of Chicago Press, 2004).

39 West, *Transforming*, 28.

40 Gerda Lerner, *The Grimké Sisters from South Carolina* (New York: Schocken, 1967), 245.

41 Angelina Grimké [Weld], Address at Pennsylvania Hall, 1838, in Karlyn Kohrs Campbell, ed., *Man Cannot Speak for Her*, vol. 2 (New York: Praeger, 1989), 27.

42 Karlyn Kohrs Campbell, *Man Cannot Speak for Her*, vol. 1 (New York: Praeger, 1989), 30. See also Stephen H. Browne, "Encountering Angelina Grimké: Violence, Identity, and the Creation of Radical Community," *Quarterly Journal of Speech* 82, no. 1 (February 1996): 55–73, 70, for a discussion of how Grimké saw "not the repression of public discourse but an opportunity for it" in violent reactions to abolitionists.

43 Karlyn Kohrs Campbell, "Agency: Promiscuous and Protean," *Communication and Critical/Cultural Studies* 2 (2005): 3, italics added.

44 Christian Lundberg and Joshua Gunn, "'Ouija Board, Are There Any Communications?' Agency, Ontotheology, and the Death of the Humanist Subject, or, Continuing the ARS Conversations," *Rhetoric Society Quarterly* 35, no. 4 (Fall 2005): 83–105.

45 Christian O. Lundberg, e-mail message to Catherine Palczewski, July 16, 2014. Correspondence with Lundberg and Joshua G. Gunn was extremely helpful regarding agency.

46 Sarah Hallenbeck, "Toward a Posthuman Perspective: Feminist Rhetorical Methodologies and Everyday Practices," *Advances in the History of Rhetoric* 15 (2012): 19.

47 Lundberg and Gunn, "'Ouija Board,'" 98.

48 Saenz, Arlette. "Ted Cruz Apologizes for Joe Biden Joke after Son's Death." ABCNews.com. http://abcnews.go.com/Politics/ted-cruz-apologizes-joe-biden-joke -sons-death/story?id=31513207 (accessed June 5, 2015).

49 Peter L. Berger, *The Sacred Canopy: Elements of a Sociological Theory of Religion* (New York: Anchor, 1967), 20.

50 Barry Brummett, "Some Implications of 'Process' or 'Intersubjectivity': Postmodern Rhetoric," *Philosophy and Rhetoric* 9, no. 1 (1976): 21–53, 28–29.

51 Caglar Irmak, Beth Vallen, and Stefanie Rosen Robinson, "The Impact of Product Name on Dieters' and Nondieters' Food Evaluations and Consumption," *Journal of Consumer Research* 38 (August 2011): 390.

52 Irmak et al., "Impact," 401

53 Kevin Michael DeLuca, "The Speed of Immanent Images: The Dangers of Reading Photographs," in Hope, *Visual Communication*, 81.

54 George A. Kennedy, *A New History of Classical Rhetoric* (Princeton, NJ: Princeton University Press, 1994), 7.

55 George A. Kennedy, *Classical Rhetoric and Its Christian and Secular Tradition*, 2nd ed. (Chapel Hill: University of North Carolina Press, 1999), 1–2; George A. Kennedy, *Comparative Rhetoric: A Historical and Cross-Cultural Introduction* (New York: Oxford University Press, 1998), 1–28.

56 David Phillips, *Athenian Political Oratory: Sixteen Key Speeches* (New York: Routledge, 2004), 6.

57 Eric W. Robinson, *Ancient Greek Democracy: Readings and Sources* (Malden, MA: Wiley-Blackwell, 2004).

58 I. F. Stone, *The Trial of Socrates* (New York: Anchor, 1989); Plato, *Apology*, trans. Benjamin Jowett, classics.mit.edu/Plato/apology.html (accessed July 9, 2015).

59 Kennedy, *Classical Rhetoric*, 1–5, 29–30.

60 John Poulakos, "Toward a Sophistic Definition of Rhetoric," *Philosophy and Rhetoric* 16, no. 1 (1983): 37.

61 Aristotle, *On Rhetoric*, trans. George A. Kennedy (New York: Oxford University Press, 1991). See Kennedy's "Prooemion," x–xi.

62 Aristotle, *On Rhetoric*, 1.2.1 [1355].

63 Aristotle, *On Rhetoric*, 1.3 [1358b].

64 Aristotle, *On Rhetoric*, 1.2 [1356a–60], italics added.

65 John Poulakos, *Sophistical Rhetoric in Classical Greece* (Columbia: University of South Carolina Press, 1995), 113.

66 Poulakos, *Sophistical Rhetoric*, 132–133.

67 Poulakos, *Sophistical Rhetoric*, 135.

68 Ted Abram, "Obama and UNIVISION: Sophistry and Missed Questions," States News Service, September 27, 2012, LexisNexis; "Supreme Court Sophistry," *New York Post*, June 29, 2012, LexisNexis.

69 Burke, *A Rhetoric*, 37–46.

70 Campbell, "Agency," 3.

71 Gerard A. Hauser, "Rhetorical Democracy and Civic Engagement," in *Rhetorical Democracy: Discursive Practices of Civic Engagement*, ed. Gerard A. Hauser and Amy Grim, 1–16 (Mahwah, NJ: Erlbaum, 2004), 11.

72 Bruce Gronbeck, "Citizen Voices in Cyberpolitical Culture," in Hauser and Grim, *Rhetorical Democracy*, 17–32, 28.

[73] Robert Asen, "A Discourse Theory of Citizenship," *Quarterly Journal of Speech* 90, no. 2 (2004): 189–211.

[74] Asen, "A Discourse Theory," 191.

[75] Asen, "A Discourse Theory," 201.

[76] Asen, "A Discourse Theory," 195.

[77] Abraham Lincoln, "Gettysburg Address," November 19, 1863, http://www.americanrhetoric.com/speeches/gettysburgaddress.htm.

[78] Justice Oliver Wendell Holmes, *Abrams v. United States* 250 US 616, argued October 21–22, 1919, decided November 10, 1919, http://www.tedford-herbeck -free-speech.com/abrams.html.

[79] We the People, https://petitions.whitehouse.gov.

[80] We the People, https://petitions.whitehouse.gov/how-why/introduction.

[81] David Zaret, *Origins of Democratic Culture: Printing, Petitions, and the Public Sphere in Early-Modern England* (Princeton, NJ: Princeton University Press, 2000).

[82] Michael Scherer, "Why the White House Loves Your Death Star Petition," *Time,* January 31, 2013, http://swampland.time.com/2013/01/31/we-the-people.

[83] Scherer, "Why."

[84] Karlyn Kohrs Campbell, *The Rhetorical Act,* 2nd ed. (Belmont, CA: Wadsworth, 1996), 9–17.

[85] Mary Church Terrell, "What It Means to Be Colored in the Capital of the United States," in Campbell, *Man Cannot,* vol. 2, 421–432.

[86] US Catholic Conference, quoted in Jeffrey Overstreet, "Harry Potter and the Sorcerer's Stone," *Christianity Today,* January 1, 2001, http://www.christianitytoday .com/ct/2001/januaryweb-only/harrypotter.html?paging=off.

[87] Ida B. Wells, "Southern Horrors: Lynch Law in All Its Phases," in Campbell, *Man Cannot,* vol. 2, 385–420.

[88] Wells, "Self Help," 1892, http://www.gutenberg.org/files/14975/14975-h/14975-h.htm.

[89] Robert Galant, "The Most Trusted Man in America," CNN.com, June 5, 2012, http://www.cnn.com/2012/06/05/opinion/brinkley-walter-cronkite (accessed July 24, 2014).

[90] "The Fateful Day in Dallas Unfolds," CBS News, November 22, 2013, http://www.cbsnews.com/news/jfk-assassination-the-fateful-day-in-dallas-unfolds. The video of Cronkite's announcement can be seen at the site.

[91] Paul Brandeis Raushenbush, "The Kennedy Assassination: More Important than 9/11?" Huffington Post, November 22, 2013, http://www.huffingtonpost.com/paul -raushenbush/jfk-assassination-september-11_b_4318762.html.

[92] Avis Thomas-Lester, "A Senate Apology for History on Lynching," *Washington Post,* June 14, 2005, http://www.washingtonpost.com/wp-dyn/content/article/2005/06/13 /AR2005061301720.html.

[93] Yoursi Marzouki and Oliver Oullier, "Revolutionizing Revolutions: Virtual Collective Consciousness and the Arab Spring," *Huffington Post,* http://www.huffingtonpost .com/yousri-marzouki/revolutionizing-revolutio_b_1679181.html.

[94] Marzouki and Oullier, "Revolutionizing."

[95] Marzouki and Oullier, "Revolutionizing."

[96] Ashby Jones and Jacob Gershman, "Lengthy Arizona Execution Heightens Lethal- Injection Questions: Condemned Man Dies Two Hours after Drugs Were Administered," *Wall Street Journal,* July 25, 2014, http://online.wsj.com/articles /lengthy-arizona-execution-heightens-lethal-injection-questions-1406213831.

[97] Jones and Gershman, "Lengthy."

[98] Ed Pilkington (@Edpilkington), Twitter, July 23, 2014.

[99] ACLU National (@ACLU), Twitter, July 24, 2014.

[100] Clifford Geertz, *The Interpretation of Cultures* (New York: Basic Books, 1973), 89, italics added.

[101] William B. Gudykunst, "Individualistic and Collectivistic Perspectives on Communication: An Introduction," *International Journal of Intercultural Relations*, 22 (1998): 107–134.

[102] Robert Hariman and John Louis Lucaites, "Liberal Representation and Global Order: The Iconic Photograph from Tiananmen Square," in Prelli, *Rhetorics of Display*, 121–138. Image at http://www.sbs.com.au/news/article/1171447/-Tank -man-photo-on-Google-China.

[103] Geertz, *Interpretation*, 5.

[104] Judith Butler, *Precarious Life: The Power of Mourning and Violence* (New York: Verso, 2004) and Steven Johnston, *The Truth about Patriotism* (Durham, NC: Duke University Press, 2007).

[105] Geertz, *Interpretation*, 89.

[106] Judith N. Martin and Thomas K. Nakayama, *Intercultural Communication in Contexts*, 3rd ed., (Boston: McGraw-Hill, 2004), 3.

[107] Barry Schwartz, "The Social Context of Commemoration: A Study of Collective Memory," *Social Forces* 61 (1982): 374.

[108] Carole Blair, "Communication as Collective Memory," in *Communication as . . . Perspectives on Theory*, ed. Gregory J. Shepherd, Jeffrey St. John, and Ted Striphas (Thousand Oaks, CA: Sage, 2006), 52.

[109] Maurice Halbwachs, *On Collective Memory* (Chicago, University of Chicago Press, 1992).

[110] Richard Morris, *Sinners, Lovers, and Heroes* (Albany: State University of New York Press, 1997), 26, italics added.

[111] Iwona Irwin-Zarecka, *Frames of Remembrance: The Dynamics of Collective Memory* (New Brunswick, NJ: Transaction, 1994), 4.

[112] Irwin-Zarecka, *Frames*, 217.

[113] Michael Kammen, *The Mystic Chords of Memory: The Transformation of Tradition in American Culture* (New York: Knopf, 1991), 27.

[114] Thomas J. Steele, S. J., "The Figure of Columbia: Phillis Wheatley Plus George Washington," *The New England Quarterly: A Historical Review of New England Life and Letters* 54, no. 2 (1981): 264–266.

[115] José Barreiro, ed., *Northeast Indian Quarterly: View from the Shore: American Indian Perspectives on the Quincentenary* 7 (Fall 1990), 2. See also José Barreiro, "What 1992 Means to American Indians," in *Without Discovery: A Native Response to Columbus*, ed. Ray Gonzales (Seattle: Broken Moon, 1992): 57–60.

[116] Cheris Kramarae and Paula A. Triechler, *Amazons, Bluestockings and Crones: A Feminist Dictionary*, 2nd ed. (London: Pandora, 1992), 351, italics added.

[117] John Louis Lucaites and Celeste Michelle Condit, "Reconstructing <Equality>: Culturetypal and Counter-Cultural Rhetorics in the Martyred Black Vision," *Communication Monographs* 57 (March 1990): 21, n3.

[118] Lucaites and Condit, "Reconstructing," 6.

[119] Michel Foucault, "The Order of Discourse," in *Language and Politics*, ed. Michael J. Shapiro, 108–138 (New York: New York University Press, 1984), 110.

[120] Michel Foucault, *Discipline and Punish: The Birth of the Prison*, 2nd ed. (New York: Vintage, 1995), 206.

[121] Michel Foucault, *The History of Sexuality* (New York: Vintage, 1980), 93.

[122] Michel Foucault, *The Final Foucault*, ed. James Bernauer and David Rasmussen (Cambridge, MA: MIT Press, 1987), 12.

[123] Michael Dutton, "Street Scenes of Subalternity: China, Globalization, and Rights," *Social Text* 60 (1999): 65.

[124] Bernard L. Brock, Mark E. Huglen, James F. Klumpp, and Sharon Howell, *Making Sense of Political Ideology: The Power of Language in Democracy* (New York: Rowman and Littlefield, 2005), 39.

[125] Brock, et al., *Making Sense*, 39.

[126] Geertz, *Interpretation*, 195.

[127] Peter Berger defines legitimation in this way. We see ideology as legitimizing the social order. See Berger, *The Sacred Canopy*, 4, 9, 29.

[128] Burke, *Language*, 6.

[129] Stuart Hall, "Ideology and Communication Theory," in *Rethinking Communication Theory*, vol. 1, ed. Brenda Dervin, Larry Grossberg, Barbara O'Keefe, and Ellen Wartella, 40–52 (Newbury Park, CA: Sage, 1989).

[130] Antonio Gramsci, Raymond Rosenthal, and Frank Rosengarten, *Letters from Prison* (New York: Columbia University Press, 1993).

[131] Rosemary Hennessy, "Subjects, Knowledges, ... and All the Rest: Speaking for What," *Who Can Speak? Authority and Critical Identity*, ed. Judith Roof and Robyn Weigman, 137–150 (Urbana: University of Illinois Press, 1995), 145–146.

[132] Joseph P. Zompetti, "Toward a Gramscian Critical Rhetoric," *Western Journal of Communication* 61, no. 1 (Winter 1997), 66–86, and John M. Murphy, "Domesticating Dissent: The Kennedys and the Freedom Rides," *Communication Monographs* 59, no. 1 (March 1992), 61–78.

[133] Stuart Hall, "Encoding, Decoding," *The Cultural Studies Reader*, ed. Simon During, 90–103 (London: Routledge, 1993), 98–102.

[134] Bonnie J. Dow, *Prime-Time Feminism* (Philadelphia: University of Pennsylvania Press, 1996), 13.

[135] William L. Nothstine, Carole Blair, and Gary A. Copeland, *Critical Questions: Invention, Creativity, and the Criticism of Discourse and Media* (New York: St. Martin's, 1994), 40.

II

Forms of Symbolic Action

2

Language

KEY CONCEPTS

characterizations

condensation symbol

connotation

denotation

discursive symbolism

doublespeak

dramatism

euphemism

gestalt

ideograph

inflated language

metaphor

presentational symbolism

public vocabulary

resignification

semiotics

terministic screen

theory of
    linguistic relativity

truncated passives

Language can elicit a complex range of responses in people: it can induce fear, it can awe, it can make people weep with sadness or with joy, it can motivate people to action, or it can bore them into a stupor. Language is a tool with which to transmit information, but it is also a rich, complex, transactional web that defines who you are and how you see the people, objects, and actions that enmesh you in daily life.

If you doubt the importance of language, think about times when disagreement arises over what word to use to name a particular individual or action. Depending on how you name their actions, your reaction to the people and their actions shifts. A crime is viewed as worthy of punishment because it represents an instance in which one human being, motivated by personal gain or animosity, harmed another. An act of terrorism is viewed as worthy of even greater condemnation because it represents an instance in which one human being, motivated by hatred of a group, harmed another human being in order to terrorize all members of the group to which that person belonged. While a crime affects the person attacked (and that person's friends and family), terrorism also affects the larger social group to which the person belongs. For example, *Colorlines*, a daily news site that foregrounds issues of race, began a "Drop the I-word" campaign in September 2010.[1] Because it believed that using the word "illegal" was an inaccurate and dehumanizing way to describe people who immigrate into the United States without required documentation, *Colorlines* sought to change the way news outlets talked about immigration. By Spring 2013,

41

several news outlets (*USA Today*, the *Los Angeles Times*, and the *San Francisco Chronicle*) had agreed to stop using the "I-word." The Associated Press altered its stylebook, a major guide for US newspapers, to change "how we describe people living in a country illegally."[2] The AP Stylebook directs writers, "use *illegal* only to refer to an action, not a person: *illegal immigration*, but not *illegal immigrant*. Acceptable variations include *living in* or *entering a country illegally* or *without legal permission*."[3] By keeping the focus on the action, and not the person, the guidelines remind people "no human being is illegal."[4]

We open this chapter with a discussion of theories that describe how language constructs social reality. We will then identify four concepts that offer a vocabulary with which to describe how language functions as symbolic action: terministic screens, public vocabulary, discursive and presentational forms, and resignification. Finally, we will examine some ways in which language can be misused. This chapter demonstrates how language is more than a tool to transmit information about the world in which you live; it is a way in which you make that world.

LANGUAGE AND THE CONSTRUCTION OF SOCIAL REALITY

Early studies of language relied on the correspondence theory, which assumes that each word simply refers or corresponds to some thing in the world. For example, the word "dog" corresponds to a barking, wagging, furry member of the family *Canidae*. Understanding between people is based on each person's ability to know the meaning of the word "dog" and to what thing in the world it corresponds, but subtle differences in meaning emerge for a word. Although one basic function of communication is information transmission, the correspondence theory fails to fully explain the power of language. Theorists now see language as much more than a tool used to reference specific things in the world. People use language to construct social reality, not just to refer to reality. In this section, we discuss theories that explain how language makes meaning.

Semiotics

In the mid-1800s, US philosopher Charles Sanders Pierce coined the term **semiotics** to describe *the relationship among signs, meanings, and referents*. Around the same time, Swiss linguist Ferdinand de Saussure pushed forcefully for a semiotic approach, arguing that a science that "studies the role of signs as part of social life" should be a part of psychology and linguistics.[5] Semiotics rejects the correspondence theory of language. It urges people to consider signifying practices—how language does not *have* meaning but, as a social practice, *makes* meaning.

Semiotics recognizes a relationship between a sign and a referent, but that relationship is rather complex. Semiotics defines a sign as composed of two parts: the signifier (the sound/image of the sign or the form it takes) and the signified (the concept referenced by the signifier).[6] A sign still refers to some thing in the world (the creature wagging its tail), but it is composed of the signifier (the word "dog") and the signified (the idea of what a dog is that never perfectly corresponds to the creature wagging its tail, otherwise how can a Great Dane and a teacup Chihuahua both be dogs?). In semiotics, people understand a sign's meaning by decoding the concept that is signified, and not just what the sign refers to.

The semiotic recognition of the signified enables a distinction to be made between the denotation of a word and its connotation. **Denotation** is *the literal, commonsense meaning of a sign, ostensibly value-free and objective.* "Dog" would denote a domesticated, carnivorous, four-legged, hair-covered mammal of the family *Canidae*. If this definition sounds like something you would find in a dictionary, it is because dictionary definitions attempt to provide the denotative meaning of a word. Denotation is where the correspondence theory of meaning stops in its explanation.

Connotation is *the emotional or cultural meaning attached to a sign; it is what is signified.* Connotative meanings are usage-specific. They emerge when the sign's denotative meaning is not sufficient to completely communicate a concept. Even though the same canine can serve as the referent for "dog," "cur," and "mutt," the change in what is signified influences your understanding of that canine. "Dog" likely induces a neutral or positive valuation, while "cur" and "mutt" would induce a negative valuation. The denotations of signs may be easily decoded, but their connotations require a more nuanced process of decoding.

The same term can have very different connotations in different contexts, because a sign does not correspond to a single concept or thing. For example, at a dog show, different categories of competition exist for each breed, including puppy dog, American-bred dog, open dog, puppy bitch, American-bred bitch, and open bitch. In that context, "bitch" has a very specific denotative meaning: a female canine. Because the word carries no negative connotation, it is common to hear a person comment to another: "Your Brittany bitch is gorgeous." In another context, "bitch" carries very negative connotations. When used as a derogatory term for a woman, it likens a human woman to a vicious and moody female canine.

Linguistic Relativity

Attention to the way that language structures meaning led to the development of the Sapir-Whorf hypothesis, also known as the **theory of linguistic relativity,** *the idea that the structure of a language influences the way people perceive the world.* Anthropologist and linguist Edward Sapir explains that a person lives in both an objective reality and a social reality constructed through language. Thus, multiple social realities exist. Sapir explains:

> Human beings . . . are very much at the mercy of the particular language which has become the medium of expression for their society. It is quite an illusion to imagine . . . that language is merely an incidental means

of solving specific problems of communication or reflection. The fact of the matter is that the "real world" is to a large extent unconsciously built upon the language habits of the group. . . . The worlds in which different societies live are distinct worlds, not merely the same world with different labels attached . . . . We see and hear and otherwise experience very largely as we do because the language habits of our community predispose certain choices of interpretation.[7]

Although people may know things exist apart from their language, they do not know what those things mean, or how they are to react to them, except through language. In other words, meanings are relative to the symbol system, or code, that produces them.

A number of studies on the linguistic relativity theory support the idea that people's language does, indeed, affect their perceptions. For example, the range of linguistic categories for color affect whether a person sees changes in hues.[8]

An example from the art community also illustrates the power of language to structure meaning. Artist Marcel Duchamp is credited with developing the form of art known as "readymade," in which an artist elevates a found object to the highest levels of art "by the simple performative utterance of calling it 'art.'"[9] In 1916, Duchamp became a member of the Society of Independent Artists, "founded in that year with the express purpose of holding exhibitions for any artist who cared to exhibit something. There were no juries, and no work would be refused."[10] To test the group's conception of art and its purpose, Duchamp submitted, under a pseudonym, an upended urinal he titled "Fountain." The committee rejected the piece. Duchamp resigned in protest because the group had violated its own commitment to accept all submissions.

This story illustrates the power of naming: a committee was given the power to determine what was, and was not, art. The example also raises the possibility that what people think of as a discarded urinal could be called art, and that as a result their reaction to that object—what it means to them—could change. In fact, even though "Fountain" originally was rejected as a work of art, its importance to contemporary art has attached both meaning and value to it. It is now recognized as a piece of art so important it sold in a 1997 Sotheby's auction for $1,762,500.[11] The symbolic act of Duchamp calling it "Fountain" and the controversy surrounding it made a discarded urinal into art.

People are capable of thinking beyond the limits set by language, but it takes effort. Sapir writes that "language is . . . a prepared road or groove."[12] Feminist lexicographer Julia Penelope explains that a person's language creates paths of least resistance through which she or he can understand the world. The more a person travels those paths, the deeper and more difficult it becomes to think outside the grooves, because "language focuses our attention on what we believe we know . . . and we neglect to glance aside at . . . the much larger, but apparently formless lands of all that we do not, but might know if we stepped outside the mainstream."[13] For example, even though language habits in the 1800s named black people as slaves, less than fully human, activists such as British parliamentarian William Wilberforce, the Quaker Grimké sisters, former slaves

Sojourner Truth and Frederick Douglass, and US social reformer William Lloyd Garrison were able to see outside of the groove of white supremacy to name the immanent humanity of all people, regardless of color.

LANGUAGE AS SYMBOLIC ACTION

Kenneth Burke, one of the most significant rhetorical theorists of the twentieth century, described himself as a "word-man."[14] His theories about language continue to influence scholars in communication studies, English, philosophy, theatre, and sociology. Burke's theory is known as **dramatism,** *an idea that is premised on two interlocking assumptions: (1) "language is primarily a species of action . . . rather than an instrument of definition," and (2) the best way to understand human relations and motives is through an analysis of symbolic action.*[15] When people use symbols, they engage in a form of human action that relies on the mobilization of symbols, rather than physical force, to act in the world. When using language, people *do* things; they induce cooperation, foment division, create identification, constitute identity, and shape social reality.

Burke's dramatistic approach offers many concepts to explain language's power, and inspired scholars to develop even more. A few key concepts that share Burke's basic assumption that language is a species of action include terministic screens, public vocabulary, discursive and presentational form, and resignification.

Terministic Screens

Words can shape human beings as much as human beings use words to shape the world. Burke asks: "Do we simply use words, or do they not also use us?"[16] For example, we think of sex and race as purely biological, but they are not. How people see other human beings in terms of sex and race is a social construction achieved through symbolic action. The English language has long described the sexes of human beings in a binary and dichotomous way: a human being is one of two sexes—male or female—and those sexes are "opposite," as in the phrase "opposite sex." More than two sexes exist, however. Many recent medical studies have determined that about one in two thousand babies are born both/and or neither/nor, and that even more people have more subtle sex anatomy variations that do not appear until later.[17] This example shows how words begin to "use us" when you consider what was done to babies who did not fit into the male/female binary. From the 1950s (when surgical intervention became a possibility) to the 1990s, doctors embraced the concealment model, which calls for radical surgical intervention. In many cases, doctors did not even consult the parents but simply made surgical adjustments to make a baby's body fit the sex the doctor "assigned."[18] Literally, babies' bodies were surgically altered to fit the linguistic binary.[19] Since the early 1990s, new language has emerged that makes space for bodies that do not fit the sex binary, starting with biology professor Anne Fausto-Sterling's declaration that at least five sexes exist along a continuum (male, merm, herm, ferm, female).[20] Activists embraced the term "intersex" to describe a person who "is born with a reproductive or sexual anatomy that doesn't seem to fit the typical definitions of female or male."[21] They also demanded a shift from a concealment approach to a more patient-centered model. Language has power to reinforce binaries that use people in real ways.

People often assume that race, like sex, is a biological (and hence objective and unchanging) designation, but history and recent studies show that race is socially constructed. In 1751, US founding leader Benjamin Franklin worried that Germans would take over Pennsylvania and would "Germanize us instead of our Anglifying them, and will never adopt our Language or Customs, any more than they can acquire our Complexion."[22] Franklin's reference to "complexion" reveals that he did not see Germans as the same ethnicity. Irish, Italian, Russian, and Spanish immigrants generally were thought of as "colored" until the 1960s.[23] Historian Noel Ignatiev conducted a book-length analysis of *How the Irish Became White.*[24]

Just as a group's racial designation may shift, so too can an individual's. Recent studies show that "how individuals are racially classified by others and how they identify themselves . . . both change over time."[25] In a series of studies, sociologists Andrew M. Penner, Aliya Saperstein, and their colleagues discovered the following:

- "Cirrhosis decedents are more likely to be recorded as American Indian on their death certificates, and homicide victims are more likely to be recorded as Black [by medical examiners and funeral directors even if they were not identified as such by next of kin], . . . suggest[ing] that seemingly non-racial characteristics, such as cause of death, affect how people are racially perceived by others and thus shape U.S. official statistics."[26]

- "individuals who are unemployed, incarcerated, or impoverished are more likely to be seen and identify as black and less likely to be seen and identify as white, regardless of how they were classified or identified previously."[27]

- Not only does "incarceration increase[e] the likelihood that people are racially classified by others as black, and decreas[e] the likelihood that they are classified as white," but "even one arrest significantly increases the odds of subsequently being classified as black, and decreases the odds of being classified as white or Asian."[28]

These researchers explain the role of daily communicative interactions on people's understanding of race: "Our results emphasize not only that racial divisions are drawn by macro-level decision making but that race and racial inequality are constantly created and renegotiated in everyday interactions."[29] National Public Radio science desk correspondent Shankar Vedantam notes, "Strong stereotypes lin[k] race with crime. . . . this research suggest[s] [that] it's not just our perceptions of race that drive our stereotypes, but our stereotypes that drive our perceptions of race." Such studies illustrate the social nature of race. Race is a concept developed by people rather than a function of biology.[30]

Language's ability to use us is explained by the idea of a **terministic screen,** which Burke describes as *a screen composed of terms through which humans perceive the world, and that direct attention away from some interpretations and toward others.* For Burke, language always acts to direct attention, making all communication persuasive because "[e]ven if any given terminology is a *reflection* of reality, by its very nature as a terminology it must be a *selection* of reality; and to this extent it must function also as a *deflection* of reality."[31] Your words screen what you see.

Every single time you think about something, the words you use to articulate your thoughts have directed your attention in one way rather than another. The terms "male," "female," and "opposite sex" contribute to a terministic screen that induces humans to see only males or females; without a term such as "intersex," the existence of people who do not fit the sex binary is deflected. Terms such as "black," "white," and "Indian" also induce people to see a person's race first, as a thing that differentiates one person from others, rather than to see people's shared humanity. Because people tend to associate some races with crime and others with alcoholism, if a person is a criminal, they see the person as black. If the person dies from a drinking-related disease, they see the person as a Native American. Because people also tend to think in binaries in terms of race, they see someone as *either* black *or* white. For example, even though Barack Obama is the son of a white woman and an African man, he is often referred to as black.

Because US society has symbols that stand for money (currency), people tend to judge the quality of an item through its monetary value: attention is directed to a thing's cost, rather than its intrinsic characteristics. This monetary symbol system directs people's attention so powerfully, people judge the same thing to be of a higher quality when *only* the price assigned to it is changed. In a fascinating study that tested the power of marketing, researchers at the California Institute of Technology and Stanford University told volunteer subjects they would be tasting different wines sold at different prices, when actually they were given the same wine over and over. Not only did the subjects indicate that the supposedly more expensive wine tasted better, their medial orbitofrontal cortexes (the part of the brain that processes feelings of pleasantness) reacted differently.[32] Because the dollar symbol directed their attention to read "more expensive" as "better quality," they were not able to see (or taste) what their own senses could have imparted—that all the wine was exactly the same.

Another example of the effect of terministic screens comes from the reproductive freedom and abortion controversy, a rhetorically charged issue in the contemporary United States. Two main sides have long dominated the controversy: pro-life and pro-choice. People who are pro-life tend to refer to the reality as a "baby" while those who are pro-choice tend to refer to the reality as a "fetus." Each term selects, deflects, and reflects reality in a particular way, and calls forth different clusters of terms that flesh out the contours of the screen.[33]

"Baby" accurately reflects reality insofar as people often ask "when is the baby due?" and feel pain at miscarriages as the loss of a baby. The term also selects a particular aspect of reality to highlight: it focuses your attention on the idea that the reality is a fully formed human being, separable from its gestational location. A person could leave a baby in a room unattended (though safely ensconced in a crib). However, when the baby is in the womb, it cannot be separated from its location. The term also selects a particular type of relationship to other human beings: "babies" have mothers and fathers, not women and men. "Baby" also calls forth positive associations because US culture is pronatal—it celebrates the arrival of babies—and perceives babies as innocent and pure. Once people think of the reality as a separate and distinct human being, to terminate its existence means that someone has murdered the baby. Babies can be murdered; people do not talk about "terminating" babies.

In the process of selecting some parts of reality to highlight, the term "baby" also deflects part of reality. It deflects that the reality is located within a woman's body, as well as the possibility that women can be anything more than mothers. It also deflects the fact that recognized development stages exist in the human as it undergoes gestation: from zygote, to blastocyst, to embryo, to fetus.

In the same way that "baby" reflects, deflects, and selects parts of reality, so too does the term "fetus," which selects those parts of reality that "baby" deflects. "Fetus" notes that the reality is described in medical and scientific terms, that gestational stages exist through which the fetus eventually becomes a complete human being, and that a fetus cannot exist without a woman to carry it. In fact, "fetus" reverses the order of the relationship created by "baby": babies have mothers, while women carry fetuses. The "baby" is an entity that has agency and rights—a baby has a mother, and focus is literally on the baby first. With "fetus," the woman is the entity that has agency and rights—she carries the fetus, and focus is on her first.

In selecting the medical reality of the fetus, the term highlights that the fetus is not a complete human being. Although people may think fondly of sitting in a rocking chair and cuddling with a baby, the image of cuddling with a fetus is not quite the same.

In the process of selecting, "fetus" also deflects attention away from things the term "baby" selects. "Fetus" deflects the emotional attachments people have to small human forms, as well as the possibility that the fetus can be murdered. Fetuses are not murdered; instead, pregnancies are terminated.

The clusters of terms around "baby" and "fetus" form terministic screens through which individuals construct and view reality. Those screens form a context that infuses the terms with particular connotations, even though each term ostensibly refers to the same referent. As terms direct people's attention in one way rather than another, they "affect the nature of our observations." Burke posits that "much that we take as observations about 'reality' may be but the spinning out of possibilities implicit in our particular choice of terms."[34]

Public Vocabulary

Because rhetoric constructs, maintains, and transforms your understanding of reality, to understand some event in the world or some policy enacted by the government, one must ask not just "What is it?" but also "How do we talk about it?" Communication scholar Celeste Condit argues that the "process of convincing" involves more than just acceptance of a particular policy; it also requires "that a given vocabulary (or set of understandings) be integrated into the public repertoire."[35] John L. Lucaites and Celeste Condit describe this **public vocabulary** as the *"culturally established and sanctioned" terms that compose people's taken-for-granted understanding of the world.*[36] A public vocabulary forms a society's terministic screen. In debates about civil rights, the public vocabulary includes words such as "equality" and "justice," stories of racism such as Rosa Parks being forced to sit at the back of the bus and the murder of Emmet Till, and characterizations of the United States as a place that must "let freedom ring." Daily, people in a community call upon this vocabulary to justify social actions, but when conditions call for social change, "the public vocabulary needs to be managed and reconstituted in ways that require" rhetorical skill.[37] Rhetors can try to "rearrange and revivify" the existing vocabulary, or they can introduce new vocabulary.[38] Ideographs, characterizations, narratives, and metaphors are key elements of the public vocabulary.

Ideographs. Michael Calvin McGee, a communication scholar, coined the term **ideograph** to represent *"an ordinary language term found in political discourse. It is a high-order abstraction representing collective commitment to a particular but equivocal and ill-defined normative goal. It warrants the use of power, excuses behavior and belief which might otherwise be perceived as eccentric or antisocial, and guides behavior and belief into channels easily recognized by a community as acceptable or laudable."*[39] Words such as "freedom" and "security" are examples of ideographs: they are abstract words, used in ordinary language, that warrant the use of power. People cannot point at freedom or security, yet US troops are ready to give their lives to defend them. On September 11, 2001, when physical structures (the World Trade Center and the Pentagon) had been attacked, President George W. Bush used abstract language to declare: "our very freedom came under attack."[40] Because freedom was under attack and US security was undermined, Bush called for a collective commitment to the War on Terror. Such a call was a clear attempt to warrant the use of presidential power, both in the invasion of Afghanistan and the later attack on Iraq.

It may seem strange to think of military action as antisocial, but consider this: typically, we do not condone one person taking the life of another and, hence, name it "murder." However, in a time of war, people do condone taking lives, and tend to speak of it as killing (the enemy) rather than as murder. Killing in the name of freedom is not murder. An antisocial behavior is condoned, in part because the abstraction calls for the people to condone the use of that power. The ideograph of "freedom" warrants the use of deadly force.

Scholars have studied a range of ideographs, including family values,[41] equality,[42] choice, and life.[43] In each case, the word offers a way to track ideology as expressed through language.

Characterizations and Narratives. **Characterizations** are *the labels and descriptions rhetors attach to acts, agencies, agents, scenes, and purposes.* These five terms constitute what Burke calls the dramatistic pentad. An *act* is "what took place, in thought or deed"; *scene* is "the background of the act, the situation in which it occurred"; *agent* is the "person or kind of person" who "performed the act"; *agency* is the means by which the act was accomplished; and *purpose* is the justification for the act.[44] Whenever you analyze a rhetorical act, you should be able to identify the way a rhetor characterizes each of these elements.

By exploring where differences arise among rhetors' characterizations of these elements, you can identify motives and reasons for disagreement. As Burke explains, people "may violently disagree about the purposes behind a given act, or about the character of the person who did it, or how he [or she] did it, or in what kind of situation he [or she] acted; or they may even insist upon totally different words to name the act itself."[45] Thus, to understand human communication, you need to understand the stories told and the way in which the elements of the stories are characterized. Characterizations are never neutral but, according to Lucaites and Condit, "integrate cultural connotations and denotations while ascribing a typical and pervasive nature to the entity described."[46] These labels guide the way a society attaches values to people or actions. Depending on how an agent, scene, or act is characterized, your reactions to that agent, scene, or act may change.

For example, when the "Don't tase me, bro!" video went viral on YouTube in September 2007, characterizations influenced people's reactions.[47] The video was made when US Senator John Kerry addressed a Constitution Day Forum at the University of Florida. Andrew Meyer, a senior telecommunication major, asked why Kerry had conceded the 2004 presidential election and whether Kerry was a member of the Yale secret society Skull and Bones. As Meyer's questions exceeded the time allowed, university police officers attempted to escort Meyer out of the lecture hall. Meyer insisted he had done nothing wrong and declared his right to stay in front of the microphone. His microphone was turned off. The officers began to escort him outside forcibly. When he resisted, the officers drew a taser. Meyer screamed: "Don't tase me, bro!" as one of the officers fired the taser at him.

Initially, serious questions arose about an apparent use of excessive force against a college student. The act of tasing was characterized as unwarranted; the officers as out of line. As descriptions of Meyer emerged, however, the focus shifted from the officers' (agent) unwarranted (purpose) excessive use of force (act) and to Meyer as the agent. Media outlets described Meyer's purpose not as the exercise of free speech, but as seeking attention. One day after the incident, CNN reported that Meyer had brought his own camera and had a friend videotape him.[48] The *International Herald Tribune* reported that Meyer had begun his question only after he confirmed the other student had started videotaping, and noted that Meyer had a "penchant for practical jokes."[49] ABC's *Good Morning America* reported that Meyer "has a reputation for practical jokes, and stars in short comedy films he posts on the Internet."[50]

As this incident demonstrates, the same act and person can be characterized in very different ways. In one version, the officers acted in an unnecessarily violent way against an innocent college student exercising his free speech rights. In another version, an obnoxious practical joker pushed the officers to an extreme reaction by abusing the decorum of a public forum. Once the event became characterized by the juvenile request of "Don't tase me, bro," the focus firmly shifted to Meyer, and characterizations of Meyer affected the way people interpreted the tasing incident. It became a laughable practical joke, rather than an excessive use of state power.

Characterizations are the building blocks of narratives, or stories. Narratives direct people to see particular relationships between characterizations and, thus, offer explanations about how reality makes sense and works.[51] You tell stories about family members, daily events, classroom incidents, and yourself; and to explain why others should (or should not) take a specific course or professor. People's reliance on stories to better understand the world in which they live led moral philosopher Alasdair MacIntyre to describe the human being as "a story-telling animal."[52] (Chapter 5 explores narratives in more depth.)

Narratives play a significant role in public communication. They form and maintain public memory and teach cultural values. Communication scholar Walter Fisher identifies the way narratives offer good reasons in public deliberation and help people make sense of the world.[53] The dominant social narrative that informs the US public vocabulary is the American Dream, most vividly illustrated by Horatio Alger's stories. Alger wrote hundreds of books in the 1800s about young working-class men pulling themselves up by their boot-straps in order to improve their positions in life and achieving rags-to-riches success. These stories embodied the US ideal that regardless of where people start out, if they work hard enough, they can achieve success. Rhetorical critics Robert C. Rowland and John M. Jones suggest that when public figures refer to the "American Dream," they tap into this narrative and its characterization of the people in the United States as being "on a progressive journey to a better society."[54]

Metaphors. A **metaphor** is *a figure of speech in which two dissimilar things are said to be similar, offering a new perspective on a known issue.* For example, when Plato's *Republic* refers to government as the ship of state,[55] "ship" is a metaphor for government. Most people define government as the administrative arm of a state, but the power of government to direct the future of a state is not really made clear in that definition.

Burke explains that metaphor provides "perspective" insofar as it is "a device for seeing something *in terms of* something else. It brings out the thisness of a that, or the thatness of a this."[56] In Plato's metaphor, people learn something about government by looking at it as a ship; they gain perspective on the ship-ness of government. By thinking about government as a ship, one begins to think about government as having a direction, navigating through troubled waters, and needing a captain.

Insofar as metaphors enable you to see one thing in terms of something else, linguistics professor George Lakoff and philosophy professor Mark Johnson believe, they enable a person to "elaborate a concept . . . in considerable detail" and "find appropriate means for highlighting some aspects of it and hiding others."[57] Burke's observation that language selects and deflects is echoed by Lakoff and Johnson's description of how metaphors function.

A range of metaphors populates language ("range" and "populate" both being metaphors themselves). Lakoff and Johnson argue that metaphor is not only a "device of the poetic imagination" but a matter of "ordinary language."[58] They believe people's "ordinary conceptual system is metaphorical in nature,"[59] which means you cannot understand language unless you understand metaphor. Every sentence you use contains metaphors. In the previous sentence, "contains" is a metaphor. Sentences are words, and cannot really contain anything; but if you think of a sentence as a structure with sides, it can hold other things ("structure," "sides," and "hold" all being extensions of the metaphor "contains").

The power of metaphor resides in its ability to structure thought. Metaphors help people make sense of the world. Lakoff explores the metaphors "tax relief" and "tax burden" to demonstrate. According to Lakoff, "relief" implies that one has some affliction. In this case taxes are a burden, from which people need to be relieved. Within this metaphor, the person who relieves another of a burden is a hero, while anyone who would interfere with relief is a villain. What if, instead, people think of taxes as a patriotic obligation for living in the United States and reaping the benefits of its infrastructure? Lakoff points out:

> As Oliver Wendell Holmes famously said, taxes are the price of civilization. They are what you pay to live in America—your dues— to have democracy, opportunity and access to all the infrastructure that previous taxpayers have built up and made available to you: highways, the Internet, weather reports, parks, the stock market, scientific research, Social Security, rural electrification, communications satellites, and on and on. If you belong to America, you pay a membership fee and you get all that infrastructure plus government services: flood control, air-traffic control, the Food and Drug Administration, the Centers for Disease Control and so on. . . . It is an issue of patriotism! Are you paying your dues, or are you trying to get something for free at the expense of your country? It's about being a member.[60]

The metaphors of "dues" and "burden" structure your understanding of taxes in different ways.

Metaphors are ubiquitous and inconspicuous at the same time. They populate language, yet few people are aware of their presence. Metaphor's stealth nature is part of its power to structure thought. Political scientist Riikka Kuusisto warns that if people do not recognize that metaphors express a particular and necessarily limited perspective, the implications of these metaphors may be heard as "objective factual descriptions and come to define the only way of seeing and doing things in a specific situation."[61] Instead of offering *a* perspective, the metaphor comes to be *the* perspective. If you do not hear how metaphors direct your attention, you will begin to accept a metaphorical interpretation of the world as fixed and objective reality.

In her analysis of Western metaphors concerning the war in Kosovo, Kuusisto identifies the ways US President Bill Clinton, British Prime Minister Tony Blair, and French President Jacques Chirac described the conflict through the metaphors of heroic fairy tale, athletic game, and business deal. All these metaphors operated in subtle ways to structure people's understanding of the conflict: "they made participation in the conflict chivalrous and reassuring (heroic tales), exciting and fun (games), and profitable and rational (trading)."[62] In the process, the metaphors downplayed "the misery, pain, and turbulence often associated with deadly quarrels."[63] Kuusisto concludes the metaphors "brought the complicated and destructive conflict into the sphere of the well-known and harmless."[64] The metaphors enabled people who lived outside the conflict zone and had no direct experience of the horrors of war to understand the war, but also provided a very particular understanding, one that "tied the progression of the events to a logic of responding and accepting the challenge, a logic that could not easily be reversed into negotiating or giving the enemy a second chance."[65] The metaphors of war as fairy tale, game, and trading directed attention toward reassurance, fun, and rationality, and deflected attention away from the horror of war.

Discursive and Presentational Forms

Susanne Langer, a prominent philosopher, significantly contributed to understanding the primary role symbols play in constructing meaning within cultures and individuals, and how rhetors and audiences achieve meaning collaboratively.[66] Langer explored all forms of symbol use, including those related to art, myth, ritual, and science. To highlight the diverse functions that symbols perform, she advanced an important distinction between two types of symbols: discursive and presentational.

Discursive symbolism is *language use with a linear structure that operates through reason and not intuition*—for example, deliberative discourse. Discursive form breaks down complex relationships into an easy-to-follow linear structure, such as problem/cause/solution. In contrast, **presentational symbolism** is *"a direct presentation of an individual object"* that *"widens our conception of rationality far beyond the traditional boundaries, yet never breaks faith with logic in the strictest sense."*[67] Art and music are Langer's primary examples of presentational symbolism, but she also highlighted how some uses of language participated in presentational form. Langer uses the metaphor of clothing to explain the differences between the two forms:

> All language has a form which requires us to string out our ideas even though their objects rest one within the other; as pieces of clothing that are actually worn one over the other have to be strung side by side on the clothesline. This property of verbal symbolism is known as *discursiveness:* by reason of it, only thoughts which can be arranged in this peculiar order can be spoken at all; any idea which does not lend itself to this "projection" is ineffable, incommunicable by means of words.[68]

If you wanted to share your experience of seeing a moose in the wild, you could do so discursively or presentationally. Discursively, you would articulate what you saw in a linear format, word after word, breaking down the experience into a description of the time, the place, the sounds, the smells, and your emotions. The experience would unfold bit by bit. In contrast, presentationally, you could offer a painting or a photograph; or you could create a virtual experience of the moose all at once, the time, place, sounds, and your emotions all contained in the presentational form, taken in by your audience not over time as your words unfold, but all at once as they look at the image. You could also use a metaphor and say that seeing the moose was a "thrill ride."

Metaphors are verbal symbolic acts that function on a level beyond the discursive and, thus, are presentational. Even though verbal metaphors are presented in discursive form (through language), they operate presentationally. In fact, Langer argues, "Metaphor is our most striking evidence of *abstractive seeing*, of the power of human minds to use presentational symbols."[69] Metaphors encourage people to see one thing in terms of something else. In so doing, they collapse, rather than string out on a line, all the points made about the thing. A metaphor takes a complex subject with many components (say, war) and collapses them into a single easy-to-grasp concept (say, fairy tale). Langer's main argument is that discursive action is not the only form of "articulate symbolism."[70] Presentational symbols that operate on the level of intuition and the gestalt can be both articulate and reasonable.

The German word "Gestalt" refers to a shape or form. In contemporary usage, **gestalt** is *a pattern or structure whose parts are so integrated that one cannot really describe the pattern simply by referring to the parts.* Langer explains, "The symbolic materials given to our senses, the *Gestalten* or fundamental perceptual forms which invite us to construe the pandemonium of sheer impression into a world of things and occasions, belong to the 'presentational' order."[71] An example often used to illustrate how human beings make sense of random impression is the "dog picture" attributed to R. C. James.[72] At first glance, the picture appears to be a random series of dots, but because the human brain possesses the perceptual form of "dog," the image of a Dalmatian emerges.

Gestalt explains how metaphors condense a series of impressions into a single understandable thing. For example, the metaphor of a computer virus uses the existing understanding of "virus" (a microscopic infectious agent that replicates inside living cells) to make sense of the pandemonium that happens when a software program is introduced into your computer to make it do something you do not want, often causing harm to your computer and your data and, in the process, replicating itself so that it can be transferred to other computers. Many things happen when you execute a software program on your computer, but the key thing on which the metaphor of "virus" focuses your attention is the idea of replication causing harm.

Presentational form helps people make sense of a barrage of impressions by ordering them into a form, but a form that is more than just the sum of its parts. Just as language can name and condense a large category of things into a single term, presentational symbolism can "telescope" many concepts into a single image that psychoanalysts call a condensation symbol.[73] In psychology, a condensation symbol is a single symbol that represents multiple emotions, ideas, feelings, memories, or impulses. In relation to civic discourse, political science scholar Doris Graber defines a **condensation symbol** as "*a name, word, phrase, or maxim which stirs vivid impressions involving the listener's most basic values*" *and readies the listener for action.*[74]

Within rhetoric, scholars study ideographs, as well as god and devil terms, as the primary forms of condensation symbols.[75] Rhetoric scholar Richard Weaver describes *god term* as an "expression about which all other expressions are ranked as subordinate," and that has the "capacity to demand sacrifice."[76] In contrast, *devil terms* are "terms of repulsion."[77]

Condensation symbols, including ideographs and god and devil terms, whether verbal or visual, operate presentationally because they do not lay out a series of ideas side by side, but instead condense them into an inseparable whole. "My country," "Old Glory," "American Dream," "un-American," and "family values" are examples of presentational form because they create a picture of the referent that possesses intense emotional or affective power. Langer's emphasis on these symbols reflects her interest in how symbolic action always involves emotional appeals and not merely rational claims. Groups often try to use these forms to advance a cause. For example, the Human Rights Campaign, the largest national lesbian, gay, bisexual, and transgender (LGBT) civil rights organization, uses the verbal condensation symbols of "Human Rights" and "Equal Rights" in its campaigns.[78] Those who oppose extending legal protections to LGBT people often refer to those legal protections as "special rights."[79] To counter the idea that those rights are special, the Human Rights Campaign highlights that the rights it fights for are human rights and *equal* rights. It supplements these powerful terms with a mathematical symbol that condenses their meaning into a symbolic form: the "=" symbol, which the campaign hopes will appeal to the United States's historic commitment to equality.

We end our discussion of discursive and presentational symbolism with an example that highlights the difference between them. On July 9, 2011, a young woman named Regan posted a four minute and forty-one second, black-and-white video, titled "Retarded," to YouTube.[80] As of January 2, 2015, the video had over 94,288 views and numerous repostings on Pinterest, websites, and blogs. Throughout the video, the Rocket Summer's song "Walls" is playing. During the first four minutes and twenty seconds, Regan silently holds fifty-three hand-written sticky notes up to the camera. The notes mostly contain terms such as "waste of time," "awful," "ugly," "beastly," "crap," "loser," and "worthless." Her notes then tell us all these words are related to one word, "retarded" and, thus, to one person: "my brother." Her next note says that on urbandictionary.com, these are the top-voted definitions for "retarded" (misspelled on the video) and that her brother will never be able to speak to her, but because he means the world to her, she will be his voice. Her last notes ask people to think about what "retarded" (and "retarted") mean before using the word. The last twenty seconds show her interacting with her brother Russell, who has Down Syndrome and autism. On the YouTube page, she asks viewers to go to urbandictionary.com to vote down these definitions.

If you watch the video, think about how our discursive description cannot really capture its presentational power. Although the words Regan presents are central to the video, more is going on than the discursive request to stop using the term and to vote down the definitions. Note after note after note with pejorative terms builds an impression of hurt and pain. Her distraught face, the accumulation of the notes, and the mournful music all build an impression that exceeds the words themselves. In fact, even the words are more than discursive symbols: the hurtful power of the words is made present by their accumulation. The video ending, with her brother laughing and smiling, shows that he is not worthless. In reducing the video to only the words used, to the discursive appeal, you miss the power of the video as a presentational whole.

Viewers responded by voting down the definitions on urbandictionary.com. Regan thanked them in a follow-up video.[81] In fact, if you visited urbandictionary.com in June 2014, the top definition of "retarted" focused on the hurt and pain that the word causes even when it is spelled correctly. Entries on the site also encouraged people to stop using the word in hurtful ways and to join the Spread the Word to End the Word movement.[82]

Resignification

The concepts of terministic screens, public vocabulary, and discursive and presentational form explain how language constructs social meaning and effects social change. Language itself can also be the focus of change—where the meanings of words, as words, are challenged and transformed. Burke noted this possibility when he wrote "a Dramatistic approach to the analysis of language starts with problems of terministic catharsis," which he describes as "when a major term is found somehow to have moved on, and thus to have in effect changed its nature either by adding new meanings to its old nature, or by yielding place to some other term that henceforth takes over its functions wholly or in part."[83] A term might be "moved on" when its connotations are challenged.

Resignification is *a process in which people reject the connotation of a symbol, expose how the meaning of the symbol is constructed, and attempt to change its connotation.* If a group is labeled with a particular word, it can reject the sign, saying "That word does not accurately denote us," or resignify the sign, saying "That word does denote our group, but its connotation is one we reject." Words with an intense connotation, words many are loathe to utter, are words that demand resignifying. If a term is so powerful it can do damage to a person labeled with it, then its power should be challenged. In some cases, the challenge takes the form of resignification. If a term is mild and noncontroversial, the group would not need to resignify it; thus, the examples to follow are trigger words or loaded terms.

Lawyer and civic activist Urvashi Vaid, in her analysis of lesbian and gay rights, finds that gay men originally used "queer" as a form of self-naming. By the 1920s, men who thought of themselves as different because of their homosexual attraction to other men called themselves "queer."[84] The term later developed its negative connotation when it began to be used as an epithet in playgrounds and streets. This connotation did not develop overnight. As rhetoric scholar Judith Butler explains, "'Queer' derives its force precisely through the repeated invocation by which it has become linked to accusation, pathologization, insult."[85] The connotation of a term is not an inherent or fixed part of it: what is signified develops over time, as people repeatedly use the term in contexts that infuse it with negative (or positive) meaning.

The fact that terms have histories explains the difficulty involved in resignifying them. People cannot simply decree that the connotation of a term changes. If a connotation develops as the result of repeated usage in contexts that derogate, it can only change as the result of repeated usage in contexts that infuse the term with new, positive connotations. Resignification requires the repeated invocation of a term, linking it to praise, normalization, and celebration. The meaning of "queer" has altered with the emergence of queer theory and queer studies in the academy, Queer Nation's chant "We're here! We're queer! Get used to it!" and queer theory scholars such as Vaid reclaiming the term. Unfortunately, even when a term is resignified within a group, its new meaning may not carry beyond that group, which is why "queer" is still used as an epithet against people. Even though resignification is possible, it is difficult.

SlutWalks are another example of resignification.[86] Historically, the word "slut" referred to a slovenly girl; in contemporary usage, it has risen to the status of a "four-letter word"[87] referring to a sexually promiscuous woman. Illustrating this usage, in January 2011 a police officer at a York University (Canada) panel on campus safety said women should stop dressing like "sluts" if they wanted to avoid sexual assault.[88] Campus activists responded by planning SlutWalks. In so naming them, organizers meant to signal that they could be both pro-sex and anti-rape.[89] Organizers of SlutWalk Seattle made clear the importance of the term: "One of the most effective ways to fight hate is to disarm the derogatory terms employed by the haters, embracing them and giving them positive connotations."[90] SlutWalks, and the activism around them, have embraced the term "slut" and sought to change its meaning.[91] In 2011 alone, tens of thousands of people marched in over two hundred cities and forty countries.[92]

Resistance to reclaiming "slut" illustrates the complexity of resignification. Sociology professor Gail Dines and law professor Wendy J. Murphy describe the attempt to change the meaning as a "waste of precious feminist resources," because the term is "so saturated with the ideology that female sexual energy deserves punishment."[93] A group of black women also challenge the SlutWalk movement to rename and rebrand itself. Calling for an intersectional approach, they argue: "As Black women, we do not have the privilege . . . to play on destructive representations burned in our collective minds, on our bodies and souls for generations."[94] They explain that, given the power of historical and contemporary stereotypes about black women's sexuality, the word "slut" carries more intense emotional baggage for them and, thus, is less open to being resignified when applied to black women's bodies. A feminist blogger also noted the challenges in resignifying the term, given its repeated invocations:

I have been called a slut for having sex, for not having sex, and for
being coerced into sex. . . . I wish that this word did not hold the power
it does. . . . Regardless of whether or not I decide to redefine the word.
It continues to be used in this way. And so I still 'grapple' with the
word, 'slut'.

This is not to say that attempting to change language is not a
purposeful endeavour. Or that to take away the power a word has to hurt
and abuse people is impossible. But rather that this is something that we
must not only agree upon, as the oppressed group who has decided to
reclaim the oppressive word, and that this takes time. While the argument
has been made that the intent is not to force this supposed "reclamation"
on others, that, rather, anyone can volunteer to be a "slut or an ally,"
the very uncomfortable fact that Slutwalk pressures women (and men!)
into accepting this word, a violent word, as part of their empowerment
discourse, is not addressed. In fact it seems to go unnoticed.[95]

Although resignification is possible, it is not easy. Rhetors cannot simply snap
their fingers and declare that the connotation of a word has changed. Who uses
the term, in what context, and to what end, all matter, as does the repeated uses
of the word by others whose politics and terministic screens may not align with
the resignifiers'.

THE MISUSE OF LANGUAGE

When Burke describes human beings as "symbol-making, symbol-using, symbol-
misusing,"[96] he means that symbol use is not neutral. Symbols can be used to
create differences among people, or to denigrate groups or individuals. They can
be used to damage people, ideas, or institutions. In this section, we discuss some
misuses of language and ways to identify them. We do not provide an exhaustive
list of ethically questionable rhetoric, but introduce you to some of the unscru-
pulous ways that language can be used: doublespeak; truncated passives; and
people, places, and topics of silence. Most of this book celebrates the positive
uses of rhetoric as symbolic action, but language can also be used to deceive and
silence people.

Doublespeak

In his insightful novel *1984* (written in 1949), George Orwell depicted a society
misled by language. Orwell's fictional society developed a new form of English,
"Newspeak." In the novel, dictionaries were rewritten and words changed to alter
people's thinking. Orwell's conception of language is similar to the one we have
laid out in this chapter: language and thought are linked, so the way to manipulate thought is to manipulate language. Orwell described this new language in
the appendix of the novel: "The purpose of Newspeak was not only to provide
a medium of expression for the world-view and mental habits proper . . . [for
society], but to make all other modes of thought impossible."[97] Through the

use of Newspeak's deliberately ambiguous language, it became possible to hold views that were otherwise contradictory, enabling the ruling party of the state to have as the state slogan: "War is peace; freedom is slavery; ignorance is strength."

Unfortunately, Newspeak is not limited to the fictional world. Hitler's concentration camps used the slogan "work will set you free," even though no one was freed and the work was slave labor. More recently, the Obama administration was accused of using "newspeak" to explain its use of drones in the "war on terror."[98] In 2009, the United States intensified the war in Afghanistan with a surge in troop deployments and by "shifting use of Remote Piloted Aircraft—drones—from surveillance to targeted killing."[99] The killing was supposedly targeted, but in Pakistan alone, in the ten-year span between 2004 and 2014, drones killed 2310 to 3743 people, of whom 416 to 957 were civilians and 168 to 202 were children. Apparently the drones missed their targets over 20 percent of the time.[100] The decision on whom to "target" (meaning "kill") was based on a "disposition matrix," which journalist Glenn Greenwald called an "Orwellian euphemism for due-process-free presidential assassinations."[101]

Taking his cue from Orwell, English professor William Lutz wrote about **doublespeak,** *language used in the real world to confuse or deliberately distort its actual meaning rather than to achieve understanding.* Lutz explained doublespeak this way:

> Doublespeak is language that pretends to communicate but really doesn't. It is language that makes the bad seem good, the negative appear positive, the unpleasant appear attractive or at least tolerable. Doublespeak is language that avoids or shifts responsibility, language that is at variance with its real or purported meaning. It is language that conceals or prevents thought; rather than extending thought, doublespeak limits it.[102]

Lutz identifies two types of doublespeak: euphemism and inflated language.

A **euphemism** is *a word used to denote a thing in a way that avoids connotations of harshness or unpleasantness,* as when people refer to someone having "passed on" rather than "died." Another example can be found in how people talk about lying. A plethora of words are available in English to describe dishonesty or degrees of lying, most of which enable people to avoid saying that they lied: "white lie," "deception," "dishonesty," "untruth," "evasion," "falsehood," "fib," "fiction," "conceal," "hyperbole," "guile," "prevarication," "tall tale," "misstatement," "omission," "misleading," and so on. Very few words exist for honesty: the main examples are "blunt," "candid," and "frank."[103] Euphemisms can be unethical because they tend to lessen the harshness of something that probably should be judged harshly. In public discourse, governments have used euphemisms to distort military action. In October 1983, the Pentagon did not use the more straightforward "invasion" to describe the US invasion of Grenada, but the more obscure phrase "predawn vertical insertion."[104]

Inflated language, Lutz explains, is "*language designed to make the ordinary seem extraordinary; to make everyday things seem impressive; to give an air of importance to people, situations, or things that would not normally be considered* *important; to make the simple seem complex.*"[105] Inflated language is clearly evident in advertising. For instance, if you go to the store and see food labeled as "home-style," the language seems to suggest a type of food preparation. In reality the term is meaningless because it does not have a denotative meaning; it can be used to mean various things.[106] When television channels declare they are about to air a "special encore presentation," they are using inflated language to describe a rerun. People sometimes use inflated language on résumés when they try to make their jobs sound more impressive; for example, if you say you were a cleaning specialist instead of a janitor, or a special administrative assistant instead of a work-study student worker. (Just to be clear: you should not use inflated language on your résumé. Employers are very critical of inflated language.)

Truncated Passives

Language is much more than the words we use. Its power resides in the grammatical structure of language as well as in the individual words. Julia Penelope, a linguist who focuses on language's structures, reminds people "languages are much more than the words in their vocabularies. They are systems of rules. . . ."[107] Those rules, themselves, contain political consequences. In particular, she encourages people to watch out for **truncated passives,** *sentences that use a passive verb in order to delete the agent of action.* A sentence uses passive voice when it combines some "to be" verb with another verb and no do-er of the action appears in the sentence. Instead of active voice "I broke the toy," the passive voice "The toy was broken . . ." enables the speaker to leave out the phrase ". . . by me."

Individuals who attempt to avoid explicit responsibility for the consequences of the power they exercise often use truncated passives. When a communicator deletes the agent of action, then only the object on which the agent acted is present in the sentence. In this way, Penelope says, "Passives without agents foreground the objects (victims) in our minds so that we tend to forget that some human agent is responsible for performing the action,"[108] as in "mistakes were made" or "Hanoi was bombed."[109]

President Ronald Reagan introduced the passive phrase "mistakes were made" into public dialogue about presidential scandal, in response to the 1986–1987 Iran-Contra investigation. This phrase begged the question: mistakes were made *by whom?* Instead of saying "I made mistakes," or "This person made a mistake," the phrase made it seem as though the mistakes happened outside of human control. The phrase "mistakes were made" was resuscitated in 2014 by New Jersey Governor Chris Christie. In the "Bridgegate" scandal, his close aides, as a form of political retribution, had allegedly ordered lanes to the George Washington Bridge to be closed, resulting in a massive traffic jam. In his State of the State address, Christie said of the debacle, "Mistakes were clearly made."[110]

Penelope explains, "Agentless passives conceal and deceive when it doesn't suit speakers' or writers' purposes to make agency explicit. . . . This makes it easy to suppress responsibility" and, thus, results in "protection of the guilty and denial of responsibility, . . . the pretense of objectivity, . . . and trivialization."[111]

Identifying truncated passives is one way to identify hidden power. Once you identify a truncated passive, you begin to ask who had the power to do this thing that happened. When someone says "mistakes were made," ask "by whom?"

People, Places, and Topics of Silence

Language is not only a collection of words, but a system of rules with political consequences. Language rules influence who can speak, about what, and where. French philosopher Michel Foucault believed one could trace power by analyzing language. To truly understand language, he said, people need to understand that it is a form of power and a place where power is contested. He wrote about language rules governing people, places, and topics in his essay, "The Discourse on Language," in which he outlined "rules of exclusion" that control people's use of language:

> We know perfectly well that we are not free to say just anything, that we cannot simply speak of anything, when we like or where we like; not just anyone, finally, may speak of just anything. We have three types of prohibition, covering objects, ritual with its surrounding circumstances, the privileged or exclusive right to speak of a particular subject; these prohibitions interrelate, reinforce and complement each other, forming a complex web, continually subject to modification.[112]

Foucault recognized that there are certain topics about which people are not allowed to speak, that certain cultural practices limit what people speak about and how they can speak, and that certain topics may only be addressed by particular people (such as experts). These prohibitions also interact to create additional constraints. Who speaks, where, and about what is governed by rules of discourse. If you analyze language, then, you can discover people, places, and topics of silence.

Think about how these rules govern language use in a classroom. If a class is discussing a particular topic and a class member starts talking about something that goes beyond that topic, the other students might experience discomfort or irritation. Constraints on whose speech matters in the classroom also make power dynamics visible. For example, students rarely take notes when other students speak; nor do they direct their comments to other students, but instead funnel them through the instructor. In the classroom, the teacher is accorded credibility to speak. When students do formal presentations, they often move to the podium. People in the United States have been acculturated to the rules of discourse to recognize that the podium is a location that accords a person more power.

The rules governing people, places, and topics are in constant flux. A significant revision of the rules of discourse in the public sphere occurred as part of the US struggle to abolish slavery during the 1800s. Initially, slavery was viewed as a private economic matter, not an issue of public concern. The language of the time reflected this view. Additionally, when it came to debating issues in the public sphere, women and African Americans were not granted access. Thus, women and African Americans who were abolitionists had to justify their right to speak even before broaching the topic of slavery. They challenged the rules about who was allowed to speak. Only after they were allowed to speak were they able to demonstrate they were intellectually capable of being full citizens of the country. Their eloquence and rational argument made clear their brains were not inferior. Women's and African Americans' struggle for the podium (for the right to speak) was a challenge to the rules that governed communication in the public sphere.

The first US-born woman known to speak in public to a mixed-sex audience was African-American Maria W. Miller Stewart, who addressed Boston's African-American abolitionist community between 1831 and 1833.[113] Later, white Quaker sisters Sarah and Angelina Grimké spoke against slavery and argued that the era's dictates on womanhood were contradictory. Historian Barbara Welter, in her influential book *Dimity Convictions*, notes that during this time period, women were expected to be pure, pious, domestic, and submissive.[114] If a woman believed slavery was an affront to piety, however, she had to leave the domestic sphere to agitate against it. Ultimately, the rules governing discourse in the public sphere shifted. Slavery became a topic open to debate; women and African Americans were slowly recognized as legitimate participants in this debate; and the evidence they brought from their own experience began to count.

CONCLUSION

Language is messy, unpredictable, and fascinating. Still, people use it to make sense of their world. Language is a symbol system through which human beings construct, maintain, and transform social reality. It forms the terministic screens through which people observe and understand reality, and composes the public vocabulary central to public policy and identity formation. The role language plays in symbolic action is complex because language can operate both discursively and presentationally. Because it can operate presentationally—through metaphors and condensation symbols—it can become emotionally charged. Language is so central to reality that words, themselves, become a site for struggle, as in the case of resignification.

Language defines what people know. Human beings are both suspended in a web of signification and the spinners of the web. Language both enables and restrains; it makes sense of the world and imposes a particular sense on the world. It limits what you know, but also provides the possibility of seeing beyond the limits. Understanding that language does more than correspond to reality allows human beings to imagine a reality that may not yet exist. Language allows human beings to imagine, hope, and hypothesize.

Even though people tend to think public deliberation is at its best when purely logical and rational, in reality, the artistry of language affects its persuasiveness. Public discourse occurs within a larger cultural and symbolic context, or public vocabulary, and calls on taken-for-granted assumptions about the world. Thus, to convince another person of an idea, purely rational and objective argument is not enough because communication occurs through language that has judgments embedded within it. To convince people, you need to think about your vocabulary as much as your goal.

When responding to rhetoric and formulating rhetorical messages, people must understand, analyze, critique, and consider the language choices involved. The use of language to communicate is a symbolic action; consequently, individuals exercise choice about the nature of that action and about whether to use or misuse it.

The analysis of language requires nuanced thinking and facile imaginations. People must think not only about what was said, but what else could have been said. Why was one word chosen, and how did it direct your attention differently from the way another word might have? Identifying the difference between what was said and what could have been said will help identify the subtle ways in which rhetoric is at work. Identifying silences (of people, about topics, and in places) also enables you to identify the way language and power interact. Because language is a way to exercise power, and because power resides in language, understanding locations of silence is important.

DISCUSSION QUESTIONS

1. Can you think of an example where two different terms for the same thing direct your attention in different ways, selecting, reflecting, or deflecting different aspects of "reality"?
2. Can you think of examples of metaphors that have become so ingrained in the English language that people do not even think of them as metaphors?
3. Discuss how people, places, actions, and events are characterized in news coverage of a recent event. How were the people characterized? How did language shape the way the events, places, actions, and people were interpreted? Although news reporting is often considered to be objective, was the language in the news stories actually persuasive? How?
4. Find an advertisement and analyze the language of the ad. Can you identify a metaphor, a narrative, a characterization, an ideograph, and/or doublespeak? How does the ad use (or misuse) language?
5. Identify an example of a term undergoing resignification. How has its connotation changed? Has its denotation changed?

RECOMMENDED READINGS

Burke, Kenneth. "Dramatism." In *International Encyclopedia of the Social Sciences*, vol. 7. Edited by David L. Sills, 445–452. New York: Macmillan and Free Press, 1968.

Burke, Kenneth. "Terministic Screens." In *Language as Symbolic Action*, 44–62. Berkeley: University of California Press, 1966.

Fisher, Walter R. "Narration as a Human Communication Paradigm: The Case of Public Moral Argument." *Communication Monographs* 51, no. 1 (March 1984): 1–22.

Lakoff, George, and Mark Johnson. *Metaphors We Live By.* Chicago: University of Chicago Press, 1980.

McGee, Michael Calvin. "The 'Ideograph': A Link between Rhetoric and Ideology." *Quarterly Journal of Speech* 66, no. 1 (February 1980): 1–16.

ENDNOTES

[1] "Drop the I-Word," Colorlines, 2013, http://colorlines.com/droptheiword.

[2] Paul Colford, "'Illegal Immigrant' No More" (blog post), AP: *The Definitive Source,* April 2, 2013, http://blog.ap.org/2013/04/02/illegal-immigrant-no-more.

[3] As cited in Colford, "Illegal."

[4] Jose Antonio Vargas, quoted in Rachel Weiner, "AP Drops 'Illegal Immigrant' from Stylebook," *Washington Post,* April 2, 2013, http://www.washingtonpost.com/blogs /post-politics/wp/2013/04/02/ap-drops-illegal-immigrant-from-stylebook.

[5] Ferdinand de Saussure, quoted in Daniel Chandler, *Semiotics: The Basics* (New York: Routledge, 2007), 2–4.

[6] Sonya Andermahr, Terry Lovell, and Carol Wolkowitz, A *Glossary of Feminist Theory* (New York: Oxford University Press, 2000), 240.

[7] Edward Sapir, "The Status of Linguistics as a Science," *Language* 5, no. 4 (1929): 207–214, 209–210.

[8] Julia M. Penn, *Linguistic Relativity versus Innate Ideas* (Paris: Mouton, 1972), 39.

[9] Michael Mackenzie, "Marcel Duchamp and the Antimonies of Art Historical and Art Critical Discourse" (review essay), *Modernism/Modernity* 7, no. 11 (2000): 154.

[10] Mackenzie, "Marcel Duchamp," 154.

[11] Francis M. Naumann, "The Art of Defying the Art Market," *Tout-Fait: The Marcel Duchamp Studies Online Journal* 2, no. 5 (April 2003), http://www.toutfait.com /issues/volume2/issue_5/news/naumann/naumann1.htm.

[12] Edward Sapir, *Language: An Introduction to the Study of Speech* (New York: BiblioBazaar, 1921/1939/2007), 23.

[13] Julia Penelope, *Speaking Freely* (New York: Pergamon, 1990), 203.

[14] David Blakesley, "Introduction: Kenneth Burke, Word-Man," in Kenneth Burke, *Late Poems, 1968–1993: Attitudinizing Verse-Wise, While Fending for One's Selph, And in a Style Somewhat Artificially Colloquial* (Columbia: University of South Carolina Press, 2005), xvii.

[15] Kenneth Burke, "Dramatism," in *International Encyclopedia of the Social Sciences,* vol. 7, ed. David L. Sills (New York: Macmillan and Free Press, 1968), 447, italics added.

[16] Kenneth Burke, "Definition of Man," in *Language as Symbolic Action,* 3–24 (Berkeley: University of California Press, 1966), 6.

[17] Melanie Blackless, Anthony Charuvastra, Amanda Derryck, Anne Fausto-Sterling, Karl Lauzanne, and Ellen Lee, "How Sexually Dimorphic Are We? Review and Synthesis," *American Journal of Human Biology* 12 (2000): 151–166. See also Julie A. Greenberg, "Defining Male and Female: Intersexuality and the Collision between Law and Biology," *Arizona Law Review* 41 (Summer 1999): 265–328.

[18] Anne Tamar-Mattis, "Medical Decision Making and the Child with a DSD," *Endocrine Today,* November 10, 2008, http://endocrinetoday.com/view.aspx ?rid=32542.

[19] Suzanne J. Kessler, "The Medical Construction of Gender: Case Management of Intersexed Infants," *Signs* 16, no. 1 (Autumn 1990): 3–26.

[20] Anne Fausto-Sterling, "The Five Sexes," *The Sciences* 33, no. 2 (March/April 1993): 20–24.

[21] Intersex Society of North America, "What is Intersex?" 2008, http://www.isna.org/faq /what_is_intersex.

[22] Benjamin Franklin, "Observations Concerning the Increase of Mankind, Peopling of Countries, Etc.," 1751, para. 23, http://www.historycarper.com/resources/twobf2 /increase.htm.

[23] Judith N. Martin and Thomas K. Nakayama, *Intercultural Communication in Contexts*, 6th ed. (Boston: McGraw-Hill, 2012).

[24] Noel Ignatiev, *How the Irish Became White* (New York: Routledge, 2009).

[25] Andrew M. Penner and Aliya Saperstein, "How Social Status Shapes Race," *Proceedings of the National Academy of Sciences* 105, no. 50 (2008): 19628–19630.

[26] Andrew Noymer, Andrew M. Penner, and Aliya Saperstein, "Cause of Death Affects Racial Classification on Death Certificates," *PLoS One* 6, no. 1 (2011): e15812.

[27] Penner and Saperstein, "How," 19628.

[28] Aliya Saperstein, Andrew M. Penner, and Jessica M. Kizer, "The Criminal Justice System and the Racialization of Perceptions," *Annals of the American Academy of Political and Social Sciences* 651 (2014): 104–121. See also Aliya Saperstein and Andrew M. Penner, "Beyond the Looking Glass: Exploring Fluidity in Racial Self-Identification and Interviewer Classification," *Sociological Perspectives* 57 (2014): 186–207.

[29] Aliya Saperstein and Andrew M. Penner, "Racial Fluidity and Inequality in the United States," *American Journal of Sociology* 118, no. 3 (November 2012): 712.

[30] Shankar Vedantam, "Study: Stereotypes Drive Perceptions of Race," NPR: Code Switch, February 11, 2014, http://www.npr.org/blogs/codeswitch /2014/02/11/275087586/study-stereotypes-drive-perceptions-of-race?utm _medium=Email&utm_source=share&utm_campaign.

[31] Burke, "Terministic Screens," in *Language*, 45.

[32] Hilke Plassmann, John O'Doherty, Baba Shiv, and Antonio Rangel, "Marketing Actions Can Modulate Neural Representations of Experienced Pleasantness," *Proceedings of the National Academy of Sciences* 105, no. 3 (January 22, 2008): 1050–1054.

[33] The description of "fetus" and "baby" as illustrations of terministic screens first appeared in Victoria DeFrancisco and Catherine H. Palczewski, *Communicating Gender Diversity* (Thousand Oaks, CA: Sage, 2007), 110–111.

[34] Burke, "Terministic," 46.

[35] Celeste M. Condit, *Decoding Abortion Rhetoric: Communicating Social Change* (Urbana: University of Illinois Press, 1990), 6.

[36] John Louis Lucaites and Celeste Michelle Condit, "Reconstructing <Equality>: Culturetypal and Counter-Cultural Rhetorics in the Martyred Black Vision," *Communication Monographs* 57 (March 1990): 8.

[37] Lucaites and Condit, "Reconstructing," 8.

[38] Lucaites and Condit, "Reconstructing," 8.

[39] Michael Calvin McGee, "The 'Ideograph': A Link between Rhetoric and Ideology," *Quarterly Journal of Speech* 66 (February 1980): 15, italics added.

[40] George W. Bush, "Address to the Nation by President George W. Bush regarding Terrorist Attacks on the World Trade Center and the Pentagon," Federal News Service, September 11, 2001, LexisNexis.

[41] Dana L. Cloud, "The Rhetoric of <Family Values>: Scapegoating, Utopia, and the Privatization of Social Responsibility," *Western Journal of Communication* 62, no. 4 (Fall 1998): 387–419.

[42] Celeste Michelle Condit and John Louis Lucaites, *Crafting Equality: America's Anglo-African Word* (Chicago: University of Chicago Press, 1993).

[43] Celeste Condit Railsback, "The Contemporary American Abortion Controversy: Stages in the Argument," *Quarterly Journal of Speech* 70, no. 4 (November 1984): 410–424.

[44] Kenneth Burke, *A Grammar of Motives* (Berkeley: University of California Press, 1969), xv.

[45] Burke, *Grammar*, xv.

[46] Lucaites and Condit, "Reconstructing," 7.

[47] "University of Florida Student Tasered at Kerry Forum," YouTube.com, November 15, 2007, http://www.youtube.com/watch?v=6bVa6jn4rpE&feature=related. The authors want to thank Kaori Yamada for her research assistance with this example.

[48] "Cops on Leave after Taser Incident, Student's Behavior under Scrutiny," *CNN.com/US*, September 18, 2007, http://www.cnn.com/2007/US/09/18/student.tasered/index.html.

[49] "Florida Student Arrested, Tasered at Kerry Forum Has a Penchant for Practical Jokes," *International Herald Tribune*, September 17, 2007, http://www.iht.com/articles/ap/2007/09/18/america/NA-GEN-US-StudentTasered.php.

[50] ABC, "Taser Attack: Is Taser Use Out of Control?" *Good Morning America*, September 19, 2007, http://www.lexisnexis.com/us.

[51] Lucaites and Condit, "Reconstructing," 8.

[52] Alasdair MacIntyre, *After Virtue: A Study in Moral Theory*, 3rd ed. (Notre Dame, IN: University of Notre Dame Press, 2007), 216.

[53] Walter Fisher, "Narration as a Human Communication Paradigm: The Case of Public Moral Argument," *Communication Monographs* 51, no. 1 (March 1984): 1–22.

[54] Robert C. Rowland and John M. Jones, "Recasting the American Dream and American Politics: Barack Obama's Keynote Address to the 2004 Democratic National Convention," *Quarterly Journal of Speech* 93, no. 4 (November 2007): 430.

[55] Plato, *The Republic*, trans. Benjamin Jowett, book vi, http://classics.mit.edu/Plato/republic.7.vi.html.

[56] Burke, *Grammar*, 503.

[57] George Lakoff and Mark Johnson, *Metaphors We Live By* (Chicago: University of Chicago Press, 1980), 61.

[58] Lakoff and Johnson, *Metaphors*, 3.

[59] Lakoff and Johnson, *Metaphors*, 4.

[60] George Lakoff, "Framing the Dems," *American Prospect* 14, no. 8 (September 2003), http://www.prospect.org/cs/articles?article=framing_the_dems.

[61] Riikka Kuusisto, "Heroic Tale, Game, and Business Deal? Western Metaphors in Action in Kosovo," *Quarterly Journal of Speech* 88, no. 1 (February 2002): 54.

[62] Kuusisto, "Heroic Tale," 62.

[63] Kuusisto, "Heroic Tale," 62.

[64] Kuusisto, "Heroic Tale," 62.

[65] Kuusisto, "Heroic Tale," 62.

[66] For more on Langer's contribution to rhetorical theory, see Arabella Lyon, "Susanne K. Langer, Mother and Midwife at the Rebirth of Rhetoric," in *Reclaiming Rhetorica: Women in the Rhetorical Tradition*, ed. Andrea A. Lunsford, (Pittsburgh: University of Pittsburgh Press, 1995), 265–284.

[67] Susanne K. Langer, *Philosophy in a New Key*, 3rd ed. (Cambridge, MA: Harvard University Press, 1957), 96–97, italics added.

[68] Langer, *Philosophy*, 81–82.

[69] Langer, *Philosophy*, 141.

[70] Langer, *Philosophy*, 88.

[71] Langer, *Philosophy*, 98.

[72] For an example of the image, see http://psychology.jrank.org/pages/1286/6-Some -principles-with-examples.html, or search "dalmation gestalt picture."

[73] Langer, *Philosophy*, 191.

[74] Doris Graber, *Verbal Behavior and Politics* (Urbana: University of Illinois Press, 1976), 289, italics added.

[75] Murray Edelman, *The Symbolic Uses of Politics* (Urbana: University of Illinois Press, 1972), 6. See also David S. Kaufer and Kathleen M. Carley, "Condensation Symbols: Their Variety and Rhetorical Function in Political Discourse," *Philosophy and Rhetoric* 26, no. 3 (1993): 201–226.

[76] Richard M. Weaver, *The Ethics of Rhetoric* (Davis, CA: Hermagoras, 1985), 212, 214. See also Randall A. Lake, "The Metaethical Framework of Anti-Abortion Rhetoric," *Signs* 11, no. 3 (Spring 1986): 478–499.

[77] Weaver, *The Ethics*, 222.

[78] Human Rights Campaign, http://www.hrc.org (accessed May 1, 2009).

[79] See, for example, *Gay Rights/Special Rights—Inside the Homosexual Agenda*, Jeremiah Films, 1993, uploaded July 26, 2006, http://video.google.com/videoplay ?docid=7664929225320091404.

[80] RayMay52, "Retarded," YouTube.com, July 9, 2011, http://www.youtube.com/watch ?v=1iSlok6muY0.

[81] RayMay52, "Thank You," YouTube.com, October 18, 2011, http://www.youtube.com /watch?v=U5f5EohyhCo&list=UUxVwpX0Sjs38WHbmrlgogVA.

[82] "Retarded," *UrbanDictionary.com*, http://www.urbandictionary.com/define.php?term =retarded.

[83] Burke, "What are the Signs of What?" in *Language*, 367.

[84] Urvashi Vaid, *Virtual Equality* (New York: Anchor, 1995), 42.

[85] Judith Butler, *Bodies That Matter: On the Discursive Limits of "Sex"* (New York: Routledge, 1993), 226.

[86] This example is based on a similar section in Victoria P. DeFrancisco, Catherine H. Palczewski, and Danielle D. McGeough, *Gender in Communication*, 2nd ed. (Thousand Oaks, CA: Sage, 2014), 119–120.

[87] Geoff Nunberg, "Slut: The Other Four Letter S-Word," NPR: Fresh Air, March 13, 2012, http://www.npr.org/2012/03/13/148295582/slut-the-other-four-letter-s-word.

[88] Quoted in "Officer Tells Students Don't Dress Like a 'Slut,'" *MacLeans.ca*, February 17, 2011, http://www.macleans.ca/education/uniandcollege /officer-tells-students-dont-dress-like-a-slut.

[89] Deborah Tuerkheimer, "Slutwalking in the Shadow of the Law," *Minnesota Law Review* 98 (2014): 1453–1511.

[90] Quoted in Christie Thompson, "Taking *Slut* for a Walk," *Ms.* (Summer 2011), 14.

[91] Ratna Kapur, "Pink Chaddis and SlutWalk Couture: The Postcolonial Politics of Feminism Lite," *Feminist Legal Studies* 20 (2012): 1–20.

[92] Joetta L. Carr, "The SlutWalk Movement: A Study in Transnational Feminist Activism," *Journal of Feminist Scholarship* 4 (Spring 2013), http://www.jfsonline.org /issue4/articles/carr.

[93] Gail Dines and Wendy J. Murphy, "SlutWalk is Not Sexual Liberation," *Guardian*, May 8, 2011, http://www.guardian.co.uk/commentisfree/2011/may/08/slutwalk -not-sexual-liberation.

[94] "An Open Letter from Black Women to the SlutWalk," *Huffington Post*, September 23, 2011, http://www.huffingtonpost.com/susan-brison/slutwalk-black -women_b_980215.html.

[95] Meghan Murphy, "We're Sluts, Not Feminists. Wherein My Relationship with Slutwalk Gets Rocky," *The F Word: Feminist Media Collective*, May 7, 2011, http://feministcurrent.com/2585/were-sluts-not-feminists-wherein-my -relationship-with-slutwalk-gets-rocky.

[96] Burke, "Definition," 16.

[97] George Orwell, *1984*, ed. Irving Howe (New York: Harcourt, Brace, Jovanovich, 1982), 198.

[98] Andrew O'Hehir, "How Do You Explain Drone Killings? With Post-Orwellian 'Newspeak,'" Salon.com, February 9, 2013, http://www.salon.com/2013/02/09 /how_do_you_explain_drone_killings_with_post_orwellian_newspeak.

[99] G. Thomas Goodnight and Gordon R. Mitchell, "Drones: Argumentation in a Communication Control Society," in *Disturbing Argument*, ed. Catherine H. Palczewski (New York: Routledge, 2015).

[100] Bureau of Investigative Journalism, "Get the Data: Drone Wars: Casualty Estimates: Pakistan 2004–2014 CIS Drone Strikes," 2014, http://www.thebureauinvestigates .com/category/projects/drones/drones-graphs.

[101] Glenn Greenwald, "Obama Moves to Make the War on Terror Permanent," *Guardian*, October 24, 2012, http://www.theguardian.com/commentisfree/2012 /oct/24/obama-terrorism-kill-list.

[102] William Lutz, *Doublespeak* (New York: Harper and Row, 1989), 1.

[103] Penelope, *Speaking Freely*, 47.

[104] James Warren, "A Vertical Insertion of Doublespeak," *Chicago Tribune*, August 12, 1990, http://articles.chicagotribune.com/1990-08-12/features/9003070579_1 _double speak-award-committee-on-public-doublespeak-william-lutz.

[105] Lutz, *Doublespeak*, 6, italics added.

[106] Lutz, *Doublespeak*, 2–7.

[107] Penelope, *Speaking Freely*, xiii.

[108] Penelope, *Speaking Freely*, 146.

[109] The most recognized recent example may be Reagan's discussion of the events surrounding the Iran-Contra affair, when he remarked: "Mistakes were made." Commenting on a similar example, Penelope notes, "At a superficial level, the omission of direct and explicit reference to himself made the events seem far removed from our immediate experience, occurring in some abstract realm where human beings are not responsible for their actions" (Penelope, *Speaking Freely*, 145).

[110] Chris Christie, "2014 State of the State Address," *Washington Post*, January 14, 2014, http://www.washingtonpost.com/politics/full-text-of-new-jersey-gov-chris-christies -2014-state-of-the-state-speech/2014/01/14/8fd12f08-7d55-11e3-9556-4a4bf7bcbd84 _story.html.

[111] Penelope, *Speaking Freely*, 149.

[112] Michel Foucault, *The Archaeology of Knowledge and the Discourse on Language*, trans. R. Sawyer (New York: Pantheon, 1972), 216.

[113] Laura R. Sells, "Maria W. Miller Stewart," in *Women Public Speakers in the United States, 1825–1900*, ed. Karlyn Kohrs Campbell, 339–349 (Westport, CT: Greenwood, 1993).

[114] Barbara Welter, *Dimity Convictions: The American Woman in the Nineteenth Century* (Athens: Ohio University Press, 1976).

3

Visual Rhetoric

KEY CONCEPTS

body rhetoric

dominant reading

enactment

iconic photographs

image events

negotiated reading

oppositional reading

presence

rhetoric of display

visual culture

Images and material forms, as much as words, can be symbolic actions. A flag is material; it has a substance you can touch, but it is much more than a piece of fabric. It is visual; most people encounter a flag by looking at it (the US national anthem begins, "Oh, say! Can you see . . . ?"). The US flag is a symbol of the nation and its values. Supreme Court Justice John Paul Stevens once wrote: "The flag uniquely symbolizes the ideas of liberty, equality, and tolerance—ideas that Americans have passionately defended and debated throughout our history. The flag embodies the spirit of our national commitment to those ideals."[1] As a visual symbol, the flag can unify people behind shared ideals. To understand it, we need to ask not only what it represents (the United States) and what it means (for example, a star for every state), but also what it does.

Rhetorical forms that are other than language, or that include more than language, are typically referred to as "visual rhetoric." But as the example of the flag and the national anthem shows, more than just the sense of sight is involved.

You also encounter many forms of visual rhetoric through other senses: touch, taste, hearing, and smell. For example, the Vietnam Veterans Memorial illustrates that visual forms often stir more than the sense of sight. Located in the National Mall, the memorial includes a wall listing the names of over fifty-eight thousand service members killed during the war. (A statue of three soldiers, a flag pole, and a statue of women service members are also part of the memorial.) Visitors can not only see the wall, they can touch it as they take a rubbing of the name of a loved one, hear the weeping of others who visit it, smell the rain or fresh mown grass of the National Mall, and even taste the salt of their own tears.

Sometimes, however, people interpret visual and material artifacts[2] as merely representations of a reality, not as interpretations of it. People might see photographs, even photographs of the flag, as merely recording objective events. They might interpret the presence of the flag at the Vietnam Veterans Memorial as merely representing the nation for which the people it names fought and died. They might see the memorial as an objective listing of the war dead.

However, nonverbal symbolic action can shape people's beliefs and attitudes as much as verbal symbolic action. In fact, when the design for the Vietnam Veterans Memorial was selected, there was much outcry about the fact that it included no plans for a flag. In response, the Three Servicemen statue and a flagpole were added to the design.[3] The mere presence, or absence, of the flag means and does a great deal.

Another example shows that photographs are not just neutral records of reality. Since the Vietnam War, US government officials have been aware that images of coffins containing war dead returning home can affect public support of the war effort. Journalists coined a phrase to measure this effect: "the Dover Test." The test asks whether the US public will continue to support a war if it is faced with a stream of images of flag-draped coffins arriving at Dover Air Force base, through which, since 1955, the remains of all deceased armed forces personnel return from abroad.

The Dover Test achieved stark public awareness during President George H. W. Bush's term. In 1989, during the US invasion of Panama, twenty-three service members died. In news coverage, televisions showed a split-screen image, one half depicting flag-draped coffins arriving at Dover and the other half showing President Bush bantering with reporters during a news conference. The image created the impression that he was not concerned about the loss of life. In response, he banned media coverage of Dover arrivals during the Persian Gulf War in 1991.[4]

The ban remained in place until February 2009. The Pentagon lifted the ban after President Obama asked Defense Secretary Robert Gates to review the policy.[5] Presidents' willingness to maintain the ban showed they understood the power of a photo to influence public perception of a war. More powerful than media commentary about war casualties is a powerful image. Photos of flag-draped coffins arriving at Dover make present the cost of war.

Both material and visual forms engage in symbolic action: they can shift opinion and create meaning. It is important to be able to read visual rhetoric and understand how it functions persuasively, especially as visual forms of communication appear in more diverse spaces than they did a few decades ago (on social media, iPhones, computers, moving billboards, people's clothing, birthday cakes, and so on) and because more people are capable of producing (and reproducing) images seen on public screens (television, newspapers, computers, smartphones, and tablets).

That a person can be both a producer and receiver of images is illustrated by the haunting pictures of the 2007 Virginia Tech massacre that were taken on students' cell phones and shown on newscasts. People took it upon themselves to provide up-to-the-minute reporting, creating an entry on *Wikipedia* on April 16, 2007 (the day of the attacks) and modifying it 1860 times on that day alone.[6] The potential for anyone to visually record the news is formalized by sites such as CNN's iReport (ireport@cnn.com), which asks: "Is news happening in front of your eyes? Pull out your camera and I-Report it for CNN."[7] CNN does not ask for a written story, but for images.

These examples illustrate cultural theorists Jessica Evans and Stuart Hall's description of contemporary culture as "pervaded at all levels by a host of cultural technologies designed to disseminate viewing and looking practices through primarily visually mediated forms."[8] You live and work in a visual culture. Although scholars for many years confined the study of the available means of persuasion to the study of verbal symbols, within the last few decades they have recognized the centrality of visual and material symbolic action to the study of rhetoric.[9]

In this chapter, we explain how visual rhetoric creates presence, how the ubiquity of images has created a visual culture, and how to approach the study of visual and material rhetoric. We then outline four forms of visual rhetoric: bodies, photographs, memorials, and image events. These four forms are not all the types of visual and material rhetoric, but each one illustrates something unique about such rhetoric.

PRESENCE

Visuals such as the Dover photos are powerful because they make an event, person, or thing present. Visuals possess the characteristic of **presence** because of their *immediacy, the creation of something in the front of an audience's consciousness*. This creation may, as rhetoric scholars Chaïm Perelman and Lucie Olbrechts-Tyteca would say, "act directly on our sensibility."[10] Visuals may create virtual experiences in a particularly intense way, by making audience members feel as though they were present to witness an event. They offer a direct presentation instead of a discursive description.[11] They can make things that are distant in time or space feel current and close.

In 2006, Amnesty International in Switzerland launched an ad campaign with the slogan "It's not happening here. But it is happening now." Created by advertising agency Walker Werbeagentur, the campaign was visually stunning. Posters were placed at more than two hundred public transportation hubs (bus and train stations) in Zurich. Each poster replicated the background behind it—what you would see if the poster was not there—and superimposed, on that background, an image of an actual human rights abuse.[12] The poster at one hub showed a naked African child holding a bowl and picking grain from the steps of the hub. Another poster showed a child holding a machine gun beside a tree next to the hub. A third showed a man, probably a captive in Iraq, suspended in a bus stop shelter by chains wrapped around his wrists and ankles. Others showed police beating prisoners in bus stops, adults carrying the dead bodies of children in metro stations, child soldiers crawling onto urban train platforms, and Guantanamo detainees kneeling on city streets. The large variety of posters and their impact is illustrated by the large number of images from the campaign that are found on the Internet. The images forcefully made human rights abuses *present* that might otherwise have been ignored or forgotten.

As Amnesty International explained, "Actual human rights abuse appears to be happening in the here and now."[13] The campaign took abstract notions of human rights violations that happen in other places and grounded them in the home city of Zurich residents. One commentator said, "'It's not happening here but it's happening now' forces the viewer to confront such atrocities; to think of such actions and abuses happening on their own doorstep."[14]

The use of images in the transportation hubs of Zurich reflected an intentional effort to make the human rights abuses present. A project brief for the campaign argued that people would be more likely to identify with human rights abuses if they were set within the city of Zurich rather than across the globe.[15] The success of the campaign was demonstrated by the twentyfold increase in traffic at the Amnesty International website[16] and the discussion of the campaign in over four hundred blogs shortly after the release of the campaign.[17]

THE RISE OF VISUAL CULTURE

US and global culture are becoming, in the words of Evans and Hall, a **visual culture**—*a culture distinguished by the ubiquity of visual forms of communication that appear in multiple media outlets at the same time (such as television, the Internet, cell phones, and magazines)*.[18] Think about how you spend your time. You do not just read books; you watch movie adaptations of them. You do not simply phone friends; you send text messages with photos embedded. You do not simply read or listen to speeches; you watch them on YouTube or television. Communication scholar Lawrence J. Prelli argues that the **rhetoric of display,** *rhetoric that makes ideas present through visual display*, has become the dominant mode of communication in visual culture.[19] Even highly verbal speeches become visual events, with lavish attention paid to backdrops, clothing color, and camera angles.

Evans and Hall argue that it is impossible to understand contemporary culture without analyzing visuals, because a study of any contemporary media product—any television show, movie, advertisement, web page, blog, or magazine—would be "incomplete" if you only analyzed the words, or if you interpreted the "images as if they only functioned as artifacts to be read rather than as sights and often exhibitionist performances to be looked at."[20] Could you really explain television's power to shape contemporary culture if you only analyzed the scripts? Could you really explain the power of fashion magazines by studying only the stories? No and no. Cultural norms of fashion and body image are influenced by the actors on the screen and by the images in the magazine, perhaps even more than by the scripts and stories. People in a visual culture not only read words, they look at and interpret images.

Evans and Hall note that recognition of the importance of symbolic action means that researchers now explore how "social practices and relations" also function as "signifying practices."[21] Their point is that as you move through the world and interact with other people (in person or in mediated forms), you impart meaning to the world and your relationships; you also interpret the world and your relationships through the symbols you use. Communication, verbal and visual, is more than a means to transmit information. Television and movies are more than mere entertainment. Visual rhetoric, like language-based rhetoric, is a signifying practice through which human beings make meaning and make sense of the world in which they live.

Both visual and verbal aspects are almost always present in symbolic action, yet they operate in ways similar to and different from each other. As Evans and Hall note: "the differences between language and the visual remain significant and require further attention; that is, the different cultural technologies and industries built upon them, their characteristic forms and rhetorical devices, and the ways in which they are put to work, disseminated, and made sense of by readers and viewers."[22] You cannot explain fully the power of Dover photos by saying the photo depicts a historically real event. A Dover photo is powerful because it simultaneously captures a symbolic moment of ritual, a family's pure moment of grief, the honor of military service, a coffin containing a person, and the human costs of war. Imagine if we had started the chapter by reproducing a particular Dover photo, instead of only describing Dover photos in general. Would you have had the same reaction? If you have seen one of the Dover photos, did you have a different or more intense reaction than when you just read about them?

Visual rhetoric was not absent prior to the age of electronic media. In fact, most of the forms of visual rhetoric discussed in this chapter predate television and computers, although these forms have been adapted to mass and digital media. People have been using their bodies to make arguments as long as parades have crowded streets; events using spectacle have been around as long as audiences have listened and watched. Because electronic media make it easier to transmit images, however, and because interactive media enable everyone to be a publicist, attention to visual forms has increased. Photography first emerged in the 1820s. It became widely accessible in the 1880s when George Eastman developed film technology that replaced cumbersome photographic plates. Public monuments have played a role in the United States since the country's inception, with monuments literally being built into the bricks and stones of the nation's Capitol building. Scenes commemorating Columbus's life as a discoverer appear in the massive bronze doors that lead into the Capitol rotunda. Reliefs depicting settler-Indian relations adorn the Rotunda walls.[23] The last few decades have seen a proliferation of museums, memorials, and other memory sites.[24]

The prominence of visuals in public discourse has also increased; they are now omnipresent.[25] Photographs populate computer-mediated spaces such as Instagram, Facebook, Google Images, and Flickr. Visual rhetoric scholar Diane Hope concludes that visual communication is "a foundational core within the discipline of communication. Visual artifacts provoke intended and unintended meanings for individual and collective identity."[26]

The interaction between mediated messages and audience interpretations is in constant negotiation, with hegemonic powers dominating in some cases and audience resistance triumphing in others. The more skilled an audience is in analyzing visual and verbal messages, the more it is able to resist a hegemonic interpretation. Communication scholar Celeste Condit warns, "Audiences are not free to make meanings at will from mass mediated texts" because "the ability of audiences to shape their own readings . . . is constrained by a variety of factors in any given rhetorical situation," including "access to oppositional codes . . . the repertoire of available texts" and the historical context.[27] What you can say about a visual text depends on the vocabulary you have and the questions you have been trained to ask. If the only code you have to analyze a movie is "thumbs up" or "thumbs down," you have a limited ability to provide a detailed critical analysis of it. If you also have language to talk about race, gender, class, and nationality, you have a greater capacity to shape your own reading.

For any given text, Stuart Hall identifies three possible readings.[28] A **dominant reading** (or preferred, hegemonic meaning) is *a reading in which a reader (or viewer) takes the "connoted meaning . . . full and straight . . . the viewer is operating inside the dominant code."*[29] The viewer does not challenge the ideology behind the message or the way in which it maintains hegemonic power. A **negotiated reading** is *a reading in which the viewer accepts some of the hegemonic meanings, but also recognizes some exceptions.* In such a reading, the denotational meanings are understood, but some of the connotational meanings are challenged. An **oppositional reading** is *a reading in which the viewer correctly decodes the denotational and connotational meanings of a text, but challenges it from an oppositional perspective.*

Because of the possible levels of reading, we find persuasive Evans and Hall's description of how visual rhetoric generates meaning:

> [M]eaning is constituted not in the visual sign itself as a self-sufficient entity, nor exclusively in the sociological positions and identities of the audience, but in the articulation between viewer and viewed, between the power of the image to signify and the viewer's capacity to interpret meaning.[30]

The meaning of a text is not determined by its author, nor is the meaning solely contained in the text. Instead, audiences interpret meanings of visual texts in the process of looking. As a result, a single text or image may have multiple meanings, meanings influenced by the audience's culture and personal interpretations. Thus, when people analyze visual rhetoric, it is important to take into consideration not only the image and its producer, but also the social context surrounding the audience's interpretation of that image.

For example, American Apparel, a company that wanted its name identified as the "Made in USA—Sweatshop Free" brand,[31] ran an advertisement in *Vice* magazine. The bottom seventh of the page contains a narrative about the model, Maks, who appears in the ad. It explains that she was born in Dhaka, Bangladesh, and grew up "attending mosque as a child alongside her conservative Muslim parents," but moved to southern California at age four. Now an adult, she is a merchandiser for the company. The narrative ends by describing the jeans she is wearing and that they were "manufactured by 23 skilled American workers."

Above the script is a picture of Maks, jeans unzipped and pulled down to expose her underwear. She is wearing no top and the words "Made in Bangladesh" are emblazoned across her bare chest. American Apparel's preferred reading of this advertisement is that you should buy their products because they are made in the United States and because, just as American Apparel has helped Maks "forge her own identity," it can help you forge your own. Maks may have been made in Bangladesh, but her clothes were not.

The dominant reading would suggest that the use of a woman's body to sell clothing remains unremarkable, just part of the way things are. A negotiated reading of this image may question why a partially naked body would be used to help sell clothes, but still find the clothing attractive, partly because it is modeled by an attractive person. An oppositional reading would reject both the use of a woman's body to sell clothing and the commodification of the woman's body. The ad labels her body "made in Bangladesh" in the same way clothing is labeled, turning her into a commodity to be bought and sold just like clothing.

This oppositional reading as a form of challenge is demonstrated by *Ms.* magazine, which, in its Summer 2014 issue, included the American Apparel ad in its "No Comment" section. *Ms.* is devoted to "women's status, women's rights, and women's points of view." It eschews advertisements in its own pages and devotes its last page to a "No Comment" section[32] that reproduces advertisements that readers submit because they find them injurious and degrading to women. This section is both the result, and cause, of oppositional readings. As communication scholar Linda Steiner explains, the section reflects an oppositional reading: "*Ms.* readers call attention to [the] items in ways not encoded by their producers, precisely to make the point that *Ms.* readers are not the women inscribed in dominant media. . . . The very act of capturing these texts and setting them in an oppositional frame is an act of resistance."[33] The hope is that once others are made aware of the problematic advertisements, they will pressure companies to remove them. (The magazine includes the companies' contact information along with the advertisement.)

Although audiences may have different interpretations of the same text, often interpretations are relatively consistent. Why? The culture that constitutes the audience influences its interpretations; hence, many audience interpretations reinforce the interpretation preferred by those in power. Both media and viewers participate in the hegemonic process, in which the predominant ideology uses noncoercive legal and political forms to generate consent in the dominated. Hegemonic institutions usually do influence audiences; that is what makes them hegemonic. For example, most people in the United States take the mere existence of commercial advertising in stride; the United States, as a capitalist society, sees encouragements to consume as normal.

When critically analyzing visual rhetoric, consider the image, the viewer, and the other influences at work. Some of these may increase the audience's ability to open up the interpretive process; some may limit it. Remember that Evans and Hall are not talking about a single interaction between viewer and image, but multiple interactions that may, ultimately, seem to lead away from the image and the viewer, although they all lead back to the context understood as socioeconomic positions and identities.[34]

ANALYZING VISUAL AND MATERIAL RHETORICS

A rhetorical approach to the study of visual rhetoric does not stop at analyzing what an artifact means or whether it is aesthetically pleasing. The primary question of a rhetorical approach is: What does an artifact *do*? In an art class, you might analyze the color, content, spatial organization, and light of an image (moving or still). You might also ask what the various elements of a painting represent (for instance, the stars in the US flag). Rhetoricians are interested in more than aesthetics and meaning. They want to know: What does this image tell people about what it means to be a citizen, about the costs of war, about the values of the community, about people's own place in the world, about who is worthy of being pictured and who is not? Because a central component of rhetoric is that it is addressed, we should also ask: What type of audience does this artifact address—spectators, witnesses, or participants?[35] For example, when Sonja K. Foss analyzes visual rhetoric, she asks about the "function or functions communicated by an image"; not the rhetor's purpose but the "action the image communicates."[36] When Carole Blair analyzes monuments, she says, her concern is "not just what a text means but, more generally, what it does; and we must not understand what it does as adhering strictly to what it was supposed to do."[37]

According to the National Park Service website, the World War II Memorial, which opened to the public in 2004, "recognizes the ways Americans served, honors those who fell, and recognizes the victory they achieved to restore freedom and end tyranny around the globe."[38] The dedication ceremony speakers, however, included no representatives of Allied nations and only one veteran of World War II, and he was not recognized as a veteran. Speakers focused on the US role in winning World War II and its current role in the war in Iraq. Rhetoric scholars V. William Balthrop, Carole Blair, and Neil Michel argue that, although the memorial's intent was to celebrate service and sacrifice, the dedication ceremony makes clear the monument actually "affirms contemporary U.S. imperialism, promotes the George W. Bush administration's highly questionable policies under the revered sign of World War II, and 'speaks' more about the present than about the past the Memorial allegedly marks."[39] Words and images, often in conjunction, as in the dedication ceremony and the World War II Memorial, construct reality.

Visual rhetoric scholars Kevin Michael DeLuca and Anne Teresa Demo note that visuals, just pictures, "are important not because they represent reality, but create it."[40] Thus, when people analyze visuals, the question "What do the images represent?" is insufficient; it assumes an absolute correspondence between the image and reality. In studying visual rhetoric, DeLuca and Demo say, people should also ask "What do the images want?"—meaning what attitude toward the world do these images encourage the audience to assume, and in what ways do the images direct a person's attention in one way rather than another?[41] When an advertisement contains an image of a stylish person using a product, the image does not merely depict that person's use of the product. It also wants you to see yourself using the product in order to be like the stylish person in the ad.

The rest of the chapter offers examples of what bodies, photographs, monuments, and image events rhetorically do. These four forms do not exhaust the range of visual and material rhetorics available, but they do illustrate a rhetorical approach to their study.

TYPES OF VISUAL AND MATERIAL RHETORIC

In the sections to follow, we outline four types of visual communication that have received substantial scholarly attention. They are not necessarily the most important forms of visual rhetoric (though they are important), but they offer illustrations of how visual communication operates presentationally and can create presence, thus directing attention to some things while deflecting it from others.[42]

Bodies

Research on body rhetoric and body argument shows that verbal messages do not exist apart from a material body that creates those messages. *Who* says a message and *how* a body is made present communicate as much as *what* is said. **Body rhetoric,** then, is *rhetoric that foregrounds the body as part of the symbolic act.*

When we speak of bodies, we are not speaking of some biological entity, but of a social and individual creation, performance, and inscription. Gender, sex, race, class, sexual orientation, religion, ethnicity, ability, age, and a host of other identity ingredients enter the discussion. Additionally, body rhetoric is often used by those who are denied access to more traditional forms of verbal address and of proof. In some cases, your own body may be your only available proof for a point you want to make.

To understand the power of bodies as rhetoric, consider the technique of enactment. **Enactment** occurs when *the person engaging in symbolic action functions as proof of the argument s/he advances.*[43] As you read the following uses of enactment, think about how, if the same statement was presented by any other person, the argument would lose some of its power, even though the words might be identical. The power of the visual proof enhances the power of the words.

Barbara Jordan delivered the keynote address at the 1976 Democratic National Convention. Her main argument was that the Democratic Party was the party of inclusion and opportunity, regardless of one's race, sex, or class. She sought to answer the question: "What is it, what is it about the Democratic Party that makes it the instrument that people use when they search for ways to shape their future?" As proof of the claim that the Democratic Party was an instrument of positive change, she offered herself. She proclaimed from her black, female body: "But there is something different about tonight. There is something special about tonight. What is different? What is special? I, Barbara Jordan, am a keynote speaker. . . . And I feel that notwithstanding the past that my presence here is one additional bit of evidence that the American Dream need not forever be deferred."[44]

Mary Fisher (an artist and the daughter of a major Republican fundraiser) delivered a speech on AIDS at the 1992 Republic National Convention. Her main argument was "the AIDS virus is not a political creature. It does not care whether you are Democrat or Republican; it does not ask whether you are black or white, male or female, gay or straight, young or old." She believed everyone, Democrats and Republicans, should be concerned about AIDS because it affected everyone. She proclaimed from her Republican, white, non–drug using, heterosexual, economically privileged, married-when-infected, HIV+ body: "You are at risk."[45] She functioned as proof that everyone present at the convention was at risk.

In September 2010, in the wake of a number of bullying-induced suicides of LGBT youth, journalist and author Dan Savage launched the "It Gets Better Project," an online website on which adults can post videos in which they "show young LGBT people the levels of happiness, potential, and positivity their lives will reach—if they can just get through their teen years."[46] As of July 2014, the site contained fifty thousand user-created videos and had had over fifty million views. Each video is an example of enactment. Savage and his husband Terry begin their eight-and-a-half-minute video by talking about the violence and harassment they experienced as gay youth. A little over a minute into the video, they declare: "It gets better." They spend most of the video talking about their loving parents, the beginning of their sixteen-year relationship, their thirteen-year-old son, their travels to Paris, and their skiing trips—basically describing how good, loving, and happy their lives are. They are proof that "it gets better."

As these examples demonstrate, bodies can be rhetorically powerful as they function as evidence for a claim. However, not only may bodies function as a *part* of an argument in the form of data, they can also be the *complete* argument. Argument traditionalists often relegate the role of the body in argument to a means of capturing and holding attention, rather than as a central part of the substance of the argument, but their perspective lacks explanatory power when applied to contemporary activism. For example, in his study of the rhetoric of groups such as Earth First!, ACT UP, and Queer Nation, Kevin Michael DeLuca highlighted that the activists' bodies are "not merely flags to attract attention for the argument but the site and substance of the argument itself."[47] In the case of ACT UP and Queer Nation, two groups that focus on AIDS policy, the presence of the body is the argument, "for it is the body that is at stake—its meanings, its possibilities, its care, and its freedoms. In their protest actions, the activists use their bodies to rewrite the homosexual body as already constructed by dominant mainstream discourses—diseased, contagious, deviant, invisible."[48] Instead of presenting their bodies as passive, diseased, and dying, the activists present their bodies as active, healing, and living. Activists present integrated verbal and visual arguments about what the body means, what the government does to it, and how it is affected by disease.

The ability of bodies to induce memory and answer arguments is illustrated in recent actions by grandchildren of Auschwitz survivors. As the number of Holocaust survivors dwindles, Jodi Rudoren of the *New York Times* says, "institutions and individuals are grappling with how best to remember the Holocaust . . . after those who lived it are gone."[49] Survivors' children and grandchildren are choosing to tattoo themselves with the numbers that were

FIGURE 1
M. E. Cohen cartoon
M. E. Cohen/Artizans.com

etched into their parents' and grandparents' arms and chests in the camps. Communication scholars Linda Diane Horwitz and Daniel C. Brouwer argue that this practice resignifies the meaning of the tattoo, transforming it from a marker of power over a human to a marker of human resistance to power. They explain, "These young people articulate that they are not going to forget, and they are also going to help anyone who witnesses their tattoo in the process of never forgetting."[50]

The power of the tattooed body as evidence is also evident in another visual form. The 2006 editorial cartoon in Figure 1 responded to Iranian past president Mahmoud Ahmadinejad, who had repeatedly called the Holocaust a "myth."[51] He had also hosted a conference for Holocaust deniers, including David Duke from the United States, French lecturer Robert Faurisson, and British author David Irving.[52] The cartoon points out the overwhelming evidence of the body to refute those who deny that the genocide of the Holocaust occurred.

Sometimes, body rhetoric may be the only rhetorical option available. In societies where free speech is not sanctioned, an image (a photo) and a presence (a body) may be the only way to negate a government's denial of wrongdoing. Communication studies scholar Valeria Fabj's study of the Mothers of Plaza de Mayo is an excellent example of a situation in which discursive argument

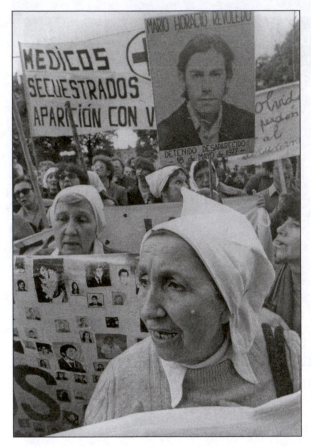

FIGURE 2
Madres de Plaza de Mayo
© Horacio Villalobos/Corbis

was not an option and a visual form was necessary.[53] The Mothers formed in 1977 to protest the "disappearance" of their children under the repressive military regime that ruled Argentina from 1976 to 1983. Wearing as headscarves their children's nappies (diapers embroidered with the children's names and dates of disappearance) and carrying pictures of their disappeared children, they marched around the Plaza at a time when public protest was prohibited. Fabj argues it was the very "myth of motherhood," the social beliefs attached to the women's bodies, that allowed them "to draw from their private experiences in order to gain a political voice, discover eloquent symbols, and yet remain relatively safe at a time when all political dissent was prohibited."[54] (See Figure 2.)

Bodies offer a powerful rhetorical resource. They can function as proof of an argument; they can be the argument; and they can argue when speech has been restricted. To really understand a rhetorical action, you must consider the body that speaks it.

Photographs

Research on the rhetoric of photographs shows that images never represent a reality that is free from the influences of symbolic action. Instead, photographs direct attention to a particular reality. Although people often think of

FIGURE 3
Cathedral Rocks, Yosemite Valley
Carleton Watkins, Library of Congress

photographs (assuming they are not obviously photoshopped) as exact representations of reality, all visual technologies (such as cameras, video recorders, and
cell phones with digital recording technology) "structure images of reality."[55]
Visual communication scholar Diane Hope explains that "what viewers see,
what they do not see, and how they contextualize images depends on structural
choices made by producers, and include editing, framing, sequencing, contrast,
focus, illumination and grounding."[56]

An example of photographs that persuaded people to see the world in
a particular way can be found in Carleton Watkins's 1860s photographs of
Yosemite Valley. (See Figure 3.) The California Geological Survey began to map
the valley in 1863. As part of his appeal to have the valley declared a public park,
survey head Josiah Dwight Whitney included twenty-eight of Watkins's original
photographs in an unprecedented use of photographs to illustrate a scientific
survey. When a bill finally was written calling for President Abraham Lincoln to
preserve Yosemite Valley, advocates attached some of Watkins's photographs to
the bill. As the images circulated, they "became iconic of an American vision of
nature itself."[57] They were central to the preservation of that area and influenced
the focus of environmental movements for years to come.

How? The images are more than a simple reflection of the Yosemite Valley.
They also select and highlight a particular understanding of nature even as

they deflect other understandings. DeLuca and Demo ask, in their analysis of these photos, "What vision of nature do the photographs authorize, warrant, and legitimate?"[58] For them, Watkins's images were not "merely evidence in a conventional political argument;" nor were they "simply representing reality or making an argument about reality. Instead . . . the pictures are constituting the context within which a politics takes place—they are creating a reality."[59] These images influenced what it meant to be an environmentalist by reducing the environment to pristine, untouched lands, rather than including all the land, sky, and water in which beings live. These images also reinforced the prevailing myth that Euro-American settlers were the only people to step foot into this pristine wilderness, wiping the presence of Native Americans from public awareness. They induced people to accept a particular view of nature as untouched by human habitation. The framing of the photos (framing being a technique that directs attention) meant that Native Americans were not present within the frame of reference.

The centrality of photographic images to a people's understanding of their identity cannot be underestimated. Watkins's images reinforced the identity of Euro-Americans as explorers and discoverers. When you study photographs, the questions are not limited to what meaning the image maker wants to transmit; they also include what the image does, how audiences read images, and how the rhetor calls a particular audience into being. You live in a visual culture and are bombarded by rhetorics of display. How do you develop an awareness of what images are asking of you, instead of just doing what they ask?

In a world increasingly dominated by electronic media, visual rhetoric scholars Robert Hariman and John Louis Lucaites argue, commonly viewed images can provide a sense of "shared experience." Even as public life seems impersonal, people develop a personal connection (an identification) with the people they see in pictures. In addition, "the daily stream of images in the public media . . . defines the public through an act of common spectatorship. All viewers *seem* to see the same thing."[60] The "Pass It On" public service billboard campaign, cosponsored by The Foundation for a Better Life and the Outdoor Advertising Association of America, relies on common spectatorship. The Foundation seeks to create a sense of community and identification by celebrating shared experiences of positive values, such as unity, dedication, strength, soul, vision, sacrifice, persistence, and commitment. Using celebrities (such as Michael J. Fox and Oprah Winfrey), historic figures (such as Mahatma Gandhi, Nelson Mandela, and Wolfgang Amadeus Mozart), and less-well-known individuals (such as Nola Ochs, who graduated college at age ninety-five, softball players who carried an injured opponent around the bases, and a Tiananmen Square protester).

Thus, when discussing public communication, one needs to consider the ways visuals form what is considered public and shared. For people in the United States, a few key photos inform how citizens see themselves. Lucaites and Hariman identify these images as **iconic photographs**: "*photographic images produced in print, electronic, or digital media that are (1) recognized by everyone within a public culture, (2) understood to be representations of historically significant events, (3) objects of strong emotional identification and response, and*

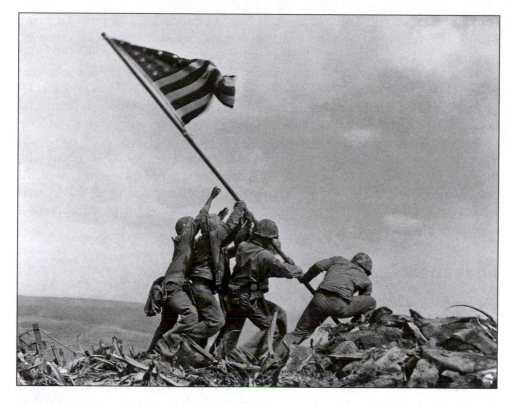

FIGURE 4
US Marines raising flag over Iwo Jima
AP Photo/Joe Rosenthal

(4) regularly reproduced or copied across a range of media, genres, and topics."[61] Examples of iconic photographs include Joe Rosenthal's 1945 photo of the flag raising on Iwo Jima,[62] John Filo's 1970 photo of a Kent State student shot to death by the National Guard[63] Nick Ut's 1972 Vietnam War photo of accidental napalm,[64] and Jeff Widener's 1989 Tiananmen Square photo of a single protester. Each of these photos contribute to the way US citizens came to see themselves.

The Pulitzer Prize–winning photo of Iwo Jima, published in the midst of World War II, presents a particular understanding of citizenship and war. (See Figure 4.) Taken by Associated Press photographer Joe Rosenthal, it depicts the US military seizing a Japanese observation post on the island. This image fulfills all the elements of an iconic photo. Most people in the United States would recognize it. It represents a historically significant event; in fact, it has come to represent all of World War II for many people. It creates a strong emotional identification, as citizens identify with the men pictured, with their struggle and victory. It is regularly reproduced; in fact, it is the most reproduced photograph in history.[65] What is most significant, however, is how the photo has come to form an understanding of US public culture.

Hariman and Lucaites argue that this photo presents two arguments about what distinguishes and defines US citizens. First, war is more an act of labor than an act of killing. The marines and Navy corpsman are not pictured firing weapons, but laboring to erect the flag. Second, even in an act of conquest (taking a strategic place), the soldiers work together, regardless of rank, thus enacting egalitarianism and civic pride. In depicting war and egalitarian cooperation, the photograph "reflect[s] social knowledge and dominant ideologies; . . . shape[s] understanding of specific events and periods; . . . influence[s] political action by modeling relationships between civic actors; and . . . provide[s] figural resources for subsequent communicative action."[66] As people in the United States look at this image, they come to a shared vision of who they are and why the nation fought. The photo reflects a particular image of US citizens as hardworking (not warlike), equal (rank is irrelevant, as all participants labor equally), and proud of their nation (the US flag is a primary indicator of civic pride).

Monuments, Memorials, and Museums

On family vacations, many people visit monuments and memorials, such as the Washington Monument and the Vietnam Veterans Memorial in Washington, DC. They often read these structures as neutral markers of historical figures and events, but monuments do more than simply record historic facts. They guide people in their thinking about those facts from the past, how to act in the present, and what possible futures to seek. It is not surprising, therefore, that controversy often arises over monuments and memorials. Although they are inanimate objects, they are not just markers of famous locations or ways to memorialize the dead; they also direct people's views of themselves.

One controversy actually resulted in renaming a national monument and adding another memorial to its space. Off I-90 in southern Montana sits the Crow Indian Reservation, the site of the most famous battle in the Indian Wars, remembered not because it was a great victory for the US Seventh Cavalry under the command of Lieutenant Colonel George Armstrong Custer, but because on June 25, 1876, the Cavalry was annihilated on this site by the superior might of Lakota (Sioux), Hinono'eino' (Arapaho), and Tsistsistas (Cheyenne) warriors. In 1879, the battlefield was dedicated as a national cemetery. In 1881, the Seventh Cavalry Memorial was erected, listing the names of all the Cavalry members and "Arikaree" (Arikara Indian, also known as Sahnish) scouts slain in the battle. In 1925, Mrs. Thomas Beaverheart (daughter of Chief Lame White Man, a Southern Cheyenne killed in the battle) initiated Native American demands for inclusion. In 1946, the Custer Battlefield National Monument was dedicated.

After years of protest by Native Americans, in 1991 the Custer Battlefield National Monument was *rededicated* as the Little Bighorn Battlefield National Monument. A national design competition was authorized for an Indian Memorial. When President George H. W. Bush signed the federal law declaring the name change, he explained: "The public interest will best be served by establishing a memorial . . . to honor and recognize the Indians who fought to preserve their land and culture."[67]

An advisory committee composed of members of all the Indian nations involved in the battle, historians, artists, and landscape architects selected the memorial's theme, "Peace through Unity," in response to the advice of elders Austin Two Moons (Northern Cheyenne) and Enos Poor Bear, Sr. (Oglala Lakota).[68] In 1997, the committee selected John R. Collins and Alison J. Towers's memorial design, which incorporated a sculpture of Spirit Warriors designed by Lakota artist Colleen "Sister Wolf" Cutschall. The Indian Memorial was dedicated on June 25, 2003.

The need for the Indian Memorial becomes clear when one considers the way Euro-Americans remembered the battle prior to the 1991 law. Not only were the sites where Native Americans died unmarked, a marker in the national cemetery that memorialized US officers who died in the Indian Wars told a distorted story, referring to "hostile Indians" without noting the reason for the hostility: for decades US troops had forcibly driven them from their homelands and onto reservations. Until the law changed the name of the battlefield and required the memorialization of Native Americans who fought, only the names of Custer's soldiers, civilians traveling with the cavalry, and the three Sahnish (Arikara) Indians who scouted for the Seventh Calvary were inscribed on the monument. The deeds of the triumphant Sioux Indian chiefs Crazy Horse and Sitting Bull were not remembered in the official space, even though Native Americans kept these deeds alive in oral histories.

The evolution of the Little Bighorn site illustrates that public memory is grounded in the present rather than the past and is continually (re)made to fit the needs of the public(s) it serves. Initially Custer Battlefield National Monument served the need to justify the westward expansion and to celebrate the actions of the military. It held Custer up as a hero who ostensibly served the cause of fighting "hostile Indians." As needs arose to account for the wrongs committed against Native Americans, the form, content, and name of the site had to change to encompass those needs.

The Little Bighorn Battlefield is a place where the US conception of citizenship and nationhood is developed and maintained, a conception that directly implicates a particular history of Native Americans. Communication scholar Richard Morris notes in another context that "the continuous struggle to gain access to and control of America's collective memory is hardly a benign process."[69] The national monument site initially argued that only Custer and his men should be remembered. As it constructed and maintained memory about Custer, it generated amnesia about Native Americans and why they fought. The new monument argues that both soldiers and warriors should be remembered, that all the lives lost are worthy of being mourned.

The question of how, and whom, to mourn is not a simple one. The Freedom Tower at Ground Zero, now called One World Trade Center, did not open until 2015. Disagreement over the form of monumental structures at the site had delayed construction until 2006.[70]

As memorials and monuments sustain public memory, they make arguments about how to think about the identities of particular groups of people. Thus monuments and memorials are rhetorical. As communication scholar Victoria J. Gallagher notes, they "perpetuate values, admonish as to future conduct, and affirm or challenge existing power relations."[71] There are two reasons why they are able to perform those functions: (1) what is remembered has less to do with what happened in the past than with the needs of the present, and (2) the process of remembering always involves an act of forgetting as well, creating both presence and absence.

Memory, and thus the architecture of memorials, monuments, and museums, serve the needs of the present. Thus, when people discuss memorials and monuments, they should question which parts of history are selected for memory, and why those elements are selected when others are not. Historians Peter Grey and Kendrick Oliver suggest that not only can a nation-state seek to remember key points in its history, such as wars, but "diverse and competing interest groups" can "seek to use constructions of the past to advance their agendas in the present."[72] One vivid example is the Vietnam Veterans Memorial. After the Vietnam War ended in 1975, the US public was deeply divided over its meaning. Even though the selection committee of eight architects and sculptors unanimously selected Maya Lin's design for the wall from among 1,421 proposals in 1981, controversy continued. Construction proceeded only after an agreement was reached to add a flagpole and Frederick Hart's Three Servicemen Statue. The wall was unveiled in 1982, the statue in 1984. Communication scholars Carole Blair, Marsha S. Jeppeson, and Enrico Pucci, Jr., point out that the tension over the monument "designates the domestic conflict over the war itself."[73] Lin's wall questions whether the war was an event worthy of admiration, while Hart's statue resoundingly affirms that it was.

The controversy over memory did not end with those two parts of the memorial. As women increasingly called for the ability to serve in combat roles and their contributions as service members were increasingly recognized, calls for a Vietnam women's memorial grew. Grey and Oliver state that in 1993, the "sacrifices made and horrors witnessed by American women—particularly nurses—during the conflict in Vietnam" were recognized.[74] Even this historically accurate reintroduction of women into the memory of Vietnam was not without controversy. People reacted negatively to the statue partly because of "its representation of a wounded soldier, drawing attention to the harsh, immediate purpose of the war, and rejecting, in the forlorn, desperate expressions of the nurses, the conventional iconic languages of healing, sacrifice and redemption."[75] Although women's absence had been corrected, people did not agree about how women should be made present in the memorial.

Objects of commemoration are historical in nature and stand for something in the past, but they are chosen as commemorative because of present day concerns.[76] So what was happening in 1993? Although women had served as medical personnel and in support positions in every war, and were admitted to the military academies in 1976, not until the late 1980s did serious debate occur about women serving in combat positions. Advocates for allowing women in combat argued that women, even in noncombat positions, faced all the dangers of war. Even noncombat nurses serving on the front lines in MASH units often ended up serving in combat. Thus, a statue recognizing women's roles in Vietnam participated in the ongoing debate about women in combat.

Research on the rhetorical power of monuments and memorials shows that architecture, itself, positions those who view the monuments (audiences) in particular ways, inducing particular reactions and foregrounding particular memories. Gallagher is among the scholars who recognize that "the symbolic, architectural, and/or textual aspects of artifacts . . . impact both people who come into contact with them and the larger society of which those people are members."[77] The preferred readings of memorials and monuments call people to remember some events, and remember them in particular ways. Because some events and people are remembered, others are not; they are deflected. As monuments make some people and events present in public memory, they also make others absent.

This dialectic of presence and absence complicates memorial practices. When actions by people and governments have erased the existence of a group, is it the correct memory practice to erase that erasure? How do you remember the past presence of a people without erasing their present absence? This is the memory conundrum with which Germans have grappled as they consider how to remember and memorialize the Holocaust. The Third Reich's genocidal policies included destroying anything associated with the Jewish people, including a fountain that had been donated to the town of Kassel by a Jewish entrepreneur named Sigmund Ashcrott in 1908. Ashcrott fountain, neo-Gothic in style, stood in front of City Hall. It was over 36 feet high and surrounded by a reflecting pool. On April 8 and 9, 1939, Nazi activists destroyed the fountain, condemning it as the "Jews' fountain." They carried it away piece by piece until, according to James Young, a professor of Judaic Studies, all that was left was "a great, empty basin in the center of the square. Two years later, the first transport of 463 Kassel Jews departed from the Central Train Station to Riga, followed in the next year by another 3,000, all murdered."[78]

In 1943, the basin was filled with soil and planted with flowers. Later, it was turned into a fountain again. By the 1960s, when people were asked what had happened to the fountain, their memory was that English bombers had destroyed it during the war. One person, who had grown up in Kassel, said, "No one wished to be reminded of the victims" nor of the collective guilt of the community; the absence of the fountain represented their desire to make the history of the role of Kassel in the Holocaust absent and forgotten.[79]

In 1984, to counter this mis-remembering, the Society for the Rescue of Historical Monuments proposed restoring a form of the fountain as a way of recovering the memory and history of the fountain and the Jews of Kassel.[80] Horst Hoheisel, the architect of the new memorial, designed the new fountain as a mirror of the previous fountain. But the new fountain was placed below the original fountain as a way of recognizing it as "a wound and as an open question" focused on emboldening the residents of Kassel to ensure "such things never happen again."[81] Where the old fountain rose 36 feet into the air, the new fountain dives 36 feet into the ground. It makes the absence of the fountain and of Kassel's Jews visible and present.

In his analysis of the new fountain, Young answers the question "How does one remember an absence?" by saying "In this case, by reproducing it. Quite literally, the negative space of the absent monument will now constitute its phantom shape in the ground."[82] Rebuilding the fountain as it originally stood would have erased the destruction wrought by pro-Nazi members of the community. Covering the space with a new memorial would have covered the scar left by the destruction. By using negative space, however, Hoheisel was able to make an absence (of the fountain and the Jews of Kassel) present.

Image Events

Kevin DeLuca opens his book, *Image Politics*, with a paradigm example. On June 27, 1975, 50 miles off the coast of California, sailed the 160-foot Russian whaling ship *Vlastny*, equipped with a 90-mm cannon that shot 160-pound exploding grenade harpoons. Six Greenpeace activists in three inflatable rubber dinghies pursued the *Vlastny*. One dinghy, carrying Bob Hunter and Paul Watson, positioned itself between the whaling ship and a fleeing whale, thinking the whalers would not fire and risk hitting humans. They thought wrong. The whalers on the *Vlastny* fired over the heads of the activists and hit the whale, with the harpoon's trajectory carrying it less than five feet from the dinghy and the people riding in it.[83]

The event was captured on tape by other Greenpeace members, and was televised on CBS, ABC, NBC and around the world during the International Whaling Commission's conference. (Before the Internet, these outlets represented comprehensive coverage.) Although Greenpeace did not save this one whale, the video opened Greenpeace's "Save the Whales" campaign, which eventually led to bans on commercial whaling and thus saved many whales.[84] Paul Watson commented:

> That thirty-second film clip that Fred had captured would be our ticket to the hot media of television.
>   Armed with the tempting media bait of dramatic visual documentation, we could now gain access to the doors of human awareness through the avenue that only television could provide. For the first time, we had some hope of inciting public indignation against whaling.
>   . . . our efforts in the past had been stymied by the fact that . . . if the public thought about whaling at all, it was the image of Moby Dick that came to mind, along with brave whaling men in puny longboats locked in a heroic struggle against a monstrous giant beast. Thanks to our activities that day, the media began to present a different image of whaling from here on in.[85]

The images created a virtual experience for people who had no understanding of whaling. They altered perceptions by challenging the norms and assumptions of the dominant public, making present the violence involved in whaling.

DeLuca labels Greenpeace's symbolic act an "image event." **Image events** are *"staged acts . . . designed for media dissemination."*[86] They may be used for protest, for example, as "mind bombs," to explode the typical ways people think about a topic, such as their relationship to the environment.[87] Image events combine visual and verbal rhetorics in order to challenge the images people have of corporations and of protestors. They are structured to elicit the attention of media outlets, so that they appear on the public screen of television, computers, newspapers, tablets, and smartphones.

Although at first glance, the Greenpeace effort might seem like a dangerous and crazy stunt (would *you* be willing to sail in a rubber dinghy between a whaling boat and a whale?), DeLuca argues that "far from being the desperate stunts of the disillusioned, image events are the central mode of public discourse both for conventional electoral politics and for alternative grassroots politics in an era dominated by a commercial televisual electronic public sphere."[88] He notes that although people today could probably name famous speakers from the civil rights era, many would be hard-pressed to name a famous environmental speaker or memorable environmental speech. Even Al Gore gained fame as an environmental speaker by using images to transmit his message in his 2006 movie on global warming, *An Inconvenient Truth.*[89]

DeLuca's description of image events challenges traditional notions of how rhetoric operates. When you acknowledge the power of visuals, he argues, you begin to question many assumptions of "traditional rhetorical theory and criticism, starting with the notion that rhetoric ideally is 'reasoned discourse,' with 'reasoned' connoting 'civil' or 'rational' and 'discourse' connoting 'words.'"[90] Although these assumptions might apply to the discourse at town hall meetings, and although there is little that is civil or reasoned about Greenpeace's image event, it is not irrational.[91] Image events, though often outrageous, should not be dismissed as "gimmicks or the antics of the unruly" or reduced to "flares sent out to gain attention."[92] They actually form the substance of contemporary activism in a world saturated by images. Radical environmental groups "are using image events to attempt both to deconstruct and articulate identities, ideologies, consciousnesses, communities, publics, and cultures in our modern industrial civilization."[93] Greenpeace's images of the dying whales and of Greenpeace activists' willingness to sacrifice themselves to save the whales generated questions about human beings' relationship to the natural world and the way human beings value it.

Image events are used by a wide range of rhetors. Any time an act of public communication is planned with the hope of media dissemination, people consider the way the event will play on public screens. Thus, one could examine all of the following as image events: the 1999 protests at the World Trade Organization meeting in Seattle, the 2009 Tea Party Taxpayer March on Washington, Occupy Wall Street's 2011 protests, Barack Obama's 2013 inaugural address, and Open Carry Texas's 2014 actions in retail outlets and restaurants. The meaning of each event is not contained solely in the verbal content of the messages; it is also contained in the visual images: people sleeping on pavements; Obama as president speaking to a crowd that overflowed the National Mall; tens of thousands of conservative protesters in Washington, DC; police using tear gas and riot batons on protesters; and people with guns standing in fast food restaurants. An image of the Taxpayer March, for example, shows the mass of bodies filling the frame and extending to the horizon as it proceeds down Pennsylvania Avenue towards the Capitol, a central symbol of US government

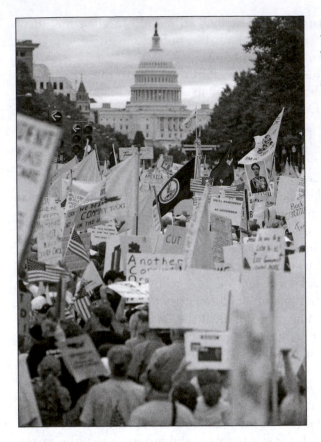

FIGURE 5
Taxpayer March,
Washington, DC.
Bill Clark/CQ-Roll Call Group/
Getty Images

power. (See Figure 5.) The Patriot Action Network estimated 1.7 million people were in attendance and provided time-lapse video of the crowd. The National Taxpayers Union, one of the organizers of the event, said 200,000 to 300,000 people attended. The diverse signs make the protest seem spontaneous rather than orchestrated.

Research on image events shows that the ability of electronic media to transmit visual rhetoric to broad audiences is a central element of visual rhetoric. Visual rhetoric, in some cases, requires its audiences to come to it (one must intentionally seek out places such as the Little Bighorn Battlefield National Monument). In contrast, image events are structured in such a way that media are induced to take the event to the audience, to transmit it so that even those who are not seeking exposure to a group's rhetoric may see the event when it is broadcast across various media.

When studying image events, keep in mind that they do not always function the same way verbal rhetoric does. As presentational symbolism, they operate holistically and not in a sequentially logical manner. In addition, they sometimes challenge, rather than invite, identification. Although Kenneth Burke believes that identification is central to rhetoric, DeLuca notes "the rhetorical tactic of image events works not so much through identification as through disidentification, through the shock or laughter that shatters" the taken for granted, the commonplace, and the meanings of fundamental ideographs.[94] In the

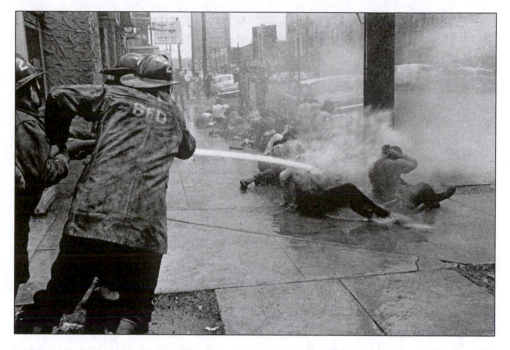

FIGURE 6
Firefighters turning hose on civil rights demonstrators
Charles Moore, Black Star

Greenpeace example, does the viewer identify with the Russian whalers, with the Greenpeace activists, or with the whales? Image events are not necessarily meant to make the audience feel similar to the rhetor. Instead, their purpose may be to alter perception, to explode the commonplace so that new ways of thinking emerge.

Instead of using identification with already formed identities, DeLuca says, image events can both reconstitute or re-form the identity of the protester and "the identity of the dominant culture by challenging and transforming mainstream society's key discourses and ideographs."[95] Civil rights activists had long faced violence, but not until the circulation of photos of civil rights marches in Birmingham in 1963 were white people's sense of themselves and the law challenged. In 1960, during lunch counter sit-ins at Woolworth's, college students faced violence from white onlookers. In 1961, angry mobs confronted the Freedom Riders as police stood by and watched. In 1962, President Kennedy had to send in federal troops when James Meredith became the first black student to enroll at the University of Mississippi and white people reacted violently. Yet, northern white people were slow to react. Then, in May of 1963, Birmingham happened.

As civil rights activists peacefully marched, Commissioner of Public Safety Eugene "Bull" Connor ordered the police to use dogs and fire hoses to disperse them. Images of police dogs and fire hoses turned against black protestors, widely televised and published in numerous print media, shook the conscience of the nation and made clear to moderate white people that racial equality would not be attained via a gradualist approach.[96] (See Figure 6.) Communication scholar

Davi Johnson argues that a photograph of officers with police dogs attacking unresisting black protestors constituted "a visual reversal where the traditional characteristic of the uniformed authorities are transposed into their opposites: the protector of order becomes the oppressor who brings chaotic brutality into the scene of civilization."[97] Instead of white people identifying with the police and accepting the ideograph of "law and order," they were induced to break their traditional patterns of identification. The photos asked white people to identify with black protestors who were breaking (unjust) laws.

It is not just protest groups that use images. Most campaign events are image oriented, positioning candidates so they look good on the evening news. Corporations, establishment politicians, and radical political groups all use images.[98] Understanding the ability of image events to reorient public discourse is essential to understanding the role of rhetoric in contemporary society and how it constitutes citizenship, participation, and meaning.

CONCLUSION

Our goal in this chapter is to assist you in becoming a critical viewer of visual rhetoric, so you can resist the hegemonic pull that many images may have on you. Because visual forms are rhetorical, and not just objective recorders of some fixed world, viewers of visual rhetoric should not ask "what do images represent?" but instead "what do the images do?" Images induce you to see the world one way rather than another. The more aware you are of the rhetorical aspects of images, the more you will be able to determine when you should assent to the arguments they advance.

In a visual culture, civic life is constituted, maintained, defined, and performed through visual rhetoric. Public bodies enact citizenship; civic identity is constituted through photographs; national memories are maintained in monuments; and image events use media outlets to call attention to issues for deliberation and action. Although people often think of civic life as occurring only through the medium of talk, language is only one form of symbolic action. Visual rhetoric is as important to civic life as language. Ignoring visual rhetoric in studies of civic life strips people of one of their core senses. People not only hear each others' appeals, they also see each other.

Visual communication scholar Diane Hope explains: "Viewing audiences are not necessarily passive. Viewers select, choose, and perceive images according to the context, knowledge, and life experience they bring to the act of viewing."[99]

DISCUSSION QUESTIONS

1. In what ways is contemporary US culture a visual culture?
2. Find an example of visual rhetoric. Identify what type it is (iconic photograph, body rhetoric, monumental rhetoric, image event, something else). Explore how the example of visual rhetoric induces you to accept a particular understanding of the world.

3. Find a monument or memorial in your area. Identify the symbolism (for example, what the various parts of the monument or memorial are meant to symbolize). Which group's memory does the monument or memorial foreground? Are any groups' memories placed in the background? What cultural values or ideologies does the monument or memorial praise? What is the message that people today are meant to take away?

4. Can you identify an iconic photograph taken in the last decade? If so, explain how it meets all the criteria of an iconic photo that Lucaites and Hariman identify. If not, is there something about contemporary US visual culture that might explain the apparent decline in iconic photographs?

5. Even though we live in a visual culture, are there instances when there is a duty *not* to look at a photograph? Has the visual culture made us always assume we should look?

RECOMMENDED READINGS

Balthrop, V. William, Carole Blair, and Neil Michel. "The Presence of the Present: Hijacking 'The Good War'?" *Western Journal of Communication* 74, no. 2 (March/April 2010): 170–207.

Birdsell, David S., and Leo Groarke, eds. "Toward a Theory of Visual Argument." Special Issue on Visual Argument, *Argumentation and Advocacy* 33 (Summer and Fall 1996): 1–10.

Delicath, John W., and Kevin Michael DeLuca. "Image Events, the Public Sphere, and Argumentative Practice: The Case of Radical Environmental Groups." *Argumentation* 17, no. 3 (September 2003): 315–333.

DeLuca, Kevin Michael. "Unruly Arguments: The Body Rhetoric of Earth First!, ACT UP, and Queer Nation." *Argumentation and Advocacy* 36 (Summer 1999): 9–21.

DeLuca, Kevin Michael, and Anne Teresa Demo. "Imaging Nature: Watkins, Yosemite, and the Birth of Environmentalism." *Critical Studies in Media Communication* 17, no. 3 (September 2000): 241–260.

Dickinson, Greg, Carole Blair, and Brian L. Ott, eds. *Places of Public Memory: The Rhetoric of Museums and Memorials.* Tuscaloosa, University of Alabama Press, 2010. Especially the "Introduction."

Hariman, Robert, and John Louis Lucaites. "Performing Civic Identity: The Iconic Photograph of the Flag Raising on Iwo Jima." *Quarterly Journal of Speech* 88, no. 4 (November 2002): 363–392.

ENDNOTES

[1] Justice John Paul Stevens, dissent in *United States v. Eichman,* 496 U.S. 310 (1990), at 321.

[2] We are aware of the equivocal meaning of "material" in relation to rhetoric. We use it here in the sense of a tactile substance: granite, fabric, photographic paper. However, we also believe in the materiality of all rhetoric (the purely

verbal included), given that we study rhetoric as symbolic action. Our emphasis throughout the book is on what rhetoric does, not just what it means.

3 Allan Cromley, "Flag, Statue Added to Resolve Vietnam Memorial Controversy," NewsOK, October 14, 1982, http://newsok.com/flag-statue-added-to-resolve -vietnam-memorial-controversy/article/1998948.

4 "Lift the Veil on the Return of the Nation's War Dead" (editorial), USA Today, February 23, 2009.

5 "Official: Pentagon Allows Coverage of War Coffins," CNNPolitics, http://www.cnn .com/2009/POLITICS/02/26/pentagon.media.war.dead/index.html (accessed February 26, 2009); Andrea Stone, "Ban on Photographing U.S. Troops' Coffins Lifted," USA Today, February 27, 2009–March 1, 2009.

6 The history can be accessed at "Revision History of Virginia Tech Massacre," http://en.wikipedia.org/w/index.php?title=Virginia_Tech_massacre&action=history (accessed February 16, 2009).

7 CNN.com I-Report home page, http://www.cnn.com/exchange/ireports/topics/forms /breaking.news.html (accessed June 7, 2007).

8 Jessica Evans and Stuart Hall, "What is Visual Culture?" in Visual Culture: The Reader, ed. Jessica Evans and Stuart Hall (London: Sage, 1999), 7.

9 Charles A. Hill and Marguerite Helmers, eds., Defining Visual Rhetorics (Mahwah, NJ: Erlbaum, 2004); Diane S. Hope, ed., Visual Communication: Perception, Rhetoric, and Technology; and Lawrence J. Prelli, Rhetorics of Display (Columbia: University of South Carolina Press, 2006).

10 Chaïm Perelman and Lucie Olbrechts-Tyteca, The New Rhetoric: A Treatise on Argumentation (Notre Dame, IN: University of Notre Dame Press, 1969), 116, italics added.

11 Diane S. Hope, in the introduction to her edited collection of essays, Visual Communication, describes the way in which presence functions in visual rhetoric, referencing the works of Chaïm Perelman and Lucie Olbrechts-Tyteca. Generally, the process of "selecting certain elements and presenting them to the audience" implies that they are pertinent and important and, thus, imbues them with presence. Hope, Visual Communication, 116. See also Prelli, Rhetorics of Display, 7. Although Perelman and Olbrechts-Tyteca discuss presence as it relates to data selection in a verbal argument, they use examples that make clear the applicability of presence to the study of visual rhetorics. Visuals and presence, alike, act "directly on our sensibility." Perelman and Olbrechts-Tyteca, New Rhetoric, 116. Although a thing exists, it does not act on a person's thoughts unless it is made present. The item need not be physically present. Instead, it can be rhetorically present, through the use of verbal or visual forms of communication.

12 D&AD, "Amnesty International: It's Not Happening Here, But It's Happening Now," 2010, http://www.dandad.org/en/amnesty-international-not-here-but-now. See also "Amnesty—It's Not Happening Here, But It Is Happening Now" (video), YouTube, http://www.youtube.com/watch?v=M2hYauBsKRk.

13 "Amnesty."

14 D&AD, "Amnesty."

15 "It's Not Happening Here, But It's Happening Now, for Amnesty," Where Good Grows, http://wheregoodgrows.com/works/view/45. See also "Amnesty International's Hyper-Local and 'Hyper-Visual' Public Service Denouncements," BagNews, October 31, 2013, http://www.bagnewsnotes.com/2013/10/amnesty -internationals-hyper-local-and-hyper-visual-public-service-denouncements.

[16] "It's Not."

[17] "Amnesty."

[18] Jessica Evans and Stuart Hall, eds., *Visual Culture: The Reader* (Thousand Oaks, CA: Sage, 1999), 7.

[19] Prelli, *Rhetorics of Display*, 1–3.

[20] Evans and Hall, *Visual Culture*, 7.

[21] Evans and Hall, *Visual Culture*, 2.

[22] Evans and Hall, *Visual Culture*, 7.

[23] Barry Schwartz, "The Social Context of Commemoration: A Study of Collective Memory," *Social Forces* 61 (December 1982): 374–402.

[24] Victoria J. Gallagher, "Memory as Social Action: Cultural Projection and Generic Form in Civil Rights Memorials," in *New Approaches to Rhetoric*, ed. Patricia A. Sullivan and Steven R. Goldzwig, (Thousand Oaks, CA: Sage, 2004), 149.

[25] Diane S. Hope, ed., "Introduction: Identity and Visual Communication," in *Visual Communication*, 4.

[26] Hope, "Introduction," 5.

[27] Celeste Michelle Condit, "The Rhetorical Limits of Polysemy," *Critical Studies in Mass Communication* 6, no. 2 (June 1989): 103–104.

[28] Stuart Hall, "Encoding, Decoding," in *The Cultural Studies Reader*, ed. Simon During, 90–103 (London: Routledge, 1993), 98–102.

[29] Hall, "Encoding, Decoding," 101, italics added.

[30] Evans and Hall, *Visual Culture*, 4.

[31] A version of the advertisement is available at http://www.americanapparel.net /presscenter/ads/images/a9000/type3/9826_MAKS_AD_040314_LG.jpg.

[32] "HerStory: 1971–Present," *Ms.*, http://www.msmagazine.com/about.asp. The "No Comment" archive can be accessed at http://www.msmagazine.com /nocommentarchive.asp.

[33] Linda Steiner, "Oppositional Decoding as an Act of Resistance," *Critical Studies in Mass Communication* 5, no. 1 (March 1988): 2.

[34] The authors want to thank Nathan Epley for these valuable insights.

[35] Lester C. Olson, Cara A. Finnegan, and Diane S. Hope, "Visual Rhetoric in Communication: Continuing Questions and Contemporary Issues," in *Visual Rhetoric: A Reader in Communication and American Culture*, ed. Lester C. Olson, Cara A. Finnegan, and Diane S. Hope (Thousand Oaks, CA: Sage, 2008), 3.

[36] Sonja K. Foss, "A Rhetorical Schema for the Evaluation of Visual Imagery," *Communication Studies* 45 (Fall–Winter 1994): 213, 216–217. She also asks how well that function is communicated, given the visual's stylistic and substantive elements, and whether the effects sought by the image are legitimate.

[37] Blair encourages asking these questions: "(1) What is the significance of the text's material existence? (2) What are the apparatuses and degrees of durability displayed by the text? (3) What are the text's modes or possibilities of reproduction or preservation? (4) What does the text do to (or with, or against) other texts? (5) How does the text act on people?" Carole Blair, "Contemporary U.S. Memorial Sites as Exemplars of Rhetoric's Materiality," in *Rhetorical Bodies*, ed. Jack Selzer and Sharon Crowley (Madison: University of Wisconsin Press, 1999), 23, 30.

[38] National Park Service, World War II Memorial, "Service, Sacrifice, Unity, and Victory," http://www.nps.gov/nwwm/index.htm.

[39] V. William Balthrop, Carole Blair, and Neil Michel, "The Presence of the Present: Hijacking 'The Good War'?" *Western Journal of Communication* 74, no. 2 (2010): 172.

[40] Kevin Michael DeLuca and Anne Teresa Demo, "Imaging Nature: Watkins, Yosemite, and the Birth of Environmentalism," *Critical Studies in Media Communication* 17, no. 3 (September 2000): 244.

[41] DeLuca and Demo, "Imaging," 244. See also W. J. T. Mitchell, *What Do Pictures Want?* (Chicago: Chicago University Press, 2005), especially chapter 2.

[42] Prelli, *Rhetorics of Display*, 11.

[43] Karlyn Kohrs Campbell, *The Rhetorical Act*, 2nd ed. (Belmont, CA: Wadsworth, 309–310.

[44] Barbara Jordan, "1976 Democratic Convention Keynote Address: Who Then Will Speak for the Common Good?" New York, NY, July 12, 1976, http://www.elf.net/bjordan/keynote.html. For an analysis of enactment in this speech, see Karlyn Kohrs Campbell and Kathleen Hall Jamieson, "Form and Genre in Rhetorical Criticism: An Introduction," in *Form and Genre: Shaping Rhetorical Action*, eds. Karlyn Kohrs Campbell and Kathleen Hall Jamieson (Falls Church, VA: Speech Communication Association, 1978).

[45] Mary Fisher, "1992 Republican National Convention Address: A Whisper of AIDS," Houston, TX, https://www.americanrhetoric.com/speeches/maryfisher1992rnc.html.

[46] It Gets Better Project, "About," http://www.itgetsbetter.org/pages/about-it-gets-better-project (accessed February 18, 2011).

[47] Kevin Michael DeLuca, *Image Politics* (New York: Guilford, 1999), 10.

[48] DeLuca, *Image Politics*, 17.

[49] Jodi Rudoren, "Proudly Bearing Elders' Scars, Their Skin Says 'Never Forget'," *New York Times*, October 1, 2012.

[50] Linda Diane Horwitz and Daniel C. Brouwer, "The Progenic Trauma Tattoo as Resignification: Auschwitz 157622, A-15510, 4559, . . . ," in *Disturbing Argument*, ed. Catherine Helen Palczewski (New York: Routledge, 2014), 91.

[51] Karl Vick, "Iran's President Calls Holocaust 'Myth' in Latest Assault on Jews," *Washington Post*, December 15, 2005, http://www.washingtonpost.com/wp-dyn/content/article/2005/12/14/AR2005121402403.html.

[52] Robert Tait, "Holocaust Deniers Gather in Iran for 'Scientific' Conference," *Guardian*, December 11, 2006, http://www.theguardian.com/world/2006/dec/12/iran.israel.

[53] Valeria Fabj, "Motherhood as Political Voice: The Rhetoric of the Mothers of Plaza de Mayo," *Communication Studies* 44 (Spring 1993): 1–18.

[54] Fabj, "Motherhood," 2.

[55] Hope, *Visual Communication*, 17.

[56] Hope, *Visual Communication*, 17.

[57] DeLuca and Demo, "Imaging," 242.

[58] DeLuca and Demo, "Imaging," 244.

[59] DeLuca and Demo, "Imaging," 242.

[60] Robert Hariman and John Louis Lucaites, "Performing Civic Identity: The Iconic Photograph of the Flag Raising on Iwo Jima," *Quarterly Journal of Speech* 88, no. 4 (November 2002): 365.

[61] John Louis Lucaites and Robert Hariman, "Visual Rhetoric, Photojournalism, and Democratic Public Culture," *Rhetoric Review* 20, nos. 1/2 (Spring 2001): 37, italics added.

[62] Hariman and Lucaites, "Performing Civic Identity," 363–392.

[63] Robert Hariman and John Louis Lucaites, "Dissent and Emotional Management in a Liberal-Democratic Society: The Kent State Iconic Photograph," *Rhetoric Society Quarterly* 31, no. 3 (Summer 2001): 4–31.

[64] Robert Hariman and John Louis Lucaites, "Public Identity and Collective Memory in U.S. Iconic Photography: The Image of 'Accidental Napalm,'" *Critical Studies in Media Communication* 20, no. 1 (March 2003): 35–66. Image available at http://digitaljournalist.org/issue0008/ng2.htm.

[65] Hariman and Lucaites, "Performing," 364.

[66] Hariman and Lucaites, "Performing," 366.

[67] Quoted on Friends of the Little Bighorn website, http://www.friendslittlebighorn.com /Indian%20Memorial.htm (accessed June 20, 2007).

[68] Western National Parks Association, *The Indian Memorial at Little Bighorn Battlefield National Monument: Peace through Unity* (Canada: Western National Parks Association, 2003).

[69] Richard Morris, *Sinners, Lovers, and Heroes* (Albany: State University of New York Press, 1997), 25.

[70] See letter to the editor in the *New York Times*, July 1, 2005, http://www.triroc.com/wtc /media/freedomtower/timesletters.htm.

[71] Victoria J. Gallagher, "Remembering Together: Rhetorical Integration and the Case of the Martin Luther King Jr. Memorial," *The Southern Communication Journal* 60, no. 2 (Winter 1995): 112.

[72] Peter Grey and Kendrick Oliver, "The Memory of Catastrophe," *History Today* 51, no. 2 (February 2001): 9–15.

[73] Carole Blair, Marsha S. Jeppeson, and Enrico Pucci, Jr., "Public Memorialization in Postmodernity: The Vietnam Veterans Memorial as Prototype," *Quarterly Journal of Speech* 77 (1991): 277.

[74] Grey and Oliver, "Memory," 12.

[75] Grey and Oliver, "Memory," 12.

[76] Barry Schwartz, "The Social Context of Commemoration: A Study of Collective Memory," *Social Forces* 61 (December 1982): 395.

[77] Gallagher, "Remembering," 109.

[78] James E. Young, *The Texture of Meaning: Holocaust Memorials and Meaning* (New Haven, CT: Yale University Press, 1993), 43.

[79] Quoted in Horst Hoheisel, "Ashcrott Fountain [Kassel 1985]," http://www.knitz.net /index.php?Itemid=3&id=30&option=com_content&task=view&lang=en. Images of the original fountain and the new memorial can be seen on this site.

[80] Young, *Holocaust Memorials*, 43.

[81] As quoted in Young, *Holocaust Memorials*, 43.

[82] Young, *Holocaust Memorials*, 45.

[83] For a first person account of this event, see Paul Watson, "One Day on the Water with Bob Hunter," Sea Shepherd Conservation Society web page, http://www .seashepherd.org/editorials/editorial_050510_1.html (accessed July 17, 2007). Footage of the event can be seen on National Geographic, *The Great Whales*, 1978.

[84] See also John W. Delicath and Kevin Michael DeLuca, "Image Events, the Public Sphere, and Argumentative Practice: The Case of Radical Environmental Groups," *Argumentation* 17, no. 3 (September 2003): 315–333.

[85] Watson, "One Day."

[86] Delicath and DeLuca, "Image Events," 315, italics added.

[87] Robert Hunter, quoted in Kevin Michael DeLuca, *Image Politics* (New York: Guilford, 1999), 1.

[88] DeLuca, *Image Politics*, 17.

[89] Davis Guggenheim (director), *An Inconvenient Truth* (Los Angeles: Paramount, 2006).

[90] DeLuca, *Image Politics*, 14.

[91] Traditional approaches to images events, such as Boorstin's influential book, which calls them "pseudo-events," fail to account for the full power of images. Daniel J. Boorstin, *The Image: A Guide to Pseudo-Events in America*, 25th anniversary ed. (New York: Athenaeum, 1987), 188–189.

[92] DeLuca, *Image Politics*, 17.

[93] DeLuca, *Image Politics*, 17.

[94] DeLuca, *Image Politics*, 52.

[95] DeLuca, *Image Politics*, 16.

[96] Meg Spratt, "When Police Dogs Attacked: Iconic News Photographs and Construction of History, Mythology, and Political Discourse," *American Journalism* 25, no. 2 (2008), 85–105.

[97] Davi Johnson, "Martin Luther King Jr.'s 1963 Birmingham Campaign as Image Event," *Rhetoric and Public Affairs* 10, no. 1, (2007), 14.

[98] DeLuca, *Image Politics*, 21–22.

[99] Hope, "Introduction," 17.

4

Argument

KEY CONCEPTS

argument

argument₁

argument₂

argument field

backing

burden of proof

claim

claim of definition

claim of fact

claim of policy

claim of value

conditions of rebuttal

data

enthymeme

particular audiences

personal sphere

presumption

public sphere

qualifiers

spheres of argument

syllogism

technical sphere

universal audience

warrants

The cover of the July 2008 issue of *National Geographic* shows a close-up of the face of a gorilla, with the question superimposed: "Who murdered the mountain gorillas?"[1] Mark Jenkins's feature story opens by describing the conditions in central Africa's Virunga Park, the forests of which are stripped by charcoal producers and the borders of which are crowded by refugees from the conflict in the Democratic Republic of Congo. During the summer of 2007, seven mountain gorillas were killed in the park. The story describes the killing this way:

> On July 22 of last year unknown assailants crouched in the forest, preparing to execute a family of gorillas. . . . [A]rmed with automatic weapons, the killers had hunted down the twelve-member Rugendo family, well known among tourists and well loved by the rangers of Virunga National Park. . . . On foot patrol the next morning [park rangers] found three female gorillas—Mburanumwe, Neza, and Safari—shot to death, with Safari's infant cowering nearby. The following day Senkwekwe was found dead: blasted through the chest that same night. Three weeks later the body of another Rugendo female, Macibiri, would be discovered, her infant presumed dead.
>
> Just a month earlier, two females and an infant from another gorilla group had been attacked. The rangers had found one of the females, shot execution style in the back of the head; her infant, still alive, was clinging to her dead mother's breast. The other female was never found.

All told, seven Virunga mountain gorillas had been killed in less than two months. Brent Stirton's photographs of the dead creatures being carried like royalty by weeping villagers ran in newspapers and magazines around the world. The murders of these intelligent, unassuming animals the park rangers refer to as "our brothers" ignited international outrage. . . .

One thing seemed certain from the moment the bodies of the gorillas were found last July: Poachers had not killed them. Poachers who prey on gorillas leave an unmistakable calling card: They kidnap the infants and cut off the heads and hands of the adults—to be sold on the black market. But these bodies were left to rot where they fell, and the motherless infants left to starve to death.[2]

Notice how the essay speaks of the gorillas in human terms, describing them as members of a family, calling them by name, explaining how an infant was found clinging to her dead mother, and referring to execution-style shootings. Additionally, the magazine cover is a commanding piece of visual rhetoric: it shows a close-up image of a gorilla, eyes staring directly back at the readers with a face much like their own. The essay proceeds to lay out a forensic argument about who was most likely guilty of the "murders."

In the magazine's November 2008 issue, debate emerged about this story. One letter disagreed with the use of term "murder," arguing "the word 'murder' (the unlawful premeditated killing of one human being by another) is and should be reserved for people."[3] The writer worried that not only would the term be redefined, its meaning would be minimized "by equating people to animals," which would further desensitize people to the murder of millions of people in Darfur. Another letter referred to the images of women begging for charcoal that accompanied the original story, and argued: "The plight of these human beings should be our very first concern."[4]

Which author is right? Either what was done to the gorillas constitutes murder and people should feel about and react to it the same way they would to the murder of a human family of seven, or the killing of animals is not murder even though it may be a cause for sadness and a reaction. Which position is most persuasive? Is it murder? Can a nonhuman be murdered? When a gorilla is murdered/killed, what should be the government response? What penalty is appropriate for the murderer/killer?

Many people might rightly say Jenkins and the letter writers all have a right to their own opinions, but that misses the point. You have been exposed to different opinions. Which makes the most sense to you? You cannot accept them both, even if you can see both sides. Either you agree it is murder, or you do not. Arguments require people not only to understand another person's point of view, and that person's reasons for that position, they also require them to choose between competing arguments.

THE PLACE OF ARGUMENT IN A CIVIL SOCIETY

Argument is not something to be avoided. The letter writers did not start a fight by disagreeing or attacking the *National Geographic* article's author. Instead, a reasoned exchange of arguments occurred. Such an exchange is something to encourage. Citizen participation in decision making distinguishes a democracy from all other forms of government. If that distinction is to be more than superficial, and if democracy is to remain vibrant, citizens must be trained in the skills that enable reasoned and reasonable decision making. Influential US political philosopher John Dewey explains:

> [T]he faith of democracy in the role of consultation, of conference, of persuasion, of discussion, in formation of public opinion . . . [is] faith in the capacity of the intelligence of the common man [and woman] to respond with commonsense to the free play of facts and ideas which are secured by effective guarantees of free inquiry, free assembly and free communication . . . [T]he heart and final guarantee of democracy is in free gatherings of neighbors on the street corner to discuss back and forth what is read in the uncensored news of the day, and in gatherings of friends in the living rooms of houses and apartments to converse freely with one another.[5]

Argumentation is a skill central to democracy. This section offers a definition of argument and an explanation of its role in decision making, then outlines argument as interactive, contingent and, at its best, cooperative.

Argument is a complex concept. It can be defined as *reasoned discourse that seeks to persuade by presenting support for a position*. As discussed in Chapter 1, Aristotle outlined three types of proof for an argument: ethos (proof from the character of the speaker), pathos ("disposing the listener in some way"), and "argument [logos] itself, by showing or seeming to show something."[6] Some have simplistically defined "logos" as "logic," but the Greek term "logos," like "argument," is complex. Classical rhetoric scholar George Kennedy points out that "logos" can mean "anything that is 'said,' but that can be a word, a sentence, part of a speech or a written work, or a whole speech."[7] "Logos" refers to the content of persuasion, usually the reasoning, but it is a broad concept.

"Argument" refers both to a thing one makes and an exchange in which one engages. Communication scholar Daniel O'Keefe divides argument into two types, describing argument$_1$ as a "kind of utterance" and argument$_2$ "as a particular kind of interaction."[8]

Argument$_1$ is *argument as a thing, the particular speech act in which one presents a claim and provides sufficient reasons to warrant assent to that claim.* Jenkins's story about the gorillas advances a number of arguments$_1$, including the arguments that gorillas were murdered, that there were many suspects, and that the battle over charcoal provoked the attacks. The letters responding to the story also contain examples of argument$_1$, including the arguments that gorillas by definition cannot be murdered because they are not human and that people should be more worried about the refugees than the gorillas.

Argument$_2$ is *argument as a form of interaction, the way in which arguments-as-things and the people using them interact with each other.* The exchange between the feature story and letters constitutes an argument$_2$, in which differing points of view are represented and contrasted to one another. At its best, argument$_2$ highlights areas of agreement just as much as it might represent a disagreement. It can create the conditions where agreement can be reached, not just where disagreement is solidified. For example, these authors could decide that regardless of whether the killing of gorillas rises to the level of the murder of a human, it is still an egregious act that deserves prosecution. As this example demonstrates, argument$_1$ forms the *basis* on which decisions are made; argument$_2$ is the *process* through which they are made.

In democratic systems in which members participate in decision making (systems as small as a shared household and as large as a nation-state), argument is indispensable. It provides the means through which the relative benefits and costs of a proposal can be assessed. Families may consult with each other about where to vacation. Residents of a state may debate whether to legalize marijuana, as citizens in Colorado and Washington did in 2013. In a representative democracy, such arguments may be conducted in debates among legislators. Extensive debate occurred in Congress about the Affordable Care Act (ACA) in 2009 and 2010.[9] Citizens were also involved in debates over the ACA, in town halls hosted by members of Congress and in various protests. The debate eventually turned to the courts. The Supreme Court ultimately decided that the ACA was constitutional in June 2012,[10] but that decision did not end the debate. Candidates for Congress and President Obama made the ACA an issue in the 2012 and 2014 elections. The Supreme Court heard another case on the ACA in 2015 and again upheld the law. But again, the decision did not end the debate.

These examples highlight two important themes: (1) arguments are necessarily interactive and (2) all decisions based on argument are necessarily contingent.

Argument is interactive: an exchange of arguments$_1$ creates arguments$_2$. In November 2012, for example, Colorado passed Amendment 64 with 55 percent of the vote, legalizing small amounts of marijuana for recreational use by adults.[11] It also allowed personal possession and sales at regulated retail stores, and stipulated penalties on drivers under the influence of marijuana.[12] Supporters had begun with a petition drive to get Amendment 64 placed on the ballot. Supporters and opponents crafted arguments during that drive and until the election.

The arguments that supporters and opponents made were crafted within a context of an ongoing national debate about marijuana laws, which began in 1970, when NORML (the National Organization for the Reform of Marijuana Laws) initiated some its first challenges to marijuana prohibition.[13] Even then, many arguments on both sides of the issue had already been well formulated: the issue had been debated and discussed for decades.

Supporters argued, first, that regulation of marijuana is not justified. Marijuana, they claimed, is more similar to alcohol than to other drugs banned by the federal government. In fact, the largest group supporting legalization in Colorado was called "Campaign to Regulate Marijuana Like Alcohol."[14] Supporters also argued that criminalization of marijuana had some of the same effects as prohibition of alcohol: enriching cartels, empowering gangs, promoting organized crime, as well as making otherwise law-abiding citizens into criminals.[15]

Second, supporters argued that it would be better to focus police resources on other crimes. Betty Aldworth, advocacy director of the Campaign to Regulate Marijuana Like Alcohol, wrote, "There is no arguing whether limited law enforcement resources would be better spent combatting violence and other crimes . . . . 10,000 Coloradans are arrested, prosecuted and burdened with criminal records each year."[16] The codirector of the organization, Mason Tvert, claimed that the United States "wastes billions of taxpayer dollars annually on the failed policy of marijuana prohibition."[17]

Finally, supporters argued that Colorado would gain significant tax revenues with the legalization of marijuana. The Colorado Center on Law and Policy estimated that legalization would raise more than $100 million in tax revenue annually.[18] The amendment specified that the first $40 million would go toward school infrastructure.[19]

Opponents focused on two arguments. First, they argued that health and safety risks are associated with legalized marijuana. Kenneth Buck, Colorado candidate for the US Senate in 2010, claimed that marijuana use is associated with 6.8 percent of all traffic accidents.[20] He also argued that marijuana is addictive and leads to harder drugs.[21] Other opponents focused on the connection between marijuana use and workplace safety.[22]

Opponents also argued that legalization at the state level would lead to tensions with the federal government, because marijuana would still be illegal under federal law. Michael McCallum, chair of the board of directors for the Glenwood Springs Chamber Resort Association, concluded, "Colorado employers would find it tough to compete for government business against companies in states where marijuana use remains illegal under both federal and state law."[23]

Although opponents were united against the amendment, their reasons for opposing it varied. For instance, David Martin, founder of a medical marijuana dispensary, argued that legalization would hurt jobs in Colorado because large pharmaceutical companies would begin producing marijuana, which would lower prices and force local growers out of business.[24] In other words, his argument was not against the use of marijuana; rather, he argued that there was a better system to allow for its use.

At this point, the arguments begin to interact. For instance, supporters argued that tax revenues would increase as a result of passing the amendment. However, Buck argued that for tobacco, the state faces seven dollars in health-related costs for every two dollars raised in tax revenues, suggesting that revenues from marijuana would be outweighed by increased healthcare costs. Similarly, in response to the opposition claim that marijuana would lead to harder drugs, Sean T. McAllister, a leading drug policy reform lawyer in Colorado, said "Right now, black market drug dealers control distribution for recreational purposes. Those drug dealers use violence to enforce their contracts. They push harder drugs on people only looking for marijuana."[25]

This continuing argument$_2$ illustrates our second point: argument is contingent. Human beings must make decisions and act even when complete information is lacking. In this case, people had to vote on the amendment even though debate had not finished. Thus, people make decisions that are contingent, meaning they are based on the circumstances and information available at a particular point in time, information which necessarily deals in probabilities and not certainties. These decisions are useful for the time being, but if new information arises, or times change, the conclusions people reach through argument may change.

Even when humans believe they possess all possible information, they still lack certainty. Human beings are not perfect and always possess incomplete knowledge. They often only know what is probable, not certain. That is why the goal of argument is not to achieve absolute certainty about what is true, but to resolve what is probably right and, hence, what should be done. New facts can always emerge, general beliefs change; thus, conclusions can shift. Although arguments may be presented in absolute language, the decisions based on them are not necessarily absolute, final, or the only option. The domain of argument is the probable. Still, a decision reached through argument is better than a decision made randomly.

For example, when you considered which college to attend, you used arguments to make that decision. You gathered information from various schools, came up with reasons why each school was better or worse, and came to a decision based on those information-backed reasons. When people asked you why you chose a particular school, you offered reasons, such as: "the university has a good reputation," "the university is the most affordable," "the school has a good program in the area I want to study," or "the location of the college and the programs it offers suit my interests." All these are reasons why you chose the school, and evidence for your claim that a particular school is best for you. Even if you could never be 100 percent certain that you chose the best college, these reasons enabled you to make a decision that is better than one made randomly.

An example of how the conclusions of *all* arguments are contingent, even arguments about facts, can be found in the recent debates over Pluto. First discovered in 1930, Pluto was demoted from planet status in 2006 when the General Assembly of the International Astronomical Union voted to accept a definition of "planet" that would exclude Pluto. Neil deGrasse Tyson, an astrophysicist at the American Museum of Natural History and director of the Hayden Planetarium, chronicled Pluto's rise to and fall from planet status.[26] When it was initially discovered, scientists declared the mass of rock and ice to be a planet. It was located where the scientists thought a planet should be, given the orbital path of other planets. However, Pluto is idiosyncratic: it is very small compared to the other planets; its orbit is eccentric (it crosses the orbit of Neptune) and tips more than seventeen degrees from the plane of orbit of other planets in the solar system; and other icy objects share its orbital space. Thus, the claim "Pluto is a planet" was contingent and open to revision as more information became available.

Knowing that even scientific knowledge is contingent, when they planned the new $230-million Rose Center for Earth and Space at the museum, Tyson and other exhibit planners made determinations of the "shelf life of various astrophysical subjects,"[27] in other words, of the degree of reservations attached to various scientific conclusions. Since the Copernican revolution, scientists have possessed a high degree of certainty that the earth revolves around the sun. The exhibit planners were willing to cut such claims into permanent metal displays at the museum,[28] knowing they would have a long shelf life. In the "moderate shelf-life category" resided claims about water on Mars, which were displayed with "replaceable rear-lit transparencies." For knowledge claims with a brief shelf life, the exhibit would show videos that could easily be swapped out.[29]

Given that the subject of argument is the contingent and probable, people need an attitude toward argument that induces a willingness to argue. Just because a conclusion has been reached does not mean it cannot be reconsidered. Thus, the process of argument$_2$ works best when it is a cooperative, rather than combative, process. People need to want to engage in argument, to test ideas, and to work through disagreements.

Unfortunately, argument seems to have been given a bad rap. If you ask someone "Do you want to have an argument?" the other person would probably look at you as if you were crazy. People tend to view arguments as harmful rather than productive. This view is based on misconceptions about argument. People often understand argument through a structural metaphor, which organizes the concept of argument in terms of war. Linguists George Lakoff and Mark Johnson believe this understanding has implications not only for how people talk about argument, but also how they engage in it, for people "conceive of arguments, and execute them, according to the ARGUMENT IS WAR metaphor because the metaphor is built into the conceptual system of the culture in which you live."[30] People involved in argument perceive themselves "as having something to win and something to lose, territory to establish and territory to defend. In a no-holds-barred argument, you attack, defend, counterattack, etc."[31] Even in the most systematic, rational arguments, these parallels between war and argument prevail: "There is still a position to be established and defended, you can win or lose, you have an opponent whose position you attack and try to destroy and whose argument you try to shoot down. If you are completely successful, you can wipe him [or her] out."[32]

Unfortunately, the argument-is-war metaphor works against seeing argument as cooperative. If you think of those with whom you disagree as enemies, your goal is not to communicate with them, but to vanquish them. Concomitantly, they are unlikely to want to talk to you if they are beaten down by the end of every exchange. Argument-is-war induces a worldview in which people who disagree are vicious enemies, opponents are to be vanquished, and the outcome of a dispute is final, without any possibility (or desire) for reliving the fight. For example, is there a person in your life with whom you do not want to argue under any circumstances? That person may not view argument as a way to work through a disagreement, but as a way to emotionally and intellectually beat you down.

Fortunately, argument-is-war is not the only way to view argument. Consider how the way you think about argument would change if you instead used another metaphor: argument-is-play. Viewing argument as play allows you to see how it can be productive and enjoyable. Play is a way in which people learn, cooperate, and experiment. It can be quiet or raucous; a solitary enterprise or a team sport. The outcome is uncertain and the goal is indeterminate, but you'll probably have fun while playing. Just as in play, argument can be a contest with only one winner (as in organized sports) or a form of engagement in which the goal is not to win (as in role-playing or playing house). In play, the goal is not to chase others from the field (or to deter them from even entering the game), but to induce them to join the argument. In play, you do not want to completely defeat your opponent, because you want to play again. The play metaphor represents an attitude adjustment about argument, and can influence the way you engage in the process.

Using the play metaphor, people can frame the argumentative interaction differently. In contrast to a metaphor that uses combat terms, the play metaphor talks about argument in a way that encourages other people to participate. For example, when a difference of ideas occurs during a class, students can play out an idea to see all its nuances. When a student group is debating what to do, its members can see themselves as all members of the same team, working together to reach a goal.

In a democratic society, participation in argument is essential. Without it, decision making is left in the hands of the few people who are in positions of power. Arguments occur about many topics, with greater or lesser degrees of importance. If the only disagreement that people had with others was about which movie to attend, the world would be a much simpler (and more boring) place, but arguments arise over much graver issues: war and peace, life and death, justice and equality. Aristotle recognized the importance of such topics when he wrote about the subjects of political oratory in his *Rhetoric*. To be equipped to make decisions about these issues, an understanding of argument is essential. The next sections review the parts of an argument$_1$ and introduce the concept of presumption. The final section explores the various ways in which argument$_2$, as an interactional process, occurs in various spheres of argument.

CLASSICAL CONCEPTIONS

Aristotle's approach to logic has long influenced argument studies. At the heart was the concept of the **syllogism,** *a statement in which a conclusion is inferred from the truth of two premises.* You may have heard of this process as deductive reasoning, which is composed of a major premise, a minor premise, and a conclusion. In a perfect syllogism, the major premise speaks to a universal truth. The minor premise speaks to a specific example of the universal. The conclusion is the result of combining the two premises.

Major premise: All human beings are mortal.

Minor premise: John is a human being.

Conclusion: John is mortal.

The conclusion of a formal syllogism is certain only if the premises are certain. Of course, because humans are fallible, virtually no premise can be absolutely certain.

An example of deductive reasoning can be found in US Senator Pat Toomey's support for Senate Resolution 75, which he introduced in 2012, urging Iran to release members of the Baha'i faith who were in prison. After the Senate passed the resolution, Senator Toomey stated, "Religious freedom is a natural right that belongs to everyone, everywhere. As a beacon of that freedom, it is appropriate that the U.S. Senate has shown solidarity with the beleaguered Iranian people, including the Baha'i minority."[33] Toomey's argument began by establishing a major premise: that religious freedom is a natural right and belongs to everyone. He then argued that the Senate should act because the United States is a beacon of freedom.

The resolution and Senator Toomey's statement then detailed the violations of religious freedom that Baha'i faced in Iran. According to Senator Toomey's press release, "Since the Islamic Revolution of 1979, Iranian Baha'is have regularly had their homes ransacked or have been banned from attending university or holding government jobs."[34] Similarly, the Senate Resolution read, "Whereas the United States Commission on International Religious Freedom 2012 Report stated, 'Since 1979, Iranian government authorities have killed more than 200 Baha'i leaders in Iran and dismissed more than 10,000 from government and university jobs.'"[35] In these statements, the minor premise of the argument developed the idea that religious freedom has been violated.

The conclusion of the argument was that the Iranian government should be condemned and sanctions should be imposed.

The argument followed the deductive form:

Major premise: Religious freedom is a natural right.

Minor premise: Iran violates religious freedom of people of the Baha'i faith.

Conclusion: Iran should be condemned and sanctions should be imposed.

Note that this deductive argument did not follow the structure of a valid syllogism perfectly. In a valid syllogism, all parts of the conclusion should be included in the major and minor premises. In rhetorical argument, however, new terms often occur in the conclusion. In this case, the terms "condemned" and "sanctions" were not found in the premises, but the reasoning process is deductive because it moves from a general statement to a more specific conclusion.

Aristotle recognized that people typically do not speak in formal syllogisms, especially because human beings can rarely be certain of their premises and because the conclusion seldom contains only words from the premises. Thus, he developed the enthymeme, which he defined as a "rhetorical syllogism."[36] Although much scholarly debate exists over exactly what Aristotle meant by the term, the definition we find most helpful is offered by communication scholar Lloyd Bitzer, who says an **enthymeme** is *"a syllogism based on probabilities, signs, and examples, whose function is rhetorical persuasion. Its successful construction is accomplished through the joint efforts of the speaker and audience, and this is its essential character."*[37] What most distinguishes the enthymeme is not its form or content, but the process through which it is constructed—jointly by the speaker and the audience. Often the speaker will leave some premises unspoken so that the audience fills them in. Bitzer argues that the process of co-construction makes the enthymeme extremely persuasive because *"the audience itself helps construct the proofs by which it is persuaded."*[38] The concept of enthymeme also suggests that the distinction between argument$_1$ and argument$_2$ may be too rigid. The making of an argument$_1$ can also be interactive.

Enthymemes are widely used. Advertising slogans, political campaigns, and conversations with friends often rely on enthymemes. People do not systematically lay out every premise, but rely on shared beliefs and values to fill them in. An illustration of how the audience fills in reasoning can help to clarify how enthymemes function. In 1991, Gatorade developed a marketing campaign featuring Michael Jordan, arguably the greatest basketball player of all time. The slogan of the campaign was "Be Like Mike." The commercial featured highlights of Jordan playing basketball and drinking Gatorade, interspersed with images of regular people playing basketball, while the "Be Like Mike" jingle played in the background. The commercial ended with the slogan "Be Like Mike. Drink Gatorade."[39] The campaign was so successful that many people recognize the jingle more than twenty-five years later.

Given that the Gatorade marketing campaign was one of the most successful in history, it is reasonable to conclude that many members of the audience complete the reasoning by filling in the principle that, if you mimic the behavior of another person, you become more like that person.[40] The power of the campaign occurred largely because the reasoning was left for the audience to provide. If made explicit, the reasoning would have become suspect. If members of the audience had been told that by drinking Gatorade, they would become better basketball players, they would have been skeptical. When allowed to fill in the reasoning on their own, they were more likely to accept it.

Enthymemes consistently appear in presidential campaign rhetoric, as candidates tap into beliefs shared by the people they see as their base.[41] During the 2007 primary for the Republican presidential nomination, Mitt Romney's campaign aired a sixty-second spot known as the "Ocean" advertisement.[42] Within the advertisement, Romney voiced over the image of waves crashing on a beach as children played on the shoreline. He began by referring to a *Wall Street Journal* editorial, penned by Reagan speechwriter Peggy Noonan in the wake of the Columbine school shootings, in which she described contemporary culture as "the ocean in which our children swim" and a "culture of death," full of television, radio, magazines, and newspapers that bombard children with images of violence and sex, and said, "The boys who did the killing, the famous Trench Coat Mafia, inhaled too deep the ocean in which they swam."[43] Extending Noonan's metaphor of ocean, Romney explained that he wanted to: "clean up the water" where people swim. He also wanted to limit Internet pornography, drugs, and violence on TV and in video games. The advertisement concluded with the simple statement: "Mitt Romney. President."[44]

The unspoken part of the enthymeme—the part the audience was asked to fill in—is that any person who wants to clean up the culture should be supported in a bid for the presidency and that Romney was more committed to doing these things than any of the other Republican candidates. The advertisement also relied on the audience to fill in the premise that controlling pornography, drugs, sex, and violence on TV should be one of the primary goals of the president. The spoken part of the argument was that Mitt Romney would like to control pornography, drugs, and violence on TV. The main conclusion (contained in the slogan that ends the advertisement) was: you should vote for Mitt Romney for president of the United States.

The process of arguing can involve a variety of strategies. The central question is: how can you know when you have presented (or heard) a good argument? In order to present a coherent argument$_1$, you must be able to: (1) provide any parts of the argument for which other people ask or about which they are uncertain, and (2) understand what type of claim you are advancing and what type of data are needed to support that claim.

THE TOULMIN MODEL

Philosopher Stephen Toulmin was troubled by the inadequacy of the syllogism as a model for actual argument in which premises are never certain.[45] For instance, a person may understand the data offered and the conclusion advocated, but not *why* that particular data supports the conclusion. Toulmin believed an explanation of the relationship between the data and the conclusion was needed. He developed a description of argument patterns composed of the following parts: claim, data, warrant, qualifications, backing, and conditions for rebuttal. Based on Toulmin's work, argument scholars Wayne Brockriede and Douglas Ehninger developed a model that we adapt here:[46]

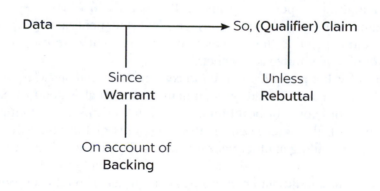

Parts of Argument$_1$

Toulmin defines the **claim** as *"the conclusion whose merits we are seeking to establish,"*[47] or what the rhetor is trying to persuade the audience to believe. For example, Mark Jenkins, the author of the article about the gorillas, claims "Poachers had not killed them."[48] Because neither he nor the readers were present when the gorillas were killed, he had to provide data for that claim.

Argumentation scholars distinguish between four types of claim: fact, definition, value, and policy. A **claim of fact** is what it sounds like, *a claim that advances an empirically verifiable statement.* In 2014, for example, a Malaysian Airlines flight was shot down over the Ukraine. Questions immediately turned to what type of missile was used to shoot it down. The claim of fact that some observers forwarded was: "A [Russian-made] Buk missile shot down the Malaysian Airlines flight."[49] Evidence to support that claim included radar images provided by US intelligence sources and the type of damage to the plane. This claim of fact can be disputed, however. In the immediate aftermath of the event, Russian media sources blamed the CIA for the incident.[50]

A **claim of definition** is *a claim that identifies how a concept or term should be defined.* Often, when people think of a definition of a word or term, they think of the established meaning. The last time you did not know the meaning of a word, you may have asked someone, "What is the meaning of the word?" or looked up the meaning of the word on the Internet. Scholars of rhetoric are interested in how words and terms attain meaning and are used in argumentation. For example, Edward Schiappa notes, "Definitions can be understood more productively as involving claims of 'ought' rather than 'is'."[51] He explores how words such as "death," "wetlands," "obscenity," and "person" have been defined in public argument.

Consider how important the definition of "murder" is to the dispute over killing gorillas or the definition of "planet" to the dispute over Pluto's status. Considerable debate over same-sex marriage has occurred in the United States over the last decade or so. One of the most important elements of that debate is the very definition of "marriage." Opponents of same sex-marriage often argue that marriage *is* defined in a particular manner, while proponents argue that marriage *should* be defined in a particular way. Definitions are rhetorically and argumentatively important because of the manner in which they structure understandings of the world. Definitions represent statements about how certain things are, and depend on the agreement of listeners. They are used to change the behavior of others and to alter beliefs.[52]

A **claim of value** is *a claim that advances a statement about what is worthy.* A claim of value may be based on arguments about what is good or bad, just or unjust, right or wrong, or beautiful or ugly. Such claims are not empirically verifiable; instead, they are based on the judgments of the audience. People often assume that killing another person is wrong, but in some instances killing another person is generally considered acceptable. The arguments about when taking another life should not be punished are arguments about claims of value. On August 9, 2014, in Ferguson, Missouri, Darren Wilson, a white police officer, shot and killed black, eighteen-year-old Michael Brown. A grand jury did not indict Wilson for any crime. In terms of police department policy and the law, Wilson had done nothing wrong, but a vibrant values debate emerged under the heading "#Black Lives Matter," a hashtag for a movement that had been created after the 2012 killing of Trayvon Martin, a black teenager, by a white man.[53] The value claim is, simply, that black lives matter, that black lives are valuable. You may infer this means laws should change. The moment you make that move, you have shifted from a value claim to a policy claim.

Finally, a **claim of policy** is *a claim that addresses what should be done*. A claim of policy usually contains the words "should" or "ought to." It is up to legislators to determine what the appropriate punishment should be for each type of crime, although juries and judges have some discretion. For example, "Marijuana should be legalized." is a claim of policy. Embedded within a claim of policy is a complex series of related arguments, wherein the arguer establishes that a significant problem exists, the proposed policy can solve the problem, the benefits of the policy outweigh any potential costs, and the policy is necessary given the limits of alternative solutions.

Most extended arguments include all these types of claims. Distinguishing among types of claims can help you figure out what is really at issue. For example, if you wanted to organize a debate about global warming on your campus, the first thing you would need to figure out is whether you want the debate to be about a question of fact (is human activity the primary cause of global warming?), a question of policy (should the federal government enact higher fuel efficiency standards for autos in order to reduce global warming?), or a claim of value (is stopping global warming more important than preserving our fossil fuel–based economy?).

The example that began this chapter is an illustration of claims of definition, which play a central role in debate. Before you could answer the question of fact, "who murdered the Virunga gorillas?" you would first need to answer the definitional question of whether killing a gorilla is murder. The controversy over regulating pornography and obscenity also illustrates how claims of definition complicate public debate. Before you can debate a question of fact (does viewing pornography encourage men to accept rape myths?), a question of value (is pornography morally wrong?), or a question of policy (should pornography be regulated through civil or criminal law?), you need to first figure out what "pornography" is. Is "pornography" best defined by activist Andrea Dworkin and legal scholar Catharine MacKinnon as "the graphic sexually explicit subordination of women through pictures and/or words,"[54] or by the US Supreme Court as that which "the average person, applying contemporary community standards would find . . . taken as a whole, appeals to prurient interest";[55] or is it just speech like other speech? Depending on how you define the term, you would answer the questions of fact, value, and policy differently.

The second element of the Toulmin model is data. Toulmin describes **data** as the *"information on which the claim is based."*[56] Data are sometimes referred to as evidence or supporting materials. Jenkins's description of the gorillas provides data to support the claim that poachers were not at fault: infants were left clinging to their dead mothers; and the gorillas' bodies had not been cut up after death.

Supplying incorrect or insufficient data to support a claim is an example of bad argument. Improperly collected statistics, poorly chosen examples, or quotations that are taken out of context are some of the ways in which evidence can be incorrect. For instance, an argument may rely on a public opinion poll, but the statistics summarizing the poll may not be useful if the poll was not properly conducted. Many television news programs conduct call-in polls in which viewers are encouraged to call and vote. The results cannot be generalized to the entire public, because only those people who are watching that particular news show and sufficiently interested in the topic will participate.[57] The data generated is not necessarily representative of the entire population's opinions.

Someone might also present a bad argument by providing insufficient evidence to justify the claim. When you reason from example, you must provide a sufficient number of examples before you can warrant a generalization. Almost everyone knows someone who has lived a long life in spite of a less-than-healthy lifestyle. If you were to justify smoking cigarettes and eating a poor diet on the basis of one person, you would be engaging in a hasty generalization. If Jenkins based his claim that poachers had not killed the gorillas on the data that only one of the seven gorillas was left unscathed, he would have provided insufficient data.

The need to guard against accepting a claim supported by insufficient data is demonstrated by social satirist Stephen Colbert's concept of *truthiness*. Once selected by *Merriam-Webster's Dictionary* as the Word of the Year, *truthiness* is defined as "1: 'truth that comes from the gut, not books' (Stephen Colbert, Comedy Central's *The Colbert Report*, October 2005) 2: 'the quality of preferring concepts or facts one wishes to be true, rather than concepts or facts known to be true' (American Dialect Society, January 2006)."[58] Colbert explains further: "It used to be, everyone was entitled to their own opinion, but not their own facts. But that's not the case anymore. Facts matter not at all. Perception is everything. It's certainty."[59] Colbert is being humorous, but he is also making a serious point. Too frequently, people jump to conclusions based on an impulsive reaction without researching the facts, and sometimes even despite facts.

To avoid relying on unjustified opinion, when presented with a claim, you need to ask: What data support this claim? Simply saying that you "feel" something is true is not sufficient. Why does Jenkins's description of the condition of the dead gorillas serve as data proving poachers were not involved?

Toulmin describes **warrants** as *bridges, or the generalizable "rules" and "principles" that link the data to the claim.*[60] Warrants show that the jump from the data to the conclusion is reasonable, that the conclusion is warranted. Toulmin's model is sometimes referred to as the jurisprudential model because he believed values could best be understood by studying argument and, in particular, legal argument. In the legal system, a judge issues a warrant, which allows the police to search a suspect's home or possessions. The warrant is issued on the basis of probable cause. By analogy, the warrant in the Toulmin model provides probable cause for an argument. The data provides probable cause that the claim is true. It does not prove the claim true beyond a doubt—if it did, it would not be an argument! Instead, the data *suggests* that the claim is true. The warrant provides the reason that the data would lead a person to believe the claim is correct.

One difficulty in understanding and identifying the warrant in an argument is that the rhetor often leaves it unstated. Recall that Aristotle suggested that enthymemes were a strong form of argument because they invited audience participation in completing the argument. The warrant of the argument is often left unstated for this reason.

A few examples illustrate how warrants function. Advocates of recreational marijuana legalization argue that marijuana should be legalized because it is similar to alcohol. The data is "Marijuana is similar to alcohol." The claim is "Marijuana should be legalized." The warrant is left unstated. What would link the data to the claim or provide probable cause for the data leading to the claim? In this case, the warrant could be "substances similar to alcohol should be regulated like alcohol" or "substances similar to alcohol should be legalized."

Jenkins uses empirical knowledge about poaching to connect his data to his claim: "Poachers who prey on gorillas leave an unmistakable calling card: They kidnap the infants and cut off the heads and hands of the adults—to be sold on the black market."[61] In this case, the claim is "Poachers did not kill the gorillas." The data is that the heads and hands of the adults were left intact. The warrant is "Poachers always take the head and hands of gorillas."

In both arguments, the warrant is left unstated. The connection between the data and the claim may be suggested, but the audience fills in the connection.

Sometimes, however, the rhetor provides the warrant to assist the audience in understanding the argument. Toulmin explains warrants are needed because a listener may not understand why the data provides proof of a claim. For example, John once told his spouse, "I need new golf clubs (claim). The grooves on my irons are smooth (data)." To him, that was sufficient. However, his spouse did not understand the connection and asked, "What does that mean?" John then explained the warrant: grooves are what put spin on the golf ball, and the spin is what makes the ball stop on the green. Thus, when the grooves are smooth, it is time to get new clubs. (Happily, John got his new golf clubs.)

One reason rhetors may leave the warrant unstated is that it is contingent rather than certain. The warrant provides only a *probable* reason that the data leads to the conclusion. When the warrant is explicitly stated, the audience may doubt or distrust the reasoning. For instance, when John explained that the grooves make the ball spin, his wife may have wondered whether he needed the specific clubs he bought or whether he had the ability to hit the ball well enough to really make it spin. (Fortunately, she did not ask such questions.)

The audience's concerns often lead to the fourth part of the Toulmin model, the rebuttal. For Toulmin, **conditions of rebuttal** indicate *"circumstances in which the general authority of the warrant"* should be set aside.[62] Conditions of rebuttal provide reasons why the argument may not be correct and offer challenges to the data or the strength of the warrant. In the gorilla story, one condition of rebuttal might be that the poachers were interrupted before they could "kidnap" the infant or take the hands and feet. That condition seems unlikely, however, given that the killings happened over many days.

Toulmin defines **qualifiers** as *those statements indicating the "strength conferred by the warrant."*[63] Not all claims have the same level of certainty. The level is often determined by the strength of the conditions of rebuttal. Claims can be qualified with terms such as "usually," "possibly," "likely," "in all probability," "presumably," and "always." Notice that each qualifier represents different levels of certainty.

One of the best examples of using qualifiers in argument is a weather report. Meteorologists make an argument when forecasting tomorrow's weather. They claim the weather will be of a particular type, based on the data from weather stations, models, and radar. Usually, meteorologists will qualify a forecast with a probability; for example, "there is a 50 percent chance of rain tomorrow." We might say: "it will *probably* rain tomorrow." That is a different claim from "it will *certainly* rain tomorrow" (a claim few, if any, meteorologists would ever make).

Jenkins provides no qualifiers in his essay. He does not say: "Poachers probably had not killed the gorillas." Instead, his statement is unequivocal: "Poachers had not killed them."

Finally, Toulmin describes **backing** as *assurances that the warrants are authoritative and/or current.* The backing says the warrant is supported. Usually, backing will provide an answer to the conditions of rebuttal. Although Jenkins provides no explicit backing for his description of poaching, if pressed he could likely point to studies and past experiences with poaching. In other words, his warrant is based on inductive reasoning, which is based on his accumulated experience of poaching.

In discursive form, an example of an argument₁ that contains all the parts of the Toulmin model would read as follows:

> Legalization of marijuana will provide additional tax revenues to the
> state (data), so marijuana should probably (qualifier) be legalized (claim),
> unless the health costs associated with marijuana use are greater than
> the additional tax revenues (conditions of rebuttal), given that sales of
> marijuana are expected to generate $100 million in tax revenue (warrant)
> because many people are expected to buy marijuana in Colorado
> (backing).

Just as most arguments are not formal syllogisms, arguments are not usually laid out following Toulmin's pattern. You will have to figure out the components. (As this example demonstrates, rigidly following the Toulmin model results in overly complex sentences.)

What would an argument containing the elements of the Toulmin model look like in prose form? What follows is an argument that Elizabeth Cady Stanton advanced in 1892 in a speech to the Committee of the Judiciary of the United States Congress. Her "Solitude of Self" speech is fascinating because it provides a philosophical foundation for granting women the right to vote.[64] As you read the following passage, which outlines her argument, notice how it fulfills each part of argument Toulmin identifies.

> The strongest reason for giving woman all the opportunities for higher
> education, for the full development of her faculties, forces of mind
> and body; for giving her the most enlarged freedom of thought and
> action; a complete emancipation from all forms of bondage, of custom,
> dependence, superstition; from all the crippling influences of fear,
> is the solitude and personal responsibility of her own individual life.
> The strongest reason why we ask for woman a voice in the government
> under which she lives; in the religion she is asked to believe; equality
> in social life, where she is the chief factor; a place in the trades and
> professions, where she may earn her bread, is because of her birthright

to self-sovereignty; because, as an individual, she must rely on herself. No matter how much women prefer to lean, to be protected and supported, nor how much men desire to have them do so, they must make the voyage of life alone, and for safety in an emergency they must know something of the laws of navigation. To guide our own craft, we must be captain, pilot, engineer; with chart and compass to stand at the wheel; to match the wind and waves and know when to take in the sail, and to read the signs in the firmament over all. It matters not whether the solitary voyager is man or woman.[65]

Stanton's argument could be broken down as follows:

Qualifier, Claim: "woman [should be given] all the opportunities for higher education . . . a complete emancipation from . . . all the crippling influences of fear." In this passage, "all . . . most enlarged . . . complete" make clear the claim is unqualified; Stanton does not recognize a less than exhaustive application.

Data: "the solitude and personal responsibility of her own individual life"

Warrant: each person has a "birthright to self-sovereignty"

Backing: "as an individual, she must rely on herself"

Rebuttal: Stanton anticipates that someone might argue "women prefer to lean" on men, so she says "No matter how much women prefer to lean" they ought to experience full freedom.

Because Stanton delivered this speech toward the end of her career, after decades of debate on the issue of woman suffrage, it makes sense that she would deliver the argument₁ in its most complete form. As people engage in argument₂ and are challenged to explain themselves, the various parts of an argument₁ are filled in. In other words, argument₂ usually is necessary to call forth a complete argument₁.

Knowing the parts of an argument₁ will help you understand what a person is arguing, become better at constructing an argument, and understand where you disagree with someone. For example, is the disagreement on the level of the data or the warrant? The answer allows you to locate the point of disagreement. Knowing the parts of an argument also helps you critique and analyze an argument. You can understand whether someone is making a warranted argument; that is, you can determine whether a rhetor's claim is supported by data and reasons, or parts of the argument are missing.

This knowledge also will help you understand when people introduce an argument that is irrelevant—that does not speak to the claim, data, or warrant, but introduces an irrelevant issue. For example, *ad hominem* attacks are arguments against the person making the claim that are irrelevant to the claim. The title of Al Franken's 1999 book, *Rush Limbaugh is a Big Fat Idiot,*[66] contains an ad hominem attack. Even if some of Limbaugh's arguments are wrong, Franken cannot demonstrate this by highlighting Limbaugh's girth or by calling him an idiot. If someone attacks you, rather than a part of your argument, you could point out that the attack is irrelevant: your claim is still warranted.

Ad hominem arguments are not always irrelevant. During the 2007 presidential primary campaign, they can be seen not only in verbal comments, but also in multimodal forms, such as YouTube videos. In what is considered the first video to go viral during that campaign, ParkRidge47 (Phillip de Vellis) posted an attack advertisement against Hillary Clinton and supporting Barack Obama, titled "Vote Different."[67] A mashup of the famous "Apple/1984" advertisement,[68] the "Vote Different" video replaces the original advertisement's image of a movie screen, showing a male face speaking to undifferentiated and gray-clad masses, with a screen showing Hillary Clinton's face.[69] In both advertisements, amid the wash of gray, sprints a woman in red and white running shorts and top. At the end of the ad, she flings a sledgehammer at the screen, smashing it and freeing the masses. The original commercial ended with the January launch date of the Macintosh computer and a hint that this is a reason why 1984 will differ from George Orwell's *1984*. The mashup remake ends with a reference to *1984*, then jumps to a simple graphic "BarackObama.com" accompanied by a mashup of the Apple and Obama logos.

The advertisement represents an ad hominem attack insofar as it does not offer an assessment of Hillary Clinton's policies, but instead creates a visual analogy between Clinton and the controlling face and voice of the Orwellian dystopia. The mashup wants you to see Clinton as controlling and dangerous.

When a question of character is at issue, or when arguers claim they should be believed because of their characters (in other words, their characters are what warrants their arguments), ad hominem arguments become relevant. Particularly in contemporary politics, when candidates run on their personalities and images as much as on their political positions, arguments concerning their characters become highly relevant.[70] To the extent that Hillary Clinton's campaign argued that she was the better candidate because her experience formed her character as presidential, the advertisement had a point. It argued one could engage in politics as usual, voting for a person perceived to be part of the Washington establishment, or one could "vote different."

A statement that sounds as if it has all of the parts of a complete argument does not necessarily justify assent. It may provide bad data. A warrant may be nonsensical. A qualification may not be strong enough. The connections between the data, claim, and warrant may be weak. Not only must people be able to identify the parts of an argument, they also need to be able to assess the strength of those parts.

Argument Fields

Although a complete argument should contain all the component parts outlined by Toulmin, not all arguments sound alike. An argument between friends about what movie to see proceeds differently from an argument in a legislative hearing about what regulations should be placed on movies. In a debate between friends, the argument "It's my turn to pick," may be perfectly reasonable, but a legislator who said "It's my turn to have a law passed" would likely be laughed out of the assembly.

The idea that the norms and rules of argument change from field to field was introduced most completely by Toulmin. He explained that an **argument field** is *an argument type in which the types of data used and conclusions reached are of the same logical type*. Arguments "come from different fields when the backing or the conclusions in . . . arguments are not of the same logical type."[71] The elements involved in argument (claim, data, warrant, and so on) do not change, regardless of the field in which the argument occurs, but the criteria for examining an argument do vary. Toulmin pointed to argument in the fields of law, marine biology, and mathematics, which are field dependent because they each use different types of data and warrants to support claims. In law, citing previous court decisions as precedent is a central way to provide data, but court decisions would be unpersuasive at a presentation on marine biology. All fields require data and the other parts of the Toulmin model, but what counts as legitimate data, warrants, and so on, varies from field to field.

PRESUMPTION AND BURDEN OF PROOF

Regardless of the type of claim, your argument will not take place in a vacuum. All arguments have claims and data that precede them; thus, audience members are predisposed to believe one side more than the other. Presumption as a concept was developed in 1828 by Richard Whately, Anglican Archbishop of Dublin, in his book *Elements of Rhetoric*. He defined **presumption** as *a predisposition to believe that a claim is correct until overwhelming evidence proves otherwise*.[72] This definition makes clear that arguments do not occur in a political or social vacuum; instead, as rhetorical scholar Karen Whedbee explains, they are "'grounded' within a context of commonly accepted opinions, practices, and institutions."[73] Whately's view is that the most commonly and widely held ideas deserve presumption and should only be set aside if there is good reason to do so.

The Pluto controversy described earlier contains appeals to presumption, with defenders of Pluto arguing that until exploratory missions had flown to Pluto and "additional factual details" were uncovered, Pluto should remain a planet.[74] One Pluto defender articulated a particularly strong presumption for maintaining Pluto's planet status: "I believe that until we land on Pluto and find incontrovertible evidence that that world does not wish to be called a planet, that we should leave things as they are."[75] Despite substantial evidence that Pluto is not like other planets, Plutophiles argued that overwhelming evidence was necessary to overcome the presumption that Pluto was, indeed, a planet.

Whately also explained the relationship between presumption and the **burden of proof,** or *the obligation to offer reasons sufficient to overcome presumption*. Whately claimed that the burden of proof "lies on the side of him [or her] who would dispute" the claim presumed correct.[76] Burden of proof is an important concept for determining when you should assent to a claim that another person advances. The burden of proof lies on people who support ideas that lack presumption.

People most commonly hear of presumption and burden of proof in relation to courts of law. The accused are "presumed innocent." This does not mean they *are* innocent, or that they are more likely innocent than not. Instead, it means that before anyone concludes the accused is guilty, the prosecution must meet its burden to prove the accused is guilty. Presumption is almost always fixed and unchanging in a criminal court of law. Presumption can be overcome and the burden of proof fulfilled if the prosecution provides evidence proving guilt beyond a reasonable doubt, but it cannot shift from the defense to the prosecution (unless there is a defense such as insanity, in which case the defense bears the burden of proving insanity).

In other debates, presumption may not be predetermined, and debate may begin with determining where presumption rests and who, then, carries the burden of proof. Often, arguers spend time establishing that presumption is on their side and that, if doubt exists in the audience's minds, the audience should side with them. For example, the science behind the personal health and environmental effects of fracking are, for the most part, unsettled. Although some studies have been conducted on the possible link between fracking and birth defects, or between fracking and earthquakes, the results are often described as "uncertain."[77] Kate Galbraith, a journalist who has covered oil and gas stories in Texas, claims, "Frankly, we don't know many of the answers."[78]

In such a situation, presumption becomes an important consideration. If decision makers do not know the health and environmental consequences of fracking, should it be permitted, controlled, or banned? People from all sides use presumption in making their arguments. Opponents of fracking argue that it must be banned or regulated in light of the uncertainty. *Scientific American* reports that "Still, for some, waiting for additional science to clarify those uncertainties before adopting more serious safeguards is misguided and dangerous. As a result, a number of researchers and local activists have been pushing for more aggressive oversight immediately."[79] Others argue that in the absence of conclusive studies, fracking should be allowed because of the economic benefits. Both sides' arguments are based on presumption. Opponents argue that presumption should lie in protecting health and the environment, and that the burden of proof lies on those who believe fracking is safe. Supporters argue that presumption should lie with the economic benefits of fracking, and that the burden of proof lies with those who claim that fracking harms health or the environment.

Another example of a presumption appeal comes from the debates over the 2003 invasion of Iraq, which was justified at the time by the claim that Iraq president Saddam Hussein possessed weapons of mass destruction (WMDs). As time passed and no WMDs were found, administration officials were pressured to justify the invasion. On August 5, 2003, Secretary of Defense Donald Rumsfeld held a Pentagon press briefing. When asked why the United States had not yet found the weapons that were the reason for the war, he answered: "as we all know, the absence of evidence is not evidence of absence."[80] This statement clearly located presumption with those who believed Iraq possessed WMDs. According to Rumsfeld, the burden of proof was not on those who believed weapons existed, but on those who argued that they did not.

SPHERES OF ARGUMENT

Although many arguments in which you engage on a daily basis may be technical (such as the communication in a classroom as you discuss specialized scholarly articles) or personal (such as the interpersonal interactions you have with friends), one purpose of this book is to orient your thinking about communication toward a public sensibility. How can people resolve disagreements about public issues such as global warming, immigration, economic policy, abortion, or desegregation? To understand the dynamics of public argument, it helps to understand the distinctions between the processes of public, personal, and technical argument.

Philosopher Chaïm Perelman emphasizes that arguments are always addressed to an audience.[81] Although people often think of the strength of an argument in terms of how well it will convince a **universal audience,** that is, *an audience composed of all reasonable and competent members of humanity,* the reality is that people address arguments to **particular audiences,** or *actual audiences.*[82] The debate between creationism/intelligent design and evolution provides an example. For scientists, only peer-reviewed scientific data count when determining which theories should be taught; thus, citing evidence from the Bible to explain creation would be unpersuasive to an audience of scientists. In contrast, evidence from the Bible might be sufficient to persuade a religious audience that nonscientific data pointing to intelligent design should be taught as a theory. In each case, the arguers are addressing particular audiences. Arguments are different according to their audiences and purposes (resolving a technical dispute, working through a personal issue, or developing public policy).

Communication scholar G. Thomas Goodnight recognizes that the persuasiveness of an argument and the form it takes depend on the sphere of argument in which it occurs.[83] According to Goodnight, **spheres of argument** are *"branches of activity—the grounds upon which arguments are built and the authorities to which arguers appeal."*[84] Goodnight recognizes that what is persuasive depends on the purpose of the argument. To explain how different grounds for argument emerge, he posits three spheres of argument: personal, technical, and public. He argues that particular warrants and data count differently depending on the sphere in which they are argued.

Think about the last time you and friends were talking. What did you talk about? Music? Your favorite TV show? The newest movie? What a friend should do about a family conflict? You and your friends may have covered a range of topics, from art to interpersonal relations. It is unlikely that any of you declared another friend incapable of speaking about a topic because s/he was unqualified. The next day, probably no one in your group remembered the specific arguments. Your experience in this instance is an example of the **personal sphere,** *the place where the most informal arguments occur, among a small number of people, involving limited demands for proof, and often about private topics.*

Argument in the personal sphere tends to be ephemeral, meaning it is not preserved. No preparation is required. Many things count as evidence, which is pulled from memory. All topics are open to discussion even if the participants have no special knowledge about them. Expertise is not necessary; anyone can talk on any subject. The test of what constitutes a valid argument in the personal sphere is truthfulness: are the people with whom you disagree honestly representing their beliefs? The time limits imposed probably have nothing to do with the nature of the disagreement, and more to do with when people must leave. Ultimately, the relationships involved do not require agreement among everyone.

Contrast this to the **technical sphere,** *the argument sphere that has explicit rules for argument and is judged by those with specific expertise in the subject.* An example of a technical sphere argument occurs any time medical professionals try to publish their scholarship in a specialized journal such as *Journal of the American Medical Association* or *The Lancet.* Technical arguments are judged by referees, or peer reviewers, who have special expertise in the area being discussed. When the arguments are deemed valuable, they are preserved and published. Other members of the specialized medical community may then join the discussion.

The function of this type of argument is, as Goodnight states, to "advance a special kind of knowledge."[85] It takes special expertise to contribute to a technical dispute. It also takes special expertise to read or understand it. Terms, phrasings, and the complexity of the argument make it relatively inaccessible to anyone not trained in medicine. The argument in a medical essay may be difficult for you to follow because the data being used is unknown to you, or because the warrants were left unstated and you did not know how to provide them.

Another example of technical argument can be found in courts of law. Judges oversee disputes between trained lawyers and must themselves possess special expertise in order to apply the rules of argument fairly. Lawyers must not only have received training, they must also have passed a test (the bar exam) that deemed them competent to practice law. Very specific rules govern who may speak, when they may speak, and what they may say. The proceedings are recorded. Not all evidence counts. (For example, hearsay evidence is usually excluded in criminal cases.) The ultimate authority for determining punishment is the law; a jury may decide a case, but its decision is bound by the rules of law and the judge's instructions. Many times, the test of argument in the technical sphere is truth, either in terms of objective facts or in terms of which claim best approximates people's understanding of the world.

In many ways, the technical and personal spheres of argument represent two extremes. The **public sphere** is *the argument sphere that exists* "to handle disagreements transcending personal and technical disputes."[86] Ultimately, the issue at hand is broader than the needs of a group of friends or of a specialized technical community. For example, arguments about whether the university should raise tuition, a parking ramp is the best way to solve the parking problem downtown, or a local school bond referendum should be passed are public sphere arguments. Generally, the issues affect a broad range of people and, hence, a broad range of people may speak to them. The demands of proof are not as rigid as in technical argument or as fluid as in personal argument. The test of validity for such an argument tends to be whether it is right, as in "just" (not as in "correct"). People, as members of a community, try to serve the community's interests with public argument and, thus, need to assess whether they can come to agreement about what is the right thing to do.

The Pluto controversy offers an example of the distinction among public, personal, and technical claims. In the February 1999 issue of *Natural History*, Tyson wrote an essay titled "Pluto's Honor." In it, he argued:

> As Citizen Tyson, I feel compelled to defend Pluto's honor. It lives deeply in our twentieth-century culture and consciousness and somehow rounds out the diversity of our family of planets, like the troubled sibling of a large family. Nearly every schoolchild thinks of Pluto as an old friend. And there was always something poetic about being number nine. As Professor Tyson, however, I must vote—with a heavy heart—for demotion. Pluto was always an enigma to teach.[87]

In other words, Tyson recognizes that arguments that might matter in a personal or public sphere (such as public perception, schoolchildren's beliefs, and the poetry of nine) are not relevant in the technical realm, where technical questions of how planets are grouped are the only criteria. Children's sadness at not finding Pluto along with the terrestrial and gas giant planets in the Scales of the Universe exhibit (which portrays the relative size of things in the solar system) simply does not count as relevant data in the debate.

Other scientists also recognized this distinction among argument spheres. In a debate Tyson organized at the American Museum of Natural History, astronomer Jane Luu argued that Pluto was not a planet and that continuing to refer to it as a planet "would only be due to tradition and sentimental reasons. . . . So, in the end, the question goes back to this: Should science be a democratic process, or should logic have something to do with it?"[88] Luu was basically asking: Is this a technical or public sphere debate? Substantial public outcry arose over the International Astronomical Union's vote to demote Pluto from planet status, but the data used by the scientific community was what mattered. As Tyson explains, "Science is not a democracy. As is often cited (and attributed to Galileo), the stated authority of a thousand is not worth the humble reasoning of a single individual."[89]

Just because an argument belongs in the public sphere does not mean technical arguments are irrelevant. In debates over what individuals and governments should do to combat global warming, technical debates about the causes and rate of warming, as well as about the effectiveness of solutions, play an important role. Other arguments might start in the technical sphere, but become public sphere arguments. Communication scholars Valeria Fabj and Matthew J. Sobnosky explore how HIV/AIDS activists challenged the medical establishment's drug-testing protocol (a technical issue) because it failed to serve public interests. The traditional requirements of double-blind studies to administer placebos to terminal patients seemed to magnify, rather than lessen, the public health crisis of HIV/AIDS.[90] Fabj and Sobnosky argue that public sphere deliberation was enhanced by activists' introduction of a personal and technical issue (individuals get diseases that doctors treat) into the public sphere of deliberation. Activists trained themselves in the technical language of medicine so they could persuasively argue that public, and not just technical, concerns should govern drug-testing protocol.

Spheres of argument do not denote locations. The most technical arguments might occur in the most private locations: imagine two doctors debating the best treatment for a patient while in the restroom, or two lawyers having a heated personal discussion, while preparing for court, about where they should eat lunch. Spheres of argument do influence argumentative practices—the norms and rules that govern how the argument ought to proceed and that may influence who is allowed to speak, from what location, and on what topics.

The person, topic, or location also do not determine the sphere; instead, the sphere influences who may speak on what topic and in what location.

CONCLUSION

"Argument" refers both to the complex relation of claim, data, warrant, backing, qualifications, and conditions for rebuttal and to the process by which people engage each other in the exchange of reasons. Most important, however, arguments are a central part of communication in a democratic society. The attitude people take into argument influences how they engage in argument. Believing argument is war induces you to treat people with whom you disagree as enemies to be vanquished. This perspective is not conducive to creating an environment that encourages open communication. In contrast, if you conceive of argument as play, you are likely to see debate as a cooperative enterprise. Argument only works in deliberation and judgment if people are willing to change their minds when they hear a sound argument. Interlocutors are not enemies, but fellow humans, vulnerable to the same dangers, injuries, and harms as other humans, and thus deserving of the full measure of respect due to people considered to be friends.

We do not mean to imply that argumentative processes are just play without real consequence. The outcomes of argument have real consequences to which campus project is funded, which job candidate is hired, which political candidate wins, whether or not a country is invaded, and so on. Our objective with this argument-is-play metaphor is not to suggest the stakes involved in argument are less important, but to heighten our sense of responsibility to the people with whom we argue.

Deliberation, judgment, and decision making—all crucial elements of democracy—require that members of a community be able to explain and justify their positions. Deliberation also requires that people compare and contrast competing arguments so they can make decisions even when faced with incomplete information. Every person makes decisions every day; and it is always better to make a decision based on sound evidence, strong reasoning, and warranted conclusions. When argument is conceived of as a cooperative enterprise in decision making, its utility as a way to resolve differences, rather than magnify them, becomes clear.

You may have found that an argument that works for one audience is not persuasive to another. As you listen to public discussion of a policy, you realize the way that argument progresses is different from the way that you and a friend may resolve a disagreement. Argument is a process: the best argumentative engagements are those in which people engage with each other and are open to persuasion.

We think a good principle for arguing is as follows: you should be as open to persuasion and change as you hope the person with whom you are arguing is. When you walk into an argument$_2$, you should be willing to alter your position in the face of other arguments. The willingness to alter your own position is the basis of democratic government, the First Amendment, and the marketplace of ideas, all of which rely on the assumption that people will make reasoned decisions when presented with information and arguments. As an argument progresses, data is accepted and discarded, warrants are challenged and reinforced, qualifications and reservations are added to claims, and claims are rejected or accepted. Rejection of a claim influences the other arguments$_1$ offered, because that claim may actually function as backing or warrant for other arguments. As particular arguments are abandoned, the argument$_2$, itself, evolves.

DISCUSSION QUESTIONS

1. Does the word "argument" have a positive or negative connotation to you? Why? What would change the connotation?
2. Read an article advocating a policy, a letter to the editor, or an editorial. Diagram one of its arguments, identifying as many components of the Toulmin model as you can.
3. Read a newspaper or magazine in which a public policy issue is discussed. Identify places where appeals to presumption are used.
4. Identify a topic about which much debate proceeds. Create examples of the four types of claims (fact, definition, value, policy) that could be made in relation to that topic. In other words, craft four topics that people could debate, each topic focusing on a different type of claim.
5. In 2014, the American Dialect Society named "#BlackLivesMatter" as the Word of the Year. Is the message an enthymeme? If so, what are the elements of the Toulmin model? If not, why is it not an argument?

RECOMMENDED READINGS

Fabj, Valeria, and Matthew J. Sobnosky. "AIDS Activism and the Rejuvenation of the Public Sphere." *Argumentation and Advocacy* 31 (Spring 1995): 163–184.

Goodnight, G. Thomas. "The Personal, Technical, and Public Spheres of Argument: A Speculative Inquiry into the Art of Public Deliberation." *Argumentation and Advocacy* 18 (Spring 1982): 214–227.

O'Keefe, Daniel J. "Two Concepts of Argument." *Journal of the American Forensic Association* 13 (1977): 121–128.

ENDNOTES

[1] Mark Jenkins, "Who Murdered the Virunga Gorillas," *National Geographic*, July 2008, 34–65. The full story is available online at http://ngm.nationalgeographic.com/2008/07/virunga/jenkins-text. A video that accompanies the story is available at: http://ngm.nationalgeographic.com/2008/07/virunga/gorillas-video-interactive.

[2] Jenkins, "Who Murdered," 39, 45.

[3] Chris Falzon, letter to the editor, *National Geographic*, November 2008, 8.

[4] Bryan Berry, letter to the editor, *National Geographic*, November 2008, 8.

[5] John Dewey, "Creative Democracy," *1939–1941/Essays, Reviews, and Miscellany*, vol. 14, *John Dewey: The Later Works, 1925–1953* (Carbondale: Southern Illinois University Press, 1988), 227.

[6] Aristotle, *On Rhetoric*, trans. George A. Kennedy (New York: Oxford University Press, 1991), 1.2 [1356a].

[7] George A. Kennedy, *A New History of Classical Rhetoric* (Princeton, NJ: Princeton University Press, 1994), 11.

[8] Daniel J. O'Keefe, "The Concepts of Argument and Arguing," *Advances in Argumentation Theory and Research*, ed. J. Robert Cox and Charles Arthur Willard (Carbondale: Southern Illinois University Press, 1982), 3–23, esp. 3–4, and "Two Concepts of Argument," *Journal of the American Forensic Association* 13 (1977): 121–128.

[9] Emily Smith, "Timeline of the Health Care Law," CNN.com, June 28, 2012, http://www.cnn.com/2012/06/28/politics/supreme-court-health-timeline.

[10] Smith, "Timeline."

[11] "Amendment 64—Legalize Marijuana Election Results," *Denver Post*, November 8, 2012, http://data.denverpost.com/election/results/amendment/2012/64-legalize-marijuana.

[12] Sadie Gurman, "Colorado Legalizes Recreational Use and Sale of Marijuana," *Contra Costa Times* (Walnut Creek, CO), November 6, 2012.

[13] Keith Stroup, "Legalization Needs the 'Marijuana Middle' to Win," NORML.com, December 15, 2014, http://blog.norml.org/2014/12/15/legalization-needs-the-marijuana-middle-to-win.

[14] Carrie Click, "Colorado Amendment 64 Pot Legalization Gaining Support on Both Sides of Aisle," *Aspen Business Journal*, October 20, 2012, http://www.aspenbusinessjournal.com/article.php?id=7350.

[15] "Opponents, Supporters of Amendment 64 Speak Out," *Post Independent* (Glenwood Springs, CO), October, 8, 2012, http://www.postindependent.com/article/20121008/VALLEYNEWS/121009882.

[16] "Opponents, Supporters."

[17] Click, "Colorado Amendment."

[18] "Opponents, Supporters."

[19] "Opponents, Supporters."

[20] Kenneth R. Buck, "NO: Colorado Can't Put Our Kids at Risk," *Denver Post*, September 23, 2012.

[21] Buck, "NO."

[22] "Opponents, Supporters."

[23] "Opponents, Supporters."

[24] Quoted in Carrie Click, "Weeding through the Pros and Cons of Amendment 6," *Post Independent* (Glenwood Springs, CO), October, 25, 2012, http://www.aspenbusinessjournal.com/article.php?id=7358.

[25] Sean T. McAllister, "Guest Opinion: The Real World Impacts of Marijuana Prohibition," *Daily Camera* (Boulder, CO), October 5, 2012.

[26] Neil deGrasse Tyson, *The Pluto Files: The Rise and Fall of America's Favorite Planet* (New York: Norton, 2009).

[27] Tyson, *Pluto*, 63.

[28] Tyson, *Pluto*, 64.

[29] Tyson, *Pluto*, 64.

[30] George Lakoff and Mark Johnson, *Metaphors We Live By* (Chicago: University of Chicago Press, 1980), 63–4.

[31] Lakoff and Johnson, *Metaphors*, 62.

[32] Lakoff and Johnson, *Metaphors*, 63.

[33] Quoted in "Sen. Toomey's Resolution Urging Release of Religious Prisoners in Iran Passes Senate," December 20, 2012, http://www.toomey.senate .gov/?p=press_release&id=1233.

[34] "Toomey's Resolution."

[35] "Toomey's Resolution."

[36] Aristotle, *On Rhetoric*, 1.2 [1356].

[37] Lloyd F. Bitzer, "Aristotle's Enthymeme Revisited," *Quarterly Journal of Speech* 45, no. 4 (December 1959): 399–408, 408, italics added. See also Thomas M. Conley, "The Enthymeme in Perspective," *Quarterly Journal of Speech* 70 (1984): 168–187.

[38] Bitzer, "Aristotle's Enthymeme," 408.

[39] The full video is on YouTube at http://www.youtube.com/watch?v=b0AGiq9j_Ak.

[40] Darren Rovell, *First in Thirst: How Gatorade Turned the Science of Sweat into a Cultural Phenomenon* (New York: AMACOM, 2005).

[41] Kathleen Hall Jamieson, Erika Falk, and Susan Sherr, "The Enthymeme Gap in the 1996 Presidential Campaign," *PS: Political Science and Politics* 32, no. 1 (March 1999): 12–16.

[42] The spot can be viewed on YouTube, at http://www.youtube.com/watch?v= vFyDWjATbok.

[43] Peggy Noonan, "The Culture of Death," *Wall Street Journal*, April 22, 1999, http://peggynoonan.com/article.php?article=40.

[44] Script for "Ocean," http://www.mittromney.com/News/Press-Releases/Ocean_Ad.

[45] Stephen Toulmin, *The Uses of Argument* (Cambridge, UK: Cambridge University Press, 1969), 130.

[46] Wayne Brockriede and Douglas Ehninger, "Toulmin on Argument: An Interpretation and Application," *Quarterly Journal of Speech* 46, no. 1 (February 1960): 44–53.

[47] Toulmin, *Uses*, 97, italics added.

[48] Jenkins, "Who Murdered," 45.

[49] Jessica Durando, "Malaysian Airlines Flight 17: What We Know Now," USA Today Network, July 21, 2014, http://www.usatoday.com/story/news/nation-now /2014/07/21/malaysia-airlines-flight-mh17-crash-investigation/12936419.

[50] Taylor Wofford, "Russian State Media Says CIA Shot Down Malaysia Airlines Flight MH17," Newsweek.com, July 22, 2014, http://www.newsweek .com/russian-state-media-says-cia-shot-down-malaysian-airlines-flight-mh -17-260381.

[51] Edward Schiappa, *Defining Reality: Definitions and the Politics of Meaning* (Carbondale: Southern Illinois University Press, 2003), 5.

[52] Schiappa, *Defining*, 32.

[53] Black Lives Matter, "About Us," http://blacklivesmatter.com.

54 Andrea Dworkin and Catharine A. MacKinnon, *Pornography & Civil Rights: A New Day for Women's Equality* (Minneapolis: Organizing Against Pornography, 1988), 138–139.

55 U.S. Supreme Court, *Paris Adult Theatre I et al.* (413 U.S. 24) 1973.

56 Toulmin, *Uses*, 97, italics added.

57 Doug Muzzio, "The Savvy Voter: Analyze a Poll," PBS's *By The People: Election 2004*, http://www.pbs.org/elections/savvyanalyze.html.

58 "Truthiness," Merriam-Webster's Word of the Year 2006, http://www.merriam-webster.com/info/06words.htm.

59 Stephen Colbert, interview by Nathan Rabin, January 25, 2006, http://www.avclub.com/articles/stephen-colbert,13970.

60 Toulmin, *Uses*, 98, italics added.

61 Jenkins, "Who Murdered," 45.

62 Toulmin, *Uses*, 101, italics added.

63 Toulmin, *Uses*, 101, italics added.

64 For an analysis of the speech, see Karlyn Kohrs Campbell, "The Humanistic Underpinnings of Feminism: 'The Solitude of Self,'" *Man Cannot Speak for Her*, vol. 1 (New York: Praeger, 1989).

65 Elizabeth Cady Stanton, "The Solitude of Self," *Man Cannot Speak for Her*, vol. 2, ed. Karlyn Kohrs Campbell (New York: Praeger, 1989), 373.

66 Al Franken, *Rush Limbaugh Is a Big Fat Idiot* (New York: Dell, 1996).

67 Chris Cillizza, "Creator of Hillary Attack Ad Speaks," washingtonpost.com Politics Blog, March 30, 2007, http://blog.washingtonpost.com/thefix/2007/03/author_of_hillary_attack_ad_sp.html.

68 "1984 Apple's Macintosh Commercial," YouTube video, http://www.youtube.com/watch?v=OYecfV3ubP8 (accessed November 21, 2007).

69 "Vote Different," YouTube video, http://www.youtube.com/watch?v=6h3G-lMZxjo (accessed November 21, 2007).

70 John F. Cragan and Craig W. Cutbirth, "A Revisionist Perspective on Political *Ad Hominem* Argument: A Case Study," *Central States Speech Journal* 35, no. 4 (Winter 1984): 228–237.

71 Toulmin, *Uses*, 14, italics added.

72 Richard Whately, "From *Elements of Rhetoric, The Rhetorical Tradition*," in *The Rhetorical Tradition: Readings from Classical Times to the Present*, ed. Patricia Bizzell and Bruce Herzberg (Boston: Bedford, 1990), 846–847.

73 Karen Whedbee, "Authority, Freedom and Liberal Judgment: The Presumptions and Presumptuousness of Whately, Mill and Tocqueville," *Quarterly Journal of Speech* 84 (1998): 176.

74 Julian Kane, quoted in Tyson, *Pluto*, 66.

75 David Levy, quoted in Tyson, *Pluto*, 100.

76 Whately, *Elements*, 847, italics added.

77 Kristin Jones, "CU Study on Fracking's Effects Is Stirring Debate," *Daily Camera* (Boulder, CO), February 9, 2014, LexisNexis.

78 Kate Galbraith, "Fear of Russia, Fear of Fracking: Let's Find a Way to Produce More Independent Information about Fracking, Urges Energy Writer," *Pittsburgh Post-Gazette*, April 13, 2014, LexisNexis.

79 Naveena Sadasivam and ProPublica, "Drilling for Uncertainty: The Latest in Fracking Health Studies," *Scientific American* March 5, 2014, http://www.scientificamerican.com/article/drilling-for-certainty-the-latest-in-fracking-health-studies/?&WT.mc_id=SA_SP_20140310.

[80] Donald Rumsfeld, "DoD News Briefing—Secretary Rumsfeld and Gen. Myers," August 5, 2003, United States Department of Defense, http://www.defenselink.mil /transcripts/2003/tr20030805-secdef0525.html.

[81] Chaïm Perelman, *The Realm of Rhetoric,* trans. William Kluback (Notre Dame, IN: University of Notre Dame Press, 1982), 9–20.

[82] Perelman, *The Realm,* 14.

[83] G. Thomas Goodnight, "The Personal, Technical, and Public Spheres of Argument: A Speculative Inquiry into the Art of Public Deliberation," *Argumentation and Advocacy* 18 (Spring 1982): 214–227.

[84] Goodnight, "The Personal," 216, italics added.

[85] Goodnight, "The Personal," 219.

[86] Goodnight, "The Personal," 219, italics added.

[87] Neil deGrasse Tyson, "Pluto's Honor," *Natural History* 108, no. 1 (February 1999): 82.

[88] Quoted in Tyson, *Pluto,* 71.

[89] Tyson, *Pluto,* 127.

[90] Valeria Fabj and Matthew J. Sobnosky, "AIDS Activism and the Rejuvenation of the Public Sphere," *Argumentation and Advocacy* 31 (Spring 1995): 163–184.

5

Narrative

KEY CONCEPTS

character development

comic frame

myth

narrative

narrative fidelity

narrative probability

personal memory

personification

plot

public memory

representative anecdote

social truth

tragic frame

vivacity

For many people, the notion of home is a pleasant one. They want to live close to their parents and the people with whom they grew up. Basketball player LeBron James had the opportunity to live that life. He grew up in Akron, Ohio; played for the St. Vincent–St. Mary High School team; and was drafted by the Cleveland Cavaliers when he graduated from high school. His commute from his hometown of Akron to the arena where he would play his NBA games was less than an hour. He seemed to be living the dream life, in his hometown and near his family.

In 2010, James became a free agent: he could negotiate a deal with any team in the NBA. After weeks of public speculation, in a live special on ESPN, James announced, "I'm going to take my talents to South Beach."[1] There, he would be playing for the Miami Heat and teaming up with two of the best players in the NBA: Dwyane Wade and Chris Bosh. Speculation immediately turned to how many NBA Championships the Miami Heat would win. But James also faced a good deal of criticism. Seemingly, he was walking away from his home.

Again, in 2014, James became a free agent. This time, he announced his decision through a letter titled "I'm Coming Home" on the *Sports Illustrated* web site, in which he said, "Before anyone ever cared where I would play basketball, I was a kid from Northeast Ohio. . . . People there have seen me grow up. I sometimes feel like I'm their son. . . . I want to give them hope . . . . I want to inspire them . . . . My relationship with Northeast Ohio is bigger than basketball. I didn't realize that four years ago. I do now."[2] Throughout the letter, James reflected on his desire to return to his home and raise his family in the area where he grew up. He concluded, "I'm ready to accept the challenge. I'm coming home."[3]

Despite novelist Thomas Wolfe's admonition that "You can't go home again,"[4] James was willing to try. Although no individual's story may be exactly the same as his, many people express a desire to return to their homes at some point during their lives. Few, if any, will be able to move home and get millions of dollars to play basketball, earn millions more in endorsements, and be the idol of adoring fans. Instead, they move home to be near family, care for ailing parents, or take over the family business. Whatever the reason, the decision typically involves remembrance of the stories of the past and anticipation of the events of the future. In that way, stories that describe those decisions are often similar.

Interpretations of James's decision to return home were varied. Joe Posnanski, a prominent sportswriter who grew up in Cleveland, talked about how Cleveland had not won a sports championship since 1964 and how, in the years since, the city had declined. The winters seem colder, he said; people moved away, and the river caught on fire. He saw James's return as a reason for Clevelanders to be happy. Posnanski wrote that James was "a superstar . . . coming back home to try and win a championship for a city that hasn't had one in a half century. There will probably be movies about it."[5] Posnanski claimed that James's decision to return home was "unprecedented." Superstars typically go to teams that can provide the best opportunity to win championships or pay them the most money. James's decision was based on returning to his home in Ohio.

The "coming home" story is called upon often, if not always in the same way. Most of us can immediately relate to the story as it is told. It relies on a set of common assumptions that the listener can draw upon. Listeners can follow the story and provide the common assumptions because of the ways stories (or narratives) function.

Narratives are everywhere. Narratives, or stories, inform people's personal lives. Families tell stories about their pasts that affect the ways family members perceive their families. Most people can cite stories from books that have changed the way they live their lives. People who belong to a particular religious tradition possess identities grounded in that tradition's narratives. Christians, for instance, rely on the stories of the birth, death, and resurrection of Jesus as the basis of their faith. Buddhists rely on the stories and teachings of Siddhartha Gautama's life.

Narratives also inform public life. Political views are shaped by the stories that politicians tell. People often vote for candidates who have life stories they find particularly appealing. Newspapers, TV news shows, and Internet sites are filled with narratives about the issues and personalities of the day. Often, when people think of stories in the news, they think of gossip about personalities such as Oprah Winfrey, Tiger Woods, LeBron James, Justin Bieber, and the Kardashians, but those stories are a small fraction of the stories in public discourse. People also tell stories about the effects of inadequate health care on individuals, the manner in which the Islamic State group developed, how the IRS targeted certain groups, and the history of the nation. These stories play an important role in framing the way members of the public remember what has happened. Narratives are an important way to understand the world in which people reside.

Quite simply, narratives are rhetorical. In the next section, we describe the form and function of narrative. We then review criteria used to judge narratives: aesthetics, authorial intent, empirical truth, and social truth. Throughout the chapter, we examine narratives at the micro level of the individual story and the macro level of the overarching myth that structures a culture. Our goal is to help you understand how narratives function within all areas of civic life.

FORM AND FUNCTION OF NARRATIVES

Gerald Prince, a professor of romance languages, defines **narrative** as *"the representation of at least two real or fictive events or situations in a time sequence, neither of which presupposes or entails the other."*[6] As representations, narratives are a form of symbolic action. They are referential, meaning they depict or describe events; they are not the event themselves. Prince's reference to at least two events emphasizes the temporal component of narratives; a story moves across time as events relate to each other. The events do not presuppose or require one another: a causal or logical relationship is not necessary for the two events to exist. Instead, the narrative itself develops the relationship between them.

Obviously, not all communication is narrative. Statements such as "Two plus two equals four" or "A penny saved is a penny earned" fail to meet the definition of narrative. To be a narrative, a rhetorical action must organize people's experiences by identifying relationships among events and across time. Narratives have several important functions, including the formation of memory and the creation of a sense of cultural identity and community.

Forming Memory

Narratives form two types of memory: personal and public. They give people a personal sense of who they are as individuals with a history, as well as a public sense of who they are as members of a community that also has a history.

Personal memory is *the manner in which individuals remember their pasts.* People remember events through the narratives told about them. Individuals recollect events from their daily lives as stories that they keep in their own personal memories or share with others. The ability to remember narratives seems almost innate within humans. Think for a moment about what you did yesterday. The way you remember yesterday's events is most likely a narrative or a series of narratives. As you think about your more distant past, the memories become even more grounded in narratives. What do you remember from your grade school days? Probably all that you remember from that time are narratives: events that happened one day on the playground or on a particularly memorable birthday. However, these memories are based on the narrative you have created about that day. They certainly do not include everything from that day.

The narratives people remember are not mental videos of their pasts. They select which bits of information they will remember. Most daily experiences are rapidly forgotten. For instance, can you remember what clothes you wore last Thursday? Probably not—unless something happened to cause you to remember exactly what you wore that day. One author of the text remembers exactly what he wore one day in July 2014. He was supposed to meet with high school students who were thinking about attending his university, so he wore a white shirt with an emblem of the university mascot on it. Right before the meeting, he spilled coffee on his shirt. He remembers the white shirt with the university mascot emblem because it is an important part of the story. The spilled coffee would not have mattered as much if he were not meeting with potential students.

In this story, the clothing is important. It was chosen to provide a good image of the university, but the coffee stain probably sent a different message. The account of this day is highly selective. The author already cannot recall what else happened, what other meetings he had, or who else he met that day. He selectively remembers some events of the day because he places them in the context of a narrative. He likely will not wear a white shirt for a recruitment event again unless he has an extra shirt with him. The story becomes memorable because it implicates many of the author's values. He likes to make a good first impression on strangers, especially those who might consider attending his university. The story also tells you something about the author: he is likely to spill coffee on himself and is willing to let others know that. Many stories that you remember may tell a great deal about how you view yourself.

Narratives serve as retrospectives.[7] They make sense of events of your life by placing them in relation to one another, thus imbuing them with significance.[8] In rhetoric, narratives tap into what English professor Marshall Grossman describes as "an essential activity of the human mind."[9] Audience members are accustomed to narratives; they remember their own pasts as narratives that they tell to other people, so they understand narrative form easily.

Just as narratives can form and maintain individual memory so, too, can they form and maintain the memory of collectives of people. Collective memory occurs whenever people who compose a group share memories. For instance, the members of a community often participate in retelling stories and developing a collective memory of a place.

In May 2008, the small town of New Hartford, Iowa (population 516), was hit by a mile-wide tornado with winds of 200 mph. Two weeks later, to the day, the town was flooded, after a storm moved through the area and dropped over 31 inches of rain in less than three days.[10] Almost all the homes, churches, and businesses, even the school, were damaged by either the tornado or the flood.[11] As soon as the floodwaters receded, citizens of the small town began cleaning up and renovating the school and the town. Students, teachers, and other residents of the school district all helped. By the beginning of the school year, the school reopened.

The experience is encapsulated in many stories people from New Hartford tell each other and outsiders. The stories are important because they represent the pride the people have in their small town, their work ethic, and their resilience, and because they are an important part of their collective memory.

Not all stories are so positive, however. For example, part of the collective memory of the people of Newtown, Connecticut, has been shaped by the shootings in Sandy Hook Elementary School on December 14, 2012, when twenty students and six adults were killed. The memories will continue to affect people in that community for decades to come.

As discussed in Chapter 1, **public memory** is *a particular type of collective memory that combines the memories of the dominant culture and fragments of marginalized groups' memories, and enables a public to make sense of the past, present, and future.* Communication scholar Richard Morris explains that "public memory is perhaps best conceived as an *amalgam* of the current hegemonic bloc's cultural memory and bits and pieces of cultural memory that members of other cultures are able to preserve and protect."[12] Although a particular memory may become dominant (for example, the story of Columbus's arrival in the Americas), bits and pieces of marginalized stories persist and can be used as the basis to challenge the dominant public memory (for example, indigenous people's memories of colonization).

Another example of public memory that is driven by a dominant perspective, yet also contains bits and pieces of marginal memories, can be found by comparing stories told in the 1950 film *The Jackie Robinson Story* and the 2013 film *42* with the story told in Robinson's memorialization at the Negro League Baseball Museum in Kansas City, Missouri. In dominant memory, as influenced by the films, Robinson is an exceptional figure in Major League Baseball, which celebrates Jackie Robinson Day every April 15 and, in 1997, retired his jersey number 42, making it the first number retired from the entirety of a major US sports league. The dominant narrative in the films describes Robinson as an exceptional player who faced severe difficulties while playing in the majors (poor travel conditions, hotels that refused him entry, fans and other players who called him names). In these films, Robinson overcomes his difficulties by working hard, maintaining his cool in difficult situations, and relying on the help of white owners and teammates.

In contrast, the Negro League Baseball Museum does not focus on the story of Robinson in the Major Leagues, or even on Robinson. Instead, it tells the story of Robinson's days as a player in the Negro Leagues, portraying him as an above average, but far from great, player who, like all black players, faced racism, including Jim Crow segregation laws. On the museum website, Robinson is not foregrounded. Instead, visitors can read about all the players, who are listed alphabetically. The first images a visitor sees are of John "Buck" O'Neil, Verdell Mathis, and the Hilldale Giants.

The difference between the two narratives is striking. In the dominant story, the white scene (Major League Baseball) is the dominant scene. The story dominating public memory focuses on the integration of Major League Baseball; the key actor is Robinson; the key event celebrated is the integration of the Major Leagues. In the museum, the African-American scene (the Negro Leagues) is the dominant scene; Robinson is only one figure among many; and the integration of the Major Leagues has a downside: "While this historic event was a key moment in baseball and civil rights history, it prompted the decline of the Negro Leagues," which had become "centerpieces for economic development in many black communities."[13] When Robinson's career is framed by his role in the Negro Leagues, it is a much different story. Through narratives, public memory is formed, but different publics have more or less power to have their version of events remembered.

Narratives are important to the creation of public memory because some narratives are held in common by a society and become the dominant narratives of a culture. They affect the way that members of a culture view the world in which they live, but they are not universally shared. There are variations of the dominant story. Some people may develop narratives that run counter to the dominant narrative.

One of the most important narratives for a group is its origin narrative, a story of the moment in which the group was formed. That story provides meaning for the group. In families, wedding anniversaries and birthdays are celebrated. In the United States, people celebrate the Fourth of July as the birthday of the nation. In each of these instances, part of the celebration involves telling an origin story. Fourth of July celebrations include the story of the colonies' small army taking on the superior armies of King George, which suggests to members of the culture that the United States and its people can overcome great difficulties when they work together.

Sociologist Barry Schwartz explains how origin stories function:

> the magnetism of social origins resides not simply in their priority and ordering power, but in the *meaning* of this priority and ordering power, as defined by later generations and in light of their own experiences, problems, and needs. While the object of commemoration is usually to be found in the past, the issue which motivates its selection and shaping is always to be found among the concerns of the present.[14]

In other words, a public comes to understand itself in the present by telling stories of its historical past. Such stories form public memory.

In the United States, most citizens know the origin narratives of the country, including Columbus's 1492 landing in the Americas, the Pilgrims' difficult first winter in 1620, and the 1773 throwing of tea into Boston Harbor to protest British taxation without representation. (The narrative of throwing tea into the Boston Harbor inspired the name of a more recent political movement, the Tea Party.) Many people also know the story of Patrick Henry justifying the Revolutionary War with a speech featuring the line: "Give me liberty or give me death."[15] Schoolchildren still learn stories about Abraham Lincoln, including the story that as a young store clerk, "Honest Abe" walked miles to return a penny to its rightful owner. Hollywood tells the story of Lincoln's success in the 2012 movie, *Lincoln*. Many citizens can recite stories of successes in World War II, such as those retold in the 1998 film *Saving Private Ryan* and the 2001 television miniseries *Band of Brothers*. Each of these stories assists in creating US public memory.

Creating Culture and Community

Members of a society understand their nation and their place in it through the stories that are told about it. Political scientist Eloise Buker says that narratives, whether historical or imaginative, help "celebrate our great events, but they also allow us to explore new ways of living together."[16] Narratives create culture and community by teaching cultural values, explaining causality, and entertaining.

Teaching Cultural Values. Dominant narratives imbue a culture with a set of values. For example, more than seventy years after it occurred, people still tell stories about the D-Day invasion of Normandy on June 6, 1944. Filmmakers have produced more than twenty movies and documentaries about D-Day. Authors have written numerous books and articles about it. Very few of the books and movies stop with the end of the day. Instead, they move past the events of June 6 in order to give meaning to the day. The official home page of the US Army describes the impact of the invasion: "The D-Day cost was high—more than 9,000 Allied Soldiers were killed or wounded—but more than 100,000 Soldiers began the march across Europe."[17] At the top of the page, the words "Freedom Brotherhood Sacrifice Victory" highlight the lessons of D-Day. To mark the seventieth anniversary of the invasion, major TV networks followed veterans to Normandy to hear their tales of heroism.

Dominant US culture remembers and retells many stories that provide a basis for its values. Think of the narratives many schoolchildren read and the values that such stories teach. What value is taught in the story of "Honest Abe" returning a penny to its rightful owner? In the stories of the colonists' success in the Revolutionary War and US service members' success in the World Wars?

Even stories told in popular culture teach values, regardless of whether the stories are grounded in real or fictitious events. The movie *Captain Phillips* is partly fictitious, but it is based on the true story of a ship that was taken over by Somali pirates in the Indian Ocean in 2009. The movie, nominated for an Academy Award for Best Picture, told the story of Captain Phillips's heroic efforts to save his ship and crew. At one point in the movie, Phillips offered to be taken hostage in exchange for his crew. The message is clear: Captain Phillips was a hero who saved his ship and crew because he was willing to sacrifice himself for others. Heroism is something to which an audience can relate and aspire.

A myth is a particular form of narrative that teaches cultural values as it structures how you think about yourself, other people, and the society. Communication scholar Martha Cooper defines **myth** as "*a dramatic vision that serves to organize everyday experience and give meaning to life.*"[18] According to feminist scholars Sonya Andermahr, Terry Lovell, and Carol Wolkowitz, myths are a dramatic vision because they contain a story of conflict that is not about an actual event, but is "the imagined past of a culture"[19] that guides future action. They organize life because they explain people's relations to one another. They justify particular actions and hierarchies. Rhetorical critic V. William Balthrop argues that myths give meaning because they provide a "cultural image of perfection."[20] They enable a culture to visualize and understand what is good or evil, right or wrong.

Yet myths are ethereal; we may not be aware of their presence. They may be taken for granted, as objective reality. If, as anthropologist Clifford Geertz argues, culture is a "system of inherited conceptions expressed in symbolic forms," then myths are one of the central symbolic forms because they "communicate, perpetuate, and develop knowledge about and attitudes toward life."[21] According to Balthrop, the meanings contained in myths constitute the essence of the culture and represent that which is taken for granted, the point at which one cannot further explain the reasons for an action or a belief.[22]

Myths help people learn values and form beliefs through the dramatic telling of social lessons. They impart an identity to people who identify with the story. Myth is not the only symbolic form that maintains culture, transmits ideology, and structures values, beliefs, and attitudes, but it is a central and distinctly symbolic one. Myth is a narrative form whose power does not rely on truth or falsity, but on its appeal to a sense of social truth.

The melting pot myth (and metaphor) has held particular power in the United States, where citizenship is defined by a series of rights and responsibilities rather than by a particular ethnicity or birthplace. The melting pot myth offers a story to explain who the US people are. It valorizes giving up a person's individual cultural identity for the good of the nation. Citizenship is open to people of all races, but the melting pot myth means that when one becomes a US citizen, all vestiges of one's earlier culture melt away.

This story of immigration and assimilation came into general usage in 1908 with the publication of Israel Zangwill's play, *The Melting Pot*. The myth emerged during industrialization, when the form and function of a melting pot were widely understood. A melting pot is a vessel that can withstand extremely high temperatures and not lose its shape, even as its contents are melted into an indistinguishable and fluid mass. When various ores and metals are added to the pot and mixed together, they form a substance stronger than the individual ingredients. The United States was the vessel, impermeable to the high temperatures caused by the pressures of immigration; within the United States, diverse peoples represented the ores and metals that would be fused together into a homogenous and strong mass.

Historian Amy Maria Kenyon describes one particularly telling dramatization of this myth as a ritual enactment of the narrative of citizenship. Henry Ford, the founder of Ford Motor Company and the key developer of modern assembly-line techniques, sought to integrate his workers, many of whom were immigrants, into US culture. In 1914, he instituted English courses, in which the first thing workers learned to say was: "I am a good American." At the end of the course, workers would participate in a "melting pot" ceremony. Historian Robert Lacey provides a vivid description:

> "Across the back of the stage was shown the hull and deck of an ocean
> steamship at Ellis Island," described one eyewitness to the graduation
> ceremony. A gangway led down from this ship and, in the dim light,

a "picturesque figure" appeared at the top of the gangway, dressed in foreign costume and carrying his possessions wrapped, Dick Whittington–like, in a bundle tied to a stick over his shoulder. It was the first graduate of the after-hours language classes, and one by one the other graduates followed him down the gangway into "an immense cauldron across which was painted the sign *Ford English School Melting Pot.*" Each successful graduate entered the Melting Pot in his foreign costume, carrying a sign indicating the country he had come from. But minutes later they all emerged from the great cauldron "dressed in American clothes, faces eager with the stimulus of new opportunities. . . . Each man carried a small American flag in his hand."[23]

Kenyon describes this myth as creating a "cultural image of perfection": "the melting pot is the 'cooking up' of social identities, a fictional process that closes the circle by constant reference back to utopia, or rather to the myth of the American people as 'colorless' (i.e., white) blend of once-present, but now mercifully absent (albeit nostalgia-laden), manifestations of ethnic difference."[24] When a single myth becomes dominant in a culture, it often defines and delimits that culture. The myth of the melting pot influences definitions of what it means to be American, declares it is the responsibility of immigrants to assimilate, and makes the predominance of white culture seem normal. Even if you do not overtly think of the melting pot, it may influence your attitudes toward and beliefs about immigration.

Implying Causation. Because a narrative relies on a chronological telling of events, the event that happened first is seen to be the cause of later events. Literary theorist Seymour Chatman maintains that all good narratives possess the elements of causality, or at least contingency.[25] If one event in the story did not cause another, then at least the events are related in such a way that they bring into being or evoke a particular situation.[26] Even when a narrative does not explicitly offer causal reasoning, the audience members will supply it as they listen to the story.

A story about the end of the Cold War exemplifies implicit causal reasoning. The National Museum of American History website describes the end of the Cold War this way:

Throughout the 1980s, the Soviet Union fought an increasingly frustrating war in Afghanistan. At the same time, the Soviet economy faced the continuously escalating costs of the arms race. Dissent at home grew while the stagnant economy faltered under the combined burden. Attempted reforms at home left the Soviet Union unwilling to rebuff challenges to its control in Eastern Europe. During 1989 and 1990, the Berlin Wall came down, borders opened, and free elections ousted Communist regimes everywhere in eastern Europe. In late 1991 the Soviet Union itself dissolved into its component republics. With stunning speed, the Iron Curtain was lifted and the Cold War came to an end.[27]

Note how this narrative provides several sets of events (protracted war in Afghanistan, weakened economy, arms race, and attempted reforms) and implicitly links them to the end of the Cold War. Nowhere in the paragraph are these called "causes," but the suggestive power of the narrative format leads the reader to identify these events as causing the end of the Cold War. This is not to say the suggestion is wrong; indeed, most historians would agree that at least some of these events helped bring the Cold War to an end.

However, the causal relationship identified is not always accurate. The *post hoc ergo propter hoc* fallacy occurs when the reasoning takes the form of "after this therefore because of this." For example, according to the "The Super Bowl Indicator," if a team from the old American Football League (now the AFC) wins the Super Bowl, the stock market will decline in the next year. Conversely, if a team from the old National Football League (now the NFC) wins the Super Bowl, the stock market will rise during the next year.[28] Between 1967 and 1997, the indicator was correct twenty-eight out of thirty-one times.[29] Still, it's obvious that no causal relationship exists between who wins the Super Bowl and the future of the stock market. Students of rhetoric should scrutinize the implied causality in a narrative.

Engaging Interest. Narratives are interesting and enjoyable, even when they are about painful events. Even the scariest or saddest narratives rivet audiences' attention because they allow people to learn about the human condition. By hearing about how other people experienced pain and how they responded in the face of overwhelming circumstances, people learn about their own limits and potentials. Holocaust survivors who recount their personal histories are often among the most popular guest speakers on college campuses.

Stories develop imagination and provide new perspectives while enlightening and educating listeners. For example, Harper Lee's *To Kill a Mockingbird* has affected readers for more than fifty years. The novel is a coming-of-age story told from the perspective of Scout, a young girl growing up in the South. The writing engages readers, captures their attention, and moves listeners to respond emotionally to its narrative. The lessons are about the destructive effects of racism and the need to fight injustice. Eric Zorn, of the *Chicago Tribune*, hoped his children would "remember the biggest thing to love about *To Kill a Mockingbird*—the lesson imparted by those words that courage isn't always flashy, isn't always enough, but is always in style."[30] Countless youth have read the book in school; many claim it influenced their career choices. In 2014, NFL quarterback Christian Ponder and his wife announced that their new baby daughter, though she was named after Ponder's college football coach, would be nicknamed "Scout" after the protagonist in *To Kill a Mockingbird*.[31]

Listeners find narratives easier to follow than detailed observations or complex reasoning patterns. President Ronald Reagan made storytelling a central part of political rhetoric, consistently integrating narratives into his State of the Union addresses. Political communication scholar Kathleen Hall Jamieson argues that Reagan was not considered "the great communicator" because he was particularly eloquent, but because he understood the medium of television, which was uniquely suited to the use of memorable narratives and "vignettes that capture his central claims."[32]

The purpose of the State of the Union address is to "recommend to [Congress's] Consideration such Measures as he [the President] shall judge necessary and expedient."[33] Because a laundry list of initiatives will do little to hold audience attention or move the audience to support their proposals, presidents often incorporate stories of US citizens into their speeches. It has become traditional since Reagan's time to seat the people about whom these stories are told in the balcony of the House of Representatives.

In his 2013 State of the Union Address, President Barack Obama laid out a series of proposals to try to reduce gun violence, then told this story:

> One of those we lost was a young girl named Hadiya Pendleton. She was 15 years old. She loved Fig Newtons and lip gloss. She was a majorette. She was so good to her friends they all thought they were her best friend. Just three weeks ago, she was here, in Washington, with her classmates, performing for her country at my inauguration. And a week later, she was shot and killed in a Chicago park after school, just a mile away from my house.
>
> Hadiya's parents, Nate and Cleo, are in this chamber tonight, along with more than two dozen Americans whose lives have been torn apart by gun violence. They deserve a vote.[34]

Why would this story fit a State of the Union Address? The proposals that Obama had listed had few specific connections to people. He told the story to make real and immediate the need to act, for Congress to vote on gun and ammunition restrictions. A mere recitation of the statistics on gun violence in the United States would have been far less effective than the story of a young girl who was killed. Many listeners know fifteen-year-old girls; many know majorettes; and many know friendly teenagers. The audience can identify with the parents and their grief.

The story is engaging because it adds vivacity and a sense of humanity to Obama's speech. **Vivacity** is *a sense of immediacy or presence created through the use of descriptions, imagery, and colorful language that make an idea come alive.*[35] Narratives with vivacity are more compelling because they are rhetorical acts that engage the imagination of the audience, which, in turn, allows the audience to see the humanity of the characters portrayed. The details in narratives help listeners understand the character's actions and reactions.

Another example of vivacity can be found in Holocaust survivor Elie Wiesel's autobiographical book *Night*, originally published in the United States in 1960. Scholars of Holocaust literature maintain that his book is powerful because it humanizes Holocaust victims and helps readers understand the life that people in Nazi concentration camps were forced to live. The book opens with the story of Moishe the Beadle, a poor immigrant who was in the first wave of Jewish people deported from Sighet, Wiesel's hometown. After surviving the

Gestapo's mass murder of everyone else on the train, Moishe returned to Sighet. Wiesel's story makes real the suffering that Moishe had witnessed:

> Day after day, night after night, he went from one Jewish house to the next, telling his story and that of Malka, the young girl who lay dying for three days, and that of Tobie, the tailor who begged to die before his sons were killed.
>
> Moishe was not the same. The joy in his eyes was gone. He no longer sang. He no longer mentioned either God or Kabbalah. He spoke only of what he had seen.[36]

The power of this story comes not from statistics about train cars full of Jewish people murdered by the Nazis, but from the detailed telling of one person's story and the effect of witnessing the murders on that one person. The details engage the reader; the reader experiences the horrors of the events Moishe saw. The power also comes from the naming of each person—Moishe, Malka, Tobie— which helps personalize the event for the reader.

Narratives form personal and public memory. They create a sense of culture and community by teaching cultural values, implying causation, and engaging an audience. These functions are not neutral. Stories can be extremely enter- taining yet contain questionable values, or inform public memory by creating a false causal relationship. Thus, it is important to develop skill in assessing narratives.

JUDGING NARRATIVES

Narratives are sometimes presented in contrast to the objective world, which is grounded in the empirical or the factual. Some would argue that if humans could only understand the empirical world, narratives would no longer be needed. Theoretical physicist John D. Barrow describes this view:

> Modern physicists believe they have stumbled upon a key which leads to the mathematical secret at the heart of the Universe—a discovery that points towards a "Theory of Everything," a single all-embracing picture of all the laws of Nature from which the inevitability of all things seen must follow with unimpeachable logic. With possession of this cosmic Rosetta Stone, we could read the book of Nature in all tenses: we could understand all that was, is, and is to come.[37]

We believe such an accounting of the world is unlikely as well as uninspiring. Even Barrow wonders whether the goal tells more about the understanding of math than about the understanding of the natural world.

Moreover, much of scientific and mathematical understanding, itself, is grounded in narratives. In medicine, for example, patients typically describe their symptoms to their physicians in narrative form. They describe their symp- toms and when they first noticed them. Often, they will even describe what they think led to the symptoms. For instance, one of the authors recently went to the doctor with back problems. He explained his bad back to his doctor this way: "I was helping my neighbors clean their basement after a flood. I felt a tweak when I dumped a bucket of water. Then it seemed to get better, but almost a week later, I was carrying a door in our house and I probably twisted or something. That afternoon I went to pick up my iPad and my back spasmed." The physical symptoms of a sore back are explained with a simple story.

Physicians are learning the importance of narratives to diagnosis. Rita Charon, an MD with a PhD in English, became convinced of the need to understand narratives better as she was listening to patients. In her book, *Narrative Medicine*, she proposes that health care providers use the "narrative skills of recognizing, absorbing, interpreting, and being moved by the stories of illness."[38] Through these skills, health care providers can understand patients better. Trisha Greenhaigh, of the Royal Free and University College London Medical School, and Brian Hurwitz, of the Imperial College School of Medicine at St. Mary's in London, write:

> We "dream in narrative, daydream in narrative, remember, anticipate, hope, despair, believe, doubt, plan, revise, criticise, construct, gossip, learn, hate and love by narrative." Episodes of sickness are important milestones in the enacted narratives of patients' lives. Thus, not only do we live by narrative but, often with our doctor or nurse as witness, we fall ill, get better, get worse, stay the same, and finally die by narrative too.[39]

Medicine is not the only part of the objective and empirical world that is understood better through narratives. Nate Silver, a statistician, rose to fame because of the accuracy of his predictions in two presidential elections. Silver had previously developed a system for predicting how baseball players would perform in coming seasons. His book, *The Signal and the Noise*, examines how predictions are made in a variety of fields, ranging from weather forecasting to global climate change, from baseball to online gambling.[40] The book is about mathematical modeling and why it works; yet, Silver uses a narrative approach to frame his discussion. He talks about the interviews he conducted and the personal histories of some of the people he interviewed. His work on mathematical modeling becomes more understandable when it is interwoven with narratives.

If narratives are important even to our understanding of medicine and mathematical modeling, skills in reading and interpreting narratives and the surrounding empirical and mathematical results are also important. Narratives can and should be judged on several levels: aesthetics, authorial intent, empirical truth, and social truth. Assessing narratives is more than a matter of awarding a thumbs-up or a thumbs-down. It is a complex process.

Aesthetics

The narratives most capable of affecting people are typically developed in a particular way. They hold the attention of listeners through two common characteristics: plot and character development.[41]

Plot is *the "chain of causation" of events within a narrative.*[42] It is critical because it relates the meaning of the events in the narrative by laying out a story line, or the arc of the story. A good plot captures the audience's attention by providing a mechanism for understanding how the narrator selected the various events and related them to each other. Most narratives rely on a plot that reveals information in a chronological manner and provides the relevance or connectedness of the information as the narrative develops. Sometimes, a plot develops in a way that the connection of the events may not be understood until the end of the narrative. Some plots use flashbacks, a technique that violates strict chronology, but most unfold chronologically to develop the connections as the story progresses. For example, a presidential candidate's biography video shown at the national convention will probably present a chain of events that makes the candidate seem destined for the presidency.

Character development, a second characteristic of good narratives, is *the process of describing the actions of and relationships among actors within the story.*[43] Characters in narratives should conform to the behaviors that the audience expects. If those behaviors are antithetical to audience expectations, the narrative is likely to be dismissed. Consider the way politicians attempt to portray themselves in political campaigns: they try to develop an image that corresponds to what voters desire. When Mitt Romney campaigned for president in 2012, for example, he relied heavily on his experience as a businessperson. In his speech accepting the Republican nomination, he pointed to his experience in starting Bain Capital, which he described as a "great American success story."[44] He said, "In America, we celebrate success, we don't apologize for it."[45] Romney was relying on an analogy that running a company is like running the country.

During the campaign, several advertisements were released that attacked Romney for actions he had taken at Bain. They featured people who had been laid off from their jobs after Bain purchased their companies.[46] The 2012 presidential campaign, like many campaigns, became a contest between competing narratives.

Characters are often the human beings in the story, but they need not be. Aesop's fables, the *Harry Potter* and *Star Wars* movies, and the Bible all contain numerous nonhuman characters. Nonhuman characters in other narratives include nations and the environment. Even nonhuman characters typically act in ways consistent with human activity, however. This *attribution of human characteristics to nonhuman characters in a narrative* is called **personification.** One primary way personification occurs is through nonhuman characters' use of symbols. In Aesop's fable of the tortoise and hare, the hare laughs when the tortoise challenges him to a race. Obviously, a tortoise cannot speak to a hare, nor can a hare laugh, but personification allows for teaching morals in fictional settings that can be applied to people's lives.

Within any narrative, plots and characters may be more or less complex, depending, in part, on the audience's willingness to accept the story. People often reject simplistic accounts of complex events. On the evening of September 11, 2001, for example, a five-year-old commented that it was an "unlucky day."

In one sense, the child's explanation was perfectly accurate: a day on which two planes had crashed into the two main buildings of the World Trade Center would have to be considered a bad day. But this narrative was not sufficiently complex to satisfy most adults' need to understand that event. The collapse of the buildings was not the result of random motion (say, an earthquake) but human action.[47] While this is an extreme example, it demonstrates how narratives lacking in complexity may be rejected.

On the other hand, an audience may reject overly complex narratives. Conspiracy theories typically offer complex explanations for events by claiming that people worked together (conspired) to produce them.[48] Such theories seem to defy simpler explanations of events and are thus rejected by the vast majority of people. One conspiracy theory, for example, suggests that Barack Obama was actually born in Kenya and that his rise to the presidency was part of a plan to have a Muslim president of the United States. For that theory to be true, however, his long-form birth certificate would have to have been fabricated in Hawai'i, along with newspaper announcements, at the time of his birth. The people involved in the fabrications would have to have foreseen his rise to the presidency even before he was born. They would have to have had the ability to ensure his acceptance into prestigious academic institutions to prepare him for a career in politics. And they would have to have known that someone who had been a US Senator for less than a full term could be elected president.[49] Such a chain of events seems, at best, improbable.

We don't want to sound too much like Goldilocks, but we would suggest that narrators seek to find the "just right" level of plot and character development. Detail in character and plot development is necessary to create vivacity and audience engagement, but adding detail just to entertain may detract from the story's ability to transmit values and memory. It is also important to remember that just because you have told an aesthetically appealing story, you have not necessarily told a *good* story. Issues of truthfulness, truth, and social truth must be considered as well.

Authorial Intent

This judgment standard calls for a critic to determine whether the rhetor intends to make factual claims.[50] Authorial intent is not always easy to determine. Still, there is utility in asking: Is the author attempting to tell a story grounded in events that have actually occurred? Critics should begin by determining whether rhetors claim to be reporting facts, as well as which parts of the narrative they claim are factual. Then the audience can assess the narrative's empirical truth. When watching a news story on television, for example, an audience believes the story is based on actual events. For example, during the summer of 2004, Dan Rather of CBS News reported that he had received a fax documenting that George W. Bush's service in the Alabama Air National Guard had been reduced through his father's influence. When Rather reported the story, he intended to report something that had happened, but it became increasingly apparent afterward that the fax had been forged.[51] Rather's story was called into question.

Despite his attempts to defend the overall accuracy of the narrative, Rather ultimately stepped down as *CBS Evening News* anchor, partially in response to complaints about the inaccuracy of the facts of his story.

On the other hand, if one were to approach Stephen King about the movie based on his novel *The Shining* and say to him, "Excuse me, Mr. King. But Danny never said 'Red rum. Red rum,'" Stephen King would probably look at you as if you were deranged. The difference between Dan Rather and Stephen King as authors is that one is attempting to base a story on factual events while the other is not. The difficulty occurs when a rhetor mixes the factual and the invented within a given story or speech. When a rhetor attempts to make a factual claim, however, that claim may be judged from an empirical standpoint.

Empirical Truth

What is the relationship between narratives and empirical truth? On one level, audiences should be able to expect that a narrative meant to depict actual events reports the events as accurately as possible. Audiences should ask: did those events really happen? A paradigmatic case of uncritical acceptance of a compelling personal narrative carrying serious risks is the US Congress's acceptance of the October 1990 testimony of Nayirah, a Kuwaiti teen who claimed she witnessed Iraqi soldiers throwing babies out of incubators. Then-President George H. W. Bush repeated the story at least ten times in the weeks following her testimony, significantly contributing to Congress's willingness to go to war. Her story would later be determined to be false. Nayirah was a member of the Kuwaiti royal family. Her testimony was part of a well-funded PR campaign to induce the US government to fight on behalf of Kuwait. In a segment critical of the public relations campaign, *60 Minutes* noted that her powerful story had "mesmerized the nation and the world."[52]

Narratives based on facts, especially historical facts, can teach lessons. The 1986 movie *Hoosiers*, based on factual events, teaches much the same moral that Aesop's fable of the tortoise and the hare teaches. The empirical truth of *Hoosiers* is that a basketball team from one of the smallest towns in Indiana can beat every team in the state if it works hard enough and has enough persistence. The 2007 movie *The Great Debaters* tells a similar story about a group of African-American debaters from Wiley College in Texas who defeated the national championship team from Harvard University by working hard, overcoming incredible racism, and speaking a truth learned not only from books but also from their own personal stories.[53] The 2012 movie *Lincoln*, based on Doris Kearn Goodwin's book *Team of Rivals: The Political Genius of Abraham Lincoln*,[54] tells a story that suggests Lincoln was successful because he included some of his strongest opponents in his cabinet. The lesson is that it is important to seek out diverse opinions. Alan Jackson's song "Where Were You When the World Stopped Turning" is about people's reactions to the events of 9/11. His song shows that some responses to the events are personal rather than political, and argues that those different personal emotions and responses are equally legitimate.

A complication to the empirical truth test is that rhetors may be completely truthful, telling events as known through their subjective experience, yet not be telling the empirical truth. For example, witness misidentification in trials is the leading cause of wrongful conviction. Those testifying believe what they say and are trying to do the right thing, but they still contribute to the incarceration of an innocent person.[55]

A second complication is that it is possible for a narrative to be based entirely on factual statements, and yet for the narrative to be false as a whole. When children, teens, and politicians are suspected of doing things they should not be doing, they often base the narratives explaining their actions on numerous factual statements. How can the narrative then be false? First, the narrative can omit significant details in its development. At some point, for example, someone may have asked you, "What did you do last night?" You may have given a complete account. If you omitted some events, the story you told was not exactly false, yet it was certainly not the most accurate account of what you did. Second, the narrative can incorporate the correct events and details, but fashion them in a way that leads to a false inference. For instance, the Internal Revenue Service (IRS) was involved in a scandal in late 2013 and 2014 based on its investigations of certain nonprofit groups that received contributions from people who were taking tax deductions for those contributions. It is illegal for such nonprofits to be political groups. The IRS certainly did target groups: everyone agreed on that. However, there was significant disagreement about what types of groups were targeted. Republicans claimed the IRS only targeted conservative groups.[56] Democrats noted that the IRS also investigated groups associated with liberal and progressive issues.[57] Both sides based their claims on facts, but their conclusions were very different.

This example points to an important conclusion about empirical truth. For any given set of facts, incompatible narratives may be created. Most historians recognize that evidence inconsistent with any given narrative will always exist. Philosopher Michael Krausz writes: "Yet, no matter how widely one might cast the evidential net—no matter how richly the evidence may be described—it may still underdetermine any one single interpretation."[58] Krausz's point is that the world is extremely complex. Narratives attempt to simplify that world so it can be understood, but the process of simplification means that no narrative can account for all the empirical facts that might be relevant. Narratives about Christopher Columbus's discovery of the Americas exemplify how incompatible narratives can be based on the same evidence. No one disputes the evidence historians use when discussing Columbus's voyages, but assessments of Columbus vary, viewing him as the "first American" for his willingness to explore,[59] as a genocidal imperialist,[60] or as lucky in that he became famous for being so lost that he thought Cuba was Japan.[61]

Facts never fully determine the validity of a narrative. Incompatible narratives may be derived from the same facts. People may even believe a narrative when they are confronted with evidence that is incompatible with it. At this point, you may fear a form of total relativism in which no narrative can make claims to any type of truth and all narratives are equally true. Such a conclusion would be incorrect. In judging competing narratives, says historian Peter Stansky, a historian must "take all the available 'facts,' which are often contradictory, and judge which interpretation [or narrative] of them may seem the most [right and] 'truthful.'"[62] The same is true of audiences.

To say that many narratives are possible is not the same as claiming that every possible narrative is equally correct, nor that every possible narrative must be considered. Sometimes, writes historiographer Donald Spence, narratives are "just plain wrong."[63] Some, however, contain social truth. Narratives supporting the existence of the Easter Bunny, Santa Claus, and the Tooth Fairy lack an empirical basis. Most people over the age of ten know that they are just plain false, but the stories persist because of the social truths they possess. Young children who insist on the existence of Santa, the Easter Bunny, and the Tooth Fairy are being truthful.

One might argue that we should only believe stories if they are empirically true; if the events recounted in the story actually happened, in the order told; and if the actions were done by the people to whom they were attributed. This is the standard to which histories are held, but empirical truth as a standard for all stories, imaginative and historical, is not enough.

Social Truth

The relationship between narratives and truth is complex. Historians, literary critics, philosophers, and rhetoricians have argued about the connection between narratives and truth at least since the time of Aristotle. Mark Twain explained the relationship between imaginative fictional stories and historical stories: "Truth is stranger than fiction, but it is because Fiction is obliged to possibilities; Truth isn't."[64] Twain's point is that fictional stories must be consistent with listeners' expectations of the way the world works. By conforming to expectations, fictional narratives can be quite effective and speak to social, if not empirical, truths. Lee's novel *To Kill a Mockingbird* had a profound impact on readers. Aesop's fables teach audiences specific moral lessons.

The complexity of narratives lies in the different types of truth claims that they can advance. German sociologist Jürgen Habermas identified claims that can be made about three worlds: the objective world, the subjective world, and the intersubjective world. The test of the validity of a claim about the objective world is truth: can the claim be empirically verified? The test of a claim about the subjective world is truthfulness: does the person making the claim believe it to be true? The test of a claim about the intersubjective world is rightness: can reasonable people, through communication, reach agreement about what is right?[65]

We use the concept of **social truth** to refer to *those beliefs and values that do not refer to some objective reality, but to social reality—those beliefs about what is right that people have arrived at together.* An example of a social truth is that liberty is one of the US's highest values; that it is guaranteed and should be preserved. The Declaration of Independence declares "life, liberty, and the pursuit of happiness" are "unalienable rights." The story behind this declaration is that a creator endowed people with the right to liberty. The value of liberty is a social truth because it cannot be empirically proven or demonstrated. In fact, cultures that are more collectivist in nature are less likely to value liberty. The value of liberty is established primarily through communication, including the stories told within the culture that help to establish that value. Through communication, people can reach an inter-subjective idea (neither fixed and objective, nor totally random or completely subjective) of what is right. The nature of that intersubjective social truth is complex.

Narratives play an important role in the formation of memory and values. The social truth of a narrative does not necessarily lie in the objective *truth* of the individual statements that compose the narrative, but in the *meaning* of the story. Moral philosophy professor Jonathan L. Gorman notes: "Plots have a truth, but it is not a scientific one;" it is "not a truth about the subject the plot purports to be about."[66] But these truths are important. Joan Didion's book *We Tell Ourselves Stories in Order to Live* summarizes the importance of narratives in its title.[67]

Examples of fictive narratives that teach social truth abound. The parables of the New Testament are not usually taken as historical events, even by many Christians who believe the Bible is the literal word of God. Jesus introduced or concluded some of the parables with the statement: "He who has ears to hear, let him hear."[68] His point was that the parables were stories whose truths would only be understood by believers. Many parables are understood as illustrative stories that teach the social truth about heaven even though their settings were the present locations of the listeners.[69] Aesop's fables are another example of fictive narratives. Animals do not really talk; hares and tortoises do not really race; foxes do not really reject unreachable grapes as sour; and wolves do not really don sheep's clothing; but the fables teach lessons such as "slow and steady wins the race" or "appearances are deceptive."

The narratives in novels also contain a type of truth, although they are about imaginary events. Even simple children's stories can teach important lessons. Dr. Seuss's *Oh, The Places You'll Go* has been read to and by children for more than two decades.[70] Its lesson is that all people have unique abilities and can succeed. The book is obviously fictional, but Dr. Seuss meant for it to teach a lesson to children and people of all ages.

As these examples show, the traditional distinction between fiction and nonfiction (or historical and imaginative) stories is too simple. In fact, the relationship between the two is highly complex. Scholars of narrative typi-cally maintain that fiction actually must be truer than nonfiction, in the sense that the events must be believable. Nonfiction, on the other hand, ultimately resorts to the claim that the events actually happened. If someone had created a fictive narrative a few years ago of a man who was born of a Kenyan father and a Kansan mother, grew up in Hawaii and Indonesia, went to college at Columbia and Harvard, was elected to the Senate from Illinois in 2004, was elected presi-dent of the United States in 2008, won the Nobel Peace Prize in 2009, and was reelected in 2012, most people would have concluded that the story was fanciful and rejected it out of hand. However, these events comprise a portion of the narrative of Barack Obama.

Fictive narratives can be socially true, and stories based in facts always have elements of fiction because of the artistry inherent in the creation of stories: the rhetor creates the story. The events recounted in narratives have no necessary starting or ending point; narrators select the beginning and ending points according to the ideas they are trying to communicate. In addition, the rhetor determines what counts as facts.

Think about how different people tell different stories about the same person, event, or place. This is often the case with families. Filmmaker Sarah Polley, in the 2012 documentary *Stories We Tell*, set out to examine the stories her family tells of her deceased mother. The people she interviews—her siblings; her father and her mother's husband; her biological father and her mother's distant, extramarital lover; and her mother's friends—all tell quite different stories. Some begin with meeting her mother; others before meeting her. They include different events, interpret the same events in different ways, and conclude very differently. Yet, each story claims to be true. In her review of the film, Manohla Dargis notes that the differing stories are not an endorsement of relativism. Rather, the documentary tells stories from different perspectives. Dargis writes: "Everyone has his or her memories . . . but most adhere to the communally accepted facts. . . . What matters . . . is how each person organizes those memories, with love, humor, regret, self-interest."[71] Dargis's point is that the narrators choose facts and frame those facts in ways that are consistent with their narratives. This does not mean that all narratives are equally true or that narratives are grounded in relativism, as our narratives must provide reasonable explanations of the facts.

Another example of competing narratives grounded in the same set of historical events is the debate over the effect of the New Deal in the 1930s. Looking at the same set of historical events, narratives differ about the impact of President Franklin Delano Roosevelt's policies on the economy. Traditionally, historians have held that the New Deal stimulated the economy. William Edward Leuchtenburg, in his famous treatise on the New Deal, argues that FDR's decisive policies ended the Great Depression.[72] Historian Burton W. Folsom, Jr., however, argues that the New Deal actually exacerbated it.[73] Both narratives are grounded in historical evidence, but each emphasizes different aspects of the historical record. Readers must evaluate each narrative on the basis of the historical evidence, plot, and character development it presents.

A narrator tells the audience which events are important by placing them within the structure of a narrative and omitting those considered irrelevant. The narrator also helps direct the understanding of the events, by ordering and structuring them.

Multiple stories of a single event might seem problematic or confusing, but a single story dominating understanding is really more so, given the complexity of the world and the diversity of its peoples. Nigerian novelist Chimamanda Ngozi Adichie describes "the danger of a single story" in a TedTalk lecture. She explains that when people base their understandings of others on a single story, they deny the full humanity of those others. If the only story you know of Africa is of catastrophe, famine, conflict, poverty, and disease, then you cannot see the ingenuity, passion, integrity, creativeness, vibrancy, and humanity of the people, like Adichie, who populate that continent. She explains that power and narratives are related: "How [stories] are told, who tells them, when they are told, how many stories are told, are really dependent on power. Power is the ability not just to tell the story of another person, but to make it the definitive story of that person."[74] In other words, the first step in trying to understand an event or people is not to find the definitive stories, but to search for all the stories.

Sophisticated audiences evaluate the narratives they hear. As we discussed when we talked about social truth, audiences must be able to do two things. First, they must be able to assess which narratives are just plain wrong. Second, they must be able to employ standards that will assist them in determining which narratives are better, even in the face of multiple, incompatible narratives, all of which could be plausible.

Several aspects of narratives can help us assess their social truth claims. These aspects are not intended to be considered in evaluating the empirical or factual claims of the narrative, only in evaluating the social truth claims. They include narrative fidelity and narrative probability, the representative anecdote, and the comic frame.

Narrative Fidelity and Narrative Probability. These aspects of narratives are derived from rhetorical critic and theorist Walter Fisher's writing on the narrative paradigm. Fisher developed two standards for evaluating narratives: narrative fidelity and narrative probability. **Narrative fidelity** asks *whether the events included in the story correspond to the experiences and understanding of reality of the audience.*[75] This standard focuses on the external consistency of the story by asking people to look at "whether the stories they experience ring true with the stories they know to be true in their lives."[76] **Narrative probability** asks *the question "what constitutes a coherent story?"*[77] *or, more simply, does the story hang together?* This standard focuses on the internal consistency of the story, requiring people to look at the development of characters and plot, and asking whether the characters react the way we would expect people to react. Narrative probability and fidelity can be used to judge both fiction and nonfiction. Fisher writes, "Formal features are attributes of narrative probability: the consistency of characters and actions, the accommodation of auditors, and so on."[78]

A narrative should have both narrative fidelity and narrative probability, but it may have one of the two and lack the other, or it may lack both. Such narratives are relatively common. For example, a son of one of the authors once lost his cell phone. He told his parents a story about dropping it somewhere when he got off the bus for a football game. The phone would never be found, he said, because the battery was almost dead and the phone was set on silent mode. His parents questioned the story, which in their view, lacked narrative fidelity because their son was typically very careful and responsible and because he insisted that no effort be made to find the phone. The story also lacked narrative probability because the phone was new and freshly charged, and, according to the story, had been lost in a rather small parking lot. Eventually, the true narrative was revealed. The son was nervous before the football game. When he went to the bathroom the phone fell out of his pocket and into the toilet as it was being flushed. The parents did not believe the original story due to its lack of narrative fidelity and narrative probability.

Certain types of narratives are, perhaps, more likely than others to exhibit strengths in either narrative fidelity or narrative probability. Narratives of trauma survivors, for instance, sometimes lack narrative probability (they might lack internal consistency because trauma, by definition, is unusual and extraordinary) while having a great deal of narrative fidelity (they report what actually happened). For example, one author of this book was once in a very bad van accident. His story about the accident is that he was sleeping, felt the van swerve, woke up, asked what was happening, was told a deer had run in front of the van, turned in his seat, and went back to sleep before being thrown from the van. Given the speed at which the accident happened, it does not seem likely that all those events took place in those few short seconds. The story lacked narrative probability, but the injuries and destroyed van give it narrative fidelity.

A story may be true and yet lack narrative fidelity. Invisible Children is an organization seeking to "end the use of child soldiers in Joseph Kony's rebel war and restore Northern Uganda to peace and prosperity."[79] One difficulty the organization faces is that the stories of children being abducted and forced to serve as soldiers, while empirically true, lack narrative fidelity for many people in the United States, who find it difficult to understand that anyone would force children to fight to the death in a war. Consequently, Invisible Children has relied on activism, peaceful protests including sit-ins, and videos. The videos, in particular, present stories with strong narrative probability.

Representative Anecdotes. A **representative anecdote** is *a narrative that summarizes a person, thing, or situation.* The concept, developed by Kenneth Burke, helps critics understand the appropriateness of the narrative.[80] If a narrative claims to speak to a social truth, then it should be representative of the social truth. Burke developed his notion of the representative anecdote as a response to the behaviorist argument, which dominated the first half of the twentieth century, that the world—even human behavior, as complex as it is—could eventually be understood through science and mathematics. Burke rejected such notions. His discussion of the representative anecdote borrows some of the language of the social sciences, but he redefines those terms for his own uses. Social scientists use the term "representative," for instance, to discuss how a sample should be drawn from a population. Burke writes of a representative anecdote: "*It must have scope. Yet it must also possess simplicity; in that it is broadly a reduction of the subject-matter.*"[81] For Burke, the issue was not whether the anecdote was statistically representative; rather, he believed that a single powerful anecdote could represent a complex human experience.

The representative anecdote is not subject to the tests of statistics and the social sciences. Rather than examining the statistical accuracy of the sample, for instance, Burke argues that an appropriate representative anecdote will contain, in a nutshell, the essence of the item being represented. Think about your family or the household in which you grew up. If someone were to ask you about the way you were raised or your family life, you might tell a story that would summarize or encapsulate your experiences. You would not tell your entire life history, but you might pick a moment from when you were five years old, or ten, or fifteen, that would represent all that you are. It would not be representative from a social scientific perspective—indeed, the story might be about an atypical and unrepeated moment or event—but it would demonstrate the essence of your childhood to the listener.

This notion of the representative anecdote leads to two important ideas. First, the narrative must be relevant to the point being made, not simply interesting. Second, the narrative must capture or summarize the most important aspects of the subject it is meant to represent, even though it may not be typical of that subject. For instance, in the aftermath of the Sandy Hook Elementary School shootings, blogger David Waldman began a series on the progressive website *Daily Kos* about gun accidents. The initial post, "Today in GunFail News," grew into a weekly series[82] in which Waldman described press reports of gun accidents. These are representative anecdotes, because the stories are not typical in a statistical sense of what happens when people have guns in their homes or in their possession. People who have guns in their homes typically have the proper motives, Waldman argues. They do not want to get involved in dangerous situations, nor do they want to use their guns. Most gun owners have the "best of intentions"; however, sometimes bad things happen and "often people die because of it. These are the stories you should think about every time you handle a weapon."[83] Waldman's stories are intended to show the dangers of guns in a way that a statistical analysis cannot.

Burke suggests that one way to test a narrative is by determining whether it is representative. When Waldman tells of the gun accidents each week, he is claiming that they are representative of the dangers of guns, regardless of how seldom such accidents occur. When you assess public rhetoric, it is important to determine the representativeness of the narrative.

Comic and Tragic Frames. The final aspect of narrative that is useful in assessing its social truth claims is its frame or narrative worldview. We turn to Kenneth Burke's description of tragic and comic frames.[84] In general, a **comic frame** is *a viewpoint that would have you see others as mistaken rather than as evil.* If a person does something you perceive as wrong, then the solution is not to destroy the person, but to correct her or him. As part of recognizing the inherent fallibility of humanity, a comic frame would also induce you to ask whether you are as mistaken as those with whom you disagree. The comic orientation ultimately asks for humility, not in the face of some higher power, but in the face of the human condition.

In contrast, the **tragic frame** is *a viewpoint that would have you see others as vicious and evil rather than as mistaken.* Because "evil" implies that a person has an inherent defect, correction is not possible as a solution. Destruction is the only solution to a wrong action, the only way to rid the world of evil. The tragic frame also induces humility, but only because if you become too arrogant, a higher power will put you in your place. As Burke explains, the tragic "frame of acceptance admonished one to 'resign' himself [or herself] to a sense of his [or her] limitations."[85]

Imagine, for example, that a friend passes you in the hallway but does not say "Hi." With friends, people tend to operate in a comic frame, creating a story to explain the event that assumes the best of them. You might construct a story containing the explanation that your friend was probably having a bad day, or was really busy and may not have seen you. Your friend did not intentionally snub you, but instead just made a mistake, a mistake you are just as likely to make in similar circumstances. In contrast, imagine that someone you do not really like passes you in the hallway and does not say "Hi." In this case, you might operate in a tragic frame and construct a story that attributes pernicious motives to the person. You might conclude that the person was being rude, snubbed you, intentionally ignored you, or was just being vicious. Your story assumes the worst of the person, even though the action was the same as your friend's. The point of the comic frame is to induce you to give people the benefit of the doubt, to think about the reasons they might take actions and not immediately attribute malicious motives to them. As Burke explains: "Like tragedy, comedy warns against the dangers of pride, but its emphasis shifts from *crime* to *stupidity*."[86]

In a passage that highlights the differences between meanings, attitude, and character in the comic and tragic frames, Burke concludes that a comic frame offers the most humane equipment for living: "The progress of humane enlightenment can go no further than in picturing people not as *vicious*, but as *mistaken*. When you add that people are *necessarily* mistaken, . . . you complete the comic circle, returning again to the lesson of humility that underlies great tragedy."[87] The comic frame is preferable because it "should enable people *to be observers of themselves, while acting*. Its ultimate would not be *passiveness*, but *maximum consciousness*. One would 'transcend' himself [or herself] by noting his [or her] own foibles."[88] In other words, a key characteristic of the comic frame is self-reflexivity, meaning that you would turn whatever criticism you lodge against someone else back against yourself to see whether you engage in the same action or had contributed to the other person's mistaken deeds.

Even though the comic frame might sound as though it involves frivolity or comedy, that is not the case. The comic is no less serious than the tragic. Religious studies professor John Morreall explains: "Comedy is not 'time out' from the world; rather it provides another perspective on the world, a perspective no less true than the tragic perspective."[89] Frames structure responses to events in the world. If you operate in the tragic frame, you tend to construct stories about evil, which must be destroyed. If you operate in the comic frame, you tend to construct stories of mistakes from which everyone can learn. In a comic frame, disagreement is a sign that someone is mistaken, and you are just as likely as the other person to be mistaken. In a tragic frame, a disagreement is usually seen as evidence that another person is being vicious, if not evil. As Burke constantly reminds us, a name for something often contains within it an attitude toward that thing and, thus, also contains "cues of behavior."[90] Thus, it makes sense that how you name someone else is influenced by your frame, and that the name influences the actions toward the other person. As Burke explains, "Call a man [or woman] a villain, and you have the choice of either attacking or cringing.

Call him [or her] mistaken, and you invite yourself to attempt setting him [or her] right. Contemporary exasperations make us prefer the tragic (sometimes melodramatic) names of 'villain' and 'hero' to the comic names of 'tricked' and 'intelligent.'"[91]

When Burke was writing, "contemporary" meant 1937. The preceding years had seen the United States emerging from the Great Depression; Japan leaving the League of Nations; Adolf Hitler coming to power in Germany, stripping German Jews of their citizenship rights, and creating with Mussolini the Rome-Berlin Axis; Italy invading Abyssinia (Ethiopia); the Spanish Civil War breaking out; and the abdication crisis rocking Great Britain. Still, Burke's comment remains apt over seventy years later.

The 1990s and 2000s saw a host of events that appear to be the handiwork of villains and that are often rhetorically presented as evidence of evil in the world. In US public discourse, "evil" was invoked to describe the two students who on April 20, 1999, killed twelve other students and one teacher at Columbine High School before committing suicide. News stories referred to "Columbine Evil Revisited."[92] One *New York Times* editorial concluded: "Columbine . . . was about evil."[93] The connection between school shootings and evil was revisited after the April 16, 2007, shootings at Virginia Tech, in which the shooter killed thirty-two people before committing suicide. Columnist Cal Thomas remarked, "My prayers are with the Virginia Tech community that had this evil unleashed upon them."[94] In May 2014, when a young man opened fire in Isla Vista, California, killing six people and injuring thirteen before killing himself, a commentator described him as "a narcissistic, evil man whose sex desires got in the way of his humanity."[95]

Rhetoric about the war on terror has caused communication scholars to consider the invocation of evil. President George W. Bush's speech on the evening of September 11, 2001, described the acts of that day as evil, declaring: "Thousands of lives were suddenly ended by evil, despicable acts of terror. . . . Today our nation saw evil, the very worst of human nature. . . . The search is underway for those who were behind these evil acts."[96] From that evening on, every speech he gave about the events of September 11 would refer to "evil." Not only would the term "evil" be used to describe the actions (as in "evil, despicable acts of terror"), evil itself would become an entity. In his address from the Cabinet Room on September 12, Bush concluded, "This will be a monumental struggle of good versus evil, but good will prevail."[97] In his remarks on September 14, during a National Day of Prayer and Remembrance ceremony, he used the tragic frame, making clear that evil cannot be corrected, but must be obliterated: "Our responsibility to history is already clear: to answer these attacks and rid the world of evil."[98] He would eventually expand the descriptor of "evil" to apply to more than those who perpetrated 9/11. In his January 2002 State of the Union address, he declared that the countries of Iran, Iraq, and North Korea "constitute an axis of evil." Toward the conclusion of his speech, he declared: "We've come to know truths that we will never question: evil is real, and it must be opposed."[99]

Despite Bush's invocation of evil as a verifiable fact, the reality is that "evil" is an evaluative word, not a statement of fact.[100] A number of political science and communication scholars have discussed Bush's use of the word. Political science journals such as *International Affairs* and communication studies journals such as *Rhetoric and Public Affairs* published special issues exploring "how 'evil' is produced, deployed, used, and misused in public discourse."[101]

Discussions of the decision to launch the war in Iraq based on the belief that Iraq possessed weapons of mass destruction (WMDs) also provide an example of tragic and comic plot lines. Ultimately, no WMDs were found in Iraq.[102] Some commentators frame the decision to enter the war tragically. They maintain that the intelligence was intentionally manipulated to allow the Bush Administration to lead the US into war.[103] Other commentators place the decision in a comic frame, suggesting that the decision to attack Iraq was based on mistaken intelligence.[104] Burke would suggest that, in most cases, the comic frame of acceptance is superior because of the willingness to admit mistakes and acknowledge the humanity of the people on the other side of the issue.

Our point here is not that there are no tragedies. Tragedies do happen, in part because people operate in a tragic frame. Even in the face of tragedy, however, a comic frame may be more humane. When an act of violence occurs, do not assume that locking up the person who committed it will end all violence. Instead, ask: what have I done to contribute to a world in which tragedies occur; and how can I change the world—the social structures, the culture, the rhetorical formations—so that such acts are less likely to happen again?

CONCLUSION

Narrative, in the most basic sense, is the placement of two or more events in a time sequence. The human instinct to structure thinking and communication sequentially has several ramifications for rhetoric. The narrative structure leads audiences to perceive causation, helps them to remember, and entertains them. Sometimes, because these functions of narratives are so powerful, audiences are more susceptible to accepting narratives that are wrong, in either the factual or ethical sense.

It is vital for members of an audience to understand the human side of the narrative by participating with the characters of the story, and to understand what the narrative is teaching about the nature of living through its character development and structure. As a member of an audience, however, you also must remain vigilant in applying the standards for evaluating narratives.

Narratives, the stories people tell each other, are central to civic life. They maintain public memory and teach cultural values. They are part of the warp and woof that holds the fabric of civic life together. They help place people in relation to one another, and to the history of the group, the nation, and the culture.

DISCUSSION QUESTIONS

1. LeBron James embraced the common narrative of returning home to explain his decision to sign with the Cleveland Cavaliers. Is the narrative

of returning home necessarily a positive one? What factors helped make James's narrative successful?

2. Identify a story that members of your family tell over and over. Why is that story repeated? What does it tell you about your family's values? Use the standards identified in this chapter to judge the narrative.

3. Novels and songs often tell narratives that affect people's lives and values. Identify a novel or song that has affected you. Why did it have such an effect on you?

4. People often describe commercial TV news coverage and newspaper articles as "stories." Given the definition of narrative in this chapter, are such things stories? Why?

5. Pick a current controversy on your campus or in your state or nation. Describe it, using the comic frame and the tragic frame.

RECOMMENDED READINGS

Braden, Waldo W. "Myths in Rhetorical Context." *The Southern Speech Communication Journal* 40 (Winter 1975): 113–126.

Fisher, Walter R. "Narration as a Human Communication Paradigm: The Case of Public Moral Argument." *Communication Monographs* 51 (1984): 1–22.

Rowland, Robert C., and Kirsten Theye. "The Symbolic DNA of Terrorism." *Communication Monographs* 75, no. 1 (March 2008), 52–85.

ENDNOTES

[1] Hal Habib, "LeBron Coming to Miami," *Palm Beach Post*, July 9, 2010, http://www.palmbeachpost.com/news/sports/basketball/impact-lebron-james-could-have-on-heat-nba-and-sou/nL8MZ.

[2] LeBron James, "I'm Coming Home," *Sports Illustrated*, July 11, 2014, http://www.si.com/nba/2014/07/11/lebron-james-cleveland-cavaliers.

[3] James, "Coming Home."

[4] Thomas Wolfe, *You Can't Go Home Again* (Garden City, NY: Garden City Books, 1940).

[5] Joe Posnanski, "Posnanski: LeBron James Proves He's a True Clevelander," *Pro Basketball Talk*, July 11, 2014, http://probasketballtalk.nbcsports.com/2014/07/11/posnanski-lebron-james-proves-hes-a-true-clevelander.

[6] Gerald Prince, *Narratology: The Form and Functioning of Narrative* (New York: Mouton, 1982), 4, italics added.

[7] J. B. Schneewind, "Virtue, Narrative, and Community: MacIntyre and Morality," *Journal of Philosophy* 79 (1982): 659.

[8] Barbara DeConcini, *Narrative Remembering* (Lanham, MD: University Press of America, 1990), 112.

[9] Marshall Grossman, *The Story of All Things* (Durham, NC: Duke University Press, 1998), 34.

[10] Eilene Guy, "American Red Cross Stands Up for Iowa Tornado, Flood Victims," *ReliefWeb*, July 16, 2008, http://reliefweb.int/report/united-states-america/american-red-cross-stands-iowa-tornado-flood-victims.

[11] Josh Hinkle, "Floods Ravage New Hartford Weeks after Deadly Tornado," KCRG.com, June 9, 2008, http://www.kcrg.com/news/local/19684209.html.

[12] Richard Morris, *Sinners, Lovers, and Heroes* (Albany: State University of New York Press, 1997), 26.

[13] "Negro Leagues History," http://www.nlbm.com/s/history.htm (2004).

[14] Barry Schwartz, "The Social Context of Commemoration: A Study in Collective Memory," *Social Forces* 61 (1982): 395.

[15] Patrick Henry, "Give Me Liberty or Give Me Death," March 23, 1775, at Henrico Parish Church, Richmond, Virginia, Second Virginia Convention, http://www.americanrhetoric.com/speeches/patrickhenrygivemeliberty.html.

[16] Eloise Buker, *Politics through a Looking-Glass: Understanding Political Cultures through a Structuralist Interpretation of Narratives* (New York: Greenwood, 1987), 1.

[17] US Army, "D-Day: June 6, 1944," http://www.army.mil/d-day (accessed September 6, 2010).

[18] Martha Cooper, *Analyzing Public Discourse* (Prospect Heights, IL: Waveland, 1989), 161.

[19] Sonya Andermahr, Terry Lovell, and Carol Wolkowitz, *A Glossary of Feminist Theory* (New York: Oxford University Press, 2000), 174.

[20] V. William Balthrop, "Culture, Myth, and Ideology as Public Argument: An Interpretation of the Ascent and Demise of 'Southern Culture,'" *Communication Monographs* 51 (December 1984), 341.

[21] Clifford Geertz, *The Interpretation of Cultures* (New York: Basic Books, 1973), 48, 89.

[22] Balthrop, "Culture," 342.

[23] Robert Lacey, *Ford: The Men and the Machine* (New York: Little, Brown, 1986), 126.

[24] Amy Maria Kenyon, *Dreaming Suburbia: Detroit and the Production of Postwar Space and Culture* (Detroit: Wayne State University Press, 2004), 126.

[25] Seymour Chatman, "Towards a Theory of Narrative," *New Literary History* 6 (1975): 318.

[26] Seymour Chatman, *Coming to Terms: The Rhetoric of Narrative in Fiction and Film* (New York: Cornell University Press, 1990), 9.

[27] National Museum of American History, "Cold War Timeline: The End of the Cold War," 2000, http://americanhistory.si.edu/subs/history/timeline/end (accessed July 29, 2014).

[28] "The Super Bowl Indicator," Snopes.com, April 15, 2011, http://www.snopes.com/business/bank/superbowl.asp.

[29] "The Super Bowl Indicator."

[30] Eric Zorn, "'Mockingbird' Still Sings after 50 Years," *Chicago Tribune*, July 9, 2010, http://featuresblogs.chicagotribune.com/printers-row/2010/07/to-kill-a-mockingbird-harper-lee.html.

[31] Chris Chase, "Christian Ponder Named His Baby Daughter after Bobby Bowden," *USA Today*, July 22, 2014, http://ftw.usatoday.com/2014/07/christian-ponder-bobby-bowden-named-daughter-samantha.

[32] Kathleen Hall Jamieson, *Eloquence in an Electronic Age: The Transformation of Political Speechmaking* (New York: Oxford University Press, 1988), 119.

[33] US Constitution, Article II, Section 2.

[34] Barack Obama, "Remarks by the President in the State of the Union Address," February 12, 2013, http://www.whitehouse.gov/the-press-office/2013/02/12/remarks-president-state-union-address.

[35] George Campbell, *The Philosophy of Rhetoric* (Edinburgh, Scotland: George Ramsey, 1808; Google Books), 163–165.

[36] Elie Wiesel, *Night*, rev. ed. (New York: Hill and Wang, 2006), 7.

[37] John D. Barrow, *New Theories of Everything*, 2nd ed. (Oxford, UK: Oxford University Press, 2007), 1–2, http://site.ebrary.com/lib/rodlibrary/docDetail.action?docID =10183335.

[38] Rita Charon, *Narrative Medicine* (New York: Oxford University Press, 2006), 4.

[39] Trisha Greenhaigh and Brian Hurwitz, "Why Study Narrative?" *BMJ*, 1999, http:// www.bmj.com/content/318/7175/48.1?variant=full-text.

[40] Nate Silver, *The Signal and the Noise: Why So Many Predictions Fail—but Some Don't* (New York: Penguin, 2012).

[41] Although most scholarly works devoted to narratives identify a number of other characteristics, such as narrator and setting, plot and character development are the two most important. See, for instance, Paul Cobley, *Narrative* (London: Routledge, 2001).

[42] Cobley, *Narrative*, 239, italics added.

[43] Ronald Jacobs, "Narrative, Civil Society and Public Sphere," in *Lines of Narrative: Psychological Perspectives*, ed. Molly Andrews, Shelley Day Sclater, Corinne Squire, and Amal Treacher, 18–35 (New York: Routledge, 2000).

[44] "Transcript: Mitt Romney's Acceptance Speech," NPR.org, August 30, 2012, http:// www.npr.org/2012/08/30/160357612/transcript-mitt-romneys-acceptance-speech.

[45] "Romney's Acceptance."

[46] Paul Barrett, "Mitt Romney's Private Equity Nightmare," *Bloomberg Businessweek*, May 21, 2012, http://www.businessweek.com/articles/2012-05-21/mitt-romneys -private-equity-nightmare.

[47] Robert C. Rowland and Kirsten Theye, "The Symbolic DNA of Terrorism," *Communication Monographs* 75, no. 1 (March 2008): 52–85.

[48] G. Thomas Goodnight and John Poulakos, "Conspiracy Rhetoric: From Pragmatism to Fantasy in Public Discourse," *Western Journal of Speech Communication* 45, no. 4 (Fall 1981): 299–316.

[49] Robert Schlesinger, "Obama's Birth Certificate Release Won't End Conspiracy Theories," *US News*, April 27, 2011, http://www.usnews.com/opinion/blogs/robert -schlesinger/2011/04/27/obamas-birth-certificate-wont-end-conspiracy-theories.

[50] This standard is derived partially from the work of John R. Searle, "The Logical Status of Fictional Discourse," *New Literary History* 6 (1975): 319–332.

[51] William Safire, "First, Find the Forger," *New York Times*, September 22, 2004, http:// query.nytimes.com/gst/fullpage.html?res=9A02E5DE1339F931A1575AC0A962 9C8B63.

[52] Morley Safer, "Iraqis Stealing Incubators from Babies May Have Been a Fraud," *60 Minutes*, January 19, 1992, LexisNexis: CBS News Transcripts.

[53] This movie illustrates how historical narratives can be changed to achieve narrative truth. Although the movie depicts a debate between Wiley and Harvard, the debate that actually occurred was between Wiley and the University of Southern California, the national championship team in 1930.

[54] Doris Kearns Goodwin, *Team of Rivals: The Political Genius of Abraham Lincoln* (New York: Simon & Schuster, 2005).

[55] See Elizabeth Loftus and Katherine Ketcham, *Witness for the Defense* (New York: St. Martin's, 1991), reprinted at http://www.pbs.org/wgbh/pages/frontline/shows/dna /photos/eye/text_06.html as part of *Frontline*, "What Jennifer Saw," 1997, http://www .pbs.org/wgbh/pages/frontline/shows/dna.

[56] John Hayward, "House GOP Report: The IRS Did Not Target Progressive Groups," *Human Events*, April 7, 2014, http://humanevents.com/2014/04/07/house-gop -report-the-irs-did-not-target-progressive-groups.

[57] Abby Ohlheiser, "New Documents Show the IRS Targeted 'Progressive' and 'Tea Party' Groups for Extra Scrutiny," *The Wire*, April 23, 2014, http://www.thewire .com/politics/2014/04/new-documents-show-the-irs-targeted-progressive-and-tea -party-groups-for-extra-scrutiny/361125.

[58] Michael Krausz, *Rightness and Reasons: Interpretation in Cultural Practices* (Ithaca, NY: Cornell University Press, 1993), 47.

[59] Samuel Eliot Morison, *Admiral of the Ocean Sea: A Life of Christopher Columbus* (Boston: Little, Brown, 1942).

[60] Noam Chomsky, *Year 501: The Conquest Continues* (Boston: South End, 1993).

[61] Helen Wallis, "What Columbus Knew," *History Today* (May 1992): 17–23.

[62] Peter Stansky, "The Crumbling Frontiers of History or History and Biography: Some Personal Remarks," *Pacific Historical Review* 59 (1990): 6.

[63] Donald Spence, "Saying Good-Bye to Historical Truth," *Philosophy of the Social Sciences* 21 (1991): 247.

[64] Mark Twain, *Following the Equator: A Journey around the World Part 2* (Hartford, CT: American, 1897), 156.

[65] Jürgen Habermas, *Reason and the Rationalization of Society*, vol. 1, *The Theory of Communicative Action* (Boston: Beacon, 1984).

[66] J. L. Gorman, review of *Writing History*, by Paul Veyne, *History and Theory* 26 (1987): 99–114, 110, 113.

[67] Joan Didion, *We Tell Ourselves Stories in Order to Live* (New York: Knopf, 2006).

[68] See, for instance, the parable of the sower in Luke 8.

[69] Simon Kistemaker, *The Parables of Jesus* (Grand Rapids, MI: Baker, 1987).

[70] Dr. Seuss, *Oh, The Places You'll Go* (New York: Random House, 1990).

[71] Manohla Dargis, "Family Opens Its Diary, with Mother as Subject," *New York Times*, May 9, 2013, http://www.nytimes.com/2013/05/10/movies/stories-we-tell-written -and-directed-by-sarah-polley.html.

[72] William Edward Leuchtenburg, *Franklin D. Roosevelt and the New Deal, 1932–1940* (New York: Harper and Row, 1963).

[73] Burton W. Folsom, Jr., *New Deal or Raw Deal: How FDR's Economic Legacy Has Damaged America* (New York: Threshold, 2008).

[74] Chimamanda Ngozi Adichie, "The Danger of a Single Story," TEDGlobal 2009, July 2009, http://www.ted.com/talks/chimamanda_adichie_the_danger_of_a _single_story#t-584723.

[75] Walter Fisher, "Narration as a Human Communication Paradigm: The Case of Public Moral Argument," *Communication Monographs* 51 (1984): 8.

[76] Fisher, "Narration," 8.

[77] Fisher, "Narration," 8, italics added.

[78] Fisher, "Narration," 16.

[79] Invisible Children, http://www.invisiblechildren.com/home.php.

[80] Kenneth Burke, *Grammar of Motives*, rev. ed. (1945; Berkeley, CA: University of California Press, 1945 and 1969), esp. part 3. For a detailed description of this standard, see Arnie Madsen, "Burke's Representative Anecdote as a Critical Method," in *Extensions of the Burkeian System*, ed. James W. Chesebro, 208–229 (Tuscaloosa: University of Alabama Press, 1993).

[81] Burke, *Grammar*, 60.

[82] David Waldman, "Today in GunFail News," DailyKos.com, January 19, 2013, http:// www.dailykos.com/story/2013/01/19/1180131/-Today-in-GunFail-News.

[83] Waldman, "GunFail."

[84] Kenneth Burke, *Attitudes toward History*, 3rd ed. (Berkeley: University of California Press, 1937 and 1984).

[85] Burke, *Attitudes*, 39.

[86] Burke, *Attitudes*, 41.

[87] Burke, *Attitudes*, 41.

[88] Burke, *Attitudes*, 171.

[89] John Morreall, *Comedy, Tragedy, and Religion* (Albany: State University of New York Press, 1999), 3.

[90] Burke, *Attitudes*, 4.

[91] Burke, *Attitudes*, 4–5.

[92] Austin Fenner and Corky Siemaszko, "Columbine Evil Revisited: Colo. Pauses, Honors Memory of Slain 13," *Daily News* (New York), April 21, 2000.

[93] Alan Wolfe, "Littleton Takes the Blame," *New York Times*, May 2, 1999.

[94] In Bob Beckel and Cal Thomas, "What about the Guns?" *USA Today*, April 19, 2007.

[95] Joel Mathis, "Can 'Culture' Explain the Isla Vista Shootings?" *Desert Sun* (Palm Springs, CA), May 30, 2014, http://www.desertsun.com/story/opinion/columnists /2014/05/31/red-blue-america-isla-vista-shooting/9803497.

[96] George W. Bush, "9/11 Address to the Nation: A Great People Has Been Moved to Defend a Great Nation," September 11, 2001, http://www.americanrhetoric.com /speeches/gwbush911addresstothenation.htm.

[97] George W. Bush, "The Deliberate and Deadly Attacks . . . Were Acts of War," September 12, 2001, http://www.americanrhetoric.com/speeches /gwbush911cabinetroomaddress.htm.

[98] George W. Bush, "Remarks at the National Day of Prayer and Remembrance," September 14, 2001, http://www.americanrhetoric.com/speeches/gwbush911prayer &memorialaddress.htm.

[99] George W. Bush, "State of the Union Address," January 29, 2002, http://www .whitehouse.gov/news/releases/2002/01/20020129-11.html.

[100] William Casebeer, "Knowing Evil When You See It: Uses for the Rhetoric of Evil in International Relations," *International Relations* 18, no. 4 (2004): 441–451.

[101] Dana L. Cloud, "Introduction: Evil in the Agora," *Rhetoric and Public Affairs* 6, no. 3 (2003), 509.

[102] Senate Committee on Intelligence, *Postwar Findings about Iraq's WMD Programs and Links to Terrorism and How They Compare with Prewar Assessments*, 109th Cong., 2d sess., September 8, 2006, http://intelligence.senate.gov /phaseiiaccuracy.pdf.

[103] Cynthia Cotts, "Reason to Deceive: WMD Lies Could Be the New Watergate," *Village Voice*, June 17, 2003, http://intelligence.senate.gov/phaseiiaccuracy.pdf.

[104] Richard Norton-Taylor, "We Got It Wrong on Iraq WMD, Intelligence Chiefs Finally Admit," *Guardian.co.uk*, April 8, 2005, http://www.guardian.co.uk/politics/2005/apr /08/uk.iraq.

Components of Symbolic Action

6

Rhetors

KEY CONCEPTS

authority

ethos

identity

image

intersectionality

performance

persona

polysemous

polyvalance

postmodernism

social power

strategic essentialism

On June 25, 2013, Wendy Davis, a Texas state senator, engaged in an eleven-hour-long filibuster on the floor of the Texas Senate Chamber.[1] Speaking from 11:18 a.m. to 10:07 p.m., she sought to stop passage of Senate Bill 5 (SB 5), a law that would create additional restrictions on abortion access and likely result in closing thirty-seven of the forty-two Texas clinics that provide abortions as part of their services.[2] During a filibuster, Texas Senate rules prohibit a person from eating, drinking, or having a bathroom break, and require that person to stand when speaking and confine "remarks to the bill before the Senate."[3] If ruled out of order three times, the senator must yield the floor and the filibuster ends.

To stop the vote on SB 5, Davis had planned to speak until midnight, the end of that special legislative session. She turned to Twitter to declare her intentions to speak for the women of Texas even if the legislature was unwilling to listen to women. She, and people around the nation, began using #SB5 and #txleg to allow Twitter users to follow the filibuster.[4] In fact, people following her on social media, including Twitter and her own web site, helped Davis develop material for the filibuster. As she prepared to speak for up to thirteen hours with rhetoric germane to SB 5, she asked the people following her to provide crowdsourced stories she could share.[5] They did so. One commentator noted, "The Internet was hugely involved in Davis's effort, with thousands of testimonials pouring in through her website."[6] Davis's filibuster included newspaper articles, seven statements from medical professionals and organizations, sixty-two statements from her constituents (fifty-four from women), and lengthy exchanges with other senators. Davis did not see herself as the lone rhetor performing the filibuster; she viewed it as a collective work relying on the words of Texans to oppose the Texas legislature.[7]

Over 200,000 people watched the filibuster on *The Texas Tribune*'s YouTube live stream.[8] People who did not watch Davis could access her speech in 140-character tweeted fragments from people in the gallery and lawmakers watching from the floor.[9] A newspaper reporter tweeted images of Davis in her tennis shoes as the filibuster began. As it progressed, President Obama's Organizing for American Twitter account sent out a special message supporting Davis and picking up on the trending hashtag #StandWithWendy.[10] That hashtag alone amassed more than 547,000 Tweets.[11] Davis's personal Twitter account jumped from 6,000 to 48,000 followers throughout the day. Allies used Twitter to recruit people to fill the Senate Chambers.

When Lieutenant Governor David Dewhurst assigned Davis her third strike at 10:07 p.m., other senators sought to delay the vote by making points of order that Twitter users, consulting *Roberts Rules of Order*, provided to them.[12] Throughout the filibuster, as strikes were called on Davis, supporters in attendance chanted, "Let her speak!"[13] At 11:45 p.m., when Senator Leticia Van de Putte's motion to adjourn was not recognized, she asked, "At what point does a female senator have to raise her hand in order to be recognized over a male senator?" In response, the crowds filling the rotunda shouted so loudly that order could not be restored until after midnight.[14]

The role of social media in this event cannot be underestimated: "Through it all," *The Daily Dot* reported, "Twitter chronicled the debate in dramatic images, humor, and emotion."[15]

This social media event did not arise serendipitously or accidentally. Like the speech, it was organized and planned, and not by Davis alone. NARAL Texas used Facebook to arrange rides for supporters. Progressive women's group Annie's List livetweeted from the gallery.[16] As allies tweeted about the event, and other groups retweeted, the Tweetstorm grew in strength.[17] The rhetorical action did not end with the chaotic post-midnight vote. Activists around the country, in response to other state legislators restricting reproductive services access, have reread large portions of her filibuster at pro-choice protests around the nation.[18]

If you were asked to name the rhetor in this example, who would it be? Davis? The crowd? Those who were tweeting the filibuster? The organizations who organized the crowd? The people whose testimonies Davis read? The newspaper reporters whose stories she read? People who have reread Davis's words?

This filibuster raises interesting questions in the multimodal world of social media. First, it demonstrates the need for flexible thinking about who counts as a rhetor delivering a text. Davis's text cannot be attributed to a single rhetor. Second, it complicates what counts as a text. The transcript of the filibuster, its retweeted fragments, the crowd noises that delayed the vote, and the actions of other senators are all part of the text of the filibuster; again, multiple rhetors are involved. Third, it shows that no simple, objective standard determines which rhetors garner attention from broadcast news networks. As the social media statistics demonstrate, "Twitter and Facebook were aflame with arguments over the filibuster as it was happening, while TV news networks generally paid little or no attention, at least at first."[19] In fact, during the tumultuous conclusion of the filibuster, CNN's Anderson Cooper and Piers Morgan conversed about the calorie count of blueberry muffins; MSNBC and Fox News aired reruns.[20] For breaking news, one might do better to rely on the Internet than on twenty-four-hour news channels. As one commentator noted, "The coverage of the filibuster itself marks a clear example of social media's ability to provide viewers with accurate information in real time—however disjointed it might have been,"[21] given the variety of people tweeting about the filibuster. Finally, this story establishes rhetors can rise to national prominence as a result of their rhetorical actions. A *New York Times* story explained, "[Davis] was a state senator Tuesday morning. By Wednesday, she was a political celebrity known across the nation."[22]

In this chapter, we discuss the rhetor as an essential part of any symbolic action. As rhetors produce symbolic action, they are also produced by it. To explore this process, we outline the general concept of "persona," then discuss its various facets: ethos, roles, identity, authority, and image. An analysis of a speech on same-sex marriage to the Iowa House illustrates these concepts. We end with a consideration of the complexities of the rhetor.

PERSONA AS PERFORMANCE

During her filibuster, Wendy Davis (and the people and media recirculating the filibuster) created a complex persona. In the first few minutes, she claimed authority as a legislator, critiquing the decision to depart from past Senate procedure to discuss SB 5 in a special session. But she quickly moved from that role to claiming an identity as a Texan and an amplifier for Texan voices: "I'm rising on the floor today to humbly give voice to thousands of Texans who have been ignored."[23] She also made clear that part of her character was defined as a representative of a "minority voice" as a Democratic senator; and that, as a member of the minority party, she had a special obligation to speak. Later during the filibuster, she assumed the role of a lawyer, discussing the details of the *Roe v. Wade* decision, then returned to her legislative role as she conducted a "bill analysis bit-by-bit." Davis assumed many personae. Depending on what parts of the filibuster were recirculated, other personae emerged.

The rhetorical **persona** is *the ethos, roles, identity, authority, and image a rhetor constructs and performs (or that others construct for a rhetor to perform) during a rhetorical act.* Central to this definition is an understanding that a persona is something a rhetor does, not something a rhetor innately has. A rhetor, through symbolic action, constructs and performs a persona, which the audience perceives to be the source of the symbolic action. As a result, as communication scholar James Jasinski notes, the persona becomes "a human presence that saturates a text."[24]

This definition is informed by English literature scholar Wayne Booth's examination of authorial persona. Booth drew a distinction between the identity of the actual author of a work of fiction and the identity that the author performed in that work. In his book *The Rhetoric of Fiction*, Booth refers to that performed identity as the author's "second self" or "implied author" who "chooses, consciously or unconsciously, what we read; we infer him [or her] as an ideal, literary, created version of the real man [or woman]; he [or she] is the sum of his [or her] own choices."[25] Booth sought to raise awareness of the fact that works of literature did not reflect an authentic authorial self, but were rhetorical. An authorial persona is performed when a person presents particular elements to the world as definitive of who she or he is; it is not just a neutral reflection of the person.

Narratives, whether in a novel or in an explanation of why you need a homework extension, attempt to influence an audience to see an event in a particular way. Your narratives are told from a particular perspective—your persona. Personae appear not only in works of fiction, but also in every rhetorical action. Because every act of communication contains its own drama, every act of communication also contains characters, including the persona of the rhetor.

Sociologist Erving Goffman uses a drama metaphor to explain how people in social situations perform roles. He defines a **performance** as *"all the activity of a given participant on a given occasion which serves to influence in any way any of the other participants."*[26] When you give a public presentation, you engage in a performance. You not only present your speech, you also enact a role. Your choice of what to wear, whether to speak from the front of the room or from your seat, what level of formality to display, what evidence to use, and what attitude to take toward the audience and topic all influence the way others perceive you and your message. Thus, in order to completely understand how rhetoric works, you must recognize how persona invites assent both to the request made and to the person making it. Communication scholar Randall Lake notes that "arguments seek assent not only to the claim stated but also to the claim enacted."[27] Your symbolic actions seek affirmation of what you say and as whom you say it.

When people think of a performance, they may think of an actor who memorizes a script and performs it in front of an audience. A person's daily interactions with others, as well as the public interactions of a rhetor with an audience, are not scripted (although they might sometimes be rehearsed); however, they are still a performance. When you try to persuade your professor to give you an extension on a paper, you probably plan what you will say: you produce a loose script to respond in a way that is consistent with the professor's expectations and the image you wish to convey. A script is not written for you, but you may draft one in your head, rehearse it, edit it, and then finally perform it for its target audience.

Why do you feel the need to rehearse? You want to perform a persona that enhances your persuasiveness by directing the audience's interpretation of the message. The message will also inform the audience's perception of you. Depending on how you make your request, your professor may perceive your character as trustworthy because you displayed the identity of a hardworking student, or lacking because you appear to be a procrastinator. The professor may grant your request because you played the role of student and asked politely, or refuse it because you played the role of superior and demanded an extension, thus assuming an authority you do not possess.

Although personae are rhetorically constructed, an archetypal form for the persona may preexist the rhetorical action in which it is performed.

Communication scholars B. L. Ware and Wil A. Linkugel clarify that *"persona* does not refer to the personality" of the actor as a person, but to "the characteristics assumed by the actor when [she or] he dons the mask."[28] A rhetor does not create a persona out of nothing; rather, the persona can "reflect the aspirations and cultural visions of audiences."[29] For example, when you perform the role of good student, you do not create from scratch the characteristics and habits of a good student. Instead, a prototype of the good student already exists within cultural expectations. The university culture generally agrees that the qualities of a good student include being prepared, serious, engaged, focused, and interested, as well as being a critical thinker. You bring individual characteristics to the role, but the archetype existed prior to your performance of the persona.

FACETS OF PERSONA

To highlight the ways in which persona is performed and is itself a symbolic action, we describe the various facets of persona in the following sections. Ethos, roles, identity, authority, and image are interlocking parts of a person's persona. We use the metaphor of "facet" because these concepts are interconnected parts of a larger whole, yet each concept offers a distinct perspective. The distinctions among the facets are not absolute, however. When people seek to develop authority, they often seek to portray the image of a leader. In addition, people perceive particular identities to fit particular roles better. For example, people's perception of sex roles makes female nurses and elementary school teachers less remarkable than male nurses or teachers. All these facets of persona have two things in common: (1) skillful choices about each can enhance symbolic action and (2) each facet is produced by symbolic action.

Ethos

In Chapter 1, we defined **ethos** as *that which is "in the character of the speaker"*; more completely, it is *the character of a rhetor performed in the rhetorical act and known by the audience because of prior interactions.* This understanding of ethos is informed by two classical scholars: Aristotle and Cicero.

Aristotle defined ethos as an appeal based on a rhetor's "presentation of character" within a persuasive act.[30] For Aristotle, ethos, as an artistic proof, is created by the rhetor and comprises three dimensions: practical wisdom, virtue, and goodwill.[31] Rhetors demonstrate practical wisdom (*phronesis*) through the display of common sense and sound reason. For example, if a rhetor attempts to persuade an audience with arguments that the audience perceives to be irrational, unbelievable, or unrealistic, the rhetor's character is harmed and the audience will probably not be persuaded. Rhetors are perceived to possess virtue (*arête*) when they share the values the audience considers worthy of merit. Virtue is defined by the culture and the situation, so the values that an audience esteems determine whether a rhetor is perceived to be virtuous. Rhetors who possess goodwill (*eunoia*) are perceived as being motivated by their audiences' best interests, as putting the needs of their audiences ahead of their own interests and motives, much as a friend would. If an audience perceives a rhetor to be trustworthy and to possess the character qualities and virtues it esteems, it will be more open to the rhetor's message.

Roman rhetorician and statesperson Cicero described ethos as composed of elements of character outside the rhetorical act.[32] He included "the customs, the deeds, and the life" of the rhetor of which the audience was already aware.[33] For Cicero, the rhetor's character known from previous acts was more important to demonstrating ethos than the appeals a rhetor made in the speech.

Ethos is developed both prior to and within a rhetorical act. For example, when Richard Nixon was president in the early 1970s, he normalized relations with "Red China." After World War II, the People's Republic of China had become a communist country. The United States cut off all ties with it and viewed it as an enemy. In 1972, Nixon became the first US president to visit China and began developing diplomatic ties. The US people accepted Nixon doing this because of his ethos. He was known as a staunch anticommunist; if he thought it was acceptable to work with the Chinese, it must be. Nixon did not rely on his past character alone, however. In his messages to the US public, he explained and justified his foreign policy decision, using his authority as president and praising the virtue of closer US-PRC ties.[34]

Roles

People perform various roles in their daily lives, as well as across their lifetimes. On any given day you probably assume several roles, each having particular functions, qualities, characteristics, and communication patterns. Suppose you make three requests during a day: You ask your professor to extend the deadline on a paper, your friend to let you borrow something, and your subordinate at work to perform a required task. In each of these situations, you play a different role: student, friend, or manager. You perform different personae, each calling for different attitudes toward the audience. As a student, you are a subordinate to the audience, as friend a peer, and as manager a superior. You are the same person, but the role you perform to make the request influences the request. At the same time, the nature of the request places you in a particular role. By becoming aware of social roles and the way they affect perceptions of the rhetor, you can become more aware of the factors that influence reception of rhetorical acts.

Ronald Wilson Reagan, president of the United States from 1981 to 1989, is known as the "Great Communicator."[35] As president, his personal popularity was consistently high, averaging 61 percent (with a high of 81 percent), even though his job approval averaged 53 percent (with a low of 35 percent). During the 1982 recession, Gallup polls found that "when only about 4 in 10 Americans approved of the job Reagan was doing as president, 6 in 10 Americans rated him on the positive end of a 10-point rating scale."[36] This gap between the public's assessment of his personal popularity and its approval of his policies was unprecedented and perplexed political observers.[37]

Why did people who disagreed with Reagan's policies still find him to be a credible and persuasive speaker? One factor contributing to his persuasiveness was his ability to inhabit the role of the president. Not only was he the legally elected president of the United States, he acted the part. Communication scholar J. Jeffery Auer explains, "A president must project a positive public persona, an identifiable personality, character and image. . . . Ronald Reagan . . . [has] a clearly identifiable personality, and a steady image."[38] American studies professor James Nuechterlein argues that Reagan's "leadership was, above all, a triumph of personality. His eloquence, charm, courage . . . and remarkable sense of self revived Americans' pride in the presidential office and, by extension, in the nation itself."[39] English literature professor M. E. Bradford says that "in his virtues and personal style [Reagan] symbolized our national character, not necessarily as it is, but as we wish it to be."[40] As a former movie star, Reagan had played roles that possessed iron will, strong character, and perseverance. Rhetoric scholars Karlyn Kohrs Campbell and Kathleen Hall Jamieson point out that, as president, Reagan performed the roles of president: commander-in-chief, legislative leader, and symbolic head of state.[41] He rhetorically constructed an image composed of interlocking performances of his trustworthy character, his identity as a proud American, and his authority as president. This image, as Auer writes, was "bigger than the man."[42]

If the rhetor plays a role that is held in high regard and consistent with the values of the society, Goffman explains, the audience may be more receptive to the message.[43] During performances, he says, individuals "tend to incorporate and exemplify the officially accredited values of the society."[44] People dress up for job interviews because US society equates professional dress with a professional work attitude. A potential employer can see you more easily in the role of worker if you perform the role of a worker. Thus, when you interview for a professional job, you likely dress in a way you think others perceive to be professional, rather than in blue jeans, flip-flops, and a ripped T-shirt; speak in a professional manner, using complete sentences and limited slang; and move in a professional way, sitting up in your chair rather than slouching with your feet on the table.

However, people can also perform roles in ways that challenge the society's values in order to highlight unspoken (and sometimes contradictory) norms attached to particular social roles. For example, in discussing third-wave feminism, Rita Alfonso and Jo Trigilio note that Riot Grrls (members of the underground feminist punk movement) dressed "in baby doll dresses, usually worn with combat boots, colorful but torn stockings, and any number of tiny plastic hair barrettes, but writing 'slut' on their bodies to preempt society's judgment of them."[45] Riot Grrls intentionally performed contradictory roles: young children in feminine baby doll dresses and tough adults in masculine combat boots, innocent girls wearing plastic barrettes and adult women with torn stockings. Riot Grrls played with roles because they wanted to challenge the officially accredited social values.

Identity

Identity refers to *the physical and/or behavioral attributes that make a person recognizable as a member of a group.* Identity ingredients that have attained social significance and functioned as the basis for group identification include, but are not limited to, race, class, sex, sexual orientation, veteran status, religion, nationality, citizenship status, ability or disability, education, and profession. Your answer to the question "who/what are you?" provides a clue about how you understand identity.

Identity as Rhetorical. Assuming an identity when speaking is not a politically neutral act. When people say they are speaking as members of a race, class, sex, sexuality, nationality, or other group, they are assuming personae. For example, Joshua Packwood, the first white valedictorian at historically black, all male Morehouse College, said: "What Morehouse stands for at the end of the day, and what Dr. King epitomized, it's not about black or white, it's about the content of [a person's] character. It's about me, representing Morehouse in that light—not as a white man or a black man."[46] Packwood made clear he was not speaking as a white man, but as a Morehouse man. His persona was tied to belonging to a group defined by attendance at the school, not by a race.

Rhetoric involves not only *what* people communicate (the words and images), but also *as whom* they communicate—the identities they foreground. Joni Ernst, the 2014 Republican nominee for an Iowa seat in the US Senate, foregrounded particular identities on her campaign web site and in her biography. She stressed that she was a mother, a grandmother, a soldier, a conservative, a hard worker, a Christian, and a friendly neighbor, and that she came from a lower-middle-class family.[47] Her campaign slogan was "Mother, Soldier, Conservative." Her breakout primary campaign advertisement,[48] "Make 'Em Squeal," used her identity as an Iowan child of farmers to make her policy position clear by comparing her work on the farm of castrating hogs with a willingness to cut pork spending in Congress.[49] Early in the primary race, she trailed in the polls. After the ad, she led her nearest competitor. Reporters argue that "the flashy farm-girl persona defined" by this ad, as well as another showing her getting off a Harley-Davidson, wearing a black leather jacket, and firing a handgun directly at the viewer (and at ObamaCare)[50] "transformed her candidacy."[51] She won the general election, becoming the first woman to represent Iowa in either chamber of the US Congress.

The range of personae available to rhetors is constrained by the various identities in which the rhetors can participate. This does not mean that identities are fixed, immutable, or one-dimensional. In fact, scholars argue that identity should be understood as intersectional. Legal scholar Adrien Katherine Wing defines **intersectionality** as *the nature of identity as "multiplicative" rather than additive.*[52] Identity makes more sense if you think of its facets of identity as integral, interlocking parts of a single whole, rather than as the addition of each element on top of another. The way a person performs "man" is influenced by his race, gender, sexuality, religion, education level, and class. The way people perform "white" is influenced by the same characteristics.

The metaphor of "ingredients" helps explain intersectionality.[53] Just as a cake is composed of discrete parts (eggs, flour, milk, sugar, and so on), the parts become inextricably intertwined when they are melded together through the alchemic process of cooking. The eggs affect the flour, which affects the milk, and so on. The interaction among the initially discrete ingredients makes a cake a cake. Similarly, the interaction among identity ingredients as they meld together makes a person a person.

Intersectionality in identity emphasizes that your sex influences your performance of class, your class influences your performance of race, your race influences your performance of nationality, and your nationality influences your performance of sex. In other words, you cannot understand what it means to have a certain identity without examining how all your identity ingredients interact with and infuse each other. Thus, scholars have begun to explore how Protestant religion and masculinity intersect in their studies of "muscular Christianity,"[54] how race and sex intersect in their studies of black masculinity[55] and hegemonic white masculinity;[56] and how class, sex, and race intersect in their studies of motherhood.[57]

Studies of motherhood show how a woman's identity as mother intersects with her race and class. Many people (mostly upper-class white people) might think of "mother" as the gentle soul who provides unconditional love and protective nurturing. In contrast, sociologist Patricia Hill Collins describes a form of motherhood that developed among women who had to prepare children to face discrimination. She shows that many working-class people and African Americans think of "mother" not as the gentle nurturer who soothes all wounds, but as the person who gave them the strength and the ability to handle life's hard knocks. Communication scholar Mari Boor Tonn labels this identity as "militant motherhood."[58]

Militant motherhood appears not only in families, but also in public discourse. In her study of labor activist Mary Harris "Mother" Jones, Tonn describes how militant motherhood uses "assertive, even aggressive, modes of presentation. Militant mothers not only confront their children's enemy, but must also train their children to do likewise if the threat they face is ongoing and systematic."[59] Militant motherhood is not sweet and gentle, but uses "bawdy, rowdy, and irreverent personal expression . . . . Such mothers also may bait, tease, and otherwise provoke children in order to acclimate them to attack, to provide practice at fighting back, and to sharpen their emotional control."[60] The way a woman performs the identity of "mother" is influenced by her race and class. That identity is not static and fixed: multiple performances of "mother" exist. Thus, multiple "mother" personae exist.

Intersectionality theory highlights the unique combinations of characteristics that make up each individual and calls attention to the ways interlocking forms of privilege marginalize members of some groups. Legal scholar Kimberlé Crenshaw first used the word "intersectionality" to explain why existing civil rights law, which treats race and sex discrimination as two discrete forms of discrimination, did not work for black women. She explains, "Because the intersectional experience is greater than the sum of racism and sexism, any analysis that does not take intersectionality into account cannot sufficiently address the particular manner in which Black Women are subordinated."[61] As demonstrated in the cases Crenshaw studied, black women were not discriminated against simply because they were black, or simply because they were women, but because they were black women.

As feminist philosopher Sandra Harding points out, one should remember "that it is not just the marginalized who have a gender, race, and so on."[62] Intersectionality explains the complexity of all people's identities. "Man" is as much an identity as "woman"; "middle class" is as much an identity as "poor"; and "white" is as much an identity as "black" or "Hispanic" or "Asian," but people who belong to a dominant identity do not perceive it to be an identity. Because it is the norm, the dominant identity becomes invisible. In their article on whiteness as a strategic rhetoric, communication scholars Thomas K. Nakayama and Robert L. Krizek identify the ways whiteness is created and maintained rhetorically as (1) closely tied to power, (2) the norm, (3) natural, (4) indicative of nationality and citizenship, (5) beyond the necessity of racial identity labels, and (6) consciously tied to white people's European ancestry.[63] To illustrate the hidden nature of race, think about references you may have heard to "the Asian doctor," "the Hispanic lawyer," or the "black accountant." Some people may suggest that these are only objective descriptions, but consider "white" as a descriptor: "the white doctor," "the white lawyer," or the "white accountant." Do these phrases sound strange? The fact that they sound odd suggests that "white" is an identity that receives preference for positions of power and authority. A complex interaction between audience, the rhetor, and identity exists, a relationship that calls for an analysis of power.

People's identities are not fixed, but developed through the choices they make, even as those choices are delimited by cultural norms that have been reiterated across time. Political communication scholar Thomas A. Hollihan explains, "Although all human beings actively participate in the creation of their own images, these images are not painted on a blank canvas."[64] It may be difficult for a man to play the role of mother, because social norms have linked women with the mother role and men with the father role. An audience's past experience with a rhetor, as well as its perception of the rhetor's race, sex, class, sexual orientation, nationality, and religion, influence the rhetor's ability to create and perform a persona. When delivering the graduation address at Morehouse College, valedictorian Packwood could not speak "as a black man" because US society perceives race to be a binary; one is either black or white. Thus, Packwood created an identity shared with his fellow students based not on race, but on their common Morehouse experience. Likewise, it would be difficult for Barack Obama to speak "as a white man" even though he is as white as he is black. US society sees him as a black man because the racial binary induces people to place others in the either/or identity category.

Scholars, such as feminist scholar Paula M. L. Moya, recognize that identities are fluid even as the performance of those identities are constrained by the existing relationships between social groups and "the historically produced social facts which constitute social locations."[65] The social roles that people are allowed to play and the level of social authority that they are granted are constrained by their identities. For example, a 2014 study conducted by three business scholars found that professors were less likely to respond to prospective students' requests to discuss research opportunities if the students' names signaled their sex as female and/or their race as not white. E-mails, identical save for the name of the sender, were sent to "over 6,500 professors at top U.S. universities drawn from 89 disciplines and 259 institutions."[66] The researchers found "that faculty ignored requests from women and minorities at a higher rate than requests from Caucasian males, particularly in higher-paying disciplines and private institutions." Professors in business colleges ignored requests from women and minorities at 2.6 times the rate of requests from white males.[67] In other words, female and minority students' identities, as indicated only by their names, marked them as less deserving of responses, regardless of the messages' performances of student.

Audiences read rhetors' personae through the identities they apply to the rhetors (hence, there is never a "blank canvas"), and often do not recognize that identities are intersectional. Thus, when some people look at United States Representative Keith Ellison, the first Muslim elected to the US Congress, they might see only Muslim or black, rather than US citizen, middle-class, college-educated, Muslim, African-American, man.[68] In the United States, people who are categorized as black, Latino/Latina, Native American, Muslim, or Asian are subjected to stereotypes on the basis of those categories.

People assume they know the rhetor's persona even before the rhetor performs it. These social assumptions are why identity matters: identities have real effects on how people live their lives. Moya argues that the external construction of peoples' identities influences their experiences, which then inform what they know and how they know it. She urges everyone to remember that although "people are not *uniformly* determined by any *one* social fact, . . . social facts (such as gender and race)" do influence who people are.[69] Even if identities are fictions, those fictions matter because they influence what and how people know.

Although social imposition of an identity may limit the range of persona options, identity is not fixed. It can be both an obstacle and an opportunity in constructing a persona. Communication scholar Karlyn Kohrs Campbell explains one may have the opportunity to choose to speak from an identity that has been accorded social power, or face the obstacle of speaking from an assigned identity that lacks social power. For Campbell, the concept of persona captures the "shifting but central character of the roles that we assume in the plays in which we participate."[70] Barack Obama had both an obstacle and an opportunity arising from his status as the first US president of African descent. The obstacle arose from the 5 percent of the electorate who said they would never vote for a black candidate;[71] they might never see Obama as the legitimate president even though he won the election. However, his race also provided an opportunity. He could use his race, his own self, as proof of the promise of the United States of America. In his first inaugural address, he stated:

> This is the meaning of our liberty and our creed—why men and women
> and children of every race and every faith can join in celebration across
> this magnificent mall, and why a man whose father less than sixty years

ago might not have been served at a local restaurant can now stand before you to take a most sacred oath.[72]

President Obama foregrounded his racial identity in order to make a point about the nation's progress toward equality. He spoke the oath for the highest office in the land in a city that, years earlier, had used Jim Crow segregation laws to deny equal treatment to people like him and his father.

Many rhetors call forth particular ingredients in their identities, just as President Obama did with his race, to form their personae in particular speech acts. Rhetors may speak as and for women, men, women of color, African Americans, whites, immigrants, Muslims, US citizens, and so on. Even though each of those identity ingredients may be fluid and shifting, the rhetor chooses to fix one ingredient momentarily in order to speak from the social location attached to that identity. Claiming that identity becomes a strategic part of the communication act.

Strategic Essentialism. The differences among races or between women and men are not nearly as extensive as most popular culture literature would have you believe, but people often treat each other as more different than they really are. Thus, when others label you with an identity that is perceived as essential, meaning that it is fixed and immutable, how might you use that identity? If you have been assigned an identity by the larger society, thus limiting your range of personae, how might you use that assigned identity to enhance your communicative actions? A rhetor may have limited power because of sex, race, class, or nationality, yet still find creative and artistic ways to communicate.

Literary critic Gayatri Chakravorty Spivak describes **strategic essentialism** as *the process of making an identity ingredient the core part of one's persona that legitimizes the right to speak.*[73] It is strategic because it is an intentional construction of persona based on that single identity ingredient. A rhetor consciously picks an identity ingredient to foreground. That choice is essentialist because it positions one element of identity as fixed and determinative of the rhetor's identity and seeks to create group identification through the appeal to that one shared identity ingredient. Strategic essentialism chooses to ignore intersectionality, and instead focuses on a single identity ingredient. For example, in the 1960s and 1970s, African Americans appealed to the single identity ingredient of race with their slogan "Black Power";[74] women appealed to the single identity ingredient of sex with their proclamation that "Sisterhood is Powerful";[75] and Native Americans appealed to their nationality/race with "Red Power."[76] Marginalized groups tend to be the ones to employ strategic essentialism because they are the people who are fighting misrepresentations of their group identity and struggling for a right to speak with social power.

Strategic essentialism as a rhetorical technique has two important characteristics. First, the ostensibly essential attributes of the group are defined by the group members themselves. The members of a marginalized group accept their identity as a group, but seek to control how they are defined. Instead of passively being labeled by the dominant group, they actively take possession of an identity and define it in their own terms. "Black" does not mean powerless and enslaved, but powerful. "Sisterhood" means women are not divided cat-fighting individuals, but unified and powerful. Native American identity is not extinct, but vibrant and alive. Second, even as the group members engage in essentialism, they recognize that identity is always artificially constructed. Spivak recognizes that strategically appealing to an essential understanding of identity can sometimes be politically productive, but it must be done "in a scrupulously visible political interest."[77] Thus, people must *consciously* appeal to an essential identity in order to achieve a particular goal for their group; once that goal has been achieved, they should consciously question that essentialism. If they are to have agency or some degree of control over persona production, they must consciously perform and question that persona.

Throughout this discussion, we have tried to make clear that as identities are used to form a persona, they should also be critically examined. Sometimes, people strongly embrace an identity ingredient in order to create a sense of belonging. Other times, identity ingredients are de-emphasized so alliances can be built on the basis of other ingredients. Identities can be defined in order to create unification, but the process creates divisions. If a group unifies on the basis of a common ethnic background, it excludes those who do not share that background. Thus, the deployment of identity must be carefully considered in order to avoid creating a permanent division. Chicana author, scholar, and activist Gloria Anzaldúa offers an elegant metaphor for this multi-layered process in her essay "Bridge, Drawbridge, Sandbar or Island: Lesbians-of-Color *Hacienda Alianzas*."[78] Groups who build bridges to other groups find, at times, that moments of separation are needed, and raise the drawbridge. Sometimes no bridge is built, because the group needs the isolation of an island. Sometimes permanent bridges are built so the connections to others can always be maintained.

Identity is performed. Thus, when people are seeking to present a particular persona by strategically foregrounding an identity ingredient, they should remember that a persona is a mask, which can become suffocating if it is fixed and permanent.

Authority

Authority is *a rhetor's possession of socially recognized power.* Sometimes rhetors are able to persuade audiences because of their authority. If a classmate stands up before the professor arrives and instructs everyone to take out a pen and paper for a quiz, the other students probably would ignore these instructions because they do not recognize the student's authority to give them. If the professor arrives and instructs the students to get ready to take a quiz, however, they would likely follow the professor's instructions because they recognize the professor's authority. To show how authority is a facet of persona, we first outline the way authority operates as social power. Second, we apply the concept of authority to the performance of identity to show how authority both enables and constrains.

Social Power. **Social power** is *the influence that people possess within a particular social structure, and that enables them to induce others to act.* For example, students in a course will probably follow the directives of their instructor not because of the instructor's ethos (although it helps induce cooperation), but because of the instructor's position in the social structure of the university. Instructors have ethos because students assume they possess the qualifications to teach the class. They also work to develop ethos during their classes so the coercive power of the grade book is not their only source of influence. Upon entering a classroom for the first time, however, students usually defer to instructors, not because they necessarily perceive the instructors' credibility, but because social power is attached to the role of instructor.

The social power a rhetor brings to a situation is relevant only insofar as the audience perceives it. People do not have or lack power in an absolute sense; rather, they have more or less power in relation to others. Rhetors can possess various types and degrees of social power, including reward power (the perceived authority of the rhetor to reward or benefit the audience), coercive power (the perceived authority of the rhetor to punish the audience), expert power (the perceived authority of the rhetor stemming from knowledge, talent, or skill), referent power (the perceived authority of the rhetor due to the audience's identification with the rhetor), and legitimate power (based on the audience's perception of the rhetor's assigned position in a social structure).[79] For example, you might be responsive to your professors' messages because you believe they have expert power when discussing their particular subjects. You also might perceive their reward and coercive power, related to giving grades and course credit. Professors also have some degree of legitimate power because they have particular positions in a university that grants authority within that social structure. Additionally, they might be perceived as having legitimate power or authority beyond the university, in the larger society, if the society places social importance on the teaching profession. Finally, you might admire professors' knowledge and want to identify with them, thus granting them referent power.

A professor's race, sex, citizenship status, and sexuality interact with the ability to exercise the various forms of power. Research indicates that Euro-American white professors are more likely than minority professors to possess referent power with white students,[80] male professors more easily exercise expert power than female professors,[81] and professors perceived to be straight are more likely to be granted legitimate power than professors perceived to be gay.[82]

Identity and social power intersect. People's positions in a social structure are influenced by all ingredients of their identities. Even though a police officer may have legitimate power, an audience may place limits on that power because of the officer's sex. In an ethnographic study of the traditionally masculine profession of police officer, women officers on the Pittsburgh police force talked about learning "not to smile" to reduce the risk that others would see them as incompetent or unprofessional.[83] In other words, they managed their smiling behavior to comply with public expectations for officers. Recognizing that their sex negatively impacted their legitimate power, they sought ways to perform the persona of police officer in a way that would maximize its legitimate power.

Social power can be altered as a result of changes in organizational structures and rules. For example, for a long time, women carried no power in conflict resolution. They did not appear at the negotiating table as generals of armies (with coercive power), managers of wealth (with reward power), professors (with expert power), representatives of people (with referent power), or leaders of nations (with legitimate power). The United Nations found this situation problematic, so in 2000, it adopted Resolution 1325 to urge "Member States to ensure increased representation of women at all decision-making levels in national, regional and international institutions and mechanisms for the prevention, management, and resolution of conflict."[84] In 2010, this action was incorporated in the *United States National Action Plan on Women, Peace, and Security*, which declares its goal is "to empower half the world's population as equal partners in preventing conflict and building peace in countries threatened and affected by war, violence, and insecurity."[85] This policy declared that knowledge belongs not only to the supposed experts on conflict and borders, but also to people who contend with the effects of conflict on a daily basis. It has had real effects. Then–Secretary of State Hillary Clinton, in explaining why the State Department embraced the UN policy, told the following story:

> Women have skills and practical knowledge that enrich discussions about peace and security. . . . there was a recent negotiation over how to end part of the long, terrible conflict in Darfur, and the men in the room spent days arguing over who would get territory around a certain river. Finally, a woman outside the door said, "That river's been dry for years." (Laughter.) Because, after all, it wasn't men that went looking for water every day, it was women. (Laughter.) So we have to find more ways to tap the vast talents and resources of half the population in the world. . . .
>
> That's why, at the State Department, I've instructed our leadership in Washington and at embassies around the world to prioritize advancing rights and opportunities for women. We are working to increase women's political participation, strengthen their economic position, ensure that women have a seat at every table, including tables that discuss peace and security.[86]

Authority to Perform. Audience bias about identity limits a person's ability to access authority. Harvard professor Cornell West tells of a time the police stopped him:

> Years ago, while driving from New York to teach at Williams College, I was stopped on fake charges of trafficking cocaine. When I told the police officer I was a professor of religion, he replied "Yeh, and I'm the flying Nun. Let's go, nigger!" I was stopped three times in my first ten days in Princeton for driving too slowly on a residential street with a speed limit of twenty-five miles per hour.[87]

Professor West had attained a level of social power because of his educational and professional status, but the police denied him access to it because of race bias. The police officer who stopped West did not believe West's performance of his power because he did not believe a black man had the authority to perform the role of professor.

Social power is a resource, but it is constrained when people are not given the authority to perform particular roles. When women activists struggled for their rights during the 1960s and 1970s, they sought to perform a new form of womanhood, but they were not totally free to perform "womanhood" in any way they wanted, free from social sanction. Communication scholar Karlyn Kohrs Campbell notes that the social status of women placed them at odds with the persona of "rhetor," which called for "self-reliance, self-confidence, and independence."[88] If a woman performed the persona of "woman," then she did not enact the persona of "rhetor;" if she performed the persona of "rhetor," then she might not be perceived as enacting "woman." Campbell argues that feminist rhetoric during this era, "no matter how traditional its argumentation, how justificatory its form, how discursive its method, or how scholarly its style, . . . attacks the entire psychosocial reality, the most fundamental values, of the cultural context in which it occurs."[89]

When a persona pushes at the social expectations attached to the body performing it, the audience may reject the performance as unauthorized. Because not all rhetors have equal authority to perform a role, analysis of performances should focus on the power to perform, rather than on the truth of a performance. As Goffman states: "Sometimes when we ask whether a fostered impression is true or false we really mean to ask whether or not the performer is authorized to give the performance in question, and are not primarily concerned with the actual performance itself."[90] Even though personae are performances, people are not free to play any role they wish.

For example, a person's gender identity (tending toward feminine, tending toward masculine, or a creative mix of both) is a performance. Gender is something people do, not something they are—a performance, a series of repeated actions, postures, and statements. Rhetoric professor Judith Butler aptly describes the relationship between gender and identity: "Gender is the repeated stylization of the body, a set of repeated acts within a rigid regulatory frame that congeal over time to produce the appearance of substance, of a natural kind of being."[91] Consider the ways you do gender through your dress, hairstyle, body posture, language choice, hand gestures, areas of interest, and so on. When humans (consciously or unconsciously) behave in gendered ways, they construct, maintain, and transform their own and others' notions of gender identity. These performances are repeated so frequently they become unconscious, if not involuntary, and might even appear natural and determined rather than performed. Yet, they are still actions, not some inherent identity a person possesses.

Butler explains that even though "gender is a kind of doing, an incessant activity performed, in part, without one's knowing and without one's willing," it is not "automatic or mechanical."[92] She asks people to think about gender as "a practice of improvisation within a scene of constraint."[93] It is a performance, but one where the actors maintain only some level of control over the content of the scene. When you wake up every day, you make choices about how to do gender; about how to dress, move, sit, and talk. You could choose to "do gender" differently, but first you would have to see those choices as options. If a man wanted to do his gender differently, he would need to see wearing a dress and heels as a viable option; most men do not. Although women can now wear pants and still be perceived as feminine (which was not true until the latter half of the twentieth century), a man who decided to wear a skirt would face serious social censure. Thus, the performance of gender is constrained; the script has already been written with only limited space for improvisation.

Race is another identity ingredient that affects a rhetor's authority to perform particular personae. Whiteness in US society operates as a form of privilege that nonwhites cannot access. White rhetors of European ancestry have an advantage with many US audiences, without explicitly stating the fact that they are white, because white is defined as the norm. The Birther Movement's challenges to President Obama's citizenship highlight the way in which people consider whiteness to be interlinked with US nationality and citizenship. Despite an officially recognized Hawaiian birth certificate and Honolulu newspaper birth announcements, the Birther Movement refuses to accept that Obama was born in the United States, as the Constitution requires the president to be.[94] Birthers' implication is that Obama does not have the authority to perform the role of president. Some people argue that part of their questioning of his authority is related to his race, and that challenges to his citizenship would not have gained as much traction if he were perceived as white.

Image

The year 2013 was transformative for singer and songwriter Justin Bieber's image. Bieber's commercial career began in 2008 when US talent manager Scooter Braun discovered him on YouTube. The fourteen-year-old Bieber had "the voice of a cherub and the face of a cherub on a diet."[95] Within a year, he was topping the Billboard charts with song after song and amassing a horde of diehard Beliebers, ranging from adolescents to middle-aged women. He had the image of "a squeaky-clean gentleman."[96]

Starting in January 2013, several alleged incidents would challenge that image: joyriding in his Ferrari "dangerously quickly, endangering nearby children and pets"; smoking pot; and writing in the guest book at the Anne Frank House, "Anne was a great girl. Hopefully she would've been a belieber."[97] In 2014 he spent $75,000 at a Miami strip club, and was arrested for DUI and drag racing a rented Lamborghini.[98] He spent a night in jail, his gleefully smiling mug shot gracing social media.

Rolling Stone covers track the evolution of his image from the clean-cut kid to a reckless teenager out of control. The March 3, 2011, cover showed him wearing a white tank and black leather jacket, alluringly sliding off one shoulder; touted him as "Super Boy"; and explained "To the Beliebers, Justin is the most adorable, talented, sensual kid in the world."[99] The August 2, 2012, cover showed a clear-skinned Bieber, still sporting a white tank top; touted him as "Hot, Ready, Legal"; and said, "Five years later, the phenomenon shows no signs of abating. Teenage girls are still camping out in shantytowns for days on end to get a good spot for his concerts."[100] The March 11, 2014, cover, though, told a new story. It showed a shirtless and tattooed Bieber in underwear-exposing leather pants with the caption "Bad Boy." An accompanying article declared, "There's a fine line between having more fun than any teenager alive and completely melting down."[101]

Bieber is just one of a long line of teen stars who have struggled with their images as they entered adulthood. Their changeability shows that those images are created, rhetorical constructions. An **image** is *a verbal and visual representation, emphasizing particular qualities and characteristics, that creates a perception of the rhetor in the audience's minds*. Image is an aspect of persona, but also an effect of it. Across time, an image is created by the performance of persona. An image is most persuasive, according to historian Daniel Boorstin, when it builds a reputation and does not outrage common sense.[102] Bieber built an image so clean, it was "pretty squeaky."[103] This image played off his androgynous looks; tween attraction would not horrify parents.

In his book critiquing the rise of hollow images and pseudo-events, Boorstin identifies several characteristics of an image. His purpose in analyzing images is to condemn them, but these characteristics can be useful in studying how image works more generally. For Boorstin, an image is (1) synthetic, (2) believable, (3) passive, (4) vivid and concrete, (5) simplified, and (6) ambiguous.[104]

By *synthetic*, Boorstin means that an image is "planned: created especially to serve a purpose, to make a certain kind of impression."[105] Yet an image must be perceived as authentic to be effective: It must be *believable*. As Boorstin explains, an image "serves no purpose if people do not believe it."[106] The believability of the image is not determined simply by the rhetor's ability to project an image, but also by the audience's willingness to accept it. Initially, young Bieber as angelic was believable. Now, though, the image is not as believable, as there is "some question whether he's just the latest teen star gone wild."[107] In early March 2013, "he was booed by his beloved fans when he showed up late to a concert."[108] The audience was no longer willing to accept Bieber as an angel who could do no wrong.

Although images are actively constructed, they are most believable when they appear *passive*, not something the rhetor strives for, but that occurs naturally. Conformity and image go hand in hand, because conforming to norms always appears easier than challenging them. This may be what Bieber has chosen to do: not actively fight, but conform to his new image. If the March 2014 cover of *Rolling Stone* is any indication, Bieber is embracing the "bad boy" image, conforming to the new social expectations of who he is.

In order for constructed images to influence an audience, they must be *vivid* and *concrete*, yet *simplified*. Because they are meant to invite identification, they must be *ambiguous* enough for multiple audiences to feel similarity, yet vivid enough to give them a sense of who the rhetor is. Bieber's early image was simply that he could be anyone's boyfriend. As one reporter explained, "The female fantasy about Bieber has a lot to do with wanting him to be your first real boyfriend—or, for older women, with the way that he hearkens back to the time when you had your first boyfriend."[109] The fact that he could be any (young or old) female's ideal also shows the fantasy's ambiguity.

Images are not always positive creations meant to enhance a rhetor's appeal. Sometimes, negative images are imposed on a rhetor. Gerald Ford, who served as president from 1974 to 1977, was arguably one of the most athletic presidents in the nation's history. He had been a star athlete on the University of Michigan football team, and had turned down contract offers from the Detroit Lions and Green Bay Packers. Nevertheless, he was painted as a well-meaning nice guy whose incompetence was reflected in his physical bumblings. After news footage showed him slipping on the steps as he exited Air Force One and hitting golf spectators with the ball, comedian Chevy Chase began lampooning Ford on *Saturday Night Live.* Chase did not wear makeup or hairpieces to make him look like Ford. He just fell down, stumbled over flagpoles, and knocked over Christmas trees, thus cementing the public's image of Ford[110] and of his (in)effectiveness as president. This image is so persistent, it reappeared in a 2010 Funny or Die video (with 5.6 million views as of May 2014). The "Presidential Reunion" shows Chevy Chase walking into the White House presidential bedroom only to trip over a table.[111]

Although Boorstin is extremely critical of images (especially as deployed by those with power), referring to them as "pseudo-events," contemporary scholars find that image events have a productive role in contemporary protest. Movements, groups, and organizations outside the mainstream political order also can construct images. Images not only conform, keep things the way they are, and squelch dissent; they also shake things up. Particularly in an increasingly multimediated world, rhetors recognize the need to have their images appear on the public screen. (See Chapter 3 on image events.)

RHETOR ANALYZED

On April 3, 2009, the Iowa Supreme Court unanimously ruled that the state's Defense of Marriage Act violated the equal protection clause of the state constitution, making Iowa the third state in the nation to recognize same-sex marriage.[112] In response, the legislature considered whether to amend the state's constitution via House Joint Resolution 6, specifying "marriage between one man and one woman shall be the only legal union valid or recognized in this state."[113] A public forum on the resolution was scheduled for February 1, 2011. Over seventy people testified, including college student Zach Wahls. The next day, the Iowa House Democrats uploaded his speech on YouTube. There, it amassed over eighteen million views by the end of the year, leading YouTube to award it "Top Political Video of 2011," surpassing President Obama's White House Correspondents' Dinner speech, Texas Governor Rick Perry's Republican primary advertisement, and President Obama's statement on the killing of Osama bin Laden.[114]

Prior to the speech, Wahls was not known to the legislators to whom he was speaking or to the audience in the gallery. When the speech was posted to YouTube, the millions who watched it also had no preconception of who Wahls might be. As Wahls performed his identity in this speech, he artistically used elements of his identity to craft ethos. The speech lasted only three minutes, but in it, Wahls made evident the power of enactment and strategic use of identity.

He showed that who the rhetor is may be as important as what the rhetor says. As you read the speech, consider how Wahls constructed his persona by identifying his various roles, how his identity functioned as a resource for his argument, and how he created an image of his character to grant him authority on the topic.

Zach Wahls
"Zach Wahls Speaks about Family"
Iowa House of Representatives Public Forum
January 31, 2011

1. Good evening Mr. Chairman, my name is Zach Wahls. I'm a sixth-generation Iowan and an engineering student at the University of Iowa, and I was raised by two women.

2. My biological mom Terry told her grandparents that she was pregnant, that the artificial insemination had worked, and they wouldn't even acknowledge it. It actually wasn't until I was born and they succumbed to my infantile cuteness that they broke down and told her that they were thrilled to have another grandson. Unfortunately, neither of them lived to see her marry her partner Jackie of fifteen years when they wed in 2009.

3. My younger sister and only sibling was born in 1994. We actually have the same anonymous donor, so we're full siblings, which is really cool for me.

4. You know, I guess the point is that our family really isn't so different from any other Iowa family. When I'm home, we go to church together. We eat dinner. We go on vacations. But, you know, we have our hard times too; we get in fights. My mom, Terry, was diagnosed with multiple sclerosis in 2000. It is a devastating disease that put her in a wheelchair, so, we've had our struggles. But, you know, we're Iowans. We don't expect anyone to solve our problems for us. We'll fight our own battles. We just hope for equal and fair treatment from our government.

5. Being a student at the University of Iowa, the topic of same sex marriage comes up quite frequently in classroom discussions. You know, the question always comes down to, well, "Can gays even raise kids?" And the conversation gets quiet for a moment, because most people don't really have an answer. And then I raise my hand and say, "Actually, I was raised by a gay couple, and I'm doing pretty well."

6. I scored in the 99th percentile on the ACT. I'm actually an Eagle Scout. I own and operate my own small business. If I was your son, Mr. Chairman, I believe I'd make you very proud.

7. I'm not really so different from any of your children. My family really isn't so different from yours. After all, your family doesn't derive its sense of worth from being told by the state, "You're married, congratulations!" No. The sense of family comes from the commitment we make to each other to work through the hard times so we can enjoy the good ones. It comes from the love that binds us. That's what makes a family.

8. So what you're voting [for] here is not to change us. It's not to change our families, it's to change how the law views us, how the law treats us. You are voting for the first time in the history of our state to codify discrimination into our constitution, a constitution that but for the proposed amendment is the least amended constitution in the United States of America. You are telling Iowans that "Some among you are second-class citizens who do not have the right to marry the person you love."

9. So will this vote affect my family? Would it affect yours? In the next two hours, I'm sure we're going to hear plenty of testimony about how damaging having gay parents is on kids. But in my nineteen years not once have I ever been confronted by an individual who realized independently that I was raised by a gay couple. And you know why? Because the sexual orientation of my parents has had zero effect on the content of my character.

10. Thank you very much.[115]

You may have known nothing of Wahls before his speech began, but by its end you know about the elements of his identity he chooses to foreground: he is a sixth-generation Iowan, a University of Iowa student, an engineering major, a brother, an Eagle Scout, a small business owner, not "different"; he is church-attending, smart (or at least skilled at standardized tests), and nine-teen years old. His discursive descriptions of himself are supplemented by his presentational symbolism. He physically presents himself in a particular way, wearing a subdued gray suit, blue shirt, and striped tie; sporting a short haircut; and standing 6'5" tall. These elements may appear to be unremarkable, but they were not irrelevant to the speech. The development of those identities was not accidental. As he explains, he "spent hours writing, editing and re-working the testimony I delivered to the Iowa House Judiciary Committee."[116] Quite simply, he assumed the persona of a traditionally masculine Iowan man.

Explicitly naming his identity characteristics and presenting a traditional masculinity were central to Wahls's ability to enact his argument. His argument, at heart, is that same-sex couples can raise children who do "pretty well," who are considered to be normal Iowan children. In his second sentence, he asserts his right to speak to the state legislature: he is not some visitor from the coasts, but part of a long line of Iowans. (Notice, also, how he defines the *Iowan* char-acter: independent, self-sufficient, and committed to equality and fairness.) He associates himself with traditionally masculine endeavors: scouting, engineering, and enterprise. What he leaves unspoken, but that is a presence that saturates the text, is his masculinity. Wahls quite overtly performs the archetypal form of tradi-tional masculinity. He does normative gender.

Imagine if, instead, Wahls had long flowing hair, sported eyeliner, wore a kilt and a floral shirt, was part of his community theatre and loved performing in musicals, majored in nursing, and disclosed that his small business was a design firm for prom dresses. Would the speech have functioned the same way? Granted, we just employed a range of stereotypes. That is our point. Wahls fit stereotypes of masculinity and, thus, reassured the audience that two women could raise what is considered a "normal boy." But why would any of those imagined characteristics actually weaken his *ethos*? Why would any of them disqualify him from speaking about the "content of his character"? They should not, but because rhetors face social expectations when they speak, we doubt his speech would have gone viral if he had not been as normatively masculine as he was. Wahls's ability as a rhetor to fit into a stable and essential male identity enables him to make an argument that challenges constricting interpretations of family and love. His persona of high achieving, "regular" Iowan male reflects, in Linkugel's terms, "the aspirations and cultural visions of audiences." Wahls, because of his apparent identity, was authorized to perform masculinity in a way that might assuage those who were concerned that same-sex parents could not raise children who would comport to socially determined gender norms.

This short speech catapulted Wahls into the national spotlight, landing him spots on the *Ellen DeGeneres Show*, the *Last Word with Lawrence O'Donnell*, the *Daily Show with Jon Stewart*, MSNBC, CBS, and the *Late Show with David Letterman*, as well as a speech at the 2012 Democratic National Convention. In addition to demonstrating the concept of persona and enactment, his speech also demonstrates that a young person can make rhetoric that matters and that three minutes may be all you need to make a powerful statement.

RHETORS IN A POSTMODERN WORLD

To end the chapter, we want to make clear the complex role the rhetor plays in symbolic action. Just as a rhetor may be an inventor of symbolic action, the rhetor is invented by symbolic action. In fact, the very idea of an author/rhetor may be a rhetorical invention, because rhetors' identities are constructed within the play of larger social forces. Thus, we offer four caveats about studying "the rhetor": (1) authorial intent does not determine the meaning of a text; (2) no text has a single author; (3) rhetors, themselves, may be the rhetorical constructions of others; and (4) in a networked age, algorithms, rather than people, may author the web content you see.

These insights are informed by postmodern theory. **Postmodernism**, broadly defined, is *the theory that places into question singular explanations, meta-narratives, categories, and the certainty of supposedly objective interpretations of the world*. Because human beings only access the world through the symbols they use, explanations tend to be limited by the symbolism used. In particular, postmodernism induces questioning the definition of the rhetor as possessing a stable identity and as the sole origin of the meaning of a text.

First, authorial intent does not determine a rhetorical action's meaning. The most extreme version of this argument can be dated to a 1967 essay by French literary theorist Roland Barthes, "The Death of the Author."[117] Barthes proposes that the author of a text does not determine the meaning of a text, because "to give an Author to a text is to impose upon that text a stop clause, to furnish it with a final signification, to close the writing."[118] Instead, Barthes proposes, the audience determines the meaning of a text:

a text consists of multiple writings, issuing from several cultures and entering into dialogue with each other, into parody, into contestation; but there is one place where this multiplicity is collected, united, and this place is not the author . . . but the reader.[119]

The readers, Barthes argues, provide meaning to the text through the experiences (including other works they have read) they bring to their interpretations. Barthes warns against relying on an author's intent or biography to determine the meaning of a text. The centrality of audiences to making meaning led communication theorist Michael McGee to declare *"text construction is now something done more by the consumers than by the producers of discourse."*[120]

However, as communication scholar Karlyn Kohrs Campbell declares, "reports of the death of the author are greatly exaggerated."[121] Although we agree that audiences are central to understanding rhetorical action, we also believe rhetors still carry ethical responsibilities with them when they engage in rhetorical action. In other words, we advocate a necessary fiction of the rhetor in order to talk about the civic and moral responsibilities that attach to rhetorical action.

An author's identity is only relevant to understanding the meaning of a text when it is part of that text, and your only access to an author is through the meanings you draw from his or her texts. In our analysis of Wahls's speech, we do not include any additional information about him (such as the fact that he was on his high school's speech team). The only information we discussed was that which was presented in the speech. The text's construction of Wahls, as perceived by the audience, was important to the text's meaning; Wahls's intent was not. Although Wahls's intent was probably to challenge hegemonic social norms of gender and sexuality (for example, the normative views that two women cannot raise a masculine boy and that homosexuality is taboo), his speech also (perhaps unintentionally, but actually) reinforced the normative power of masculinity. His performance of and appeal to traditional notions of hegemonic masculinity were central to the meaning of the speech.

Another example that shows the limit of intent is the use of the derogatory term for Native Americans, the "R-word," as the team name for the Washington, DC, football team. Every dictionary definition of the term says it is a racial slur. For decades, every major Native American group has called for athletic teams to drop the use of American Indian names and mascots (unless the team is connected to an American Indian school). In 2006, the NCAA began banning their use in postseason tournaments.[122] In 2013, the Oneida nation launched an advertising campaign on radio and the Internet to induce Washington team owner Dan Snyder and league Commissioner Roger Goodell to change the Washington football team's name. The National Congress of American Indians also launched a photo project calling for Native Americans to submit pictures, accompanied by statements, of what they are proud to be.[123] In 2013, the Leadership Conference on Civil and Human Rights adopted a resolution that demanded the Washington team change its name.[124]

In May 2014, after fifty US Senators sent a letter to Goodell asking him to change the name,[125] NFL spokesperson Brian McCarthy defended the team's name as intended to be complimentary to and respectful of Native Americans.[126] Clearly, regardless of the NFL and team's intent, the term is perceived as disrespectful and derogatory. On June 18, 2014, the US Patent Office cancelled six federal trademark registrations owned by the team because the team name was "disparaging to Native Americans."[127] (The team appealed, however.)[128]

Where does meaning reside? Barthes critiqued the idea that the rhetor's intent determines the meaning of a text, but one insight of contemporary rhetorical and communication theory is that meaning does not really reside in the intent of the author (if one can be identified) or in the text, but in the interaction between an audience and a text. Media studies have extensively theorized this relationship because many mediated texts (such as reality TV shows, movies, dramas, and situation comedies) do not have a single author to whom intent could be attributed; the writers, directors, actors, and editors all play a part in creating meaning in mediated shows.

Media scholar John Fiske argues that the meanings of texts are open to multiple interpretations by audiences, and that audiences are not just passive recipients; they are able to create their own meanings.[129] Fiske believes people actively and creatively engage with media, using a range of tactics to make media meet their needs. He believes diverse readings are possible because media messages have multiple meanings. He uses the term **polysemous** (*poly* meaning *many* and *sema* referring to *sign* or *symbol*) to represent *the multiple meanings of a single text.*[130]

Fiske claimed that mediated messages were not open to an endless range of interpretations, but some scholars thought he did not devote enough time to the things that limit interpretations. Mediated messages do not occur in a vacuum, but in a particular place, at a particular time, and to particular audiences. Communication scholar Celeste Condit explains that a rhetorical approach reminds the researcher that "audiences are not free to make meanings at will from mass mediated texts" because "the ability of audiences to shape their own readings . . . is constrained by a variety of factors in any given rhetorical situation" including "access to oppositional codes . . . the repertoire of available texts" and the historical context.[131] In other words, one should be trained to engage in critical reading. Condit argues that instead of the concept of polysemy (multitude of meanings) researchers should use **polyvalence** (*or multitude of valuations*), which "occurs when audience members share understandings of the denotations of a text but disagree about the valuation of these denotations to such a degree that they produce notably different interpretations."[132] Polysemy implies that audiences interpret different denotative meanings from a text, while polyvalence implies that they extract different connotational meanings.

The reaction to Joni Ernst's advertisement about castrating hogs illustrates the difference. Illustrating polysemy, some people interpreted the ad as a real and effective political advertisement; others thought it was a joke. Charles C. W. Cooke, a writer for the *National Review*, called Ernst's line "the greatest opening line in the history of campaign commercials."[133] On Twitter, however, people suggested that the ad might be a spoof created by television host and comedian Jimmy Kimmel.[134] Denotatively distinct interpretations emerged: real versus fake advertisement.

Illustrating polyvalence, almost everyone was able to interpret the core meaning of the ad: Joni Ernst castrated hogs and she would cut pork in Washington. Yet, how people valued this message differed. Some found it problematic and distasteful. A veteran Republican operative in Iowa working with Ernst's opponent thought the ad was "bizarre . . . I was embarrassed by it."[135] Others analyzed it as a campaign strategy. Media strategist Brain Donohue said the ad was effective because it created a "Buzzfeed effect," whereby an audience not only forms an opinion but feels compelled to share it.[136] Stephen Colbert declared "Sold! Joni, you had me at castration" and explained that "while the other little girls were reading *Charlotte's Web*, Joni was out back with tin snips making a soprano out of Wilbur."[137]

Although the advertisement may have induced gasps on the coasts, in Iowa (which leads the nation in hog production) the ad spoke to an experience many people might share or at least understand. As a result, the ad helped Ernst jump to the head of the pack before the primary.[138] Depending on the audience and how they valued the commitment to cut pork, the advertisement meant Ernst was qualified to be senator, was not qualified to be senator, was an effective campaigner, or was laughable.

The concepts of polysemy and polyvalence challenge the idea that the rhetor determines a text's meaning. Different audience members might come away from the same rhetorical event with radically different interpretations of what the event meant. Thus, for students of rhetoric, the goal of analysis "is not to locate *the* message" a rhetor might have intended, but to identify "the multiple, frequently conflicting, messages."[139] Given postmodern insight into the *poly* creation of meaning, a singular, unitary reading of a text's meaning is inaccurate.

This does not mean people should manipulate texts in a way that refuses to recognize another person's creative intent. For example, in Spring 2014, the world was horrified by the story of Boko Haram kidnapping more than 250 girls from their boarding school in Nigeria and auctioning them to the highest bidder. The attack on a school is not accidental, nor the first. (The name Boko Haram roughly translates to "Western education is forbidden.")[140] Nevertheless, little effort was made to find the girls, even as television networks devoted seemingly endless coverage to a "major international search" for a missing Malaysian airliner.[141] But the girls' parents persisted. With other protestors, they marched in the capital to pressure Nigerian President Goodluck Jonathan to do something.[142] In support, a social media campaign was launched on Change.org, Facebook, and the White House website: #BringBackOurGirls. Eventually, the Nigerian government began accepting assistance from other countries in their search for the girls. (As this book went to press, however, they had not been freed.)

As part of the #BringBackOurGirls campaign, three photographs of girls were tweeted and retweeted thousands of times.[143] The problem: the photos were not of the girls who had been kidnapped; in fact, the girls were not even from Nigeria. The photos had been taken by photojournalist Ami Vitale, of girls from Guinea-Bissau (which is over a thousand miles from Nigeria). Whoever had created the twitter images had taken the photos from Vitale's website or from another website. Although she supported the campaign, Vitale was deeply concerned about the misuse of these photos, explaining:

Can you imagine having your daughter's image spread throughout
the world as the face of sexual trafficking? These girls have never been
abducted, never been sexually trafficked.[144]

An additional concern was that Vitale's project had focused on the beauty
of Africa, which existed between the dominant narratives of it as a war-torn
wasteland or an exotic land of safari. Vitale's story was that the girls she photographed "are not victims," but these girls had now become the international face
of victimization. Unfortunately, the images have been misused, not only in this
campaign, but in many others. If you search for "crying little black girls," Vitale's
images come up, and might then be used in a variety of ways.

Second, no text has a single author. Although we often talk of *the* rhetor, all
symbolic actions are actually the creation of multiple rhetors, some of whom can
be identified and others of whom cannot. In some cases, a multitude of authors is
easy to recognize, as when a politician works with a speechwriter, a social movement generates a website or protest action, a group creates and solicits signatures
for a petition on Change.org, or a campus group advocates for increased funding
from the student government. Multiple rhetors/authors are at play in the Ernst
ad: Ernst, the advisors she met with to develop her stump speech, the debate
crowd that lit up when she used the one-liner about castrating hogs, Todd Harris
(her media consultant) who thought "building a provocative ad around that line
might get her attention they could not afford,"[145] and late night comics who
recirculate (even as they spoof) the ad.

Even when a speech seems to be authored by a single individual, multiple
authors are present. Campbell's statement about the death of the author echoes
Mark Twain's statement, upon hearing that newspapers had reported his
death, that such a report was "greatly exaggerated." An echo of another author
is also present in the last line of Wahls's speech: "the sexual orientation of my
parents has had zero effect on the content of my character." Does any part of
that sentence sound familiar? Martin Luther King, in "I Have A Dream," said,
"I have a dream that my four little children will one day live in a nation where
they will not be judged by the color of their skin but by the content of their character."[146] The phrase "the content of our character" has taken on a meaning of
its own; it is often cited by authors and speakers.

Rhetors knit together recognized turns of phrase, metaphors, ideographs,
narratives, myths, and public vocabularies. As Campbell notes, because rhetors
"are linked to cultures and collectivities" they cannot create meaning independently. Instead, they are inventors, "points of articulation" who link together the
components of symbolic action as they invent speeches, personae, identities, and
communities.[147]

Third, rhetors may be rhetorically constructed by others. Who people think
a rhetor is, even the words attributed to that rhetor, are constructions. You may
have heard of Sojourner Truth and the 1851 speech "Ain't I a Woman" that is
attributed to her,[148] and that is extensively read in middle school and high school
curricula. According to Campbell, the way Truth's speech was perceived and
recorded provides insight into how social power and privileges affect the perception of a rhetor's persona.[149]

What is known of Truth is that she was born into slavery in upstate New York some time in 1797 and freed in 1827. She spoke English as a second language, having been owned by a Dutch master; thus, her accent was likely Dutch rather than Southern Black dialect. She was involved with a range of religious, socialist, transcendental, women's rights, and antislavery groups. According to rhetoric scholar Roseann M. Mandziuk, your perception of her might be any of the following: "tragic victim of slavery, a religious pilgrim, a comic caricature, and a fiery orator and advocate for women's rights."[150]

Most people came to know Truth through the 1851 speech, but even it is a construction. The transcript of her speech, by Frances Dana Gage, a white woman suffrage and abolition advocate, was not created until twelve years later. It still defines how the speech is remembered, but both the content and the dialect preserved in Gage's version are vastly different from reports of the speech published in papers at the time.[151] The transcript uses speech styles found in racist caricatures and blackface minstrel shows; it does not reflect what historians know of how Truth spoke.[152] Truth's persona, as preserved in Gage's version of the speech, imposed on Truth the social perceptions of slaves as ignorant. Although illiterate, Truth was not ignorant, and there is no certainty that the speech attributed to Truth is anything like the words she actually spoke. Truth is unquestionably a historically significant rhetor. Nevertheless, who you think Truth was is a rhetorical construction; and that construction has an effect. Rhetorical scholars Mandziuk and Suzanne Pullon Fitch, in "The Rhetorical Construction of Sojourner Truth," compellingly argue, "paradoxically, because the colorful and complex crusader for multiple causes effectively is reduced to a single, false rhetorical moment in contemporary invocations of her, Truth's persona and power actually are diluted and diminished."[153] Perceptions of rhetors and their persona are filtered through the symbols of their times.

The very idea of a rhetor is also constructed. For years, the study of public address assumed that the rhetor of a text was a stable, singular entity. But as the example that opened this chapter illustrates, what we think of as the rhetor may not be so simple. Wendy Davis's filibuster was composed not only of her words, but also scores of other people's words. In addition, many people's access to Davis's speech was not the speech itself, but the fragments other people tweeted. For the people who followed only the tweets, their understanding of the filibuster came to them through other people's judgments about what was relevant to tweet.

Fourth, in a networked age, algorithms, rather than people, may author the web content you see. If you use Google to conduct your Internet searches (which 67.5 percent of people in the United States did as of March 2014),[154] who is the author of those results? The author is as much you (or at least a combination of information about you that the Google algorithm used) as it is the organizations and people who wrote the documents that the algorithm thought might interest you. What you find when you search the web is not some universal or objective result. Instead, it is the result of an algorithm specific to you, the audience.

In 2005, Google announced on its official blog that the results of its searches were now "customized search results for you based upon 180 days of search activity linked to an anonymous cookie in your browser."[155] Fifty-seven signals (including location, previous searches, bookmarked sites, and type of computer) would influence the search results. In 2009, Google refined this algorithm with its "social search" feature, which highlighted results from people you knew.[156] In 2012, it proclaimed "We're transforming Google into a search engine that understands not only content, but also people and relationships" by adding additional personalization features.[157] The result: When two people use exactly the same search terms, they do *not* receive the same search results. The audience, *you*, determine the content you receive. Internet activist Eli Pariser, author of *The Filter Bubble*, provided the following illustration. When the Deepwater Horizon Oil Rig exploded and began "spewing crude oil into the Gulf of Mexico," he asked two of his friends to conduct a search. Even though they were similar in terms of sex, location, education, and politics, their results were remarkably different: one saw "investment information about BP. The other saw news. For one, the first page of results contained links about the oil spill; for the other, there was nothing about it except for a promotional ad from BP."[158] This discovery led Pariser to title the second chapter of his book "The User is the Content."

The networked, digital age demands rethinking the relationship between the rhetor and the audience, recognizing that sometimes people are simultaneously neither and both. Media studies professor Siva Vaidhyanathan argues that people need to think of themselves not as Google's "customers," but "its product. We—our fancies, fetishes, predilections, and preferences—are what Google sells to advertisers."[159] Instead of reading what Google offers you as only the results of other rhetors' work, recognize that it is also a creation of you (or at least of Google's records of your past computer activities). Vaidhyanathan urges people to be critical of Google's "claims of omniscience, omnipotence, and benevolence" and quit granting its search results "inordinate and undeserved power."[160] That critical perspective is important when you participate in civic life. To embrace "global civic responsibility,"[161] people must resist Google's pressures to be enclaved in increasingly more personalized search worlds, where they see only that with which they already agree.

CONCLUSION

Understanding the rhetor is central to understanding rhetoric. Conceiving of the rhetor through the concept of persona enables us to recognize that the rhetor simultaneously invents and is invented by rhetorical action.

As a civic actor, you play various roles even as others' rhetoric constructs your role as a civic actor. Thus, when you contemplate producing a rhetorical action, pay attention to the way you produce yourself as rhetor in that action. Because seeking agreement with a claim invites assent not only to what was said, but who says it, attention to persona is central to understanding how rhetoric operates.

Persona is a holistic term referring to the ethos, role, identity, authority, and image a rhetor performs during a rhetorical act. When you communicate, you may do so from a range of personae. You can develop ethos, play a role, embrace an identity, claim authority, or project an image.

Regardless of where you find the resources for your performance, a persona is something you do, something you perform, not merely something you are.

You possess agency not only in relation to what you say, but as whom you say it. Despite this agency, rhetors are not free to construct just any persona, because audiences and societies place meaning and value on characteristics such as gender, race, socioeconomic status, and ethnicity.

Even as you consider your responsibilities as a rhetor, do not assume a rhetor (even if you can identify that individual) is the sole determinant of a symbolic action's meaning or content. Authorial intent alone does not determine the meaning of a rhetorical message. Multiple rhetors are always involved in the production of a single symbolic action. Persona may be constructed by others and imposed on a rhetor. Nonhuman agents (such as algorithms) may be restricting the rhetoric to which you are exposed.

DISCUSSION QUESTIONS

1.   What identity ingredients are available to you as you perform a persona? In what ways do you have the privilege (or opportunity) to choose between multiple personae? In what ways do the identities that others assign to you present an obstacle to your communication acts?
2.   Give an example of a person's character getting in the way of a persuasive message. How did the person's persona create obstacles for persuasion? What could the person have done to correct these obstacles?
3.   Think about the examples of Wendy Davis, Zach Wahls, and Joni Ernst. Did any of these rhetors engage in strategic essentialism? Why do you think they did—or did not? If they did, give examples.
4.   How might you describe how meaning is created in a postmodern world? For example, who is the rhetor in a contemporary song, a television show, or a web page? How might this description affect how you understand your own agency?

RECOMMENDED READINGS

Campbell, Karlyn Kohrs. "Agency: Promiscuous and Protean." *Communication and Critical/Cultural Studies* 2, no. 1 (March 2005): 1–19.

Ceccarelli, Leah. "Polysemy: Multiple Meanings in Rhetorical Criticism." *Quarterly Journal of Speech* 84, no. 4 (1998): 395–415.

Mandziuk, Roseann M., and Suzanne Pullon Fitch. "The Rhetorical Construction of Sojourner Truth." *Southern Communication Journal* 66, no. 2 (Winter 2001): 120–138.

Nakayama, Thomas K., and Robert L. Krizek. "Whiteness: A Strategic Rhetoric." *Quarterly Journal of Speech* 81 (August 1995): 291–309.

ENDNOTES

[1] Wendy Davis, "Texas Senate Filibuster of SB5 (06-25-2013) Transcript," transcribed Ana Mardoll, 2013, https://docs.google.com/document/d/1c0xuAFFc_6klQ1nrnQ72Qd9Y-o_uG8rSykO4wDgNqFQ/edit?pli=1. We would like to thank Zoe Russell for her research assistance on this example.

[2] Heather Kelly, "Texas Filibuster on Abortion Bill Rivets Online," CNN, June 26, 2013, http://www.cnn.com/2013/06/26/tech/social-media/texas-filibuster-twitter. This article contains many powerful images of the filibuster.

[3] *Senate Rules*, adopted by the 83rd Legislature (January 9, 2013): 10, State Resolution No. 4, http://www.senate.state.tx.us/rules/SenateRules83.pdf.

[4] Wendy Davis, @WendyDavisTexas, https://twitter.com/WendyDavisTexas/status /349377951877443584.

[5] As cited in Kelly, "Texas."

[6] Aja Romano, "How the Internet and Abortion Rights Won in Texas," *Daily Dot*, June 26, 2013, http://www.dailydot.com/politics/wendy-davis-filibuster-texas-sb5.

[7] Wendy Davis, "Wendy Davis: Why I Stood Up for Texas Women," *Washington Post*, July 15, 2013, http://www.washingtonpost.com/opinions/wendy-davis-why-i-stood-up -for-texas-women/2013/07/15/07bc14fa-eb67-11e2-aa9f-c03a72e2d342_story.html.

[8] Carl Franzen, "Why Did Networks Fail at Covering Wendy Davis's Epic Abortion Bill Filibuster in Texas?" *The Verge*, June 26, 2013, http://www.theverge.com /2013/6/26/4468130/wendy-davis-tx-abortion-bill-filibuster-media-fail.

[9] Romano, "How the Internet."

[10] Kelly, "Texas."

[11] Caitlin Dewey, "Wendy Davis 'Tweetstorm' Was Planned in Advance," *Washington Post*, June 26, 2013, http://www.washingtonpost.com/blogs/the-fix/wp/2013/06/26 /this-tweetstorm-was-planned-in-advance.

[12] Romano, "How the Internet."

[13] Romano, "How the Internet."

[14] Jennings Brown, "Wendy Davis' Filibuster by the Numbers," *Esquire*, June 26, 2013, http://www.esquire.com/blogs/politics/wendy-davis-filibuster-by-the-numbers-062613.

[15] Romano, "How the Internet."

[16] Dewey, "Tweetstorm."

[17] Dewey, "Tweetstorm."

[18] Craig Jarvis, "Activists Will Read Aloud Texas Sen. Wendy Davis' Filibuster," NewsObserver.com, November 2, 2013, http://www.newsobserver.com/2013/11/01 /3331338/activists-will-read-aloud-texas.html.

[19] Scott Collins, "Wendy Davis' Filibuster Ignites Twitter; Fans Rip News Networks," *Los Angeles Times*, June 26, 2013, http://articles.latimes.com/2013/jun/26/entertainment /la-et-st-wendy-davis-filibuster-20130626.

[20] Franzen, "Why Did Networks?"

[21] Franzen, "Why Did Networks?"

[22] Manny Fernandez, "In Texas, A Senator's Stand Catches the Spotlight," *New York Times*, June 26, 2013, http://www.nytimes.com/2013/06/27/us/politics/texas-abortion -bill.html?pagewanted=all.

[23] Davis, "Texas Senate Filibuster."

[24] James Jasinski, "Persona," in *Sourcebook on Rhetoric: Key Concepts in Contemporary Rhetorical Studies* (Thousand Oaks, CA: Sage, 2001), 429.

[25] Wayne Booth, *The Rhetoric of Fiction* (Chicago: University of Chicago Press, 1961), 74–75.

[26] Erving Goffman, *The Presentation of Self in Everyday Life* (New York: Anchor, 1959), 15, italics added.

[27] Randall Lake, "The Implied Arguer," in *Argumentation Theory and the Rhetoric of Assent*, ed. David C. Williams and Michael D. Hazen, 69–90 (Tuscaloosa: University of Alabama Press, 1990), 83.

[28] B. L. Ware and Wil A. Linkugel, "The Rhetorical *Persona*: Marcus Garvey as Black Moses," *Communication Monographs* 49 (1982): 50.

[29] Ware and Linkugel, "Rhetorical," 50.

[30] George A. Kennedy, *A New History of Classical Rhetoric* (Princeton, NJ: Princeton University Press, 1994), 57–60.

[31] Aristotle, *On Rhetoric*, trans. George A. Kennedy (New York: Oxford University Press, 1991), 2.1 [1378a].

[32] James M. May, *Trials of Character: The Eloquence of Ciceronian Ethos* (Chapel Hill: University of North Carolina Press, 1988).

[33] Cicero, *On the Ideal Orator (De Oratore)*, trans. James M. May and Jakob Wisse (New York: Oxford University Press, 2001), 2.182.

[34] Denise M. Bostdorff, "The Evolution of a Diplomatic Surprise: Richard M. Nixon's Rhetoric on China, 1952–July 15, 1971," *Rhetoric & Public Affairs* 5, no. 1 (Spring 2002): 31–56; Tyler Cowen and Daniel Sutter, "Why Only Nixon Could Go to China," *Public Choice* 97 (1998): 605–615.

[35] Michael Weiler and W. Barnett Pearce, eds., *Reagan and Public Discourse in America* (Tuscaloosa: University of Alabama Press, 1992), 4.

[36] Frank Newport, Jeffrey M. Jones, and Lydia Saad, "Ronald Reagan from the People's Perspective: A Gallup Poll Review," Gallup, June 7, 2004, http://www.gallup.com/poll/11887/ronald-reagan-from-peoples-perspective-gallup-poll-review.aspx.

[37] Weiler and Pearce, *Reagan*, 4.

[38] J. Jeffery Auer, "Acting Like a President; Or What Has Ronald Reagan Done to Political Speaking?" in *Reagan and Public Discourse in America*, ed. Michael Weiler and W. Barnett Pearce (Tuscaloosa: University of Alabama Press, 1992), 101.

[39] James Nuechterlein, in Stephen E. Ambrose, M. E. Bradford, Alonzo L. Hamby, Forrest McDonald, George H. Nash, James Nuechterlein, and Karl O'Lessker, "How Great Was Ronald Reagan?" *Policy Review* (Spring 1989), http://www.hoover.org/publications/policyreview/7908317.html.

[40] M. E. Bradford, in Ambrose, et al., "How Great."

[41] Karlyn Kohrs Campbell and Kathleen Hall Jamieson, *Deeds Done in Words: Presidential Rhetoric and the Genres of Governance* (Chicago: University of Chicago Press, 1990).

[42] Auer, "Acting," 101.

[43] Goffman, *Presentation*, 6.

[44] Goffman, *Presentation*, 35.

[45] Rita Alfonso and Jo Trigilio, "Surfing the Third Wave: A Dialogue between Two Third Wave Feminists," *Hypatia* 12, no. 3 (Summer 1997), 13, 7–16.

[46] Quoted in Dana Rosenblatt and Don Lemon, "White Valedictorian: A First for Historically Black Morehouse," "Black in America 2," CNN.com/US, http://www.cnn.com/2008/US/05/16/white.valedictorian/index.html.

[47] Joni Ernst, Joni Ernst for Senate, http://www.joniforiowa.com/home (accessed May 19, 2014).

[48] Jennifer Jacobs, "Republican Joni Ernst: 'Let's Make 'Em Squeal,'" *Des Moines Register*, May 8, 2014, http://www.desmoinesregister.com/story/news/2014/03/25/republican-joni-ernst-lets-make-em-squeal-/6860595.

[49] Ernst, "Make 'Em Squeal," https://secure.joniforiowa.com/donations/squeal/?source=carousel (accessed May 19, 2014).

[50] Joni Ernst, "Shot," http://www.washingtonpost.com/posttv/national/campaign-2014-joni-ernst-shot/2014/05/05/9c4b79e0-d486-11e3-8f7d-7786660fff7c_video.html (accessed July 14, 2015).

[51] Philip Rucker and Dan Balz, "How Joni Ernst's Ad about 'Castrating Hogs' Transformed Iowa's U.S. Senate Race," *Washington Post*, May 11, 2014, http://www.washingtonpost.com/politics/how-joni-ernsts-ad-about-castrating-hogs-transformed

-iowas-us-senate-race/2014/05/11/c02d1804-d85b-11e3-95d3-3bcd77cd4e11
_story.html.

[52] Adrien Katherine Wing, "Brief Reflections toward a Multiplicative Theory of Praxis and Being," in *Critical Race Feminism: A Reader*, ed. Adrien Katherine Wing, 27–34 (New York: New York University Press, 1997).

[53] The inspiration for the metaphor of ingredients comes from Audre Lorde, *Sister Outsider* (Trumansberg, NY: Crossing, 1984), 120.

[54] Donald E. Hall (ed.), *Muscular Christianity: Embodying the Victorian Age* (Cambridge, UK: Cambridge University Press, 1994).

[55] Herman Gray, "Black Masculinity and Visual Culture," *Callaloo* 18, no. 2 (1995): 401–405.

[56] Nick Trujillo, "Hegemonic Masculinity on the Mound: Media Representations of Nolan Ryan and American Sports Culture," *Critical Studies in Mass Communication* 8 (1991): 290–308.

[57] Patricia Hill Collins, "Shifting the Center: Race, Class, and Feminist Theorizing about Motherhood," in *Representations of Motherhood*, ed. Donna Bassin, Margaret Honey, and Maryle Mahrer Kaplan, 56–74 (New Haven: Yale University Press, 1994).

[58] Mari Boor Tonn, "Militant Motherhood: Labor's Mary Harris 'Mother' Jones," *Quarterly Journal of Speech* 82 (February 1996): 1.

[59] Tonn, "Militant," 5.

[60] Tonn, "Militant," 6.

[61] Kimberlé Crenshaw, "Demarginalizing the Intersection of Race and Sex: A Black Feminist Critique of Antidiscrimination Doctrine, Feminist Theory and Antiracist Politics," *University of Chicago Legal Forum* (1989): 59.

[62] Sandra Harding, "Subjectivity, Experience, and Knowledge: An Epistemology from/for Rainbow Coalition Politics," in *Who Can Speak? Authority and Critical Identity*, ed. Judith Roof and Robyn Weigman (Urbana: University of Illinois Press, 1995), 121.

[63] Thomas K. Nakayama and Robert L. Krizek, "Whiteness: A Strategic Rhetoric," *Quarterly Journal of Speech* 81 (August 1995): 291–309.

[64] Thomas A. Hollihan, *Uncivil Wars: Political Campaigns in a Media Age* (Boston: Bedford/St. Martin's, 2001), 56.

[65] Paula M. L. Moya, "Postmodernism, 'Realism,' and the Politics of Identity: Cherríe Moraga and Chicana Feminism," in *Feminist Genealogies, Colonial Legacies, Democratic Futures*, ed. M. Jacqui Alexander and Chandra Talpade Mohanty, 125–150 (New York: Routledge, 1997), 127.

[66] Katherine L. Milkman, Modupe Akinola, and Dolly Chugh, "What Happens Before? A Field Experiment Exploring How Pay and Representation Differentially Shape Bias on the Pathway into Organizations," April 23, 2014, available at Social Science Research Network: http://ssrn.com/abstract=2063742 or http://dx.doi.org/10.2139/ssrn.2063742.

[67] Milkman, et al., "What Happens?" 35.

[68] "First Muslim Elected to Congress," MSNBC, November 7, 2006, http://www.msnbc.msn.com/id/15613050.

[69] Moya, "Postmodernism," 132.

[70] Karlyn Kohrs Campbell, "Agency: Promiscuous and Protean," *Communication and Critical/Cultural Studies* 2, no. 1 (March 2005): 5.

[71] New York Times/CBS News Poll, "Whites, Race and the Election," August 9, 2008, http://www.nytimes.com/imagepages/2008/08/09/opinion/09blow_art.ready.html?scp=3&sq=whites%20race%20election&st=cse.

[72] Barack Obama, Presidential Inaugural Address, "What is Required: The Price and the Promise of Citizenship," January 20, 2009, http://www.americanrhetoric.com/speeches/barackobamabarackobamainauguraladdress.htm.

[73] Gayatri Chakravorty Spivak, *The Spivak Reader,* ed. Donna Landry and Gerald MacLean (New York: Routledge, 1996), 159, 214.

[74] Stokely Carmichael, "Black Power," October 1966, http://www.americanrhetoric.com/speeches/stokelycarmichaelblackpower.html.

[75] Robin Morgan, ed., *Sisterhood is Powerful* (New York: Random House, 1970).

[76] Vine Deloria, Jr., and Daniel R. Wildcat, *Power and Place: Indian Education in America* (Golden, CO: Fulcrum, 2001).

[77] Spivak, *Reader,* 214.

[78] Gloria Anzaldúa, "Bridge, Drawbridge, Sandbar or Island: Lesbians-of-Color *Hacienda Alianzas,*" in *Bridges of Power: Women's Multicultural Alliances,* ed. Lisa Albrecht and Rose M. Brewer, 216–231 (Philadelphia: New Society, 1990).

[79] John R. P. French and Bertram Raven, "The Bases of Social Power," in *Studies in Social Power,* ed. Dorwin Cartwright, 150–167 (Ann Arbor: University of Michigan Press, 1959).

[80] Mia Alexander-Snow, "Dynamics of Gender, Ethnicity, and Race in Understanding Classroom Incivility," *New Directions for Teaching & Learning* 99 (Fall 2004): 21–31.

[81] Bernice Resnick Sandler, "Women Faculty at Work in the Classroom, or, Why It Still Hurts To Be a Woman in Labor," *Communication Education* 40, no. 1 (January 1991), 6–15. A 2014 study of an online course confirms sex bias. In student assessments of an online course, regardless of the sex of the actual instructor, students rated the course taught by a professor with a traditionally male name higher than the course taught by a professor with a traditionally female name. See Lillian MacNell, Adam Driscoll, Andrea N. Hunt, "What's in a Name: Exposing Gender Bias in Student Ratings of Teaching," *Innovative Higher Education,* 39, no. 6 (December 2014), DOI 10.1007/s10755-014-9313-4.

[82] Travis L. Russ, Cheri J. Simonds, and Stephen K. Hunt. "Coming Out in the Classroom . . . An Occupational Hazard?: The Influence of Sexual Orientation on Teacher Credibility and Perceived Student Learning," *Communication Education* 51, no. 3 (2002): 311–324.

[83] Bonnie S. McElhinny, "'I Don't Smile Much Anymore': Affect, Gender and the Discourse of Pittsburgh Police Officers," in *Locating Power: Proceedings of the 1992 Berkeley Conference on Women and Language,* ed. Kira Hall and Birch Moonwomon, 386–403 (Berkeley, CA: Berkeley Women and Language Group, 1992).

[84] United Nations Security Council S/RES/1325 (2000), October 31, 2000.

[85] *United States National Action Plan on Women, Peace, and Security,* December 2011, 1.

[86] Hillary Rodham Clinton, "Remarks at the National Partnership for Women and Families," U.S. Department of State, June 21, 2012, http://www.state.gov/secretary/20092013clinton/rm/2012/06/193680.htm.

[87] Cornell West, *Race Matters* (Boston: Beacon, 1993): x–xi.

[88] Karlyn Kohrs Campbell, "The Rhetoric of Women's Liberation: An Oxymoron," *Quarterly Journal of Speech* 59 (February 1973): 75.

[89] Campbell, "Rhetoric," 75.

[90] Goffman, *Presentation,* 59.

[91] Judith Butler, *Gender Trouble* (New York: Routledge, 1990), 33.

92 Judith Butler, *Undoing Gender* (New York: Routledge, 2004), 1.

93 Butler, *Undoing Gender*, 1.

94 Jeff Zeleny, "Persistent 'Birthers' Fringe Disorients Strategists," *New York Times on the Web*, August 5, 2009, http://0-www.lexisnexis.com.unistar.uni.edu/us/lnacademic /results/docview/docview.do?docLinkInd=true&risb=21_T7120640045&format =GNBFI&sort=RELEVANCE&startDocNo=1&resultsUrlKey=29_T7120640054 & cisb=22_T7120640052&treeMax=true&treeWidth=0&csi=6742&docNo=12.

95 Amy Zimmerman, "Justin Bieber's No Good, Very Bad Year: Alleged Prostitutes, Reckless Driving, and More," Daily Beast, December 13, 2013, http://www .thedailybeast.com/articles/2013/12/13/justin-bieber-s-no-good-very-bad-year-alleged -prostitutes-reckless-driving-and-more.html.

96 Zimmerman, "Justin Bieber."

97 Zimmerman, "Justin Bieber."

98 Aaron Parsley, "Justin Bieber's Mug Shot Released," *People*, January 23, 2014, http:// www.people.com/people/article/0,,20778972,00.html; "Justin Bieber Just Won't Behave: Inside *Rolling Stone*'s New Issue," February 26, 2014, http://www .rollingstone.com/music/news/justin-bieber-just-wont-behave-inside-rolling-stones -new-issue-20140226.

99 Vanessa Grigoriadis, "Justin Bieber's God, Girls and Boatloads of Swag," *Rolling Stone*, March 3, 2011, http://www.rollingstone.com/music/news/justin-biebers-god-girls-and -boatloads-of-swag-20110303.

100 Josh Eells, "Justin Bieber: Mannish Boy," *Rolling Stone*, August 2, 2012, http://www.rollingstone.com/music/news/justin-bieber-mannish-boy-the-2012 -cover-story-20120802.

101 Grigoriadis, "Justin."

102 Daniel J. Boorstin, *The Image: A Guide to Pseudo-Events in America*, 25th anniversary ed. (New York: Athenaeum, 1987), 188–189.

103 Mesfin Fekadu, "Justin Bieber Is a Good Boy Gone Bad? Faces Adult Problems as He Struggles to Grow Up," *Huffpost Celebrity*, March 31, 2013, http://www .huffingtonpost.com/2013/03/21/justin-bieber-gone-bad_n_2924957.html.

104 Boorstin, *Image*, 185–193.

105 Boorstin, *Image*, 185.

106 Boorstin, *Image*, 188.

107 Fekadu, "Justin Bieber."

108 Fekadu, "Justin Bieber."

109 Grigoriadis, "Justin Bieber's God."

110 Mark Caro, "Ford Still Defined by Chevy: Fair or Not, Ford's Enduring Image as a Bumbler Was Sealed by a National Lampoon," *Chicago Tribune*, December 28, 2006, http://archives.chicagotribune.com/2006/dec/28/image/chi-0612280251dec28.

111 Funny or Die, "Presidential Reunion," March 2, 2010, http://www.funnyordie.com /videos/f5a57185bd/funny-or-die-s-presidential-reunion.

112 *Varnum v. Brien* 763 N.W.2d 862 (2009). See also Patricia A. Cain, "Contextualizing *Varnum v. Brien*: A 'Moment' in History," *Journal of Gender, Race and Justice* 13, no. 1 (Fall 2009): 27–57.

113 House Joint Resolution 6, http://coolice.legis.iowa.gov/Cool-ICE/default.asp ?Category=billinfo&Service=Billbook&frame=1&GA=84&hbill=HJR6.

114 YouTube, "The Top Political Videos of 2011," http://youtube-trends.blogspot. com/2011/12/top-political-videos-of-2011.html.

115 "Zach Wahls Speaks about Family," YouTube, February 3, 2011, http://www.youtube .com/watch?v=yMLZO-sObzQ. Transcribed by Kiran Dhillon, April Larson, and Catherine H. Palczewski.

[116] Zach Wahls, "A Note from Zach," Zach Wahls homepage, http://www.zachwahls .com.

[117] Roland Barthes, "The Death of the Author," translated by Richard Howard, *Aspen* 5–6 (1967), reprinted at http://www.tbook.constantvzw.org/wp-content/death _authorbarthes.pdf.

[118] Barthes, "Death," 5.

[119] Barthes, "Death," 6.

[120] Michael Calvin McGee, "Text, Context, and the Fragmentation of Contemporary Culture," *Western Journal of Speech Communication* 54, no. 3 (Summer 1990): 288.

[121] Campbell, "Agency," 5.

[122] "NCAA American Indian Mascot Ban Will Begin Feb. 1," ESPN College Sports, August 12, 2015, http://sports.espn.go.com/ncaa/news/story?id=2125735.

[123] For a description of the campaign, see http://www.ncai.org/news/articles/2014/05/19 /ncai-changethemascot-org-announce-launch-of-proudtobe-photo-project-joined-by -members-of-congress-local-elected-officials.

[124] "Resolution on the Washington, D.C., Football Team Name," December 12, 2013, http://www.changethemascot.org/wp-content/uploads/2013/12/Leadership -Conference-on-Civil-and-Human-Rights-Resolution.pdf.

[125] Marc Weinreich, "Redskins Name Controversy: 50 Senators Sign Letter to Roger Goodell Urging Name Change," *Sports Illustrated*, SI Wire, May 22, 2014, http:// tracking.si.com/2014/05/22/washington-redskins-senators-urge-name-change.

[126] Darren Rovell, "U.S. Senators Send Letters to Goodell," ESPN NFL, May 22, 2014, http://espn.go.com/nfl/story/_/id/10968190/senators-puts-pressure-washington -redskins-nfl.

[127] United States Patent and Trademark Office, "Amanda Blackhorse, Marcus Briggs-Cloud, Philip Gover, Jillian Pappan, and Courtney Tsotigh v. Pro-Football, Inc.," Cancellation No. 92046185, June 19, 2014, 2.

[128] Erik Brady and Megan Finnerty, "Washington Redskins Appeal Decision to Cancel Trademark," *USA Today*, August 14, 2014, http://www.usatoday.com.

[129] John Fiske, "Television: Polysemy and Popularity," *Critical Studies in Mass Communication* 3 (1986): 391–408; John Fiske, *Television Culture* (New York: Methuen, 1987).

[130] Fiske, "Television: Polysemy,"

[131] Celeste Michelle Condit, "The Rhetorical Limits of Polysemy," *Critical Studies in Mass Communication* 6, no. 2 (June 1989): 103–122, 103–104.

[132] Condit, "Rhetorical Limits," 106.

[133] Charles C. W. Cooke, "The Greatest Opening Line in the History of Campaign Commercials," *National Review Online*, March 25, 2014, http://www .nationalreview.com/corner/374147/greatest-opening-line-history-campaign -commercials-charles-c-w-cooke.

[134] Quoted in Frank James, "In Politics, Hog Castration Cuts through the Ad Clutter," *It's All Politics*, NPR.org, March 28, 2014, http://www.npr.org/blogs /itsallpolitics/2014/03/28/295949340/in-politics-hog-castration-cuts-through -the-ad-clutter.

[135] Douglas Gross, quoted in Rucker and Balz, "How Joni Ernst's Ad."

[136] Quoted in James, "In Politics."

[137] Stephen Colbert, "Bright Prospects for the GOP in 2016," *Colbert Report*, March 26, 2014, http://thecolbertreport.cc.com/videos/q8pyub/bright-prospects-for-the-gop -in-2016.

[138] Rucker and Balz, "How Joni Ernst's Ad."

[139] Carole Blair, Marsha S. Jeppeson, and Enrico Pucci, Jr., "Public Memorialization in Postmodernity: The Vietnam Veterans Memorial as Prototype," *Quarterly Journal of Speech* 77 (1991): 263–288, 269.

[140] "Waging War in Nigeria, and Seeking new Battlegrounds," *New York Times*, May 7, 2014, http://www.nytimes.com/2014/05/08/world/africa/boko-haram-seeks-new -battlegrounds.html.

[141] Nicholas Kristof, "'Bring Back Our Girls,'" *New York Times*, May 3, 2014, http:// www.nytimes.com/2014/05/04/opinion/sunday/kristof-bring-back-our-girls. html?smid=pl-share.

[142] Adam Nossiter, "Nigerians Hold Second Day of Protests over Mass Abductions," *New York Times*, April 30, 2014, http://www.nytimes.com/2014/05/01/world/africa /nigerians-hold-second-day-of-protests-over-mass-abductions.html.

[143] James Estrin, "The Real Story about the Wrong Photos in #BringBackOurGirls," *New York Times* Lens, http://lens.blogs.nytimes.com/2014/05/08/the-real-story-about-the -wrong-photos-in-bringbackourgirls/?_php=true&_type=blogs&_php=true&_type =blogs&smid=fb-nytimes&WT.z_sma=LE_TRS_20140508&bicmp=AD&bicmluk p=WT.mc_id&bicmst=1388552400000&bicmet=1420088400000&_r=3&.

[144] Quoted in Estrin, "Real Story."

[145] Quoted in Rucker and Balz, "How Joni Ernst's Ad."

[146] Martin Luther King, "I Have A Dream," August 28, 1963, AmericanRhetoric.com, http://www.americanrhetoric.com/speeches/mlkihaveadream.htm.

[147] Campbell, "Agency," 5.

[148] Sojourner Truth, "On Women's Rights," Ohio Women's Rights Convention, Akron, OH, 1851, available at http://people.sunyulster.edu/voughth/sojourner_truth.htm.

[149] Campbell, "Agency."

[150] Roseann M. Mandziuk, "Commemorating Sojourner Truth: Negotiating the Politics of Race and Gender in the Spaces of Public Memory," *Western Journal of Communication* 67, no. 3 (Summer 2003): 275.

[151] Roseann M. Mandziuk and Suzanne Pullon Fitch, "The Rhetorical Construction of Sojourner Truth," *Southern Communication Journal* 66, no. 2 (Winter 2001): 129. Thanks also to Bonnie Dow for insights concerning this example.

[152] Campbell, "Agency."

[153] Mandziuk and Fitch, "Rhetorical Construction," 135.

[154] "ComScore Release February 2014 U.S. Search Engine Rankings" (Press Release), March 18, 2014, https://www.comscore.com/Insights/Press_Releases/2014/3 /comScore_Releases_February_2014_U.S._Search_Engine_Rankings.

[155] Bryan Horling and Robby Bryant, "Personalized Search for Everyone," *Official Google Blog*, December 4, 2009, http://googleblog.blogspot.com/2009/12 /personalized-search-for-everyone.html.

[156] "Introducing Google Social Search: I Finally Found My Friend's New York Blog," *Official Google Blog*, October 26, 2009, http://googleblog.blogspot.com/2009/10 /introducing-google-social-search-i.html.

[157] "Search, Plus Your World," *Official Google Blog*, January 10, 2012, http://googleblog .blogspot.com/2012/01/search-plus-your-world.html.

[158] Eli Pariser, *The Filter Bubble* (New York: Penguin, 2011), 1–3.

[159] Siva Vaidhyanathan, *The Googlization of Everything (And Why We Should Worry)* (Los Angeles, CA: University of California Press, 2011), 3.

[160] Vaidhyanathan, *Googlization*, 3.

[161] Vaidhyanathan, *Googlization*, 3.

7

Audiences

KEY CONCEPTS

attitudes

audience

beliefs

consubstantiality

eavesdropping audience

first persona

fourth persona

identification

pathos

public emotions

rhetorical agency

rhetorical audience

second persona

third persona

values

On May 17, 1954, the United States Supreme Court issued the *Brown v. Board of Education* decision, authored by Chief Justice Earl Warren, ordering the desegregation of public schools. Typically, judges write decisions in a style appropriate for members of the legal profession, focusing their attention on either of two types of questions: questions of fact or questions of law. Trial courts focus on questions of fact to determine what happened, who was involved and to what degree, and whether there were extenuating circumstances. Appellate courts, including the US Supreme Court, address questions of law to determine whether the court has jurisdiction, whether the legal process was followed, which precedents and legal principles apply, whether the law is constitutional, and how the law should be interpreted.[1] Given the specialized audience and evidentiary requirements, legal decisions tend to participate in technical (rather than public) argument.

In *Brown v. Board of Education*, the Court clearly articulated the technical question of law at hand: "Does segregation of children in public schools solely on the basis of race, even though the physical facilities and other 'tangible' factors may be equal, deprive the children of the minority group of equal educational opportunities?"[2] The *Brown* decision was unique. The decision, examining whether the "separate but equal" doctrine established by *Plessy v. Ferguson*[3] in 1896 violated the equal protection clause of the Fourteenth Amendment, was not written in the typical legal style. Read aloud in its entirety from the bench, it overtly declared that precedent alone did not govern the Court's interpretation of the

Constitution. It was short, deliberately written in a length that could be repro-
duced on a single page of newsprint and understood by the general public. (The
Brown decision was approximately 1,775 words. By comparison, the 1973 *Roe v.
Wade* decision was approximately 11,667 words long.)

The *Brown* decision engaged in public argument, rather than technical legal
argument. The Court explained its reliance on social factors rather than on legal
precedent:

> Segregation of white and colored children in public schools has a
> detrimental effect upon the colored children. The impact is greater
> when it has the sanction of the law, for the policy of separating the races
> is usually interpreted as denoting the inferiority of the negro group. A
> sense of inferiority affects the motivation of a child to learn. Segregation
> with the sanction of law, therefore, has a tendency to [retard] the
> educational and mental development of negro children and to deprive
> them of some of the benefits they would receive in a racial[ly] integrated
> school system.
>
>   Whatever may have been the extent of psychological knowledge at
> the time of *Plessy v. Ferguson*, this finding is amply supported by modern
> authority. Any language in *Plessy v. Ferguson* contrary to this finding
> is rejected.[4]

Compared to most court decisions, this one is easily understood by a general
audience. It avoids the use of legal jargon, focuses on the question of right and
wrong, and refuses to be governed by *stare decisis* (the legal principle that says
that, in deciding a case, a court should be governed by the precedents set in
earlier decisions). The decision refers to the psychological effects of the *Plessy*
decision on schoolchildren, a type of evidence unexpected in an appellate court
ruling that typically would look to legal precedents (not their effects) to guide
the present case.

    What induced the Court to write such an atypical decision? Chief Justice
Warren, in his memoirs written two decades after the ruling, explains: "It was
not a long opinion, for I had written it so it could be published in the daily press
throughout the nation without taking too much space. This enabled the public
to have our entire reasoning instead of a few excerpts from a lengthier document."[5] By addressing the decision to the US public, and not just the technical
sphere of the law, the Court participated in the public discussion about race and
segregation.

    Much debate ensued. Appellate judge and judicial philosopher Learned
Hand derided the decision because it failed to follow precedent and did not
exhibit judicial restraint.[6] Judge Hand's reaction can be explained in part
because the decision was not written to persuade him as a fellow legal expert
and, thus, violated the technical rules of legal argument.

    Not everyone in the public was persuaded, however. In 1956, 101 southern
senators and congressional representatives wrote a Southern Manifesto that
"pledged the signers to exert 'all lawful means' toward reversing the Supreme

Court's desegregation decision."[7] In response, Warren pointed out that the decision did not seek to end desegregation by court decree but to give Congress and the public the ability to act politically to end segregation.[8] By targeting its discourse to a wider audience, the Court also helped persuade the general public of the social and political importance of desegregation. Separate could not be equal.

This example illustrates the important role of the audience in rhetoric. The Supreme Court was a rhetor possessing both referent and legitimate power, but it did not rely solely on that social power to persuade the country. "Because we say so" was not enough to persuade the public. The Court realized its decision, alone, could not create the necessary social change if only other lawyers and judges understood the decision: the society as a whole had to change.

In this chapter, we examine the complex relationship among audiences, rhetors, and symbolic actions. First, we discuss how rhetoric is adapted to audiences. Because rhetoric is addressed to other people, understanding audience is central to rhetoric. Second, we analyze audience agency, recognizing that not all audiences possess the same degree of power to effect change in the world. Third, we discuss how audiences can be adapted to rhetoric; or how rhetoric can constitute, or bring into being, a particular audience.

ADAPTING RHETORIC TO AUDIENCES

Audience is the element that distinguishes rhetoric from purely expressive forms of communication (such as shouting "ouch" when you stub your toe, or drawing for the pure pleasure of artistic creation). Rhetorical scholar Kenneth Burke identifies the central element of rhetoric as "its nature as *addressed*, since persuasion implies an audience."[9] He describes rhetoric as "the use of words by human agents to form attitudes or to induce actions in other human agents."[10] We would expand Burke's definition to include the use of any symbolic action, but we embrace his emphasis on rhetoric as addressed to other people—an audience. In the next section, we explain what we mean by "rhetoric as addressed." We then outline a few means of adaptation: identification, pathos, and values.

Rhetoric as Addressed

Recognizing that rhetoric is addressed to an audience is not as simple as it might first appear. **Audience** can mean *any person who hears, reads, or sees a symbolic action; the group targeted by a message, even if it is not present; or the group capable of acting in response to the message.* Multiple audiences may exist for any given symbolic action.

In interpersonal interactions, the audience is usually easy to identify: it is the person to whom you are speaking (unless—in a particularly middle-school moment—you are hoping that person will pass along what you said to your intended audience). Identifying the audience is more complicated in public address. The group of people who might hear a public address is large and diverse. Its members may carry conflicting expectations. Sometimes, everyone present is the intended recipient of the symbolic action; other times, only some of those present are the audience for the message.

When you speak to a large group, not every member may be part of the **rhetorical audience,** or *the audience that "consists only of those persons who are capable of being influenced by discourse and of being mediators of change."* In this definition, rhetoric scholar Lloyd Bitzer distinguishes a rhetorical audience from all those who might hear a speech.[11] For Bitzer, a rhetorical audience preexists the rhetorical action; it is empirically real and already possesses the ability to implement the change that the rhetor calls for. In Bitzer's approach, rhetors and critics need to analyze the audience members who are agents capable of bringing about the action, not just anyone who might receive the message.

Bitzer's understanding of the rhetorical audience finds its roots in the classical tradition, which defined the audience as that group who was capable of acting in response to a message. Aristotle points out, "A speech consists of three things: a speaker and a subject on which he [or she] speaks and someone addressed, and the objective of the speech relates to the last."[12] Aristotle argues that rhetoric is persuasive to a *particular* audience, which he defines as those who make judgments concerning the issue or issues at hand. The objective of the speech is, in turn, determined by the audience, as the audience holds the power to act on the message.[13]

Philosophers Chaïm Perelman and Lucie Olbrechts-Tyteca[14] note the classical rhetorical tradition's emphasis on "the discursive ways of acting upon an audience, with a view to winning or increasing its adherence to the theses that were presented to it for its endorsement."[15] They agree with Aristotle, explaining: "It is indeed the audience which has the major role in determining the quality of argument and the behavior of orators."[16] Whenever you consider the function of symbolic action, it is essential to assess the audience to whom the rhetor addresses the message. For example, in a graduation ceremony, the students may appreciate a commencement address their parents condemn.

You can probably recall times when you made rhetorical choices according to the audience to whom you spoke; that is, you adapted to the rhetorical audience. For example, when requesting an extension on a paper due for a class, you probably tailor your request to the professor from whom you are requesting the extension. Some professors might be more persuaded by a pity appeal, while others would only be persuaded if you proved you had not procrastinated. You might not even make such a request to some professors because you believe they are not likely to grant the request. In all these instances, you frame your message to speak to the particular audience. You adapt because your audience determines and delimits the objective of your symbolic action.

When identifying the audience(s) for a rhetorical act, remember that multiple audiences may be targeted. When President Barack Obama spoke at Cairo University on June 4, 2009, commentators noted that he addressed multiple audiences in his attempt to respond to the problems that arose in US-Muslim relations in the wake of 9/11. NBC's chief White House correspondent, Chuck Todd, explained during the NBC *Nightly News* that President Obama sought "to talk to three or four different audiences, including explaining Islam to Americans, explaining America to Muslims [in the Arab world], and trying to jumpstart a conversation between Israelis and the Arab world."[17] The speech was not simply a single message to a homogenous audience, but a complex set of messages directed to heterogeneous audiences that operate from diverse cultural orientations, participate in distinct ideologies, and possess a range of different values, beliefs, and attitudes. Although he spoke to multiple audiences, he attempted to create identification with all of them. To speak effectively to all these audiences, President Obama reportedly began working on the speech even before he was elected to office.[18]

Appealing to an Audience

How might you go about adapting to an audience? A range of overlapping rhetorical techniques exists. First, you can seek to create identification, or a sense of commonality between you and the audience. Second, you can employ pathos appeals, trying to put the audience members in a state of mind where they are most open to the arguments offered. Third, you can work with factors that influence audience perceptions, which include attitudes, values, and beliefs. These factors guide audiences' assessments of symbolic action, sometimes justifiably and sometimes in the form of unwarranted bias.

Identification. The concept of identification plays a central role in describing the relationship between rhetors and audiences. As we discussed in Chapter 1, **identification** is *a communicative process through which people are unified into a whole on the basis of common interests or characteristics.*[19] Through identification, you make a connection with the audience on a psychological level, not simply on a demographic level. On the surface you might identify with another student simply because of the shared demographic characteristic—the other person is also a student. However, identification can be deeper if you do not take it for granted, but actively produce it through rhetoric. If you wanted to create identification on the basis of shared student status, you would not simply take for granted that other students would agree with you. Instead, you would use evidence based on experiences students share, speak from the persona of a student, and emphasize values and concerns that are prominent in students' lives.

Rhetors and audience members are both similar and different. Identification can be achieved by emphasizing similarities even while respecting differences. Burke explains that "two persons may be identified in terms of some principle they share in common, an 'identification' that does not deny their distinctness."[20] Notice that Burke does not reduce identification to shared demographic characteristics, but argues that a shared principle must be identified. Identification does not require that a rhetor and audience member be identical, only that points of consubstantiality be identified. These moments of **consubstantiality,** in which *two distinct things momentarily become part of a whole,* are at the heart of persuasion and rhetoric. Burke posits, "Here is perhaps the simplest case of persuasion. You persuade a man [or woman] only insofar as you can talk his [or her] language by speech, gesture, tonality, order, image, attitude, idea, *identifying* your ways with his [or hers]."[21] If you are connected to people in some way, you probably have a better chance of persuading them than if you were a stranger or completely alien to them.

Understanding the process of identification is central to understanding rhetoric as addressed. Thus, critics need to explore how rhetors seek to create identification with their audiences. In President Obama's 2009 speech at Cairo University,[22] he sought to create identification with each of several audiences. He opened by identifying with Muslims, using the customary Muslim greeting "Assalaamu alaykum."[23] He reaffirmed that identification by outlining his other personal connections to Islam: "[M]y father came from a Kenyan family that includes generations of Muslims. As a boy, I spent several years in Indonesia and heard the call of the azaan at the break of dawn and at the fall of dusk. As a young man, I worked in Chicago communities where many found dignity and peace in their Muslim faith."[24] He identified with Christians by testifying to his own Christianity, saying "I'm a Christian."[25] He highlighted the identification of political interests between the United States and Israel: "America's strong bonds with Israel are well known. This bond is unbreakable. It is based upon cultural and historical ties, and the recognition that the aspiration for a Jewish homeland is rooted in a tragic history that cannot be denied."[26] Finally, he created identification between the United States and Arab countries by recognizing the common interests they have in stopping the suffering of Palestinians:

> On the other hand, it is also undeniable that the Palestinian people—
> Muslims and Christians—have suffered in pursuit of a homeland. For
> more than 60 years they've endured the pain of dislocation. Many wait
> in refugee camps in the West Bank, Gaza, and neighboring lands for a life
> of peace and security that they have never been able to lead. They endure
> the daily humiliations—large and small—that come with occupation.
> So let there be no doubt: The situation for the Palestinian people is
> intolerable. And America will not turn our backs on the legitimate
> Palestinian aspiration for dignity, opportunity, and a state of their own.[27]

Even though President Obama spoke to audiences with different, if not conflicting, interests and identities, he was able to create the impression that he as a person, and the United States as a nation, were consubstantial with Muslims and Christians, Arabs and Israelis. His need to create identification with multiple audiences can be explained by the various audiences' abilities to effect the change for which he called.

Pathos. As discussed in Chapter 1, Aristotle defined **pathos** as an artistic proof *that leads the audience "to feel emotion."* More specifically, pathos appeals lead audience members to particular emotional states of mind. Aristotle's treatment of human emotions was perhaps the earliest systematic treatment of psychology.[28] He placed emotions in contrasting pairs: anger/calmness; friendliness/enmity; fear/confidence; shame/shamelessness; kindness/unkindness; pity/indignation; envy/emulation. The pairs were not meant to imply that one emotion one was good and the other bad. Even anger, an emotion people are often told they should suppress, has a place. Aristotle's theory of rhetoric, communication scholars Kenneth S. Zagacki and Patrick A. Bolyn-Fitzgerald explain, "maintains that there are some rhetorical situations where the public expression of anger is appropriate and where its absence is morally blameworthy."[29] Nevertheless, political communication scholar Martin Medhurst notes, "Until quite recently, appeals to the emotions or feelings of an audience were regularly condemned but seldom studied."[30]

Aristotle explained that rhetors must consider the emotional state of the audience[31] because people make judgments differently depending upon their state of mind.[32] You have thought about the emotional state of your audience when you have considered someone's mood before initiating a difficult conversation. Suppose you want to talk to a housemate about redistributing chores. If you ask a mutual friend what kind of mood your housemate is in before you talk, you are considering the emotional state of the audience in constructing your request. You might even choose not to make the request that day if you conclude that your housemate is not in the appropriate state of mind to consider your request, or you might think about how to alter your housemate's state of mind to be more open to a conversation about shared housework. Pathos appeals recognize the effect of emotion on an audience's receptiveness, so they are chosen to induce a particular emotion in order to enhance a persuasive appeal.

For example, fear is a strong emotion that can lead people to make particular choices they might not make otherwise. For Aristotle, fear is "pain or agitation derived from the imagination of a future destructive or painful evil."[33] But fear cannot be triggered merely by saying "Be afraid, be very afraid!" Rather, Perelman and Olbrechts-Tyteca observe, images provided by a rhetor invoke emotions in audiences.[34] A rhetor who is able to construct images to which an audience attaches emotions can move the audience to a particular emotional state in which it is more open to persuasion.

To illustrate the complexities involved in a pathos appeal, consider the 2009 outbreak of the H1N1 (also known as swine flu). The World Health Organization declared the flu outbreak a pandemic, outlining health concerns and warnings because the strain had never been seen before and was affecting people on several continents.[35] Although "pandemic" refers to how widespread a disease is, and not necessarily its mortality rate, the label likely induced fear because of movies such as *Pandemic* (2007), *Outbreak* (1995), *28 Days Later* (2003), and *Contagion* (2011), all of which threatened death to everyone. Media coverage of H1N1 intensified fear by including images of people wearing protective masks, footage of Vice President Joseph Biden remarking that he would advise his own family members to avoid public transportation and confined places,[36] and local news reports of confirmed cases and deaths. The anticipation of a flu outbreak and the rhetorical depictions of the flu cases created a situation in which public fear could take control of people's decision making.

To counter this fear, President Obama issued a statement noting that the government was monitoring the situation and outlining specific steps it was taking. He concluded with practical advice: "I've asked every American to take the same steps you would take to prevent any other flu: Keep your hands washed; cover your mouth when you cough; stay home from work if you're sick; and keep your children home from school if they're sick."[37] In other words, he sought to counter the heightening fear by treating H1N1 as any other strain of flu, not as something new and uniquely frightening. By explaining that people could take control of the situation, he attempted to give them confidence to overcome the fear.

The nonrational responses to the outbreak also highlight how fear can be a problematic appeal. Often, people's fear reactions are not proportional to the actual threat. Because H1N1 was initially called the "swine flu," some people thought they should quit eating pork. Egypt went so far as to order the slaughter of all 300,000 of the country's pigs, even though no evidence existed of swine-to-human infection.[38] Philip Alcabes, a professor of allied health, explores the power of dread in *Dread: How Fear and Fantasy have Fueled Epidemics from the Black Death to the Avian Flu.* He argues that epidemics have a particular power to fascinate human beings, even though they may not be the most serious threat. For example, he points out that in the United States, 40,000 people die each year from motor-vehicle crashes, yet automobile accidents are not described as an epidemic. Yet, imagine if 40,000 people a year died from H1N1. Terror would ensue. (The Centers for Disease Control estimate 9,820 H1N1 related deaths occurred from April to November 2009.) So why is epidemic rhetoric so powerful? Alcabes argues that there are two reasons. First, "officials or entrepreneurs make use of an epidemic threat to create politically and financially useful lessons."[39] Second, fear. Alcabes highlights: "We humans dread death."[40]

Public Emotion. A rhetor may induce an emotion in an audience. Rhetors and audiences can also display emotions such as anger, passion, or disgust. Such display, unfortunately, is often thought of as undermining public deliberation. Rhetoric scholars Robert Hariman and John Lucaites note that both rhetorical and political theory have "constructed, studied, and policed . . . emotional display" through "general suppression or suspicion."[41] If public emotional display is suppressed in public deliberation, however, "then emotional display can become a mode of dissent"[42] against a purely rational approach to decision making. For example, the emotional displays behind the "Black Lives Matter" protests, following the deaths of young black men in police custody, powerfully demonstrate the value and humanity of black lives.

Scholars have begun to attend to the importance of **public emotions,** which, according to Hariman and Lucaites, are *collective expressions of feeling that are "crucial elements of democratic deliberation, judgment, and action" that "comprise a language for collective life."*[43] To understand rhetoric in civic life, you need to understand the role of emotion in civic life. Hariman and Lucaites emphasize that "public reason has to be underwritten by public emotion" and that "if citizenship is to be an embodied identity, an actual mode of participation in decision making . . . , then it has to be articulated in a manner that encourages emotional identification with other civic actors."[44] Identification is not simply a rational calculation that another person shares an interest; it is an emotional connection through which one *feels* connected to another.

Public emotion moves beyond Aristotle's theory of pathos "as an individual subjective state" and instead treats emotions as "shared (intersubjective) moods created by" rhetorical action.[45] For example, when President Obama spoke about the 2012 killing of seventeen-year-old Trayvon Martin by a person who used Florida's "stand your ground" laws as a defense, he employed identification and spoke to a public grief when he said "Obviously this is a tragedy. I can only imagine what these parents are going through. When I think about this boy I think about my own kids and I think every parent in American should be able to understand why it is absolutely imperative that we investigate every aspect."[46]

As another example, consider public vigils such as those held for the twenty-six people who were killed in 2012 in the Sandy Hook Elementary School shooting in Newtown, Connecticut;[47] the six students at the University of California, Santa Barbara, who were killed in the 2014 Isla Vista shooting;[48] and the two Las Vegas police officers who were killed in a shooting spree in 2014.[49] As rhetoric scholar Dianne Emily Cram notes, "Public vigils are a rich site to explore how local, regional, or national publics respond to and publicize acts of violence" and exemplify "how grief can constitute a political community."[50] When people come together to grieve the loss of community members, they form a political community.

Cram's study of the vigils held for Angie Zapata, a transwoman murdered by an acquaintance, highlights an "emotional politics of visuality" in which Angie's self-portraits were displayed on T-shirts worn at community vigils, and by her family members sitting in the courtroom during her murderer's trial. The family's and community's public displays of grief countered the defense team's attempt to exclude Angie from the community because she was trans. Cram notes that family, friends, and allies participated in citizenship as "a category of embodied sociality, public emotionality, and performative enactment."[51] They wore images of Angie on their bodies, close to their hearts. They displayed public grief for a person whom the prosecution tried to present as deserving of disgust rather than mourning. And they performed their belief that Angie was part of their community by keeping her images alive in their midst.

When studying emotion, do not reduce it to a mere supplement to persuasive appeals. According to Hariman and Lucaites, one should recognize that public emotion is part of civic life, "intricately woven into the material fabric of a society" because "emotions flood language and all other symbolic media in a society."[52] Of course, not every emotional display, nor every attempt to induce an emotional reaction, is good for civic life. Just as with any rhetorical action, you need to assess not only the effectiveness of the action, but also its ethics.

Jon Stewart's *Daily Show* pointed out the tensions that exist in a world filled with public fear. On June 5, 2014, he aired a segment titled "Keep Gun and Carry On" in response to "open carry" demonstrations during that spring. The segment explored the problem posed by open carry advocates, who feared erosion of their Second Amendment rights, and who also tended to be "stand your ground" advocates who believed they had the right to use deadly force in fear-inducing situations.[53] Opponents said the open carry protesters induced fear themselves, by displaying weapons in restaurants and other public places. The *Daily Show* asked: when open carry advocates enter a place, and the other people in the place perceive a threat, what are the other people to do? The conclusion: "We are at the intersection of open carry road and stand your ground place." Stewart then showed a series of clips of people declaring their need to use their rights or lose them and their fear of groups of armed people in public places, as well as an explanation of stand your ground laws and a criticism of the legal "duty to retreat to avoid danger." Stewart showed the National Rifle Association as arguing that you have the right to carry a weapon that terrifies another person, while the terrified person has the right to respond with deadly force, thus creating a "perpetual violence machine" of public fear.

Values, Beliefs, and Attitudes. When rhetors perform a persona in order to create identification with an audience, their performances are influenced by the audience's expectations. Sociologist Erving Goffman observes that every performance, from public address to interpersonal exchange, "is 'socialized,' molded, and modified to fit into the understanding and expectations of the society in which it is presented."[54] Thus, any message is produced for an audience. It is consciously and unconsciously framed by the audience's social expectations. Audiences are not just passive recipients of a message, but active influences on the rhetor.[55]

If a rhetorical act is intended to move audiences in some way, from creating virtual experience to inducing action, the rhetor needs to understand the factors affecting the audience members' perceptions. Audiences are part of larger cultures that frame their worldviews and that constrain and enable rhetors' choices. Just as rhetors' cultures and ideologies influence their rhetorical choices, an audience's culture and ideology directs the way it interprets messages. Ideology influences what makes sense to rhetors and audiences by shaping their values, beliefs, and attitudes. Although it is nearly impossible to distinguish values, beliefs, and attitudes as embedded within symbolic action, for the purposes of analysis it is sometimes helpful to differentiate among them.

Values are *organizing principles and orientations that people use to interpret the world around them, including symbolic actions.* Philosopher R. Jay Wallace defines a value as "a conception of the good,"[56] a standard against which things can be judged. For example, freedom is a value toward which most audiences in the United States feel a positive orientation. The value suggests that maximization of freedom is the goal of governance and the ideal condition in which to live. When rhetors refer to principles based on freedom, such as individual choice, they are basing their arguments on a shared value.

Beliefs are *sets of knowledge that are grounded in people's value orientations.* When people come to think of an idea as incontrovertibly true, they no longer recognize it as a social construction. When you say, "Freedom is the defining and highest value of US democracy," in effect, you are saying, "*I believe* that freedom is the defining and highest value of US democracy." You do not think of your belief as changeable if you have a freedom/democracy value orientation, but as an objective truth. Although beliefs and values are resistant to change, like ideology, they are not immune to change. The fact that people convert from one religion to another indicates that changes in value orientation are possible, causing corresponding changes in beliefs.

Attitudes are *positive or negative feelings toward some person, thing, or idea.* They represent likes and dislikes, feelings of right and wrong, and approval or disapproval. Values and beliefs inform your attitudes, but do not absolutely determine them. Just because someone's value orientation is similar to yours does not mean that person will have the same attitudes you do. For example, you might share many religious values with another person, but have different beliefs about same-sex marriage and, thus, different attitudes toward it.

The distinction among beliefs, values, and attitudes is evident in recent debates about the release of classified documents regarding National Security Agency's (NSA) surveillance activities. In June 2013, the federal government was rocked by one of the "most significant leaks in US political history,"[57] when Edward Snowden, a former consultant to the NSA, released documents demonstrating that the NSA was spying on US citizens and on world leaders such as German Chancellor Angela Merkel.[58] Snowden had copied top secret documents that exposed how the NSA had "obtained direct access to the systems of Google, Facebook, Apple, and other US internet giants" in order to see e-mails, videos, photos, chats, and so on.[59] Many believed this surveillance was against the law. The NSA director absolutely denied the existence of such a program when Congress questioned him.[60] Many people, including the journalists with whom he shared the documents, considered Snowden a "whistleblower" who had exposed dangerous practices of secrecy and violations of privacy. In contrast, the US government considered Snowden's acts to be criminal, and charged him with three felonies under the Espionage Act.[61]

Depending on whether you value personal liberty or legal order, you may consider Snowden to be a noble whistleblower—or a traitorous criminal. If you believe government secrecy should always be suspect, you might conclude it is sometimes acceptable to break the law in service of a higher good. If you believe secrecy is necessary, you might feel that it is never acceptable to violate government secrecy rules. John Cassidy, a blogger for *The New Yorker*, said Snowden was "a hero. . . . In revealing the colossal scale of the U.S. government's eavesdropping on Americans and other people around the world, he has performed a great public service that more than outweighs any breach of trust he may have committed."[62] In contrast, Jeffrey Toobin, senior legal analyst for CNN, declared Snowden "a grandiose narcissist who deserves to be in prison."[63] Demonstrating an even harsher attitude, US Representative Mike Rogers, who chaired the House Permanent Select Committee on Intelligence, declared Snowden a "traitor."[64]

The health care debate in the United States also illustrates how values, beliefs, and attitudes affect perceptions of an issue. One common concern expressed by opponents of a single-payer system is that it might undermine citizens' freedom of choice (a value) concerning their health care. Michael Tanner, director of health and welfare studies at the Cato Institute (a nonprofit public policy research foundation based on the principles of limited government, free markets, individual liberty, and peace), argues:

The broad and growing trend is to move away from centralized government control and to introduce more market-oriented features.

The answer then to America's health care problems lies not in heading down the road to national health care but in learning from the experiences of other countries, which demonstrate the failure of centralized command and control and the benefits of increasing consumer incentives and choice. . . . [A] closer look at countries with national health care systems shows that those countries have serious problems of their own, including rising costs, rationing of care, lack of access to modern medical technology, and poor health outcomes. Countries whose national health systems avoid the worst of these problems are successful precisely because they incorporate market mechanisms and reject centralized government control. In other words, socialized medicine works—as long as it isn't socialized medicine.[65]

His opposition to a national or single-payer health care program is based on particular values, beliefs, and attitudes informed by a free market economic system. From that perspective, anything that does not embrace the value of freedom of choice might be labeled as socialism, which is perceived to be capitalism's opposite. If you value choice as the central principal of freedom in a capitalist economy, then you might have a negative attitude toward any program that you perceive limits your choice. We could describe Tanner's values, beliefs, and attitudes as follows:

Value: Free market (capitalism) is good; centralized government control (socialism) is bad.

Belief: Market-oriented features, such as consumer incentives and choice, work.

Attitude: Any government program that centralizes control or limits individual health care choice is suspect.

His negative attitude toward a government program is guided by the belief in individual choice and the values of a free market economy.

To respond to Tanner, a person advocating a single-payer system could focus on beliefs, attitudes, or values. For example, you could challenge his belief that the market always works, that choice actually exists now, or that free enterprise profit motives work in health care; or you could challenge his attitude that government is inept. Altering someone's values is more difficult because it requires altering core organizing principles. It would require you to challenge ideographs, perhaps by offering a competing ideograph: you could argue that access to health care is a right, not a privilege for those who can afford to pay; or that the value of individual choice does not apply to this case.

For an example of a person operating with a different set of values, beliefs, and attitudes, we turn to a radio interview with bioethicist Arthur Caplan,[66] of the Center for Bioethics and the Department of Medical Ethics at the University of Pennsylvania, and one of *Discover* magazine's ten most influential people in science. Like Tanner, Caplan points to other countries' approaches to health care, not to argue that the market is the best way to solve the health care crisis, but to show how particular values influence US beliefs about health care and attitudes toward its provision. Caplan explains that Germany, Taiwan, and England do not say you must work in order to have health insurance. It is not a perk of work or something you earn. Caplan argues this value orientation from a moral perspective, stating: "Morally, it doesn't make sense to say you have to earn your health insurance." He argues that if people are sick and without health insurance, the choice is to leave them on the street or care for them. To argue that people earn or deserve health insurance because they have jobs seems morally wrong to him. Thus, Caplan argues for universal coverage not because it is efficient or an investment, but on the grounds that it is a basic human right—and "more than anything else about the right." He seeks to make access to health insurance a prerequisite to the free market, rather than as a good provided by it.

Caplan's interview illustrates the central role values play. He is adamant that a solution to the problem of health care costs and access cannot be achieved until US citizens hold a set of common values. Unless people in the United States see health care as an ethical issue, rather than as an economic one, no solution is possible. People, he says, will apologize for the millions of people lacking health insurance but argue that "they don't have a right to it." For Caplan, aligning values is a prerequisite for changing beliefs, attitudes, and policy.

The point is that audiences are not passive recipients of a message, but active participants in the process of rhetoric. Audiences matter. In addition, if a rhetor is seeking to induce some sort of action in an audience, the rhetor must consider the limits of audience agency, of the audience's ability to take the action. You can try to adapt rhetoric to an audience in order to create a desired change, or you can try to adapt the audience to your rhetoric. In order to show why rhetors must sometimes adapt audiences to rhetoric, we need to explain the concept of audience agency.

AUDIENCE AGENCY

Recall, from Chapter 1, that Karlyn Kohrs Campbell defines **rhetorical agency** as "*the capacity to act, that is, to have the competence to speak or write [or engage in any form of symbolic action] in a way that will be recognized or heeded by others in one's community.*"[67] We amended her definition to include competence in visual rhetoric, as well as in the verbal forms of speaking and writing.

Both rhetors and audiences possess agency. Just as rhetors may possess various degrees of agency, depending on their positions in the socioeconomic order, cultural norms, or ideologies, so, too may audiences possess various degrees of agency, or various capacities to act on or respond to rhetors' symbolic actions. Campbell argues that traditional understandings of the audience, as the group to whom a symbolic action is addressed and that is capable of enacting the called-for change, are overly limiting. Not all audiences who are addressed already possess agency; some are not already rhetorical audiences, but must be constituted as such. In some cases, rhetors may need to construct audiences as agents of action.

For example, in the rhetoric of women's liberation that emerged in the 1960s and 1970s, a central goal of the rhetoric was empowerment: convincing women that they could, indeed, be agents of change. Campbell argues, "The [traditional] concept of the audience does not account for a situation in which the audience must be *created under the special conditions* surrounding women's liberation."[68] Women activists faced the challenge of figuring out how to perform the public role of rhetor when social demands on how to perform the role of woman pushed them to stay out of public affairs. In addition, although women were not equal under the law, not all women perceived inequality to be a problem. Those who did were not sure they had the ability to effect change in the law or culture. As women appealed to other women to act, they had to make clear that audience members possessed the agency with which to act; they had to construct audiences as having agency as one of their characteristics.

Given the complexities associated with the interplay of rhetoric and audience, you need to decide whether the audience is (1) the group of people who happened to receive the symbolic action, (2) the group or groups targeted by the rhetor, (3) the group with whom the rhetor sought to create identification, or (4) the audience called into being by the rhetoric. We now turn to an analysis of this last form of audience.

ADAPTING AUDIENCES TO RHETORIC

Audiences, even those already capable of acting, are molded by the rhetoric addressed to them. Rhetoric scholar Barbara Biesecker suggests that identities of audiences and of rhetors are not fixed; that rhetorical action is "an event that makes possible the production of identities and social relations."[69] Rhetors can call audiences into being. An audience can be understood not only as Bitzer's objectively identifiable empirical audience that is capable of acting, but also as a rhetorical creation.

A rhetor addresses an audience in the hope of affecting that audience in some way. However, people often take for granted what constitutes the audience, and simply assume that the audience is the people who receive the message. Think about your preparations for a speech in class. How much time do you spend thinking about who your audience is? Do you just assume it is your classmates? Or your instructor? In other words, do you assume that an audience preexists the message? Or do you think about how you could actually change the character of the class with your message, how you could target your message to only some people in your class, or even how you might address an audience who is totally absent? Your audience might come into being because of your message.

One of the most analyzed examples of bringing an audience into existence is found in scholarly examinations of "the people." Political discourse often takes for granted that a group known as "the people" exists, and is the group to whom political discourse is directed. For example, Speaker of the House John Boehner attempted to delay implementation of the Affordable Care Act (ACA) in 2013, declaring "It's time for the Senate to listen to the American people just like the House has listened to the American people and to pass a one-year delay of ObamaCare and a permanent repeal of the medical device tax."[70]

The ACA, signed into law in 2010, expanded health care coverage by improving the affordability of health insurance, expanding coverage of adult children under their parents' plans, increasing access to insurance for people with preexisting conditions, expanding Medicaid, subsidizing low-income people's plans, and creating health care exchanges. The law also contained an individual mandate: everyone must have health insurance or pay a penalty. In order to stop full implementation of the individual mandate, House and Senate Republicans attempted to link an ACA implementation delay to a vote on whether to fund the government. The Republican-controlled House passed three funding bills, each of which either did not fund the ACA or delayed its implementation. When the Democrat-controlled Senate would only consider a funding bill that did neither of those things, a government shutdown ensued. Boehner, attempting to induce the Senate to act, argued that a delay was what "the American people" wanted, but what people was he talking about? Polls from that period indicate that 59 to 63 percent of respondents did not think it was right to shut down the government in order to stop the ACA.[71]

Who, then, are "the people?" Communication scholar Michael C. McGee points out that the concept of "the people" is a rhetorical construction. He explains that "'the people,' even though made 'real' by their own belief and behavior, are still essentially a mass illusion. In purely objective terms, the only human reality is that of the individual; groups, whether as small as a Sunday school class or as big as a whole society, are infused with an artificial identity."[72] The individuals who compose an audience are real, but the belief that the collection of individuals represents a unit is a social construction. To say an audience is a social construction does not mean, however, that it is illusory or meaningless. How an audience is constructed matters to how it acts. Rhetoric matters.

Just as McGee analyzes "the people," scholars have explored the rhetorical creation of other groups. Such a creation is not the result of a single rhetorical act, but the repeated invocation of that group across multiple messages. When a rhetor constructs an audience as a group of people who identify with one another, a second persona has been created. Yet, whenever identification is created within a group, division is also created. Thus, an assessment of the third persona, the excluded or denied audience, is necessary. The rhetor may also create an audience that is a fourth persona, an audience that is indirectly or surreptitiously addressed.

Second Persona

The **first persona** is *the author implied by the discourse.* Rhetorical theorist Edwin Black posits that just as the rhetor may construct a persona for the "I" who is speaking, so too may a rhetor create a **second persona** for the "you" to whom the rhetor speaks, *the implied audience for whom a rhetor constructs symbolic actions.*[73] He challenges critics to look beyond the immediate audience and to recognize the larger social context in which symbolic action worked.

At the beginning of this chapter we discussed the example of the Supreme Court decision in *Brown v. Board of Education,* which was written for the general public. The use of public reasoning rather than legal precedent pointed to the wider public as the implied audience, the second persona, rather than to the narrower legal community. In addition, the public is but a particular type of public—one who is called to accept the equal humanity of all people. When analyzing the audience from this perspective, a critic does not ask: To what group of bodies does a rhetor speak? Instead, the more pertinent question is: What auditor is implied within the rhetorical discourse? Identifying the implied auditor is important, Black says, because "the critic can see in the auditor implied by a discourse a model of what the rhetor would have his [or her] real auditor become."[74]

Examples of second persona abound in public discourse. Franklin Delano Roosevelt's "the only thing we have to fear is fear itself,"[75] George H. W. Bush's "thousand points of light,"[76] and Bill Clinton's "spring reborn in the world's oldest democracy, that brings forth the vision and courage to reinvent America,"[77] all demonstrate appeals to an audience to be something it is not yet. Such rhetoric holds out ideals to which an audience can aspire, yet presents those ideals as already in existence, thus constituting the US citizenry as beings of a particular type (fearless, philanthropic, reborn). Each of these presidents spoke to a particular "you," constructing the audience so that it was adapted to fit the rhetorical message, rather than adapting symbolic message to fit some objectively existing audience.

Politicians often say that "we" need to do something, or that "we" as a nation believe in particular values, when in reality they are referencing a particular segment of the population who, they hope, will vote for them. Granted, it is extremely easy to fall into using "we," especially when a person wants to create a sense of identification and community. As Burke points out, however, whenever identification is used, one must "confront the implications of *division*. . . . Identification is compensatory to division."[78] When a group says "we are alike," it implies that others are *not* like them.

In one example, Manuel Miranda (a former aide to Senator Bill Frist), in a Heritage Foundation luncheon explaining how conservatives could woo the Latino/a vote, said: "Hispanic polls, Hispanic surveys, indicate that Hispanics think just like everyone else. We're not like African-Americans. We think just like everybody else."[79] By identifying Hispanics with "everybody else," then dissociating African Americans from that group, Miranda suggests that "everyone else" as a group does not literally include everyone else. Instead, Miranda's rhetoric says "everyone else" means whites, of which African Americans are not a part. Whenever a rhetor seeks to create identification among group members, disidentification is a necessary counterpart. If you create an "us," you also create a "them." From this dialectic relationship comes the reality of a third persona, an "it" who not only is excluded from address, but whose humanity is questioned.

Third Persona

If rhetors can call an audience into being, they can construct other people as lacking being. Rhetorical scholar Philip Wander labels these people the **third persona**: *"audiences not present, audiences rejected or negated through the speech and/or the speaking situation."*[80]

Recognition of such an audience is essential in tracking the ways in which rhetoric enacts ideology. Rhetoric can affirm a set of values, beliefs, and attitudes; so too can it erase or deny values. Thus, whenever we study the audience that is present in the rhetorical action, we should also ask about the audience members who have been excluded. Wander explains, "What is negated through the Second Persona forms the silhouette of a Third Persona—the 'it' that is not present, that is objectified in a way that 'you' and 'I' are not. . . . The potentiality of language to commend being carries with it the potential to spell out being unacceptable, undesirable, insignificant."[81] The third persona is the group treated as an object and dehumanized, while the second persona is the audience treated as a subject and recognized or commended. If the first persona is an "I," and the second persona a "you," then the third persona is an "it."

The construction of a third persona involves more than speaking to one group of people rather than another. Rhetors cannot speak to all people all the time. In some instances, messages really are meant for a particular audience. In many cases, however, constituting one audience by including some people necessarily excludes other people. For Wander's purposes, the third persona

> refers not merely to groups of people with whom "you" and "I" are not to identify, who are to remain silent in public, who are not to become part of "our" audience or even be allowed to respond to what "we" say. Beyond its verbal formulation, the Third Persona draws in historical reality, so stark in the twentieth century, of peoples categorized according to race, religion, age, gender, sexual preference, and nationality, and acted upon in ways consistent with their status as non-subjects. The Third Persona directs our attention to beings beyond the claims of morality and the bonds of compassion.[82]

In calling some groups into being, rhetoric also can deny the existence of others, or erase them. Wander's exploration of the third persona emphasizes the power of language to name, interpret, and construct human understandings of reality.

The clearest contemporary example of the construction of a third persona can be found in the recent debates over immigration. Instead of addressing the people who immigrate illegally (attempting to persuade them not to cross the border illegally), critics of illegal immigration turn them into a third persona, dehumanizing them by describing them as a "flood," "tide," "pollutant," "infestation," "infection," and "disease."[83] Once denied humanity, immigrants are also denied compassion. They become an infestation to be fought, a tide to be held back, a pollutant in need of cleansing.

A third persona can be created even when speakers appear to use inclusive language. Political scientist Jane Mansbridge analyzes the use of the collective "we" in political discourse to represent a particular few by making invisible a distinct other. She explains, "'We' can easily represent a false universality, as 'mankind' used to."[84] Thus, "the very capacity to identify with others can easily be manipulated to the disadvantage of" a subordinated group because "[t]he transformation of 'I' into 'we' brought about through political deliberation can easily mask subtle forms of control."[85] The earlier example from Manuel Miranda is one illustration.

The perniciousness of a falsely universal "we" is evident even in a speech that was meant to celebrate inclusion. In 1998, President Bill Clinton delivered a speech announcing his Race Initiative, a series of national conversations and policy initiatives meant to counter racism in the United States. His speech provides a review of history, which uses the inclusive language of "we," but actually excludes some groups by their absence from the historical occurrences he outlines. As you read this passage, ask yourself: who is "we"?

> *We* were born with a Declaration of Independence which asserted that *we* were all created equal and a Constitution that enshrined slavery. *We* fought a bloody Civil War to abolish slavery and preserve the Union, but *we* remained a house divided and unequal by law for another century. *We* advanced across the continent in the name of freedom, yet in so doing *we* pushed Native Americans off their land, often crushing their culture and their livelihood. *Our* Statue of Liberty welcomes poor, tired, huddled masses of immigrants to our borders, but each new wave has felt the sting of discrimination. In World War II, Japanese-Americans fought valiantly for freedom in Europe, taking great casualties, while at home their families were herded into internment camps. The famed Tuskegee Airmen lost none of the bombers they guarded during the war, but their African-American heritage cost them a lot of rights when they came back home in peace. [emphasis added][86]

The first "we" most likely does not refer to everyone, even though Clinton had earlier noted that the audience was composed of people of "many backgrounds." It refers only to white US citizens of European descent, the group granted rights by a "Constitution that enshrined slavery." Clearly, not everyone was born equal under the nation's founding documents. Although Clinton does recognize that "we" drove Native Americans off their lands, such a use of "we" is interesting because US citizens of European descent were primarily responsible for the genocide against Native Americans. This statement also implies they (Native Americans) are not part of us (Americans).

The use of "we" is complicated further by the use of truncated passives. In the first few sentences, a "we" is present. Yet, when Clinton begins to describe specific examples of discrimination, the agent of those acts becomes invisible. He explains that each new wave of immigrants "felt the sting" of discrimination, but does not identify who discriminated against them. Japanese families were "herded into internment camps," but Clinton does not identify who herded them. Finally, their "African-American heritage cost" the Tuskegee Airmen their rights; the bigotry of white people ("we") did not deny them their "inherent dignity." Thus, responsibility either lies with no one, or with the heritage of those who faced racism. Although Clinton's historical narrative might attempt to expose the hypocrisy of the dominant myths of democracy, exploration, and equality, it fails to unmask the agency of white Americans.

Indirectly Addressed Audiences

Thus far, we have explored the first persona (the implied author), the second persona (the implied audience), and the third persona (the excluded and denied audience). However, an audience type is missing from this list: the covertly or indirectly addressed audience. Scholars have written about two types of covert audiences: the fourth persona and the eavesdropper.

The **fourth persona** is *an audience who recognizes that the rhetor's first persona may not reveal all that is relevant about the speaker's identity, but maintains silence in order to enable the rhetor to perform that persona.* A rhetor's persona may require an act of passing, or convincing an audience that the rhetor's persona participates in an acceptable identity category. Gays and lesbians sometimes attempt to pass as straight. Historically, some light-skinned black people passed as white. During the Holocaust, some Jewish children passed as Christian.

Rhetors often engage in rhetorical passing, while some members of the audience are aware of the attempt to pass. Rhetoric scholar Charles E. Morris III posits that rhetors enact passing "by means of the *fourth persona*: a collusive audience constituted by the textual wink. Similar to its counterpart, the second persona, the fourth persona is an implied auditor of a particular ideological bent."[87] Passing only works if those who know otherwise enable the rhetor to perform the passing persona.

Any time you perform a persona that may not comport with the persona with which you most often operate, you rely on those people who know you differently to not interfere with your performance. You call an audience to silence, but unlike the third persona's forced silence, in this case "silence functions constructively as the medium of collusive exchange. What is not said is nonetheless performative, a speech act that can be read by certain audiences, and calls those audience members into being as abettors."[88]

An **eavesdropping audience** is *an audience whom the rhetor desires to hear the message despite explicitly targeting the message at a different audience.*[89] The targeting can be for two reasons: (1) to limit room for response by, or the agency of, the eavesdropping audience or (2) to allow the eavesdropping audience to feel empowered because they are not being criticized even as they hear criticisms made against others.

In the first instance, by constructing the audience as an eavesdropper, the rhetor limits the options available to the audience; they were not being addressed, so how can they answer or participate in the discussion? Such a technique is used when a rhetor wants to center attention on one audience in order to maximize its agency while limiting the agency of the eavesdropping audience. One powerful example is Gloria Anzaldúa's "Speaking in Tongues: A Letter to Third World Women Writers," originally written for *Words in Our Pockets*, the Feminist Writers' Guild handbook, and later appearing in two other books, *This Bridge Called My Back* and *Speaking For Ourselves: Women of the South.* All three books bring the letter to an audience broader than the one addressed in its title.[90]

Although the letter is addressed to third world women writers, first world women are an audience. In the introduction to their edited volume, *This Bridge Called My Back,* Cherríe Moraga and Anzaldúa note that the book was created "to express to all women—especially to white middle-class women—the experiences which divide us as feminists."[91] They exhort teachers to use the book in the classroom, again recognizing that white women and men are an audience. In her foreword to the second edition of the book, Anzaldúa further clarifies the existence of a complex audience: "We have come to realize that we are not alone in our struggles nor separate nor autonomous but that we—white black straight queer female male—are connected and interdependent. We are each accountable for what is happening down the street, south of the border or across the sea."[92] Anzaldúa knows first world women and men will read the letter, and she wants them to.

Despite (or because of) the broader audience, Anzaldúa addresses her letter to a specific group of women, "third world women," not to all women (and not to any men). She linguistically and symbolically reinforces this address in the first and last sections by opening with "mujeres de color,"[93] thus placing first world women (and men) in the position of reading mail unintended for them. The letter moves first world women (and all men) to a borderland when it does not address the letter to them, while it empowers third world women by literally addressing them as the primary subjects. First world women are written about. Men are just absent; they are not written to, nor do they write. Men and first world women are uninvited eavesdroppers and, hence, suspended from a critical position. They are reminded of their difference. They are reminded that they constantly tokenize third world women and deny differences among women. The letter reverses power relationships so that first world women are allowed access without input, a condition third world women often experience.

The letter's exclusive address operates heuristically; it creates, for anyone not a third world woman, an experience of exclusion from which they can learn. Men and white women are made to feel like outsiders, much like women of color are made to feel in US culture. They learn, through experience, what it means to be marginalized, and why marginalization might make people angry. When the letter addresses third world women, it knocks first world readers out of the position that assumes white, Western, and male is the norm.

At the same time that the letter marginalizes men and first world women, it creates a community in which third world women are foregrounded. It quotes numerous third world women and, through this referencing, physically and mentally centers them. They are written to and they write. They are visualized early in the letter: "Black woman huddles over a desk. . . . [A] Chicana fanning away mosquitos. . . . Indian woman walking to school or work. . . . Asian American, lesbian, single mother, tugged in all directions by children, lover or ex-husband, and the writing."[94] The letter reminds women of color of their worth and ability, of their identification with Anzaldúa, when she refers to her "brown hand clutching the pen."[95] Third world women are present throughout the letter in all the examples, thus proving that third world women *do* write. In addition, the letter form operates as empowerment by eliciting a response, encouraging women of color to write back—to answer the letter.[96]

The empowerment function points to the second way that eavesdropping can be used. Criticisms can be targeted at one audience, in the hope that another audience overhears them and feels empowered. Communication scholars Michael Leff and Ebony A. Utley argue that Martin Luther King, Jr., did just this in his "Letter From Birmingham Jail."[97] Even though the letter is addressed to "My Dear Fellow Clergymen"—meaning white moderates—it also indirectly speaks to all black people in the United States as King attempts to persuade them to risk their bodies in nonviolent civil disobedience in civil rights protests. White moderates appear unwilling to act, so it is other African Americans who must be persuaded to push for social change. Leff and Utley argue King's persona in his letter is one

> that black readers can use as a model for becoming effective actors on the American scene. Like King, they can view themselves as agents who need not and will not suffer the indifference of white moderates, who can break free of external restraints without losing self-restraint, and who can work from within American society to make fundamental changes in the way they conceive themselves and are conceived by others.[98]

Eavesdroppers' agency was not limited, but enhanced, as King modeled for them how to be an agent of action.

These examples demonstrate that the overtly addressed audience is not necessarily the only, or even the most important, audience. A careful analysis of symbolic acts is required to understand the range of audiences to whom a rhetor speaks and the way in which the rhetoric positions that audience.

CONCLUSION

Rhetoric is always addressed to another. Thus, a rhetor must consider ways to create identification with the audience or to construct the audience in such a way that it is capable of being an agent of action. Audience members should consider whether they are, indeed, the audience spoken to (the second persona), simply a body that is present, or a person who is excluded from address. The concept of audience is much more complex than just the random group of people who may be gathered to hear a message. Audiences are actively created by rhetors. They are active recipients of messages, able to accept, question, and reject them.

Civic engagement means engaging with another, an audience, but rhetoric may also exclude people. If the ideal civil society is, in principle, open to the participation of all people, then rhetoric that excludes people works against civic ideals.

DISCUSSION QUESTIONS

1. Advertisers market their products to particular audiences. Find an advertisement and figure out who its audience is. Does the advertisement construct an audience? How? What beliefs, attitudes, or values does

the advertisement use? Does it create audience agency? Does it use identification or pathos?

2. When you attempt to persuade someone, how does your audience frame and alter your message? What is an example of a particular audience that was difficult for you to persuade?

3. Identify a recent event in which expressing and sharing emotion played a central role in the rhetoric. In what ways did that emotion limit or open up possibilities for audiences' response to the event? How did others respond to these emotional expressions?

4. Find a symbolic action and identify the audiences. Who is the second persona? Who is the third persona? What is the audience agency?

5. Politicians frequently refer to "the people." Find examples of these references and explain how the rhetor is defining and conceptualizing "the people." Who is the second persona in the reference to "the people?" Who is the third persona? What does the politician's use of "the people" tell you about the rhetor and the issue?

RECOMMENDED READINGS

Balthrop, V. William. "Culture, Myth, and Ideology as Public Argument: An Interpretation of the Ascent and Demise of 'Southern Culture.'" *Communication Monographs* 51 (December 1984): 340–352.

Black, Edwin. "The Second Persona." *The Quarterly Journal of Speech* 56 (April 1970): 109–119.

McGee, Michael Calvin. "In Search of 'The People': A Rhetorical Alternative." *The Quarterly Journal of Speech* 61 (1975): 235–249.

Wander, Philip. "The Third Persona: An Ideological Turn in Rhetorical Theory." *Central States Speech Journal* 35 (Winter 1984): 197–216.

ENDNOTES

[1] Stephen Toulmin, Richard Rieke, and Allan Janik, *An Introduction to Reasoning*, 2nd ed. (New York: Macmillan, 1984), 306–307.

[2] *Brown v. Board of Education*, 347 U.S. 483 (1954). National Park Service, Department of the Interior, National Historic Site, http://www.nps.gov/brvb.

[3] *Plessy v. Ferguson*, 163 U.S. 537 (1896).

[4] *Brown v. Board of Education.*

[5] Earl Warren, *The Memoirs of Earl Warren* (New York: Doubleday, 1977), 3.

[6] Ed Cray, *Chief Justice: A Biography of Earl Warren* (New York: Simon and Schuster, 1997), 351; Learned Hand, *The Bill of Rights* (Cambridge: Harvard University Press, 1958).

[7] "The Southern Manifesto," *Time*, March 26, 1956, http://www.time.com/time/magazine/article/0,9171,824106,00.html; Jim Newton, *Justice for All: Earl Warren and the Nation He Made* (New York: Riverhead, 2006), 339–340; Ed Cray, *Chief Justice*, 320, 342–347.

[8] Warren, *Memoirs*, 297.

[9] Kenneth Burke, *A Rhetoric of Motives* (University of California Press, 1969), 38.

[10] Burke, *Rhetoric*, 41.

[11] Lloyd F. Bitzer, "The Rhetorical Situation," *Philosophy and Rhetoric* 1 (1968): 7, italics added.

[12] Aristotle, *On Rhetoric*, trans. George A. Kennedy (New York: Oxford University Press, 1991), 47 [1.3.1; 1358b].

[13] Aristotle, *On Rhetoric*, 1.2.11 [1356b], 47 [1.3.1; 1358b].

[14] Lucie Olbrechts-Tyteca's contributions to this work often are undervalued. For a discussion of her scholarship, see Barbara Warnick, "Lucie Olbrechts-Tyteca's Contribution to *The New Rhetoric*," in *Listening to Their Voices: The Rhetorical Activities of Historical Women*, ed. Molly Meijer Wertheimer (Columbia: University of South Carolina Press, 1987), 69–85.

[15] Chaïm Perelman, "Rhetoric and Philosophy," *Philosophy and Rhetoric* 1 (1968): 15.

[16] Chaïm Perelman and Lucie Olbrechts-Tyteca, *The New Rhetoric*, trans. John Wilkinson and Purcell Weaver (Notre Dame, IN: University of Notre Dame Press, 1969), 24.

[17] "Highlights of Obama's Speech to Muslim World," NBC *Nightly News* 6:30 p.m. EST, NBC News Transcripts, June 4, 2009.

[18] "Highlights."

[19] Burke, *Rhetoric*, 20.

[20] Burke, *Rhetoric*, 21.

[21] Burke, *Rhetoric*, 55.

[22] Barack Obama, "A New Beginning: Speech at Cairo University," June 4, 2009, http://www.americanrhetoric.com/speeches/barackobama/barackobamacairouniversity.htm.

[23] Stephen Prothero, "In Egypt, a Theologian in Chief," *USA Today*, June 8, 2009.

[24] Obama, "New Beginning," para. 7.

[25] Obama, "New Beginning," para. 7.

[26] Obama, "New Beginning," para. 29.

[27] Obama, "New Beginning," para. 31.

[28] George A. Kennedy, *Classical Rhetoric and Its Christian and Secular Tradition*, 2nd ed. (Chapel Hill: University of North Carolina Press, 1999), 89.

[29] Kenneth S. Zagacki and Patrick A. Bolyn-Fitzgerald, "Rhetoric and Anger," *Philosophy and Rhetoric* 39, no. 4 (2006): 292.

[30] Martin J. Medhurst, "A Tale of Two Constructs," in *Beyond the Rhetorical Presidency*, ed. Martin J. Medhurst, xi–xxv (College Station: Texas A&M Press, 1996), xvii.

[31] Aristotle, *On Rhetoric*, 2.1.2 [1378a].

[32] Aristotle, *On Rhetoric*, 1.2.5 [1356a].

[33] Aristotle, *On Rhetoric*, 2.5.1.

[34] Perelman and Olbrechts-Tyteca, *New Rhetoric*, 147.

[35] World Health Organization, "Influenza A(H1N1)," http://www.who.int/csr/disease/swineflu/en/index.html.

[36] "Foot-in-Mouth Disease: The Vice President Isn't Helping to Calm an Anxious Public," *Washington Post*, http://www.washingtonpost.com/wp-dyn/content/article/2009/04/30/AR2009043002660.html, May 1, 2009.

[37] Barack Obama, Press Conference, April 30, 2009, http://www.whitehouse.gov/blog/09/04/30/The-Presidents-Remarks-on-H1N1.

[38] Coco Ballantyne, "Will Egypt's Plans to Kill Pigs Protect It from Swine — Sorry, H1N1 Flu?" *Scientific American*, May 1, 2009, http://www.scientificamerican.com/blog/60-second-science/post.cfm?id=will-egypts-plans-to-kill-pigs-prot-2009-05-01.

[39] Philip Alcabes, *Dread: How Fear and Fantasy Have Fueled Epidemics from the Black Death to the Avian Flu* (Philadelphia: PublicAffairs, 2009), 4.

[40] Alcabes, *Dread*, 4.

[41] Robert Hariman and John Louis Lucaites, "Dissent and Emotional Management in a Liberal-Democratic Society: The Kent State Iconic Photograph," *RSQ: Rhetoric Society Quarterly* 31, no. 3 (Summer 2001): 6.

[42] Hariman and Lucaites, "Dissent," 6.

[43] Robert Hariman and John Louis Lucaites, *No Caption Needed: Iconic Photographs, Public Culture, and Liberal Democracy* (Chicago: University of Chicago Press, 2007), 139.

[44] Hariman and Lucaites, *No Caption*, 161.

[45] Hariman and Lucaites, *No Caption*, 162.

[46] Barack Obama, "President Obama Statement on Trayvon Martin Case," CNN, March 23, 2012, http://whitehouse.blogs.cnn.com/2012/03/23/president-obama-statement-on-trayvon-martin-case.

[47] Bill Chappell, "In Grief-Stricken Newtown, Vigils and Support for Victims and Families," National Public Radio, December 14, 2012, http://www.npr.org/blogs/thetwo-way/2012/12/14/167293608/in-grief-stricken-newtown-vigils-and-support-for-victims-and-families.

[48] Adam Poulisse and Susan Abram, "Thousands Mourn Slain UC Santa Barbara Students in Public Vigil," *Los Angeles Daily News*, May 27, 2014, http://www.dailynews.com/general-news/20140527/thousands-mourn-slain-uc-santa-barbara-students-in-public-vigil.

[49] "Slain Las Vegas Police Officers Remembered at Vigil," NBC News, June 10, 2014, http://www.nbcnews.com/storyline/vegas-cop-killers/slain-las-vegas-police-officers-remembered-vigil-n127131.

[50] Emily Dianne Cram, "'Angie Was Our Sister': Witnessing the Trans-Formation of Disgust in the Citizenry of Photography," *Quarterly Journal of Speech* 98, no. 4 (November 2012): 416.

[51] Cram, "Angie," 417.

[52] Hariman and Lucaites, *No Caption*, 162.

[53] John Stewart, "Keep Gun and Carry On," *Daily Show*, June 5, 2014, http://thedailyshow.cc.com/videos/mplvs5/keep-gun-and-carry-on.

[54] Erving Goffman, *The Presentation of Self in Everyday Life* (New York: Anchor, 1959), 34–35.

[55] Goffman, *Presentation*, 9.

[56] R. Jay Wallace, *Responsibility and the Moral Sentiments* (Cambridge, MA: Harvard University Press, 1994), 53.

[57] Glenn Greenwald, Ewen MacAskill, and Laura Poltras, "Edward Snowden: The Whistleblower behind the NSA Surveillance Revelations," *Guardian*, June 9, 2013, http://www.theguardian.com/world/2013/jun/09/edward-snowden-nsa-whistleblower-surveillance.

[58] Laura Smith-Spark, "Germany's Angela Merkel: Relations with U.S. 'Severely Shaken' over Spying Claims," CNN World, October 24, 2013, http://www.cnn.com/2013/10/24/world/europe/europe-summit-nsa-surveillance; Hubert Gude, Jörg Schindler, and Fidelius Schmid, "Merkel's Mobile: Germany Launches Investigation into NSA Spying," Spiegel Online International, June 4, 2014, http://www.spiegel.de/international/germany/germany-expected-to-open-investigation-into-nsa-spying-on-merkel-a-973326.html.

[59] Glenn Greenwald, "NSA Prism Program Taps in to User Data of Apple, Google and Others," *Guardian*, June 6, 2013, http://www.theguardian.com/world/2013/jun/06/us-tech-giants-nsa-data?guni=Article:in%20body%20link.

[60] Glenn Greenwald, "Boundless Informant: The NSA's Secret Tool to Track Global Surveillance Data," *Guardian*, June 11, 2013, http://www.theguardian.com/world/2013/jun/08/nsa-boundless-informant-global-datamining.

[61] Glenn Greenwald, "On the Espionage Act Charges against Edward Snowden," *Guardian*, June 22, 2013, http://www.theguardian.com/commentisfree/2013/jun/22/snowden-espionage-charges.

[62] John Cassidy, "Why Edward Snowden Is a Hero," *New Yorker*, June 10, 2013, http://www.newyorker.com/online/blogs/johncassidy/2013/06/why-edward-snowden-is-a-hero.html.

[63] Jeffrey Toobin, "Edward Snowden Is No Hero," *New Yorker*, June 10, 2013, http://www.newyorker.com/online/blogs/comment/2013/06/edward-snowden-nsa-leaker-is-no-hero.html.

[64] Laura Barron-Lopez, "Rogers Says Snowden Committed Treason," *The Hill*, December 22, 2013, http://thehill.com/policy/technology/193832-rep-rogers-says-snowden-committed-treason.

[65] Michael Tanner, *The Grass Is Not Always Greener: A Look at National Health Care Systems around the World*, Policy Analysis No. 613, March 18, 2008, 1–3, http://www.cato.org/pubs/pas/pa-613.pdf.

[66] Arthur Caplan, "Bioethics and the Obama Administration," interview with Terry Gross, *Fresh Air*, December 17, 2008, http://www.lexisnexis.com/us/lnacademic/search/homesubmitForm.do. Audio recording available at http://www.npr.org/templates/story/story.php?storyId=98387481.

[67] Karlyn Kohrs Campbell, "Agency: Promiscuous and Protean," *Communication and Critical/Cultural Studies* 2 (2005): 3, italics added.

[68] Karlyn Kohrs Campbell, "The Rhetoric of Women's Liberation: An Oxymoron," *The Quarterly Journal of Speech* 59 (February 1973): 85.

[69] Barbara Biesecker, "Rethinking the Rhetorical Situation from within the Thematic of *Différance*," *Philosophy and Rhetoric* 22 (1989): 126.

[70] John Boehner, "Speaker Boehner: Time for the Senate to Listen to the American People," Speaker.gov, September 30, 2013, http://www.speaker.gov/speech/speaker-boehner-time-senate-listen-american-people.

[71] Adam Wollner, "Government Shutdown? Not over Obamacare, Polls Say," NPR: It's All Politics, September 24, 2013, http://www.npr.org/blogs/itsallpolitics/2013/09/23/225510362/government-shutdown-not-over-obamacare-polls-say.

[72] Michael Calvin McGee, "In Search of 'The People': A Rhetorical Alternative," *Quarterly Journal of Speech* 61 (1975): 242.

[73] Edwin Black, "The Second Persona," *Quarterly Journal of Speech* 56 (April 1970): 109–119.

[74] Black, "Second Persona," 113.

[75] Franklin Delano Roosevelt, "First Inaugural Address," March 4, 1933, http://www.americanrhetoric.com/speeches/fdrfirstinaugural.html.

[76] George H. W. Bush, Inaugural Address, January 20, 1989.

[77] William Jefferson Clinton, Inaugural Address, January 21, 1993.

[78] Burke, *Rhetoric*, 22.

[79] "Manuel Miranda: Hispanics 'Not Like African-Americans, and We Think Just Like Everybody Else,'" "Manuel Miranda Third Branch Conf Call Racist?" https://www.youtube.com/watch?v=McfZHn0asyU (accessed June 6, 2015).

[80] Philip Wander, "The Third Persona: An Ideological Turn in Rhetorical Theory," *Central States Speech Journal* 35 (Winter 1984): 209, italics added.

81 Wander, "Third Persona," 209.

82 Wander, "Third Persona," 216.

83 J. David Cisneros, "Contaminated Communities: The Metaphor of 'Immigrant as Pollutant' in Media Representations of Immigration," *Rhetoric and Public Affairs* 11, no. 4 (Winter 2008): 569–602; Anne Demo, "Sovereignty Discourse and Contemporary Immigration Politics," *Quarterly Journal of Speech* 91 (2005): 291–311; Hugh Mehan, "The Discourse of the Illegal Immigration Debate: A Case Study in the Politics of Representation," *Discourse and Society* 8 (1997): 249–270; Kent A. Ono and John M. Sloop, *Shifting Borders: Rhetoric, Immigration, and California's Proposition 187* (Philadelphia: Temple University Press, 2002); and Otto Santa Ana, *Brown Tide Rising: Metaphors of Latinos in Contemporary American Public Discourse* (Austin: University of Texas Press, 2002).

84 Jane Mansbridge, "Feminism and Democracy," in *Feminism and Politics*, ed. Anne Phillips, 142–158 (New York: Oxford University Press, 1998), 152.

85 Mansbridge, "Feminism," 143.

86 William Jefferson Clinton, "Remarks at the University of California San Diego Commencement Ceremony in La Jolla, California," *Public Papers of the Presidents of the United States: William J. Clinton* (Washington: GPO, 1998), 877, italics added.

87 Charles E. Morris III, "Pink Herring and the Fourth Persona: J. Edgar Hoover's Sex Crime Panic," *Quarterly Journal of Speech* 88, no. 2 (May 2002): 228–244, 230.

88 Morris, "Pink Herring," 230.

89 This concept of audience is discussed extensively in James L. Golden and Richard D. Rieke, *The Rhetoric of Black Americans* (Columbus, OH: Charles E. Merrill, 1971).

90 Gloria Anzaldúa, "Speaking in Tongues: A Letter to Third World Women Writers," in *This Bridge Called My Back*, 2nd ed., ed. Cherríe Moraga and Gloria Anzaldúa (New York: Kitchen Table, 1981), 165–173.

91 Cherríe Moraga and Gloria Anzaldúa, "Introduction," *This Bridge*, xxiii.

92 Moraga and Anzaldúa, *This Bridge*, iv.

93 Anzaldúa, "Speaking," 165, 171.

94 Anzaldúa, "Speaking," 165.

95 Anzaldúa, "Speaking," 169.

96 This analysis is adapted from Catherine Helen Palczewski, "Bodies, Borders and Letters: Gloria Anzaldúa's 'Speaking in Tongues: A Letter to 3rd World Women Writers,'" *Southern Communication Journal* 62, no. 1 (Fall 1996): 1–16.

97 Martin Luther King, Jr., "Letter from Birmingham Jail," April 16, 1963, http://www.africa.upenn.edu/Articles_Gen/Letter_Birmingham.html.

98 Michael Leff and Ebony A. Utley, "Instrumental and Constitutive Rhetoric in Martin Luther King Jr.'s 'Letter from Birmingham Jail,'" *Rhetoric and Public Affairs* 7, no. 1 (2004): 37–51.

8

Rhetorical Situations

KEY CONCEPTS

conformity

constraints

contextual reconstruction

deliberative discourse

desecration

epideictic discourse

exigence

fitting response

forensic discourse

genres

hybrid response

nonparticipation

rhetorical audience

rhetorical situation

Different rhetors, messages, and audiences require different means of persuasion. For example, when you request an extension on an assignment, you consider many situational elements in constructing the request to your professor. You think about whether it is generally acceptable to ask for an extension for an assignment, your professor has particular rules about late assignments, the professor has given clear instructions for the assignment, and the deadlines are more or less firm. You consider your particular relationship with the professor, your performance in the class, and whether you have asked for an extension in the past. You also consider how and where you will make the request: by e-mail, face-to-face, during the professor's office hours, after class in the hallway, before class in the classroom, in a phone message, and so on.

When Aristotle defined rhetoric as "an ability in each [particular] case, to see the available means of persuasion,"[1] he made clear that the options open to rhetors and the demands placed on them differ from situation to situation.[2] The challenge to a rhetor is to determine what options exist to communicate a message in the particular situation. Communication does not occur in a vacuum, but in a particular place, at a particular time, as part of a particular socioeconomic and cultural context, about a particular topic, and to a particular audience. Some situations recur, however, and rhetors learn from their recurrence.

Aristotle offered an early description of the interplay of audience, topic, and rhetor in a situation. For Aristotle, the composition of the audience determines the rhetorical situation because the audience determines the expectations the rhetor will need to fulfill. He divided rhetoric into three situational classifications on the basis of three distinct audiences to which those speeches are delivered: deliberative, forensic, and epideictic.[3] Each of these three classifications had a particular form, style, and range of arguments, and called for different temporal orientations. Aristotle explains: "Each of these has it own 'time': for the deliberative speaker, the future . . . ; for the speaker in court, the past . . . ; in epideictic, the present is the most important; for all speakers praise or blame in regard to existing qualities, but they often also make use of other things, both reminding [the audience] of the past and projecting the course of the future."[4]

Deliberative discourse is *rhetoric that addresses broad public audiences and concerns the merits of proposals for future courses of action.* It responds to policy issues, such as ways and means, war and peace, and legislation.

For Aristotle, **forensic discourse** is *rhetoric that occurs when a designated audience (such as a jury) judges the arguments about events in the past and accusations of wrongdoing.* The language of forensic discourse tends to be "accusation" or "defense" (apologia).[5]

Epideictic discourse consists of *speeches of praise or blame, usually delivered to audiences assembled during ceremonial occasions, and oriented to the present moment, while calling on the past to inform the future.* Its focus on praise or blame means the audience is called to determine the fittingness of the values that the rhetor uses, and to judge the virtues and vices of the rhetor's subject.

For most of the history of rhetorical studies, Aristotle's model was the dominant perspective on rhetorical situations, but more complex theories have evolved since then. We begin this chapter by reviewing a theory that claims "rhetoric is situational," that rhetorical action is a response to a rhetorical situation. Next, we review a response to this theory that argues "situations are rhetorical," that we cannot understand a situation except through rhetoric. Each of these approaches, taken alone, has limits, so we combine the most insightful parts of the two approaches to explore how situations and rhetoric constantly interact with and affect each other. That is, situations can delimit a rhetor's rhetorical choices, and the rhetorical choices of a rhetor can define the situation. We conclude the chapter by reconsidering which rhetorical actions constitute a fitting response to the situation, and why we sometimes may not want to provide a fitting response at all.

RHETORIC AS SITUATIONAL

Communication scholar Lloyd Bitzer argues that "rhetoric is situational."[6] He proposes that rhetoric is produced at a specific time, for a particular audience, and in response to a particular issue. He distinguishes the "meaning-context" formed by previous communication from the "rhetorical situation" formed by a particular event in the world.

Context and situation are not synonymous for Bitzer.[7] For instance, when voting rights activist Fannie Lou Hamer delivered her testimony to the 110 members of the 1964 Democratic National Convention Credentials

Committee, she was asking the Democratic Party Convention to recognize and seat the Mississippi Freedom Democratic Party as the official delegation from Mississippi instead of the already recognized, all-white, anti–civil rights, regular Democratic Party delegation. As she detailed the repeated abuse she had faced at the hands of police because of her attempts to vote and register others to vote, she had to consider much more than the setting and immediate audience. The rhetorical situation included expectations attached to convention speeches; Hamer's relationship to the Civil Rights movement, the Mississippi Freedom Democratic Party, and the Democratic Party; the audiences she hoped to influence, ranging from the Credentials Committee to other African Americans and the nation as a whole; the social and cultural history of voting rights for African Americans; and her reputation as an activist and vice-chair of the Mississippi Freedom Democratic Party.[8] As this example shows, and Bitzer points out, all messages occur in a context, but only a rhetorical situation demands a rhetorical response, insofar as "rhetorical discourse . . . obtain[s] its character-as-rhetorical from the situation which generates it."[9] In other words, Bitzer believes that the things he labels *rhetorical situations* are distinct from context because rhetorical situations should elicit particular responses from rhetors.

For Bitzer, rhetoric is a special kind of communication, one that intends to produce some change in the world. Rhetoric is instrumental, or pragmatic; and it "is always persuasive."[10] People engage in rhetorical action to respond to some external and preexisting problem. Given this understanding of rhetoric, Bitzer defines the **rhetorical situation** this way:

> *a complex of persons, events, objects, and relations presenting an actual*
> *or potential exigence which can be completely or partially removed if*
> *discourse, introduced into the situation, can so constrain human decision or*
> *action as to bring about the significant modification of the exigence.*[11]

He defines **exigence** as "*an imperfection marked by urgency; it is a defect, an obstacle, something waiting to be done, a thing which is other than it should be.*"[12] The exigence calls for, or demands, a rhetorical response. If rhetoric cannot create a change in the exigence, then it is not a rhetorical situation. Although a hurricane is a problem, it is not a rhetorical exigence because rhetoric cannot stop the onslaught of wind and water. People's reactions to a hurricane (usually panic) do present an exigence. Rhetorical appeals not to panic, to prepare, and to evacuate in an orderly manner can alter the exigence. When Hurricane Ike threatened the Gulf Coast during the Atlantic storm season of 2008, Texas officials asked Houston residents not to evacuate and instead to remain in Houston and seek shelter in place, even though hundreds of thousands of other Texans living in low-lying areas were told to evacuate or face certain death. All Texans faced the same storm, but different exigences presented themselves to disaster officials. Evacuation from less populated areas could occur in an orderly manner, but in more densely populated areas, as the experience with Hurricane Rita in 2005 had made clear, more people might die from the evacuation than from the storm itself.[13] The exigence was people's panic, not the storm.

In the example of a student persuading a professor to grant an extension, the exigence is the looming deadline for an assignment the student cannot complete in time. Bitzer believes that rhetoric "comes into existence as a response to a situation, in the same sense that an answer comes into existence in response to a question, or a solution in response to a problem."[14] The student responds to the situation of the assignment deadline by requesting an extension. The student's request creates a situation calling for a response from the professor, which, in turn, comes into existence because of the student's request. The situation invites and guides both rhetors' responses.[15]

Another example of how situations invite a response arises when a person dies. In many cultures, discourse is expected in response to the death, such as eulogies, sympathy cards, expressions of condolences to family and friends, and obituaries. The situation gives the rhetorical acts their significance. When a situation has importance, the persuasive responses to that situation are given importance.

Bitzer urges rhetorical critics to consider whether a rhetorical situation induced a rhetorical action so they can fully understand what the rhetor was hoping to achieve, what was possible to achieve, and what was actually achieved. Placing a rhetorical act within its rhetorical situation is more complex than identifying the historical moment at which it occurred. Knowing the historical context of a speech gives you an understanding of its contextual meaning. Knowing the rhetorical situation helps you understand the rhetorical choices that the rhetor made in response to it.

Bitzer identifies three elements of any rhetorical situation: *exigence, audience,* and *constraints.* These elements are present prior to any rhetorical act and compose the "situation which calls the discourse into existence."[16] According to Bitzer, a rhetor should consider these elements when constructing a rhetorical act. When critically analyzing a rhetorical act, critics should begin by identifying the components of the rhetorical situation in which the rhetorical act occurs.

Exigence

On September 11, 2001, when planes crashed into the Twin Towers of the World Trade Center, the Pentagon, and a field in Pennsylvania, events demanded a response. The public reaction to the events created an evolving exigence. President George W. Bush delivered three statements throughout the day. His first statement (lasting 68 seconds) was from Emma E. Booker Elementary School in Sarasota, Florida, immediately after the Twin Towers had been hit. The second statement (lasting 130 seconds) was from Barksdale Air Force Base in Louisiana, after the Pentagon had also been hit.[17] Finally, on the evening of September 11, when it appeared the attacks were over, President Bush delivered a seven-minute address to the country from the Oval Office to make sense of the day's events. The magnitude of the developing events motivated him to respond rhetorically to the situation three times in one day. In each speech, he was responding to the urgency of the situation at that moment, the exigence.

President Bush had choices regarding how to respond. One choice could have been to ignore the events and not deliver any public statements. He probably felt compelled to speak directly about the events, because to ignore them could have created additional problems that would have been more damaging than the risks he faced in responding. If he had not responded, people would have believed he failed to see the magnitude of the events;[18] they would have seen the president as out of touch, incompetent, or afraid.

Rhetorical theorist Bruce Gronbeck explains the very unexpectedness of events "calls for particular messages at particular times . . . . the unexpectedness of impending harm produces public uncertainty, especially if the event is unique rather than cyclical; public uncertainty produces public fear, which consequently calls for explanation, [and] reassurance."[19] President Bush sought to calm the initial fears and uncertainties through his rhetorical acts.

Most rhetors have an inherent sense of exigence, recognizing a need to say something in response to unexpected events; they feel they are "invited" or "called" to respond to the situation. The feeling that you must say something is an indication that an out-of-the-ordinary event has occurred that demands an immediate (urgent) response. Of course, urgency must be defined relative to the situation. Explaining why you might be late to a party is less urgent than explaining to your boss that you will be late for work. If you are going to be late to a party, you might not feel that you must contact the hosts immediately, even though you might call as a courtesy. If you are late for work, however, you probably feel a greater sense of urgency. Being late for work is more important than being late to a party.

Audience

The second component of the rhetorical situation is the **rhetorical audience** (discussed in Chapter 7), which Bitzer defines as *an audience that "consists only of those persons who are capable of being influenced by discourse and of being mediators of change."*[20] Bitzer distinguishes the entire group of people who might hear a speech or read an essay from the rhetorical audience, the group to whom a rhetor targets a message because that group is composed of agents of change who can respond. Just because you are reading or watching a speech does not mean that you are the rhetorical audience for the speech. You would have to have the ability to remedy the exigence in order to be part of the rhetorical audience.

Mediators of change are those people who are capable of taking the actions that the rhetor suggests, but it can be difficult to determine who that audience is. The perceived mediators of change are not a constant, as presidential campaign strategy demonstrates. From the 1980 presidential campaign (which saw the emergence of the Reagan Democrats) until 2004, presidential campaigns tended to focus on wooing swing voters. Campaigns identified voters without a strong party identification as their rhetorical audiences because they were the people who could swing a presidential election in favor of one side or another. When Republican campaign strategist Matthew Dowd analyzed the electorate after the 2000 election, however, he discovered that "independents or persuadable voters in the last 20 years had gone from 22 percent of the electorate to 7 percent of the electorate in 2000." Using this information, campaign strategists for the 2004 Republican election campaign developed what came to be known as "the base strategy" which attempted "to focus on delivering votes from reliable Republicans."[21] These strategists saw the Republican Party's base as the key mediators of change. As a result, the Republican presidential campaign limited rallies to invitation-only events; tickets were given only to people willing to state their allegiance to George W. Bush.[22] The campaign redefined the rhetorical audience by suggesting that the key to winning elections (the exigence) was not about persuading undecided or centrist voters, but about mobilizing dedicated party supporters to go to the polls.

In 2008, however, the Republican campaign saw the rhetorical audience as broader than the base, so it used a mix of appeals to the base (including the selection of Sarah Palin as the vice-presidential candidate) and to independents (including the emphasis on John McCain as a maverick). The 2008 Democratic campaign also redefined the rhetorical audience. Instead of simply looking at voters as the audience, the Obama campaign looked at all those who were eligible to vote. On April 25, 2008, the Democrats launched a fifty-state voter registration drive to attract first-time voters, targeting youth and minority voters who might have felt disenfranchised by politics in the past.

The 2012 presidential election saw another evolution in identifying audiences. Journalist Sasha Issenberg reports that using big data and advanced analytics, forgoing focus groups, and relying on "empirical testing in the real world," the Democratic campaign would send out multiple messages via direct mail and then follow up with survey calls to determine which message had resonated with which voters (based on age, sex, race, and so on). As a result, the campaign targeted "unexpected population[s]"; for example, the campaign "found that voters between 45 and 65 were more likely to change their views about the candidates after hearing Obama's Medicare arguments than those over 65, who were currently eligible for the program." The campaign also emphasized one-on-one contact to encourage people to register, and then to vote. In a comprehensive assessment of this strategy, Issenberg concluded, "Few events in American life other than a presidential election touch 126 million adults . . . Obama did so by reducing every American to a series of numbers." The Obama campaign used those numbers to capture something other than traditional demographics. The campaign attempted to classify each individual as a set of numbers, but those numbers "measured" how each person had the potential to "change politics" rather than merely placing that person within traditional demographics.[23]

Rhetors need to determine which audiences can be influenced to effect change, then tailor their messages to those audiences. For example, to persuade Congress to pass a particular piece of legislation, the president could choose to focus on members of Congress, who are mediators of change because they actually enact the legislation. Alternatively, the president might go directly to the voters, to get them to pressure members of Congress to pass the legislation. In the latter case, the voters are the rhetorical audience that the president defines.

Sometimes rhetors cannot choose audiences; the audiences are chosen for them, and they must adjust their messages to these audiences. For instance, the plaintiff in a legal proceeding cannot choose which judge to persuade. The judge (audience) is selected for the case and the attorney (rhetor) must adapt accordingly.

Not only does the rhetor respond to the audience, the audience responds to the exigence. Bitzer believes that the audience is guided by the situation, as is the rhetor.[24] The rhetor is seeking to influence change; the audience brings about that change. The choices a rhetor faces are not only about how to respond to the audience, but also about which audiences to respond to. Because the audience is the mediator of change, the change the rhetor seeks might guide the rhetor's choice about which audience to address.

Constraints

The third component of a rhetorical situation, according to Bitzer, is **constraints,** *"persons, events, objects, and relations which are parts of the situation because they have the power to constrain decision and action needed to modify the exigence."*[25] Constraints restrain and enable choices that a rhetor might make in response to the exigence, audience, and the rhetor's own history. They do not determine or dictate a specific response to a situation; rather, they limit and provide opportunities for the rhetor's persuasive choices.[26]

People who come from marginalized groups in a society as a result of sex, race, or class often face greater constraints and have fewer opportunities than people from privileged groups. In the 1960s, for example, when engaging in lunch counter sit-ins to protest Jim Crow segregation laws, young African-American women and men would dress very conservatively and ask politely to be served. The simple reality of African Americans and whites eating together was so radical and confrontational, they had to moderate all their other actions. They also had to counteract white people's irrational perceptions that African Americans were violent and unruly. The protesters sought to counter these constraints. John Lewis, one of the participants in the Nashville sit-ins, explains, "It was like going to Church, I guess. You would put on your church-going clothes, Sunday clothes, and we took books and papers and did our homework at the lunch counter, just quiet and trying to be as dignified as possible."[27]

As a counterexample, consider performance artist Bill Talen's character of Reverend Billy. Located in New York, Talen uses street theatre to protest the rise in consumerism and the invasion of Times Square by transnational corporations such as Disney and Starbucks.[28] Reverend Billy begins his sermon in a local theatre, but takes it directly into a store to challenge shoppers. He preaches to them about the evils of consumption, or whispers in their ears that the cute stuffed Dumbo was made by sweatshop labor. His race, sex, and class provide him an opportunity, rather than a constraint. He recognizes that as a white man, he is able to get away with more. As he explains: "I don't suffer from racial profiling. If a cop stops me, he knows immediately that I have a college education and dental work."[29] He is able to gain access to spaces and command attention from those who might otherwise dismiss the message.

All rhetors are confronted with constraints. Communication scholars Karlyn Kohrs Campbell and Susan Schultz Huxman provide a more expansive assessment of constraints in their examination of "the rhetorical problem."[30] Adapting their work and applying it to the framework of the rhetorical situation, we can see constraints stemming from the exigence, audience, and rhetor.

Constraints arising from the exigence include the complexity of the exigence and its cultural history.[31] The exigence can be more or less complex; the level of expertise needed to understand it varies from subject to subject. In the case of the student requesting an extension, the exigence is fairly straightforward and clear. The student's reasons for the extension might make the exigence more complex, but the obstacles that the student must overcome include the professor's stated (or unstated) deadline policies and the academic culture of the institution or department.

In contrast, some exigences are extremely complex. When the United States was in the throes of the Great Depression, following the 1929 stock market collapse, President Franklin Delano Roosevelt faced the daunting task of explaining to the public what was happening, why, and how the government would respond. When he was inaugurated on March 4, 1933, five thousand banks had already folded; ten million people in the United States had lost their savings; 25 percent were unemployed; hundreds of thousands of families had lost their homes; and farmers were leaving crops to rot in the fields because commodity prices had fallen so far they could not afford to harvest their crops.[32] On March 12, 1933, via the relatively new medium of radio, Roosevelt delivered his first presidential fireside chat. The subject was banking.[33] He sought to explain the federal "banking holiday" he had declared, in terms that would be understood by "the average citizen."[34] He faced the exigence of an extremely complex and volatile situation, which called forth rhetoric that would explain and calm. In an interesting parallel, as the economic crisis that had begun in the October 2008 intensified during early 2009, many commentators encouraged President Barack Obama to respond to his complex exigence in the same way Roosevelt had. Mary Kate Cary of *U.S. News and World Report* argued that "one-on-one talks with the American people explaining the crisis and the government's response—as well as a go-get-'em confidence builder at the end— might work wonders."[35]

According to Campbell and Huxman, constraints arising from the audience capable of acting include whether the rhetor can reach it, as well as whether it is likely to misinterpret or misperceive the message, can be motivated to act despite potential costs, perceives itself as an agent of change, and has control over the action asked of it.[36] Even if the rhetor is able to deliver the message to the audience, the audience must perceive and interpret the situation as described in the message in a way that is consistent with how the rhetor interprets and perceives it. Further, audience members must be motivated and believe they can make a change, that they have agency to act on the exigence. In some cases, responding to an exigence will present costs to the audience, which could include money, time, or the risk of social disapproval.

When a student asks for an extension, the professor clearly is an audience with agency; control is not the most significant constraint arising from this audience. Instead, it is the cost, which, from the professor's perspective might be the perception of unfairness to other students or the time the professor needs to grade the assignment. (If the extension is granted, the professor has less time to evaluate it.)

Constraints can also arise from audience agency. If you are trying to encourage other students to join a protest against building a road through a campus green space, you might encounter apathy. You might need to persuade them that they can make a difference. You might need to motivate them to become involved, even if they agree that the road should not be built.

Finally, Campbell and Huxman say, constraints arising from the rhetor include the rhetor's reputation, ability to create identification with the audience, and social power.[37] These characteristics can also present opportunities for the rhetorician, however. A rhetor who has credibility with an audience can use that credibility to persuade it. For example, as Roosevelt's term in office progressed, he developed credibility with the public. His fireside chats and constant communication instilled confidence to such an extent that in their letters to him, people described him as "a gift from God, and a 'friend-next-door,' a supreme being and a real fellow who did not talk down to the public."[38] Because of his reputation, Roosevelt was able to persuade audiences by relying on his relationship with them. Conversely, rhetors who have negative images or tarnished reputations would have to overcome them in order to persuade their audiences.

Fitting Response and Genre

Bitzer concludes that although a rhetorical situation invites a response, not all responses are fitting. A **fitting response** is *a response that meets the expectations of the rhetorical situation.* Bitzer points out that "every situation prescribes its fitting response; the rhetor may or may not read the prescription accurately."[39] A successful persuasive message is one that is appropriate for the exigence, audience, and constraints of the rhetorical situation.

To be fitting, a response must also meet the expectations established by responses to preceding situations that the audience perceives to be analogous. When a rhetorical situation (or a particular interaction of audience, exigence, and constraints) repeatedly recurs, rhetoric scholars Karlyn Kohrs Campbell and Kathleen Hall Jamieson tell us, stylistic and substantive expectations become attached to that situation.[40] Stylistic expectations can involve the formality of language, attitudes toward the subject and audience, and the structure of the speech. Substantive expectations include the types of subjects and evidence.

The determination of what is fitting need not occur anew with every act. When a situation recurs, rhetors can look to previous responses to identify general types of form and content that seem to work. They can respond to common elements in exigences, contexts, responses, and audiences. These responses often lead to the formulation of **genres,** *rhetorical forms created by recurrent elements of rhetorical situations, which create clusters of discourse that share style, substance, and purpose.* Genres create constraints and opportunities for rhetors as they respond to situations. Thus, it is not solely the present situation that generates constraints on and resources for a rhetor, but also, according to Jamieson, the previous situations that create—"the chromosomal imprint of ancestral genres."[41]

Even if you have never given or heard a eulogy, you probably have a general sense of what it should include. As Campbell and Jamieson note, Western audiences expect that a eulogy "acknowledges the death, transforms the relationship between the living and the dead from present to past tense, eases the mourners' terror at confronting their own mortality, consoles them by arguing that the deceased lives on, and reknits the fabric of the community."[42] What people expect to hear in a eulogy is determined not just by the particular death, but by all the eulogies that have gone before. If someone were to give a speech that did not even mention the person who had died, people would probably not see that speech as fitting and say, "It wasn't really a eulogy."

Campbell and Jamieson explain that genres are "a fusion of elements, formed from a constellation of forms."[43] First, a genre is a *fusion* of elements, not just a collection of individual elements.[44] The chemical concept, fusion, emphasizes that the way components are combined is more important to examine than whether the same elements appear in multiple forms. When fusion occurs, discrete parts are combined in such a way that their discreteness is no longer observable. Second, the emphasis on "constellation" highlights that the parts of a symbolic action, like stars, are connected by human perception. The shapes we see in the stars—the Big Dipper or Orion—are not inherent in the organization of the stars; rather, people perceive relations between stars, imbue them with meaning, and create constellations symbolically. Once a constellation has been accepted, people use it to identify the stars and to navigate. Genres of discourse are human constructions, just as constellations are. The constraints that develop from these constructed genres guide rhetorical choices just as constellations guide navigational choices.

Genres guide rhetorical action because they provide a pattern to follow. Even when rhetors are presented with *un*precedented situations, they tend to look to established genres to guide their responses. When President Richard Nixon resigned from office and Gerald Ford was sworn in, Campbell and Jamieson point out, Ford's speech as president occurred in an "unprecedented rhetorical situation." Ford was not elected: he had replaced Spiro Agnew as vice-president after Agnew pleaded no contest to a felony charge and resigned, making Ford the first appointed vice president in the nation's history. Subsequently, Ford replaced Nixon, who had resigned from the presidency in the face of three articles of impeachment from the House Judiciary Committee. Because the situation was unprecedented, Ford did not have a ready-made blueprint for how to respond to that exigence, yet he had a resource on which to rely—the established expectations of an inaugural address.

When he began his first speech after taking the oath of office and assuming the presidency on August 9, 1974, Ford stated it was "Not an inaugural address, not a fireside chat, not a campaign speech—just a little straight talk among friends."[45] Yet, Campbell and Jamieson argue, Ford delivered a classic inaugural, as the speech "established that the office had been vacated, constituted the audience as the people, rehearsed basic constitutional principles, invited investiture, and previewed Ford's approach to the presidency."[46] These elements constitute the stylistic and substantive expectations attached to presidential inaugurals in the United States. Ford's speech reflected all the formal elements of the inaugural genre, enabling him to rely on that genre to guide his response to an unprecedented situation.

In some cases, a situation may call for a response that includes elements of multiple genres. Jamieson and Campbell call *symbolic actions that combine elements of two different genres* a **hybrid response**.[47] The fusion of genres can come about when a rhetor is trying to respond to a rhetorical situation that has competing demands. For example, when Lyndon Baines Johnson delivered his first address as president, five days after the assassination of President John F. Kennedy, he had to both mourn Kennedy and invest himself with the powers of the presidency. As Campbell and Jamieson explain, "Before Johnson could tell the audience where he would lead it, the office of the presidency had to be vacated rhetorically and its former occupant laid to rest in a eulogy."[48] Johnson responded to this need by playing off Kennedy's inaugural theme of "let us begin," with the theme "let us continue." After noting that "The greatest leader of our time has been struck down by the foulest deed of our time," and recounting Kennedy's accomplishments, Johnson declared: "Today in this moment of new resolve, I would say to all my fellow Americans, *let us continue.* This is our challenge—not to hesitate, not to pause, not to turn about and linger over this evil moment, but to continue on our course so that we may fulfill the destiny that history has set for us."[49] He then listed the policy initiatives on which he demanded congressional action: passage of the Civil Rights Bill, a tax bill, and education bills. As Campbell and Jamieson note, this approach allowed him to explain what the Kennedy presidency had meant and to what a Johnson presidency would be committed.

Rhetors are not required to follow general guides, however. Even if a situation calls for particular generic responses, a rhetor may strategically chose to ignore them. For example, many presidents use epideictic occasions (such as commencement addresses) to launch major policy initiatives. John F. Kennedy used his commencement address at American University to announce the comprehensive test ban treaty, banning nuclear explosions.[50] Lyndon B. Johnson used his address at the University of Michigan to lay the groundwork for affirmative action.[51] When George H. W. Bush spoke at the University of Michigan commencement, he weighed in regarding campus speech codes about hate speech.[52] Bill Clinton used his speech to the graduating class at the University of California, San Diego, to launch his Race Initiative.[53]

On the other hand, Ronald Reagan often responded to deliberative occasions by using epideictic discourse celebrating the people of the United States. He initiated the presidential practice of inviting "citizens who have distinguished themselves in some field of service or endeavor to be his personal guests in the gallery," and then highlighting them as part of his State of the Union address, which responds to a deliberative situation.[54] The result, as Campbell and Jamieson explain, was that Reagan's yearly addresses tended to be "short on policy proposals, sharply tilting the character of the address toward ceremonial and away from the deliberative."[55] As Jamieson notes: "Genres should not be viewed as static forms but as evolving phenomena. . . . While traditional genres may color rhetoric they do not ossify it."[56]

Analysis: The *Challenger* Explosion

President Ronald Reagan's speech after the explosion of the *Challenger* space shuttle illustrates how a rhetor responds to a rhetorical situation and how critics can use the concept of the rhetorical situation to analyze a rhetorical act.

On January 28, 1986, NASA launched the *Challenger* in what it believed to be a routine mission even though there had been five liftoff delays. On board were seven astronauts: Gregory Jarvis, Christa McAuliffe, Ronald McNair, Ellison Onizuka, Judith Resnik, Dick Scobee, and Michael J. Smith. NASA had been plagued by declining public interest in its space missions, but many people in the United States, particularly schoolchildren, watched the launch live because of schoolteacher Christa McAuliffe, the first member of the Teacher in Space Project. A little over a minute after the launch, the shuttle exploded in flight, killing all seven astronauts. Although the only live coverage of the launch was on newly formed CNN and via a satellite feed of NASA TV targeted at schools, one study reported that 85 percent of those surveyed had heard the news within an hour of the accident as a result of the extensive media coverage.[57]

The vivid imagery of the explosion shocked the nation.[58] Within minutes, the networks replaced regular programming with coverage of the explosion. The nation watched in horror as their televisions repeatedly showed the shuttle exploding and debris raining down. Despite all the coverage in the hours after the explosion, the public was left with a void of meaning. People did not know what had happened or why. They could have interpreted the explosion as proof that NASA was inept and the benefits of space exploration were not worth the costs, or as an inexplicable and irredeemable loss of human life. Knowing that the situation demanded a response, President Reagan cancelled his scheduled State of the Union address to speak to the country about the *Challenger* disaster.

President Ronald W. Reagan
"The Space Shuttle *Challenger* Tragedy Address"
Oval Office
January 28, 1986

1. Ladies and Gentlemen, I'd planned to speak to you tonight to report on the state of the union, but the events of earlier today have led me to change those plans. Today is a day for mourning and remembering. Nancy and I are pained to the core by the tragedy of the shuttle *Challenger*. We know we share this pain with all of the people of our country. This is truly a national loss.

2. Nineteen years ago, almost to the day, we lost three astronauts in a terrible accident on the ground. But we've never lost an astronaut in flight. We've never had a tragedy like this. And perhaps we've forgotten

the courage it took for the crew of the shuttle. But they, the *Challenger* Seven, were aware of the dangers, but overcame them and did their jobs brilliantly. We mourn seven heroes: Michael Smith, Dick Scobee, Judith Resnik, Ronald McNair, Ellison Onizuka, Gregory Jarvis, and Christa McAuliffe. We mourn their loss as a nation together.

3. For the families of the seven, we cannot bear, as you do, the full impact of this tragedy. But we feel the loss, and we're thinking about you so very much. Your loved ones were daring and brave, and they had that special grace, that special spirit that says, "Give me a challenge, and I'll meet it with joy." They had a hunger to explore the universe and discover its truths. They wished to serve, and they did. They served all of us.

4. We've grown used to wonders in this century. It's hard to dazzle us. But for twenty-five years the United States space program has been doing just that. We've grown used to the idea of space, and perhaps we forget that we've only just begun. We're still pioneers. They, the members of the *Challenger* crew, were pioneers.

5. And I want to say something to the schoolchildren of America who were watching the live coverage of the shuttle's take-off. I know it's hard to understand, but sometimes painful things like this happen. It's all part of the process of exploration and discovery. It's all part of taking a chance and expanding man's horizons. The future doesn't belong to the fainthearted; it belongs to the brave. The *Challenger* crew was pulling us into the future, and we'll continue to follow them.

6. I've always had great faith in and respect for our space program. And what happened today does nothing to diminish it. We don't hide our space program. We don't keep secrets and cover things up. We do it all up front and in public. That's the way freedom is, and we wouldn't change it for a minute.

7. We'll continue our quest in space. There will be more shuttle flights and more shuttle crews and, yes, more volunteers, more civilians, more teachers in space. Nothing ends here; our hopes and our journeys continue.

8. I want to add that I wish I could talk to every man and woman who works for NASA, or who worked on this mission and tell them: "Your dedication and professionalism have moved and impressed us for decades. And we know of your anguish. We share it."

9. There's a coincidence today. On this day three hundred and ninety years ago, the great explorer Sir Francis Drake died aboard ship off the coast of Panama. In his lifetime the great frontiers were the oceans, and a historian later said, "He lived by the sea, died on it, and was buried in it." Well, today, we can say of the *Challenger* crew: Their dedication was, like Drake's, complete.

10. The crew of the space shuttle *Challenger* honored us by the manner in which they lived their lives. We will never forget them, nor the last time we saw them, this morning, as they prepared for their journey and

waved goodbye and "slipped the surly bonds of earth" to "touch the face of God."

11. Thank you.[59]

President Reagan was called to give this speech (instead of his planned State of the Union address) because of the rhetorical situation. In Bitzer's terms, people's reaction to and public witnessing of this event established an exigence, "an imperfection marked by urgency." The unexpected explosion and the magnitude of the tragedy created urgency for President Reagan to respond. The uniqueness of the tragedy created public uncertainty about the meaning of the event and the safety of the NASA space program, and called for explanation and reassurance.

President Reagan clearly identified the exigence: "the tragedy of the shuttle *Challenger* . . . is truly a national loss" that made it a day "for mourning and remembering," but the march of progress and the call for exploration gave meaning to that loss of life. According to Reagan, the members of the space shuttle crew had "a hunger to explore the universe" and were part of a long line of explorers. The examples of the 1967 *Apollo I* fire and the 1596 death of Sir Francis Drake offered similar historical events that helped make the loss of life during exploration seem normal and expected. As Reagan explained to schoolchildren: "It's all part of the process of exploration and discovery."

The audiences in the situation were composed of people who shared the need for reassurance and the sentiment that exploration defines the character of the people of the United States: the family of the astronauts, schoolchildren, NASA workers, and the public as a whole.[60] President Reagan provided them with an explanation, not of the actual accident, but of exploration. Thus, he identified what he saw as the meaning of the situation. In so doing, he offered a response that suggested both a time of mourning and a continued faith in exploration in general, and in NASA more specifically.

President Reagan faced constraints in the situation. The exigence was unique because it was the first time a space shuttle had exploded. Death is a recurring part of the human condition, however, so he was constrained by the antecedent genre of eulogy, even as he was able to mirror the stylistic and substantive expectations attached to eulogies to structure his speech. He also faced limits and opportunities as a rhetor. As president, he could not react in a purely personal way, but he was a popular president and played the role of a grandfather, targeting a specific message to schoolchildren. This role provided an opportunity for him because he could come across as a caring and comforting leader responding to a constraint: the audiences' need for reassurance about the space program.

Reagan situated the loss of the *Challenger* crew not as an aberration, but as a normal part of exploration and discovery, practices that define the US spirit. He reminded the audience that the crew members "were aware of the dangers" and faced them bravely. He gave meaning to an event that seemed devoid of meaning.[61] His response to the exigence defined the situation in such a way that it did not mark the end of NASA, but rather was a justification to continue funding the space program; not as proof of NASA's failure, but as proof of the undying exploratory impulse in the US spirit: "The future doesn't belong to the fainthearted; it belongs to the brave. The *Challenger* crew was pulling us into the future, and we'll continue to follow them." Reagan used his eulogy of the astronauts to call for a policy of continued support of the space program, thus creating a hybrid response of eulogizing (epideictic) and advancing a policy (deliberative).

This case illustrates the components of a rhetorical situation. The rhetor, President Reagan, responded to an exigence by speaking to particular audiences in a way that accounted for constraints in the situation. However, this analysis also shows that the rhetorical situation is not as objectively knowable and fixed as Bitzer suggests. People knew an explosion had happened, but they did not know what it meant. President Reagan not only responded to a situation, he also attempted to define exactly what it meant. The complexity of this speech makes clear the need for an alternative view of the relationship between rhetoric and situations.

SITUATIONS AS RHETORICAL

In an essay that systematically responds to Bitzer, communication scholar Richard Vatz concludes: "situations are rhetorical."[62] He contends that Bitzer's claim that rhetoric is situational is inaccurate. He writes:

> The essential question to be addressed is: What is the relationship between rhetoric and situations? It will not be surprising that I take the converse position of each of Bitzer's major statements regarding this relationship. For example: I would not say "rhetoric is situational," but situations are rhetorical; not " . . . exigence strongly invites utterance," but utterance strongly invites exigence; not "the situation controls the rhetorical response . . . " but the rhetoric controls the situational response; not " . . . rhetorical discourse . . . does obtain its character-as-rhetorical from the situation which generates it," but situations obtain their character from the rhetoric which surrounds them or creates them.[63]

Vatz argues that rhetoric constructs the situation. He rejects the idea that one can find meaning in a situation, then respond to that preset meaning. Instead, he says, "meaning is not discovered in situations, but *created* by rhetors."[64] The meaning, or the definition of a situation, is not always clear. Consequently, the demand for a response is not necessarily self-evident to the audience or the rhetor. Instead, people's responses to situations make those events meaningful. Thus, "the rhetor is responsible for what he [or she] chooses to make salient."[65]

In Bitzer's formulation, the meaning intrinsic to the situation causes rhetoric. He argues that "the situation is objective, publicly observable, and historic [which means] that it is real or genuine . . . ."[66] A fitting response, according to Bitzer, would not attempt to alter or (re)define the situation; he rejects the attempt to create or alter a situation as illegitimate.

In Vatz's formulation, however, rhetoric creates the meaning of the situation. Attempts to define the situation, or challenge another's interpretation of it, are perfectly reasonable. Of the three elements of the rhetorical situation (exigence, audience, and constraints), Vatz most objects to Bitzer's notion of exigence.[67] He argues that exigence is not intrinsic to the situation, but interpreted. Thus, critics and audiences must examine how rhetors define the exigence, and not simply accept the rhetor's description of it.

The exigence is not always clear or even known. In fact, the audience members may not perceive the urgency until the rhetor introduces the problem to them. For example, in 1962 Rachel Carson, a scientist who worked for the US Fish and Wildlife Service, wrote *Silent Spring* in order to galvanize action to ban the pesticide DDT.[68] Having researched and written several articles on ecologies, she had become concerned at the rapidly increasing use of chemical pesticides. She wrote *Silent Spring* to challenge their use and warn the public of their dangers.[69]

Prior to the publication of her book, people had not known about the dangers of chemical pesticides or recognized the urgency of the problem. They did not perceive an exigence. Technological progress was accepted as an unassailable good. Few people believed that nature was vulnerable to human intervention. Carson's book created a firestorm of controversy over pesticide use, an exigence to which chemical industries and the government had to respond, ultimately by banning DDT. Carson's rhetorical actions helped create the meaning and importance of the exigence to which the audience needed to respond.

Another example of defining an exigence can be seen in President Reagan's *Challenger* speech. He began by calling the event a "national tragedy." He clarified the exigence by stating "We're still pioneers. They, the members of the *Challenger* crew, were pioneers." In this way, he gave meaning to the disaster. In his view, the accident was part of US pioneer spirit, not an indication of the failure of NASA or the end of space travel.

The disagreement between Bitzer and Vatz appears to be irresolvable because Vatz frames his response as a direct refutation of Bitzer's position. For Bitzer, the situation produces rhetoric. For Vatz, rhetoric produces the situation. Does the situation control rhetoric or does rhetoric construct the situation?

A SYNERGISTIC UNDERSTANDING OF RHETORIC AND SITUATIONS

The rhetorical situation is complex. Symbolic action constructs human beings' understanding of reality and, hence, their understanding of situations. This statement does not mean that nothing exists outside of symbolic action, but that the meaning of the material world is always mediated through symbols and language. A synergistic relationship emerges between rhetoric and situation, one in which situations guide rhetorical responses *and* rhetoric constructs situations. The interaction results in something larger and distinct from the sum of the individual effects. Events happen, but their relative importance is given to them through interpretations, which are rhetorically constructed.

Although we recognize the importance of Bitzer's work, we question his assumption of an objectively knowable situation. Although we are sympathetic to Vatz's position, we recognize that rhetoric does not occur in a vacuum. A rhetor does not, all alone, define a situation. Human beings do not come to understand situations unmediated by discourse, but no rhetor comes to a situation with only her or his own discourse as the means of mediation. Other rhetors may have already responded; a subject's cultural history may have developed across time; individuals may have watched an event on television or the Internet.

Rhetoric scholars Robert J. Branham and W. Barnett Pearce point out that rhetoric gets its meaning from the situation, but it also influences and helps create the situation.[70] For example, when you speak in class, you are aware that you are in a classroom with other students and a professor, so you probably speak differently from the way you do when you are at lunch with your friends. Once you speak in class, however, your communication shapes the class, helping to set a tone for the discussion. As people interact, the interaction begins to define the situation. Consequently, we believe a synergistic understanding of the rhetorical situation is needed, an approach that recognizes Bitzer's and Vatz's contributions.

Definition of the Situation

Argumentation theorist Robert Cox points out that a rhetor's definition of the situation determines which responses appear to be reasonable, rational, and coherent.[71] He argues that "actors' *definitions of the situation* emerge in their symbolic interactions with their environment"; they are not predetermined by the situation.[72] The way a rhetor defines a situation determines the exact nature of the exigence and, hence, what appear to be reasonable judgments about it and actions responding to it. Instead of the situation containing rules and conventions that the rhetor must discover, Cox suggests that the rhetor's proposed definition of the situation provides the "contextual rules for interpreting choices as rational, reasonable, or justified."[73]

For example, if you were asked to deliver a speech on the Fourth of July, you would likely define the situation as one of celebration, the Fourth of July being the day on which the United States officially celebrates its independence. Such a definition would direct you to choose a celebratory tone that draws the audience members together in their shared citizenship. However, the Fourth of July could be defined in other ways. When the Rochester (NY) Ladies' Anti-Slavery Society invited famed abolitionist, woman's rights activist, and former slave Frederick Douglass to deliver a Fourth of July oration in 1852, he chose to redefine the situation from one of celebration to condemnation. Speaking as "the most powerful black man in the nation" at that time,[74] he reviewed the history of the country and the significance of the day, saying: "This, for the purpose of this celebration, is the Fourth of July. It is the birthday of your National Independence, and of your political freedom. . . . Pride and patriotism, not less than gratitude, prompt you to celebrate and to hold it in perpetual remembrance."[75] He defined the situation not as a day to celebrate the ideals of the nation, but instead as a day to condemn the nation for not living up to its ideals. Douglass asked:

> Fellow-citizens, pardon me, allow me to ask, why am I called upon to speak here to-day? What have I, or those I represent, to do with your national independence? Are the great principles of political freedom and of natural justice, embodied in that Declaration of Independence, extended to us? . . . I am not included within the pale of this glorious anniversary! . . . Fellow-citizens; above your national, tumultuous joy, I hear the mournful wail of millions! whose chains, heavy and grievous yesterday, are, to-day, rendered more intolerable by the jubilee shouts that reach them.[76]

For white people the situation may have called for the celebration of liberty, but for black people the day simply placed into stark relief the inequalities between the races.

The various elements of the rhetorical situation are connected in complex ways. For instance, how rhetors define rhetorical situations determines how they respond to them. Events beyond a rhetor's control may demand a response, but rhetors can also influence which responses are perceived as reasonable and which situations rise to a level that demand a response.

Analysis: 9/11 Defined as an "Act of War"

The events of September 11, 2001, demonstrate how a rhetorical situation can be defined in multiple ways. The situation created uncertainty: the public needed answers as to why the attacks had happened, who was responsible, and whether the country was safe. Media coverage of the burning and collapse of the Twin Towers, and of the smoldering wreckage of the Pentagon, was so immediate, constant, intense, and evocative, it called for a response from the government, specifically, the president.

The initial responses were complicated by the fact that no one really knew how to name the situation. Naming an event a wedding gives a particular interpretation to the situation, as opposed to naming it a party. In the case of 9/11, naming the event was a central rhetorical act, but the situation appeared unparalleled, creating undefined exigencies and a complex set of constraints. No perfect precedent existed.

In the initial hours after the attacks, it was not known what to call the event: a terrorist attack, an act of war, an accident, a hijacking, a tragedy, a bombing, a breach of international and domestic law, and so on. Any situation with an uncertain or equivocal meaning initially creates a need for a response to define the situation. When media and government officials began to define the events as terrorist attacks and acts of war, people began to understand them in a particular way. President Bush could have chosen to define the rhetorical situation other ways. The choices were neither automatic nor obvious. In fact, they were based on ambiguous and incomplete information.

The confusion invited a response that would clarify and comfort. Thus, when the president delivered his address to the nation that evening, people were seeking not only consolation for the lives lost and the havoc wreaked, but also explanations of the meaning of the attacks.

President George W. Bush
"Address to the Nation"
Oval Office
September 11, 2001

1. Good evening.

2. Today, our fellow citizens, our way of life, our very freedom came under attack in a series of deliberate and deadly terrorist acts. The victims were in airplanes or in their offices: secretaries, business men and women, military and federal workers, moms and dads, friends and neighbors. Thousands of lives were suddenly ended by evil, despicable acts of terror. The pictures of airplanes flying into buildings, fires burning, huge—huge structures collapsing have filled us with disbelief, terrible sadness, and a quiet, unyielding anger. These acts of mass murder were intended to frighten our nation into chaos and retreat. But they have failed. Our country is strong.

3. A great people has been moved to defend a great nation. Terrorist attacks can shake the foundations of our biggest buildings, but they cannot touch the foundation of America. These acts shatter steel, but they cannot dent the steel of American resolve. America was targeted for attack because we're the brightest beacon for freedom and opportunity in the world. And no one will keep that light from shining. Today, our nation saw evil—the very worst of human nature—and we responded with the best of America. With the daring of our rescue workers, with the caring for strangers and neighbors who came to give blood and help in any way they could.

4. Immediately following the first attack, I implemented our government's emergency response plans. Our military is powerful, and it's prepared. Our emergency teams are working in New York City and Washington D.C. to help with local rescue efforts. Our first priority is to get help to those who have been injured, and to take every precaution to protect our citizens at home and around the world from further attacks. The functions of our government continue without interruption. Federal agencies in Washington which had to be evacuated today are reopening for essential personnel tonight and will be open for business tomorrow. Our financial institutions remain strong, and the American economy will be open for business as well.

5. The search is underway for those who were behind these evil acts. I have directed the full resources of our intelligence and law enforcement

communities to find those responsible and to bring them to justice. We will make no distinction between the terrorists who committed these acts and those who harbor them.

6. I appreciate so very much the members of Congress who have joined me in strongly condemning these attacks. And on behalf of the American people, I thank the many world leaders who have called to offer their condolences and assistance. America and our friends and allies join with all those who want peace and security in the world, and we stand together to win the war against terrorism.

7. Tonight, I ask for your prayers for all those who grieve, for the children whose worlds have been shattered, for all whose sense of safety and security has been threatened. And I pray they will be comforted by a Power greater than any of us, spoken through the ages in Psalm 23: "Even though I walk through the valley of the shadow of death, I fear no evil for you are with me."

8. This is a day when all Americans from every walk of life unite in our resolve for justice and peace. America has stood down enemies before, and we will do so this time. None of us will ever forget this day, yet we go forward to defend freedom and all that is good and just in our world.

9. Thank you. Good night. And God bless America.[77]

In the second paragraph of this speech, the attacks are described as "evil," "acts of terror" and "acts of mass murder," but not yet as "acts of war." Still, Bush established a rhetorical trajectory that made clear a military response was planned when he declared: "Our military is powerful, and it's prepared," then clarified that the US would "win the war against terrorism."

Not until September 12 did President Bush specifically refer to the attacks as "acts of war."[78] Naming them as "acts of war" and also declaring a "war against terrorism" defined the situation differently from the way it would have been defined if he had named the attacks as criminal acts, violations of international law, or crimes against humanity. Because President Bush was able to convince the public that the situation was an "act of war" in which terrorism was attacking freedom, a definition that media coverage echoed,[79] the course of action that appeared reasonable was a military response. He stretched the definition of an act of war to encompass acts of terrorism that were believed to be sponsored by another country but perpetrated by nonstate actors. By declaring a war against terrorism, he expanded the idea of war to targets beyond aggressive nation states.

As the 9/11 example illustrates, President Bush's definition of the situation framed the types of evidence that were admissible (only US sources counted because the attackers were evil) and the information that was relevant (the "war" began on 9/11, and no earlier). By defining the terrorist attacks as "acts of war," he limited the appropriate response to the attacks. An act of war requires some sort of military response.

The rhetorical response, the rhetorical situation, the rhetor, and the audiences all influence each other, bringing into existence a situation at their nexus.

Once a rhetor crafts a definition of the rhetorical situation and calls a particular audience into being, the rhetorical situation is defined for present, as well as future, rhetors. The events clearly happened on September 11, 2001, but what they meant was open to interpretation; depending on that interpretation, rhetors could defend particular reactions as the most reasonable. As events unfold, however, rhetorical action ensues and the rhetorical situation evolves, eliciting different interpretations. Definitions do not go unanswered or unchallenged. Competing definitions of the situation can sustain and generate arguments about what is an appropriate rhetorical response.

Analysis: 9/11 Redefined

At this point, given how deeply the US public has been immersed in rhetoric declaring 9/11 an "act of war," it seems unreasonable to think about whether a nonmilitary response would have been appropriate. At the time, over 80 percent of US citizens approved of the US-led invasion of Afghanistan as part of its war on terror.[80] The United States government declared the Afghanistan government harbored those who masterminded the 9/11 attacks. Afghanistan was controlled by the Taliban, who were supported by Osama bin Laden, who claimed credit for the 9/11 attacks.

The interpretation of 9/11 as an "act of war" is not the only way to understand it, however.[81] As Richard Vatz points out, "meaning is not discovered in situations, but *created* by rhetors."[82]

Pope John Paul II offered a different definition of the situation. In a papal audience one year later, he stated clearly that the attacks were unjustified, but that defining the attacks as an act of war was unacceptable.

Pope John Paul II
"Address to the General Audience"
The Vatican
September 11, 2002

1. Today from every corner of the globe countless persons go in thought to the city of New York, where last year on 11 September the twin towers of the World Trade Center collapsed as the result of a savage attack, taking with them in their ruin many of our innocent brothers and sisters.

2. At the distance of a year, once again we wish to remember the victims of this terrorism and commend them to the mercy of God. At the same time, we desire to renew our expression of spiritual closeness to their families and their loved ones. But we also wish to present a challenge to the consciences of those who planned and executed such a barbaric and cruel design.

3. One year after 11 September 2001, we state again that no situation of injustice, no sentiment of frustration, no philosophy or religion can justify such a deadly assault. Every human person has the right to respect for his

own life and dignity which are inviolable goods. God says it, international law sanctions it, the human conscience proclaims it, civil coexistence demands it.

4. Terrorism is and will always be a manifestation of inhuman ferocity which, as such, will never be able to resolve the conflicts between human persons. Destruction, armed violence, and war are choices that sow and generate only hatred and death. Reason and love are the only valid means for overcoming and resolving the disputes between persons and peoples.

5. However, an agreed upon and resolute effort is necessary and urgent to advance new political and economic initiatives that are capable of resolving the scandalous situations of injustice and oppression that continue to afflict a great many of the members of the human family, creating conditions that favour the uncontrollable explosion of rancour. When fundamental rights are violated, it is easy to fall prey to the temptations of hatred and violence. A global culture of solidarity has to be built that will give young people hope for the future.

6. I would like to repeat to all the words of the Bible: "The Lord . . . comes to judge the earth. He will judge the world with justice and the peoples with his truth" (Ps 96[95],13).

7. Freedom and peace can only come from truth and justice. Only on these values is it possible to build a life worthy of human beings. Without them there is only ruin and destruction.

8. On this sad anniversary, we address our prayer to God so that love may supplant hatred and, through the dedication of all persons of good will, harmony and solidarity may be affirmed in every corner of the globe. . . .

9. Today our thoughts turn to the terrible events of 11 September last year, symbolized in the destruction of the Twin Towers of the World Trade Center in New York, with the death of so many innocent people.

10. We address an ardent prayer to Almighty God for the victims of that terrorist act. No situation of pain, no philosophy or religion, can ever justify such a grave offence against human life and dignity. Violence can only lead to further hatred and destruction. It can never lead to correct solutions to the scandalous imbalances and injustices existing in the world.

11. The Lord judges the world with justice and truth (cf. Ps 95,13). May he help all peoples to seek the justice and truth that brings freedom and peace.[83]

Even though the Pope described terrorism as unjustified "inhuman ferocity," "savage," "barbaric and cruel," he did not define the attacks as an act of war. Thus, the reasonable response is not war, but rather "political and economic initiatives that are capable of resolving the scandalous situations of injustice and oppression."[84] He defined the 9/11 rhetorical situation as tragedy, which must be understood and prevented through dialogue. To further explain his position, in 2004 the Pope declared that terrorism must be confronted with "firmness and decision, in fighting the workers of death," but that "war must always be considered a defeat: a defeat of reason and of humanity."[85]

Pope John Paul II defined the attack as an act of terrorism, but unlike President Bush he did not define it as an act that requires another act of violence—namely a war. Specifically, he referred to war as a "choice," so he did not define the situation as automatically requiring military action. He provided the rules for interpreting the choice for war in this case as irrational, unreasonable, and unjustified, and argued that the correct response to terrorism is reason and love.

Additionally, Pope John Paul II argued that underlying problems create the conditions for people to "fall prey to the temptations of hatred and violence." In this way, he challenged the assumptions about why the attacks had happened and declared a global responsibility to ensure that all people have access to basic rights. He argued that the response to terrorism should not be war, but removing the conditions that generate terrorism.

Philosopher Judith Butler offered another challenge to prevailing definitions of the situation. She mused on the very question of what 9/11 came to mean for the United States when she suggested we "ask what, politically, might be made of grief besides a cry for war."[86] Her goal was not to argue that the grief over the attacks was unwarranted or to minimize the moral abhorrence people might feel toward them. Instead, her argument was:

> neither moral outrage nor public mourning [should] become the occasion for the muting of critical discourse and public debate on the meaning of historical events. One might still want to know what brought about these events, want to know how best to address those conditions so that the seeds are not sown for further events of this kind, find sites of intervention, help to plan strategies thoughtfully that will not beckon more violence in the future. One can even experience that abhorrence, mourning, anxiety, and fear, and have all of these emotional dispositions lead to a reflection on how others have suffered arbitrary violence at the hands of the US, but also endeavor to produce another public culture and another public policy in which suffering unexpected violence and loss and reactive aggression are not accepted as the norm of political life.[87]

Butler's call for a nonviolent ethics that understands the precariousness of life is at odds with the public discourse that has defined US reactions to 9/11. Her point is that invasion should not be perceived as the only option. Instead of constituting the audience as vengeful citizens of an attacked nation, she called on people to be empathic citizens of the world. If the audience members accepted Bush's definition of the situation as war, however, it would be difficult to persuade them to redefine the situation, as Butler attempted to do.

Ultimately, Butler argued that dissent is important, including dissent against definitions of situations that lead to labeling dissent as anti-American or, worse, treason. Recognition that situations are rhetorically defined is essential if we are to recognize the possibility of challenging the definition of a situation.

Redefining a situation is not easy. Once an audience accepts a definition of a situation, it can be difficult to change that definition. When the US public accepted the definition of 9/11 as an act of war against the United States and identified another country as sharing responsibility, US support for military action was strong. Such strong support should not have meant that people who disagreed were anti-American or did not support the troops, but the definition of the situation became stable and, hence, presented a particular exigence to anyone who would question the US response.

Analysis: 9/11 Redefined, Again

On May 15, 2014, the 9/11 Memorial Museum was dedicated. Its 110,000-square-foot exhibition space is located at the center of the World Trade Center site. The larger memorial space includes reflecting pools in the footprint of the two towers, surrounded by bronze plaques on which are inscribed the names of every person who died in the 2001 attack and in an earlier, 1993, attack on the Towers. During the dedication, President Barack Obama delivered these remarks:

President Barack H. Obama
"Remarks by the President at 9/11 Museum Dedication"
New York
May 15, 2014

1. Mayor Bloomberg, Governor Cuomo, honored guests, families of the fallen.

2. In those awful moments after the South Tower was hit, some of the injured huddled in the wreckage of the 78th floor. The fires were spreading. The air was filled with smoke. It was dark, and they could barely see. It seemed as if there was no way out.

3. And then there came a voice—clear, calm, saying he had found the stairs. A young man in his 20s, strong, emerged from the smoke, and over his nose and his mouth he wore a red handkerchief.

4. He called for fire extinguishers to fight back the flames. He tended to the wounded. He led those survivors down the stairs to safety, and carried a woman on his shoulders down 17 flights. Then he went back. Back up all those flights. Then back down again, bringing more wounded to safety. Until that moment when the tower fell.

5. They didn't know his name. They didn't know where he came from. But they knew their lives had been saved by the man in the red bandana.

6. Again, Mayor Bloomberg; distinguished guests; Mayor de Blasio; Governors Christie and Cuomo; to the families and survivors of that day; to all those who responded with such courage—on behalf of Michelle and myself and the American people, it is an honor for us to join in your

memories. To remember and to reflect. But above all, to reaffirm the true spirit of 9/11—love, compassion, sacrifice—and to enshrine it forever in the heart of our nation.

7. Michelle and I just had the opportunity to join with others on a visit with some of the survivors and families—men and women who inspire us all. And we had a chance to visit some of the exhibits. And I think all who come here will find it to be a profound and moving experience.

8. I want to express our deep gratitude to everybody who was involved in this great undertaking—for bringing us to this day, for giving us this sacred place of healing and of hope.

9. Here, at this memorial, this museum, we come together. We stand in the footprints of two mighty towers, graced by the rush of eternal waters. We look into the faces of nearly 3,000 innocent souls—men and women and children of every race, every creed, and every corner of the world. We can touch their names and hear their voices and glimpse the small items that speak to the beauty of their lives. A wedding ring. A dusty helmet. A shining badge.

10. Here we tell their story, so that generations yet unborn will never forget. Of coworkers who led others to safety. Passengers who stormed a cockpit. Our men and women in uniform who rushed into an inferno. Our first responders who charged up those stairs. A generation of servicemembers—our 9/11 Generation—who have served with honor in more than a decade of war. A nation that stands tall and united and unafraid—because no act of terror can match the strength or the character of our country. Like the great wall and bedrock that embrace us today, nothing can ever break us; nothing can change who we are as Americans.

11. On that September morning, Alison Crowther lost her son Welles. Months later, she was reading the newspaper—an article about those final minutes in the towers. Survivors recounted how a young man wearing a red handkerchief had led them to safety. And in that moment, Alison knew. Ever since he was a boy, her son had always carried a red handkerchief. Her son Welles was the man in the red bandana.

12. Welles was just 24 years old, with a broad smile and a bright future. He worked in the South Tower, on the 104th floor. He had a big laugh, a joy of life, and dreams of seeing the world. He worked in finance, but he had also been a volunteer firefighter. And after the planes hit, he put on that bandana and spent his final moments saving others.

13. Three years ago this month, after our SEALs made sure that justice was done, I came to Ground Zero. And among the families here that day was Alison Crowther. And she told me about Welles and his fearless spirit, and she showed me a handkerchief like the one he wore that morning.

14. And today, as we saw on our tour, one of his red handkerchiefs is on display in this museum. And from this day forward, all those who come

here will have a chance to know the sacrifice of a young man who—like so many—gave his life so others might live.

15. Those we lost live on in us. In the families who love them still. In the friends who remember them always. And in a nation that will honor them, now and forever.

16. And today it is my honor to introduce two women forever bound by that day, united in their determination to keep alive the true spirit of 9/11—Welles Crowther's mother Alison, and one of those he saved, Ling Young.[88]

The moment remembered with this speech is not the moment the planes hit the towers, but what happened after: the heroism of coworkers, first responders, and passengers who stopped a third plane from reaching its target. The situation to which President Obama responds is not one of terror, fear, or grief. Instead, he defines "the true spirit of 9/11" as "love, compassion, sacrifice."

This situation is marked by the dedication of the 9/11 museum, and as such, is constrained by the genre of dedications. The museum sustains public memory about the events, casting events of the past in terms of the needs of the present. The temporal distance between the dedication of the museum and the events of 9/11 enable Obama to focus on the values of love, compassion, and sacrifice.

Obama does not confine his remarks to what the lesson of the museum might be, but to what the spirit of 9/11 is. He uses a representative anecdote, a narrative that summarizes a situation, by telling the story of Welles Crowther. This story connects the artifacts in the museum (in this case, the red handkerchief) to the heroism Obama praises. The speech calls forth a national audience dedicated to service, selflessness, and a commitment to others.

FITTING RESPONSES RECONSIDERED

Identifying the components of a rhetorical situation and recognizing when symbolic actions have attempted to define the situation are useful steps in understanding how rhetoric functions. The relationships among the rhetor, argument, and components of the rhetorical situation (exigence, audience, and constraints) influence the range of communication possible. One way to assess the possibility of communication is to determine whether the response to the rhetorical situation is fitting. Like clothes, fit can be expansive or tight. If the situation is defined more expansively, then the issues to be considered become broader as well. As Butler asked about 9/11, do we mourn only the loss of US life, or all life? If the situation is defined expansively, it might call for a radically different response, such as the Pope's call to respect all human life and to reflect on and correct the underlying conditions that might lead people to violence. If defined narrowly, the situation tends to demand a focused response. The focus on the loss of US lives constructs a definition of the situation that suggests armed conflict is necessary to protect US lives. As time passes, the situation and the fitting response continues to alter and expand. For Obama, the response included a memorialization of the heroes on the day of the tragic events. In the next section, we identify possible influences on whether responses are fitting, including cultural variations in historical context and conscious decisions on the part of rhetors to challenge what is considered a fitting response.

Cultural Variations and Historical Context

Although the rhetorical situation is more than the historical context, placing a rhetorical act in its historical context helps us understand the choices available to a rhetor. Not all rhetors have equal access to the full range of persuasive possibilities. Moreover, meaning is not only in texts, but in the audiences who interpret the texts. Various audiences' social norms influence what they consider appropriate, even during a single historical moment.

Understanding the historical context is a necessary, but not sufficient, condition for understanding how a response fits a rhetorical situation. Communication scholars Robert J. Branham and W. Barnett Pearce point out that an audience interprets a rhetorical text within the rhetorical situation.[89] If you read the Gettysburg Address without knowing the rhetorical situation of the speech, you might read it as a piece of literature and miss how it responds to a very particular situation. Knowing that it was given on the battleground of the bloodiest battle in the US Civil War gives meaning to the speech and the persuasive choices President Lincoln made.

The context is not simply the historical facts and events surrounding a persuasive response. It also includes the participants' cultural orientations and how they influence interpretations of those events and facts. What today might be viewed as unfitting or as inappropriate language choice, form, topic, style, or approach might have been viewed as an acceptable or fitting response when a speech was first delivered. For example, expectations concerning the appropriate length of speeches have changed dramatically. In 1841, William Henry Harrison delivered a 105-minute inaugural speech. After the advent of radio in the 1920s, most speeches lasted no more than an hour. By the 1940s, the 30-minute speech was the norm; almost all major political speeches were reprinted in their entirety in newspapers. Now, most political speeches average about 20 minutes in length. Barack Obama's 2013 inaugural was barely 20 minutes long. Speakers hope to receive evening news coverage with 5-, 10-, or 15-second sound bites.[90]

The extreme time shrinkage can also be seen in political debates. When senatorial candidates Abraham Lincoln and Stephen A. Douglas debated seven times in 1858 on the single issue of slavery (particularly the expansion of slavery into the territories), each debate lasted three hours. The first person spoke for 60 minutes, the second for 90 minutes; then the first person had a rejoinder speech of 30 minutes. By comparison, in the November 22, 2011, Republican presidential primary debate in Washington, DC, in which eight candidates participated, each person was given 60 *seconds* to answer, and a 30-*second* rebuttal.

The length of speeches is not the only thing that has changed. What you might take for granted as appropriate now could have been extremely shocking in a different era. For example, political communication scholar Kathleen Hall Jamieson traces how a style that was once condemned as effeminate (soothing, ornamental, personal, self-disclosing, and using dramatic narratives), became the norm for contemporary politicians speaking in an electronic age.[91] Television is a visual medium, in which the visual elements combine intimately with the verbal elements.[92] Television has given the public a closer view of their leaders speaking than was possible before television; and people expect the words from speakers who are close-up to be intimate and personal.[93] Additionally, television gives the illusion that the rhetor is speaking to them individually, rather than to a large audience. Hence, it invites a more personal style than did the oratory of a pretelevision age.[94]

With the emergence of digital technologies, the issue of style is complicated further. As communication scholar Bruce Gronbeck notes in his assessment of citizen voices in a networked culture, "Many Web messages are both oral and literate in tone and form, sometimes chatty, at other times formal, and they can—but need not—rely on visual technologies for controlling meaning-making by the way they're laid out."[95] Tweets and e-mails can be highly personal, addressed to you personally, even when they address broad public concerns.

In fact, some rhetorical acts are intended to contribute to changes in social norms. For example, for a woman to speak (or even vote) on public policy was considered absolutely inappropriate and "unfitting" in the United States until the early 1900s. Daniel Webster (lawyer, senator, and statesperson) declared that "The rough contests of the political world are not suited to the dignity and the delicacy of your sex." Cardinal Gibbons (Catholic archbishop and the youngest prelate at the First Vatican Council) worried that "If woman enters politics, she will be sure to carry away on her some of the mud and dirt of political contact." Dr. S. Weir Mitchell (celebrated clinician and neurologist) exhorted women to "accep[t] the irrevocable decree which made her woman and not man. Something in between she cannot be."[96] Those societal norms have significantly shifted to the point that it would now be considered inappropriate to say that women have no place in public policy argument.

Responses to Rhetorical Situations

How does one explain persuasive responses that, at first glance, do not appear to fit the rhetorical situation, but still persuade an audience? Sometimes a rhetor might respond in an "unfitting" way in order to draw attention to an issue or shock an audience into awareness. Civil rights activists' lunch counter sit-ins of the 1960s and AIDS activists' die-ins of the 1980s did not persuade in a conventional way.[97]

Rhetors may choose to respond in an untraditional way if they do not interpret the situation in a conventional way. As Branham and Pearce explain, "not all texts are conventional, not all contexts are stable, and not all situations imply recognizable techniques or consensual standards of interpretation."[98] They offer four ways in which a rhetor can respond to a rhetorical situation: conformity, nonparticipation, desecration, and contextual reconstruction. We begin with their description of conformity, which echoes Bitzer's idea of the fitting response to the rhetorical situation.

Conformity. Rhetors use **conformity** when they employ *a conventional response to a situation.*[99] A person who is upset by a particular law might write a letter or an e-mail to a legislator, outlining the ways in which the law is flawed. This is a conventional way of expressing opinions about a legislative issue; it conforms to the traditional method of persuasion. Conformity adapts the persuasive message to the norms and expectations of the audience it addresses.

Societal norms affect what is considered a conforming response. Audiences have expectations that rhetors may decide to follow in order to have their messages heard and accepted. Much of our everyday communication conforms. For example, when you attempt to persuade your professor to alter an assignment that you think is too difficult or time consuming, you probably make an argument in a polite way, offering support for your position. You probably suggest alternatives to the assignment or ways to make the assignment more workable for you and your classmates. You are attempting to persuade your professor conventionally, using a style and arguments that are expected in this situation.

Nonparticipation. Some rhetors may choose not to respond to a situation within the established context because they do not believe the context is legitimate. According to Branham and Pearce, **nonparticipation** is *a response that denies the legitimacy of the rhetorical situation.*[100]

After entertainment news outlet TMZ released the audiotape in which Donald Sterling, the owner of the Los Angeles Clippers basketball team, allegedly told his girlfriend, V. Stiviano, that she should not bring African-Americans to basketball games or be photographed with them, the team met to decide what to do. They did not choose to boycott the game (which would have been an act of nonparticipation), but instead to stage a silent protest that also functioned as a form of nonparticipation. Before warming up for the fourth game in their first-round playoff series in April 2014, they took off their shooting shirts bearing the team logo and left them in a heap at mid-court, "revealing long-sleeved t-shirts that had been turned inside out so that the team's logo and name were not visible. The team also wore blue jerseys with the words 'Los Angeles' across the chest rather than a jersey design that bore the word 'Clippers,' and donned black socks."[101] During the game, they did wear the NBA required gear, but also wore black socks and sweat bands. The team symbolically indicated they were not participating in the game as Sterling's team, but as Los Angeles's team.

Nonparticipation as a strategy is not odd. In his study of how people react to the failure of an organization to provide a high quality service or product, economist and political theorist Albert O. Hirschman argues that consumers and citizens have two choices: exit or voice, "exit" representing nonparticipation and "voice" representing participation.[102] He argues that exit occupies a privileged position in US ideology, tradition, and practice, because the nation was founded by an act of exit/nonparticipation: in the Declaration of Independence, the colonies exited the British empire and declared they would no longer participate in it. Hirschman believes the countercultural movements of the 1960s and '70s followed this tradition with their calls to "turn on, tune in, drop out."[103] He explains, "Once again dissatisfaction with the surrounding social order leads to flight rather than fight, to withdrawal of the dissatisfied group and to its setting up a separate 'scene.'"[104]

Desecration. While nonparticipation refuses to grant legitimacy to a situation by participating in it, **desecration** is *a response that violates what would be considered an appropriate response; it participates, but in a way that overtly challenges expectations.* The rhetor ridicules the situation and/or those who take part in it. This response, according to Branham and Pearce, violates norms and conventions in order to question the legitimacy of the situation.[105]

The Russian punk rock group Pussy Riot has also illustrated symbolic desecration. The group engages in various forms of protest in unusual public places. Wearing balaclavas to cover their faces (and remain anonymous) they staged protests against Russian President Vladimir Putin's policies and his apparent ties to the Russian Orthodox Church.[106] They have often videotaped their actions and uploaded edited music videos to YouTube.[107] On February 21, 2012, five members, including Nadezhda Tolokonnikova, 22; Maria Alyokhina, 24; and Yekaterina Samutsevich, 29; entered Moscow's Cathedral of Christ the Saviour and performed a forty-second-long "punk prayer."[108] They began "bowing and crossing themselves in the manner of ardent believers" while singing a prayer calling on "the Lord to oust Russian President, Vladimir Putin."[109]

Although the three women did not destroy, deface, or endanger church property, they were arrested for "hooliganism with religious hatred" and sentenced to prison.[110] US Representative Steve King told reporters in Moscow that their actions "desecrated" the cathedral, and defended the prison sentences.[111] The patriarch of the church, in a liturgy delivered in Moscow's Deposition of the Robe Cathedral, condemned the performance for making fun of religion.[112] Pussy Riot mirrored the form of prayer, but by including lyrics informed by their punk sensibility, they also desecrated what was considered appropriate prayer in that space. They challenged expectations by demanding that Putin be ousted, offering a political prayer, and delivering a prayer whose words were more punk than religious.

Desecration can be funny, as the rhetor creates what Burke refers to as "perspective by incongruity" for the audience.[113] Basically, the rhetor creates a response that is funny in its absurdity, even though there are some elements of truth in that response. For example, *The Daily Show* mimics the form of a conventional news program, but at key moments departs from the form in order to expose how media outlets have failed to live up to their journalistic duty in a democratic society. Even as it appears to conform, its departure from form make clear the show is not a news show, but a "fake news program." For example, on March 4, 2009, the show criticized CNBC (the Consumer News and Business Channel) for its failure to report the financial crisis accurately. *Mad Money* host Jim Cramer, one of the more prominent faces of CNBC, took this criticism personally and started a round of appearances on other NBC-owned shows. In response, *Daily Show* host Jon Stewart focused a segment on Cramer (whose show CNBC promoted with the motto "In Cramer We Trust") and his fabulously bad advice to hold Bear Stearns stock in the days before the financial firm collapsed. Cramer indicated that Stewart had taken his advice out of context and dismissed Stewart as a "comedian" on a "variety show."[114] On his March 9 show, Stewart showed a series of clips of Cramer specifically telling people to buy the stock in the weeks before the collapse. At the end of this series, Stewart broke from the form of reporting (where reporters are supposed to be objective and not personally invested in a story), and yelled a phrase that rhymes with "MUCK YOU!"[115] Stewart literally desecrated the form of news reporting by yelling an obscenity. He also desecrated it stylistically by rejecting the decorous persona that news anchors often assume.[116]

What is most interesting, however, is that this fake program often did the job of critically reporting world events better than its supposedly real counterparts do. As host Jon Stewart explained in an exchange on *Crossfire* (an ostensibly real news show): "the absurdity of the system provides us the most material."[117] The reporters on *The Daily Show* desecrate the news to create messages about the way media report stories, as well as to desecrate the subjects of the stories themselves.

Contextual Reconstruction. **Contextual reconstruction** is *a response in which a rhetor attempts to redefine the situation.* These responses might appear to conform to the situation, but actually challenge the expectations of what they are meant to achieve, sometimes quite overtly, as part of the rhetorical act. In these instances, Branham and Pearce say, "Speaking itself is both the subject and object of such discourse."[118] Instead of "accepting the rhetorical situation as presented," a rhetor "dismantles and then reconstructs it."[119] In contextual reconstruction, the rhetor recognizes the traditional meaning of the rhetorical situation, but seeks to redefine it.

Branham and Pearce offer Abraham Lincoln's Gettysburg Address as an example of contextual reconstruction.[120] President Lincoln had been invited to make "a few appropriate remarks"[121] to dedicate a cemetery for the soldiers who had died fighting a horrific Civil War battle that saw fifty-one thousand casualties during a three-day period in July 1863.[122] Such a situation asked President Lincoln to look backward, which he appeared to acknowledge when he stated: "We are met on a great battle-field of that war. We have come to dedicate a portion of that field, as a final resting place for those who here gave their lives that that nation might live. It is altogether fitting and proper that we should do this."[123] He reinterpreted the exigence, however, by stating that the assumed exigence was not accurate: "But, in a larger sense, we can not dedicate—we can not consecrate—we can not hallow—this ground." Instead of looking backward in consecration, he shifted the orientation to the future. He reinterpreted the situation by creating a new exigence of renewal.[124]

Harkening back to Pericles's funeral oration, delivered 2,394 years earlier,[125] President Lincoln questioned whether a verbal response was even fitting: "The brave men, living and dead, who struggled here, have consecrated it, far above our poor power to add or detract. The world will little note, nor long remember what we say here, but it can never forget what they did here." Finally, he solidi-fied his reconstruction of the situation to a future orientation, calling for a renewed commitment to the war effort:

> It is for us, the living, rather, to be dedicated here to the unfinished work which they who fought here have thus far so nobly advanced. It is rather for us to be here dedicated to the great task remaining before us . . . that from these honored dead we take increased devotion to that cause for which they gave the last full measure of devotion; that we here highly resolve that these dead shall not have died in vain; that this nation, under God, shall have a new birth of freedom; and that government of the people, by the people, for the people, shall not perish from the earth.

On one level, the Gettysburg Address, considered by many to be one of the greatest speeches in US history, was not a fitting response because the purpose of the gathering was to consecrate part of the battlefield as a cemetery. Yet, as Branham and Pearce point out, President Lincoln reconstructed the situation and offered a new interpretation to the audience[126] that focused on renewal, not consecration. Lincoln knew he was faced with eulogizing the largest number of US soldiers ever killed in battle, and that the reality of the tragedy could have a demoralizing effect on Union supporters. Not all of the North was committed to the war effort. His interpretation of the meaning of the situation transformed the understanding of the battle and the memorial.[127]

CONCLUSION

As far back as Aristotle's time, students of rhetoric have recognized that rhetors make rhetorical choices when responding to a rhetorical situation. Those choices include the rhetor's definition of the situation and indicate how the rhetor wants the audience to interpret and respond to it. The rhetor's choices do not deter-mine the situation alone, however. A situation comes into existence as a result of the interplay between rhetor, audience, and context. As a result, the range of rhetorical choices available to a rhetor are limited.

When analyzing a rhetorical act, critics must recognize the reflexive relation-ship between text and context to understand how, and whether, the response functioned as the rhetor wished. In addition, critics must recognize that some rhetorical actions are called forth by recurrent rhetorical situations, which then influence audience expectations.

When analyzing the rhetorical situation, you must examine the cultural and historical context, as well as the interpretations of the context, to assess whether a response is fitting. Branham and Pearce advise employing an approach that "assumes neither that all contexts are 'fittable' nor that texts should necessarily 'fit' the contexts in which they occur."[128] They conclude, "rhetorical competence" is not based solely on "conformity to audience expectations or to standardized models of acceptable performance."[129] Sometimes, rhetoric that seems to fit a situation least is the rhetoric that is most eloquent, ethical, and elegant, even if it is not decorous.

When rhetors participate in civic life, whether they use deliberative rhetoric about policy or epideictic rhetoric that constitutes identity, they do not add their symbolic actions to a blank slate. Others have spoken before them; audiences carry with them expectations; rhetors, themselves, have histories. Symbolic actions are woven into already existing rhetorical situations. Rhetors reconstruct those situations by bringing particular audiences into being and by redefining exigencies. Rhetorical action and the situation of civic life are synergistic.

DISCUSSION QUESTIONS

1. Think of a time when you had no idea how to respond to a situation. Was the situation difficult to define? Were you unclear about what was expected? Did the participants in the event create discourse that was confusing?
2. Think about a recent political campaign or political crisis. What was the exigence to which the politicians were responding? Who was the audience? Who was the rhetorical audience? How were the two audiences different? Think about a particular speech. What was the context of the speech? What were the constraints the speaker faced prior to a speech? What choices did the speaker make?
3. Identify the generic expectations in each of the following situations:
    You are asked to deliver a speech at your best friend's wedding.
    You are selected to deliver the commencement speech at your graduation.
    You are asked to speak at a funeral.
    What are the similarities and differences among these situations? How do these similarities and differences suggest similar and different responses?
4. Identify a speech that you believe failed to fulfill its purpose. Were there elements of the rhetorical situation that led to this failure? Did the speaker present an unfitting response? What could the speaker have done to respond to the situation or to (re)define it?
5. A rhetorical approach focuses on the context as essential to understanding a rhetorical text. Find an example of a text where understanding the context changed your assessment of the text.

RECOMMENDED READINGS

Biesecker, Barbara. "Rethinking the Rhetorical Situation from within the Thematic of *Différance*." *Philosophy and Rhetoric* 22 (1989): 110–130.

Bitzer, Lloyd F. "The Rhetorical Situation." *Philosophy and Rhetoric* 1 (1968): 1–14.

Branham, Robert J., and W. Barnett Pearce. "Between Text and Context: Toward a Rhetorical Contextual Reconstruction." *Quarterly Journal of Speech* 71 (1985): 19–36.

Campbell, Karlyn Kohrs and Kathleen Hall Jamieson. *Presidents Creating the Presidency: Deeds Done in Words*. Chicago: University of Chicago Press, 2008.

Vatz, Richard E. "The Myth of the Rhetorical Situation." *Philosophy and Rhetoric* 6 (1973): 154–161.

ENDNOTES

[1] Aristotle, *On Rhetoric*, trans. George A. Kennedy (New York: Oxford University Press, 1991), 1.2.1 [1355].

[2] Aristotle, *On Rhetoric*, 1.3.1 [1358].

[3] Aristotle, *On Rhetoric*, 1.3.1 [1358b].

[4] Aristotle, *On Rhetoric*, 1.3.1 [1358b].

[5] Aristotle, *On Rhetoric*, 1.3.1 [1358b], italics added.

[6] Lloyd F. Bitzer, "The Rhetorical Situation," *Philosophy and Rhetoric* 1 (1968): 3.

[7] Bitzer, "Rhetorical Situation," 3.

[8] For a full description of Hamer's activism, see Kay Mills, *This Little Light of Mine: The Life of Fannie Lou Hamer* (New York: Dutton, 1993), esp. chapter 6. A transcript and audiotape of Hamer's testimony is available at http://www.americanrhetoric .com/speeches/fannielouhamercredentialscommittee.htm.

[9] Bitzer, "Rhetorical Situation," 3.

[10] Bitzer, "Rhetorical Situation," 4.

[11] Bitzer, "Rhetorical Situation," 6, italics added.

[12] Bitzer, "Rhetorical Situation," 6, italics added.

[13] Tom Leonard, "Hurricane Ike: Houston Residents Ordered Not to Evacuate as Deadly Storm Hits," London *Telegraph*, September 12, 2008, http://www.telegraph.co.uk /news/worldnews/northamerica/usa/2824891/Hurricane-Ike-Houston-residents -ordered-not-to-evacuate-as-deadly-storm-hits.html.

[14] Bitzer, "Rhetorical Situation," 5.

[15] Bitzer, "Rhetorical Situation," 5–6.

[16] Bitzer, "Rhetorical Situation," 2.

[17] David Kohn, "The President's Story: The President Talks in Detail about His Sept. 11 Experience," *60 Minutes*, September 10, 2003, http://www.cbsnews.com/stories /2002/09/11/ 60II/main521718.shtml.

[18] Some people perceived failure to respond. After President Bush was informed that the second tower had been hit, he continued to listen to sixteen second-graders take turns reading *The Pet Goat*. The perception of a failure to respond is most detailed in Michael Moore's controversial documentary, *Fahrenheit 9/11* (2004).

[19] Bruce E. Gronbeck, "Rhetorical Timing in Public Communication," *Central States Speech Journal* 25 (1974): 91.

[20] Bitzer, "Rhetorical Situation," 7, italics added.

[21] Matthew Dowd, "Interview from 'Karl Rove—The Architect,'" *Frontline*, January 4, 2005, posted April 12, 2005, http://www.pbs.org/wgbh/pages/frontline/shows /architect/interviews/dowd.html.

[22] Tim Harper, "It's Very Difficult to Ambush Bush: 'Bush Bubble' Keeps Fans in Line for Hours, Campaign Events Strictly Limited to Loyal Republicans," *NewsCenter*, September 24, 2005, http://www.commondreams.org/headlines04/0925-24.htm. In response to the strict control of access to campaign events, professors at Allegheny College in Meadville, Pennsylvania, created the Soapbox Alliance (http://cpp .allegheny.edu/soapboxalliance/ index.php). See Oren Dorell, "College Criticizes

Invitation-Only Political Rallies," *USA Today*, updated November 19, 2007, http://
www.usatoday.com/news/politics/election2008/2007-11-19-soapbox_N.htm. The
invitation-only strategy continued during Bush's presidency. See Michael A.
Genovese and Lori Cox Han, "The 'Invitation Only' Presidency of George W.
Bush," *HistoryNewsNetwork*, December 5, 2005, http://hnn.us/articles/18302.html.

[23] Sasha Issenberg, "A More Perfect Union: How President Obama's campaign
Used Big Data to Rally Individual Voters," *MIT Technology Review*,
December 19, 2012, http://www.technologyreview.com/featuredstory/509026
/how-obamas-team-used-big-data-to-rally-voters.

[24] Bitzer, "Rhetorical Situation," 6.

[25] Bitzer, "Rhetorical Situation," 8, italics added.

[26] Martha Cooper, *Analyzing Public Discourse* (Prospect Heights, IL: Waveland, 1989),
22.

[27] John Lewis, "John Lewis," in *My Soul is Rested: The Story of the Civil Rights
Movement in the Deep South*, ed. Howell Raines (New York: Penguin, 1977), 99.

[28] For examples, see his website: http://www.revbilly.com.

[29] Quoted in Jill Lane, "Reverend Billy: Preaching, Protest and Postindustrial Flânerie,"
The Drama Review 46, no. 1 (Spring 2002): 71.

[30] Karlyn Kohrs Campbell and Susan Schultz Huxman, *The Rhetorical Act*, 3rd ed.
(Belmont, CA: Thomson/Wadsworth, 2003), 184–198, 206–214, 224–236.

[31] Campbell and Huxman, *Rhetorical Act*, 207–212.

[32] H. W. Brands, "15 Minutes That Saved America," *American History* 43, no. 4 (October
2008): 34–41.

[33] David Michael Ryfe, "Franklin Roosevelt and the Fireside Chats," *Journal of
Communication* 49, no. 4 (Autumn 1999): 80–103.

[34] Franklin D. Roosevelt, First Fireside Chat, "The Banking Crisis," March 12,
1933, http://www.americanrhetoric.com/speeches/fdrfirstfiresidechat.html. For a
detailed analysis of this speech, see Amos Kiewe, *FDR's First Fireside Chat: Public
Confidence and the Banking Crisis* (College Station: Texas A&M Press, 2007).

[35] Mary Kate Cary, "Obama Should Make Roosevelt-Style Fireside Chats on the
Banking Crisis," Opinion, *U.S. News and World Report* online, March 12, 2009,
http://www.usnews.com/blogs/mary-kate-cary/2009/3/12/obama-should-make
-roosevelt-style-fireside-chats-on-the-banking-crisis.html.

[36] Campbell and Huxman, *Rhetorical Act*, 184–198, 212–214.

[37] Campbell and Huxman, *Rhetorical Act*, 224–236.

[38] Ryfe, "Franklin Roosevelt," 99.

[39] Bitzer, "Rhetorical Situation," 10.

[40] Karlyn Kohrs Campbell and Kathleen Hall Jamieson, "Form and Genre in Rhetorical
Criticism: An Introduction," in *Form and Genre: Shaping Rhetorical Action*, ed.
Karlyn Kohrs Campbell and Kathleen Hall Jamieson (Falls Church, VA: Speech
Communication Association, 1978), 19.

[41] Kathleen M. Jamieson, "Antecedent Genre as Rhetorical Constraint," *Quarterly
Journal of Speech* 61 (1975): 406.

[42] Karlyn Kohrs Campbell and Kathleen Hall Jamieson, *Deeds Done in Words* (Chicago:
University of Chicago Press, 1990), 37.

[43] Campbell and Jamieson, "Form and Genre," 23.

[44] Campbell and Jamieson, "Form and Genre," 21.

[45] Gerald R. Ford, "Address upon Taking the Oath of the U.S. Presidency," August 9,
1974, East Room of the White House, Washington, DC, http://www
.americanrhetoric.com/speeches/geraldfordpresidentialoath.html.

[46] Campbell and Jamieson, *Deeds*, 47.

[47] Kathleen Hall Jamieson and Karlyn Kohrs Campbell, "Rhetorical Hybrids: Fusions of Generic Elements," *Quarterly Journal of Speech* 68 (1982): 146–157.

[48] Campbell and Jamieson, *Deeds*, 38.

[49] Lyndon Baines Johnson, "Let Us Continue," American Rhetoric, November 27, 1963, http://www.americanrhetoric.com/speeches/lbjletuscontinue.html.

[50] John F. Kennedy, "A Strategy of Peace," Commencement Address, American University, June 10, 1963, http://www.geocities.com/~newgeneration/strategy.htm.

[51] Lyndon Baines Johnson, "The Great Society: Commencement Address at the University of Michigan," in *Presidential Rhetoric*, ed. Theodore Windt, 61–64 (Dubuque, IA: Kendall/Hunt, 1987).

[52] George H. W. Bush, "Remarks at the University of Michigan Commencement Ceremony in Ann Arbor," *Weekly Compilation of Presidential Documents* 27 (May 13, 1991): 563–566.

[53] William Jefferson Clinton, "Remarks at the University of California San Diego Commencement Ceremony in La Jolla, California," *Public Papers of the Presidents of the United States: William J. Clinton* (Washington: GPO, 1998).

[54] Michael Kolakowski and Thomas H. Neale, "The President's State of the Union Message: Frequently Asked Questions," CRS Report for Congress, March 7, 2006, 5, http://www.senate.gov/artandhistory/history/resources/pdf/stateoftheunion.pdf.

[55] Campbell and Jamieson, *Deeds*, 70.

[56] Kathleen Hall Jamieson, "Generic Constraints and the Rhetorical Situation," *Philosophy & Rhetoric* 6, no. 3 (1973): 168.

[57] Daniel Riffe and James Glen Stovall, "Diffusion of News of Shuttle Disaster: What Role for Emotional Response," *Journalism Quarterly* 66 (Autumn 1989): 551–556.

[58] You can watch footage of the explosion on YouTube: "*Challenger* Disaster Live on CNN" at http://www.youtube.com/watch?v=j4JOjcDFtBE.

[59] Ronald W. Reagan, "The Space Shuttle 'Challenger' Tragedy Address," January 28, 1986, http://www.americanrhetoric.com/speeches/ronaldreaganchallenger.htm. A video of the speech is available on this site.

[60] The Soviet Union was probably also an audience, especially considering Reagan's thinly veiled reference to the Soviet penchant for secrecy in paragraph 6.

[61] For additional analysis, see "Special Issue: The Space Shuttle *Challenger*," *Central States Speech Journal* 37 (Fall 1986). For analysis of the interactions between the visuals of the explosion and Reagan's rhetoric, see Kathleen Hall Jamieson, *Eloquence in an Electronic Age: The Transformation of Political Speechmaking* (New York: Oxford University Press, 1988), esp. pp. 126–133.

[62] Richard E. Vatz, "The Myth of the Rhetorical Situation," *Philosophy and Rhetoric* 6 (1973): 159.

[63] Vatz, "Myth," 159.

[64] Vatz, "Myth," 157.

[65] Vatz, "Myth," 159.

[66] Bitzer, "Rhetorical Situation," 11.

[67] Vatz, "Myth," 155–156.

[68] Rachel Carson, *Silent Spring*, 40th anniversary ed. (New York: Mariner, 1962/2002).

[69] Linda Lear, "The Life and Legacy of Rachel Carson," 1998, http://www.rachelcarson.org/Biography.aspx.

[70] Robert J. Branham and W. Barnett Pearce, "Between Text and Context: Toward a Rhetorical Contextual Reconstruction," *Quarterly Journal of Speech* 71 (1985): 19–36, 19.

[71] J. Robert Cox, "Argument and the 'Definition of the Situation,'" *Central States Speech Journal* 32 (1981): 197–205, esp. 200.

[72] Cox, "Argument," 197. Although Cox disagrees with Bitzer, his position is not identical to Vatz's. For Cox, the definition of the situation refers not only to individual interpretations, but also to broader, culturally formulated, and shared perceptions. See Cox, "Argument," 199.

[73] Cox, "Argument," 200.

[74] Robert E. Terrill, "Irony, Silence, and Time: Frederick Douglass on the Fifth of July," *Quarterly Journal of Speech* 89, no. 3 (August 2003): 216–234.

[75] Frederick Douglass, "What to the Slave Is the Fourth of July?" July 5, 1852, http://www.teachingamericanhistory.org/library/index.asp?document=162.

[76] Douglass, "What."

[77] George W. Bush, "9/11 Address to the Nation," September 11, 2001, http://www.americanrhetoric.com/speeches/gwbush911addresstothenation.htm. A video of the speech is available on this site.

[78] George W. Bush, "Remarks by the President in Photo Opportunity with the National Security Team," September 12, 2001, http://www.whitehouse.gov/news/releases/2001/09/20010912-4.html.

[79] Kenneth Mentor, "Crime or Act of War?—The Media, 9-11, and Iraq," Presentation at the November 2002 Annual Meetings of the American Society of Criminology, Chicago, IL, http://critcrim.org/critpapers/911_iraq.htm; John Domke, David Hutcheson, Andre Billeaudeaux, and Philip Garland, "U.S. National Identity, Political Elites, and a Patriotic Press Following September 11," *Political Communication* 21, no. 1 (January/March (2004): 27–50.

[80] The Pew Research Center for People and the Press, "Americans and Europeans Differ Widely on Foreign Policy Issues," April 17, 2002, http://people-press.org/reports/display.php3?ReportID=153.

[81] Many responses to 9/11 have been penned, including Noam Chomsky, *9-11* (New York: Open Media, 2001); Sara Ruddick, "The Moral Horror of the September Attacks," *Hypatia* 18 (2003): 212–222; Gayatri C. Spivak, "Terror: A Speech after 9-11," *Boundary* 2 31 (2004): 81–111.

[82] Vatz, "Myth," 157.

[83] John Paul II, "General Audience of John Paul II," September 11, 2002, http://www.vatican.va/holy_father/john_paul_ii/audiences/2002/documents/hf_jp-ii_aud_20020911_en.html.

[84] John Paul II, "General."

[85] "Pope Opposes Military Response to Terrorism," *Catholic World News*, http://www.cwnews.com/news/viewstory.cfm?recnum=32004.

[86] Judith Butler, *Precarious Life: The Powers of Mourning and Violence* (London: Verso, 2004), xii.

[87] Butler, *Precarious*, xiv.

[88] Barack H. Obama, "Remarks by the President at 9/11 Museum Dedication," May 15, 2014, http://www.whitehouse.gov/the-press-office/2014/05/15/remarks-president-911-museum-dedication.

[89] Branham and Pearce, "Between," 20.

[90] Jamieson, *Eloquence*, 9–10.

[91] Jamieson, *Eloquence*, 67–89.

[92] Jamieson, *Eloquence*, 13.

[93] Jamieson, *Eloquence*, 62–63.

[94] Jamieson, *Eloquence*, 44.

95 Bruce Gronbeck, "Citizen Voices in Cyberpolitical Culture," in *Rhetorical Democracy: Discursive Practices of Civic Engagement*, ed. Gerard A. Hauser and Amy Grim, 17–31 (Mahwah, NJ: Erlbaum, 2004), 27.

96 "Opinions of Eminent Persons against Woman Suffrage," *Pamphlet*, issued by Massachusetts Association Opposed to the Further Extension of Suffrage to Women, Room 615, Kensington Building, Boston, MA, October 1912.

97 For an exploration of these tactics, see Susan Leigh Foster, "Choreographies of Protest," *Theatre Journal* 55 (2003): 395–412.

98 Branham and Pearce, "Between," 19.

99 Branham and Pearce, "Between," 28.

100 Branham and Pearce, "Between," 28–29.

101 Ben Golliver, "Clippers Hold Silent Protest against Owner Donald Sterling before Game 4," *Sports Illustrated*, April 27, 2014, http://nba.si.com/2014/04/27/donald -sterling-clippers-silent-protest-game-4-warriors.

102 Albert O. Hirschman, *Exit, Voice, and Loyalty: Responses to Decline in Firms, Organizations and States* (Cambridge, MA: Harvard University Press, 1970).

103 Countercultural icon Timothy Leary is credited with coining this phrase in his 1967 spoken word album of the same name, produced on the Performance Records label.

104 Hirschman, *Exit*, 108.

105 Branham and Pearce, "Between," 29.

106 Carole Cadwalladr, "Pussy Riot: Will Vladimir Putin Regret Taking on Russia's Cool Women Punks?" *Guardian*, July 28, 2012, http://www.theguardian.com/world/2012 /jul/29/pussy-riot-protest-vladimir-putin-russia.

107 Henry Langston, "Meeting Pussy Riot," *Vice*, March 12, 2012, http://www.vice.com /read/A-Russian-Pussy-Riot.

108 *Pussy Riot: A Punk Prayer*, dir. Mike Lerner and Maxim Pozdorovkin, HBO Documentaries, 2013, http://www.hbo.com/documentaries/pussy-riot-a-punk-prayer.

109 Thom Nickels, "Pussy Riot and Sacred Spaces," HuffPost Religion, November 25, 2013, http://www.huffingtonpost.com/thom-nickels/pussy-riot-and-sacred-spa_b _4334415.html.

110 Nickels, "Pussy Riot."

111 Quoted in Julian Pecquet, "Rep. Steve King Defends Jail Sentence for Russian Pro-Democracy Activists," The Hill, June 3, 2013, http://thehill.com/policy /international/303029-rep-steve-king-raises-conservative-ire-with-pro-putin -comments-during-moscow-trip.

112 Quoted in "Pussy Riot Reply to Patriarch," *RT*, March 27, 2012, http://rt.com/art -and-culture/pussy-riot-clash-patriarch-567.

113 Kenneth Burke, *Attitudes toward History* (Boston: Beacon, 1959), 308.

114 Quoted in "Memo to Jim Cramer: Three Rules to Consider," *USA Today*, March 16, 2009.

115 Jon Stewart, "In Cramer We Trust," *The Daily Show*, March 9, 2009, http://www .thedailyshow.com/video/index.jhtml?videoId=220288&title=in-cramer-we -trust&byDate=true.

116 For more on this exchange, see Ryan E. McGeough, "The Voice of the People: Jon Stewart, Public Argument and Political Satire," in *The Daily Show and Rhetoric*, ed. Trischa Goodnow (Lanham, MD: Lexington, 2011).

117 Jon Stewart, "Jon Stewart's America," CNN *Crossfire* (October 15, 2004), http:// transcripts.cnn.com/TRANSCRIPTS/0410/15/cf.01.html.

118 Robert J. Branham, "Speaking Itself: Susan Sontag's Town Hall Address," *Quarterly Journal of Speech* 75, no. 3 (August 1989): 259–260.

119 Branham and Pearce, "Between," 32.

120 Branham and Pearce, "Between," 32–33.

121 David Wills, a prominent citizen, invited Lincoln to speak. See "Gettysburg," http://www.medalofhonor.com/civilwar/gettysburg.html.

122 Abraham Lincoln, Gettysburg Address, November 19, 1863 (Chicago: Sherwood Lithograph, c. 1905).

123 All references to the speech refer to Abraham Lincoln, Gettysburg Address, November 19, 1863, http://www.loc.gov/exhibits/gadd/images/Gettysburg-2.jpg.

124 Branham and Pearce, "Between," 33.

125 Garry Wills, *Lincoln at Gettysburg: The Words That Remade America* (New York: Simon and Schuster, 1992), 56.

126 Branham and Pearce, "Between," 32.

127 Branham and Pearce, "Between," 32–33.

128 Branham and Pearce, "Between," 33.

129 Branham and Pearce, "Between," 33.

9

Publics and Counterpublics

KEY CONCEPTS

counterpublics

enclaved publics

hybrid publics

networked public screen

networked publics

oscillating publics

public

public screen

public sphere

strong publics

weak publics

Immigration has long been a topic that sparks intense debate in the United States. Legislative attempts to limit immigration have occurred throughout US history, even though the United States of America was founded as a nation of immigrants and the Statue of Liberty declares:

> Give me your tired, your poor,
> Your huddled masses yearning to
> breathe free,
> The wretched refuse of your teeming
> shore.
> Send these, the homeless, tempest-tost
> to me,
> I lift my lamp beside the golden door!

Despite this welcome, immigration restrictions have, over time, targeted Asians, Eastern and Southern Europeans, and Latinos. In 1882, Congress passed the Chinese Exclusion Act, which prohibited for ten years the immigration of people from China to the United States. The Immigration Act of 1917 restricted the amount of immigration from Asia generally. During the first two decades of the 1900s, more than 14 million people emigrated to the United States, mostly from Southern Europe, Eastern Europe, and Asia. In response, the Immigration Act of 1924 sought to lock in the then-current ethnic distribution for immigration. In 1954, the United States Immigration and Naturalization Service launched "Operation Wetback," which sought the forcible deportation of 1.2 million migrant workers, mostly from Mexico. In 1994, California passed Proposition 187, which eliminated public health, education, and welfare provisions for undocumented workers.

The spring of 2006 saw public demonstrations in response to Congressional debates over immigration policy.[1] People, not just politicians, showed the stakes they held in the public discussion. Rallies across the country that demonstrated the broad public concern included gatherings of 500,000 in Los Angeles, 350,000–500,000 in Dallas, and 400,000 in Chicago. Pro-immigration rallies occurred in 140 cities across the country from March to May 2006. In addition, the anti–illegal immigration Minuteman Project held a 13-city campaign tour, culminating in a rally outside the US Capitol building.

The debates did not end in 2006. Between October 2013 and July 2014, more than 52,000 unaccompanied children, "many who were fle[eing] gang violence in Guatemala, El Salvador and Honduras," were detained after crossing the US-Mexico border without legal documentation.[2] A humanitarian crisis arose when Texas facilities were overwhelmed, leading immigration officials to disperse the immigrants to other places so they could be processed, to be either deported or united with family living in the United States. About 140 children (some with their families) were flown to a facility in Murrieta, California. Some citizens of the town responded by blockading the Border Patrol Station, waving US flags[3] while shouting "go home." Federal authorities had to reroute the buses to a facility in San Diego. Other community members counterprotested, with signs declaring "We are your babysitters, we clean your hotels, we babysit your kids" and "Our people cook your food."[4]

The debates over immigration illustrate several things about publics and public deliberation. First, they illustrate how, as people present their concerns for public consideration, they constitute a public—that is, they navigate who is entitled to participate in forming public culture and public policy. For our purposes, a **public** is formed by *people coming together to discuss common concerns, including concerns about who they are and what they should do, and as a result constructing social reality together.* The goal of public deliberation is not always consensus; sometimes it is to unsettle existing agreement. Regardless of the goal, publics use rhetoric to discuss matters of common concern (and determine what they are), constitute identity, and construct their shared reality.

Second, discussions about immigration illustrate how public discourse includes both deliberative debates about policy and cultural debates about civic identity—who can and should participate in public deliberations about national policy and national identity. Communication scholar Anne Demo notes that anxiety has grown "over the nation's changing ethnic demographics, characterized in the popular press as 'the browning of America.'"[5] As a result, according to several other communication scholars, these debates are not just about whom to let into the country, but also about what it means to be a US citizen, how to define the country's identity, and what power and privilege comes with citizenship.[6]

Third, these discussions show that "public" is a complex concept. The term carries diverse meanings. News coverage noted various ways in which these rallies and debates had a public character. Reports described the gatherings as "massive public rallies organized by immigrants' rights groups"[7] and as a "wave of public protests."[8] US Representative Tom Tancredo talked about the public as audience: "Millions of people are flaunting the fact that they are here illegally and are demanding special treatment. I don't think that flies with John Q. Public."[9] In response, rally organizers encouraged protestors to carry more US flags because they "did not want to alienate the broader public."[10] Public opinion became a thing to be moved: reports noted that the "immigrant groups face several hurdles in their attempt to sway politicians and public opinion."[11] The audience was also described as complex, containing both politicians and the public. One story noted, "it is encouraging that politicians and the public at least are thinking about" immigration issues.[12] Other stories examined whether the rallies were a possible influence on "the public debate on immigration"[13] and referenced scholarly reports that "demonstrations represent the largest effort by immigrants to influence public policy in recent memory."[14] Opponents to illegal immigration argued that immigrants were "invading" the United States, creating economic problems such as job loss, and that "illegal aliens bring diseases and drain public services."[15] Ultimately, media reports said a congressional bill was unlikely to pass because of "deep public divisions."[16] In these descriptions, at various times, the term "public" describes the rallies, a place, a people, policy, opinion, services, and nonpoliticians.

Fourth, the debates show that an understanding of the meaning of publicity and publics is central to understanding the role of rhetoric in civic life. Which issues are considered worthy of public consideration? What discussions are part of public discourse? Which people are given access to the public sphere? Who is included in the public? To understand rhetoric in civic life, you need to understand the concept of public.

Fifth, these debates show that a multitude of voices are present in the public sphere. Various perspectives and actions emerged on the issue, including former CNN news anchor Lou Dobbs's discussions of the economic impact of the "invasion of illegal aliens";[17] the Minuteman Project's frustrations with the lack of federal enforcement of immigration law; the work of La Raza, a Hispanic civil rights organization, on immigrants' rights; various governors' concerns about the fiscal impact of illegal immigration on states' budgets; President George W. Bush's attempts to link improved border security and workplace enforcement to the legalization of twelve million illegal immigrants and the creation of a temporary worker program; President Barack Obama's promise to use executive orders to make the immigration system "smarter";[18] and the citizens and city officials of Murrieta, such as protester Ellen Meeks, who believed "the country's identity has eroded with an influx of undocumented immigrants" and said "I just wish America would be America again because it's not."[19] Rhetoric scholar Gerard A. Hauser notes that this diversity of activity is central to the public sphere, for "it is only when a multitude of voices is heard that social actors begin to realize that they can do more than respond; they can choose."[20]

This chapter introduces you to an understanding of publics and the role rhetoric plays in them, but we do not end the discussion there. As with all communication, power plays a role. Not all people have equal rhetorical power. Thus, the question arises: if a group is not represented in the dominant public, how can its members develop a vocabulary that articulates their identity, interests, and needs? To answer this question, we explore the concept of *counter-public spheres*—arenas of public deliberation that arise in response to exclusions from the dominant public. We also explore the increasing role of the Internet and the challenges it poses to the very idea of what is public. Finally, we discuss the expanding roles of visual rhetoric and media proliferation, and why these call for a reconsideration of the public sphere as a public screen.

THE PUBLIC SPHERE

Most contemporary understandings of the public sphere rely on German sociologist Jürgen Habermas's groundbreaking work.[21] Habermas studied nations that shifted from monarchical and feudalistic forms to democratic societies, such as Britain, France, and Germany during the eighteenth and early nineteenth centuries. These societies had in common the emergence of a bourgeois public sphere, composed of people who influenced culture and possessed control over the means of production (artisans and tradespeople who formed guilds and companies), and who engaged in practices that enabled them to serve as an intermediary between the state (the executive power of official government) and society (associational activity among private individuals). Habermas believed the needs and interests of individuals can come together as a public to check the exercise of state power and to make sure that power always acts in the interest of those it governs.

In Chapter 4, we defined the public sphere as the argument sphere that exists "to handle disagreements transcending personal and technical disputes." That definition is rooted in Habermas's definition. His study of the social changes in European societies led to his definition of the **public sphere** as *"a domain of our social life in which such a thing as public opinion can be formed"* and that *"is constituted in every conversation in which private persons come together to form a public."*[22] By "public opinion," Habermas does not mean the survey responses that Roper tracks or the call-in polls your local evening news conducts. Instead, he says, public opinion is formed only when "a public that engages in rational discussion exists" to create informed opinion, which he contrasts to "mere opinions."[23] As an illustration, Habermas describes the coffee houses that opened in Britain and Germany between 1680 and 1730, and served as places where a variety of people (mostly men) could meet and talk about contemporary moral, literary, and political issues.[24] London, alone, had three thousand coffee houses, each with its own regulars. For Habermas, the conversations in these coffee houses were central to the formation of a public sphere.

Notice that Habermas defines the public sphere in terms of *communication.* A public sphere is not brought into being by a particular group of people, a location, or a set of topics. Instead, it is constituted by the *conversations* (rhetorical acts) of people as they discuss topics of general interest.[25] Political and social theorist Nancy Fraser describes Habermas's public sphere as an arena of discourse "in which political participation is enacted through the medium of talk" as people come together to "deliberate about common affairs."[26]

Habermas's definition is both descriptive and prescriptive. It describes the public discourse as enabled and constrained within a given society by institutions, legal rights, and norms. It also prescribes an ideal to work toward. An ideal public sphere has certain characteristics. It must (1) be "open in principle to all citizens," (2) address "matters of general interest," and (3) be free from coercion.[27] This ideal of the public sphere is central to democracy. Free and open communication, in which anyone can participate, about issues that transcend personal interest is essential to a fully functioning democracy and open society.

It is challenging to point to an example of a public sphere because it is difficult to identify a specific place or arena of discourse. Instead, one knows a public sphere has come into being because one can identify trace elements of it in rhetoric. The immigration rhetoric described in the introduction to this chapter is an example of public sphere discourse. People enacted political participation through their rhetorical acts (conversations, speeches, parades, signs, tweets, blog posts, letters to the editor, and protest meetings) about an issue of common concern. Although the hope was that public opinion, and not mere opinion, was formed, it would be difficult to prove that all the rhetorical acts in these debates were "rational discussion." Still, the debates suggest the rise of a public sphere.

Another example is the February 2011 debate over the collective bargaining rights of unions of public employees in Wisconsin. In response to record state budget deficits, Governor Scott Walker proposed a "budget repair bill"[28] to balance the budget. The bill proposed cuts to public workers' compensation and eliminated almost all collective bargaining rights for most public employees (except police, firefighters, and the state patrol). The rhetoric about the bill provides ample trace evidence of a public sphere, as citizens talked about issues of common concern: the budget deficit, the vitality of public unions, and the legislative impasse caused when fourteen Democratic state senators fled the state in order to deny a quorum to Republican senators seeking to pass the bill. A public sphere was constituted in protests as tens of thousands of citizens filled the Wisconsin state capitol square and rotunda; as union members, citizens, and students took part in public hearings; as state representatives and senators, as well as the governor, talked in various media outlets and during legislative debates; and as citizens around the state talked to each other about the bill. The constitution of the public sphere was not confined to the events at the capitol building or the statements of lawmakers; it also occurred in coffee shops such as the Coffee Vault in Dousman[29] and EVP Coffee in Madison. In the tradition of Habermas's European coffee houses, many regulars at EVP Coffee (including public sphere scholar Robert Asen) engaged in conversations about public affairs, including the governor's bill. The protests, testimony, media interviews, and coffee shop conversations across the state enacted political participation through talk.

Habermas's ideal of open, public, and coercion-free communication may never have existed in reality,[30] but more recent scholars herald it as an ideal toward which democratic societies should strive.[31] Civic engagement requires open and reasoned communication between informed citizens. Imagine if the public debates about health care were open only to those who were already covered by health insurance. A part of the citizenry would be voiceless about an issue that deeply affects them. Or imagine that during debates, people who disagreed with the government were jailed or threatened, as happened in Russia in 2014. The day after the winter Olympics ended, a judge sentenced eight protestors to two and a half years to four years in prison. Their crime: they had participated in a protest on the eve of Russian President Vladimir Putin's inauguration. Those sentenced were not the leaders of the protest, but "ordinary people, selected from the demonstration apparently at random." Even though the Russian constitution promises "Everyone shall be guaranteed the freedom of ideas and speech," it appears protestors who disagreed with Putin were selected for prosecution "for the crime of expressing their opinions." [32]

We want to warn you against conflating and confusing the complex meanings of "public" identified in the chapter's introduction.[33] When you think of "public," you might think of anything outside the domestic sphere or family. In this formulation, that which is public is not private and that which is private is not public. This formulation shapes common understanding in phrases such as "public officials" (people who work for the state), "public opinion" (as polled by Roper), and "public figures" (people whom a substantial portion of the population can identify, even if they have nothing to do with the discussion of issues of common interest). Fraser argues that this common understanding of "public" collapses four analytically distinct ideas: (1) the state, (2) the economy, (3) arenas of public discourse, and (4) people to whom the state should be accountable. When discussing public spheres in this chapter, we use Habermas's ideal as referenced in Fraser's third sense—arenas of public discourse. The public sphere is distinct from the state; ideally, discourse in the public sphere can critique and challenge state actions. The public sphere is also distinct from the economy; it is not a location in which to buy and sell, but to deliberate about policy and form collective identities. Finally, although people's discourse forms the public sphere, the people are not identical to it. Just because many people are present does not mean that a public sphere has formed.

The boundaries of the public sphere are not static. As communication scholars Robert Asen and Daniel Brouwer explain, "'Public' and 'private' are not fixed, content-specific categories that structure the public sphere prior to discourse."[34] What counts as an issue of general interest can change over time. The question of what counts as a public issue is, itself, a topic to be discussed and debated in the public sphere. Communication scholars Valeria Fabj and Matthew J. Sobnosky note that, for many years, for example, HIV/AIDS was perceived to be a personal issue, a "gay disease." As a result of public activism, it was recognized as a public health issue about which everyone should be concerned and to which the state should respond.[35]

Habermas's description of the role of public sphere rhetoric in civil society is the foundation of more nuanced descriptions of civic participation. Because power plays a role in rhetoric, we now explore how power affects publics.

Strong and Weak Publics

Although Habermas held out the ideal of an overarching public sphere that could represent universal human interests in an arena distinct from the state, other scholars have noted that it makes more sense to speak of multiple publics, the way representative assemblies of the state can function as publics, and the interactions among publics.[36] In contrast to Habermas's description of the state as distinct from the public sphere, some scholars note, democratic parliaments and legislative assemblies can participate in public sphere discourse.

Fraser distinguishes between weak publics and strong publics. She defines **weak publics** as *"publics whose deliberative practice consists exclusively in opinion formation and does not also encompass decision making."*[37] She defines **strong publics** as *"publics whose discourse encompasses both opinion formation and decision making."*[38] "Strong" and "weak" here refer to the power to make decisions or legislate, not to the general ability to dominate public opinion. In the example of the immigration rallies and debates, both the Minuteman Project and immigrant groups represent weak publics; they cannot pass laws, but they seek to affect the opinions of politicians, who are members of strong publics. A weak public also participates in the formation of identity for those who are part of it. Communication scholars Kent A. Ono and John Sloop document how the discourse of the strong public (politicians) and dominant media, both for and against California's Proposition 187, constructed an identity of illegal immigrants (and Latinos) as prone to criminality, diseased, and of value only as an economic commodity (as workers).[39] In response, according to rhetoric scholars Marouf Hasian, Jr., and Fernando Delgado, the weak public of immigrant groups sought to redefine their identity by celebrating immigrants' contributions to the United States, creating unity around a conception of La Raza, and developing counter-histories of immigration law.[40] For example, immigrant groups repeatedly used the slogan, "we didn't cross the border, the border crossed us," to highlight that much of what is the western United States once belonged to Mexico.[41]

Strong publics engage in instrumental acts of governance. Governing bodies made up of representatives of the people (such as the US Congress or sovereign parliaments) are examples of strong publics. Where a democratically elected body exists through which the people's will can be voiced, Fraser says, it can function not as an arm of the state, but as "the site for the discursive authorization of the use of state power."[42] Thus, democratically elected representative bodies begin to blur the distinction that Habermas draws so clearly between the state and civil society. Strong publics are important because "the force of public opinion is strengthened when a body representing it is empowered to translate such 'opinion' into authoritative decisions."[43] When it implements public policy (on health care, immigration, or taxes, for example), the US Congress transforms what it perceives to be public opinion into laws.

Although strong publics possess decision-making powers, weak publics also have power to create change. They can exert influence on people in decision-making roles. For example, if a school board is considering curriculum changes, a weak public can exert pressure on the school board members (a strong public) by participating in public hearings and making public comments. If the school board members are elected, then the weak public could exert pressure because board members might be concerned about re-election.

In the case of California's Proposition 187, a typically weak public (the electorate) was empowered to act as a strong public (the legislature) because of

California's initiative system. In the initiative system, proposed laws are put to a direct vote of the people. Hasian and Delgado argue that the initiative system is "a means through which like-minded citizens might give voice to their policy and legislative concerns."[44] Not only can citizens form opinion, the initiative system enables them to pass laws.

Hybrid Publics

The immigration issue demonstrates that debates about laws may also be debates about identity. Hasian and Delgado note that a debate that began as a general discussion of the dangers of a foreign "other" illegally immigrating to the United States "transformed into a complex debate regarding the meaning of American citizenship and the social and political power that comes from belonging to particular racial categories in the U.S."[45] This insight highlights that the public sphere may not just mediate between the state and society, it is also a sphere in which people develop understandings of their role in society. Fraser describes such publics as **hybrid publics:** *publics that do not choose between civic identity and deliberative politics, but instead recognize that both can exist in a mutually reinforcing relationship.*[46]

Rhetoric that forms identity and rhetoric that forms policy are equally important. Rhetoric exploring what it means to be a US citizen is as much a part of the public sphere as rhetoric defending a policy. Thus, rhetoric in the public sphere includes epideictic and forensic rhetoric about identity as well as deliberative rhetoric about policy. Hauser clarifies the link between rhetoric, the public sphere, and social reality when he writes: "Public spheres . . . are discursive spaces where society deliberates about normative standards and even develops new frameworks for expressing and evaluating social reality."[47]

Habermas's original formulation, in which there is only one state and one public that can speak to universal interests, and only those two interact, provides a model for understanding the public sphere, but does not describe actually existing democracies. Habermas himself admits that a society does not need a unitary public to have critical debate; that a "pluralistic" public composed of diverse publics can criticize state action, which is the public sphere's primary function.[48] How might critics understand a pluralistic conception of publics?

PUBLICS, COUNTERPUBLICS, AND TRANSNATIONAL PUBLICS

Publics are not equally powerful. A dominant public tends to emerge, one that has the strength to translate its beliefs into actions affecting even people who do not share its beliefs. Unfortunately, the power of a dominant public often masks the existence of other publics and makes it more difficult to recognize that not everyone's needs and interests are being represented. English literature professor Michael Warner explains: "Some publics . . . are more likely than others to stand in for *the* public, to frame their address as the universal discussion of the people."[49] Other publics may be active. For example, scholars argue that a black public sphere exists in the United States,[50] constituted by media, aesthetic forms, and memories that are owned by and targeted at black people. The existence of a black public sphere demonstrates that there is more than one public sphere, and that what is thought of as *the* public sphere does not represent universal human concerns.

Scholars have identified several limits to Habermas's original formulation of the public sphere: A single universal public does not explain actually existing democracies. The state is no longer the sole site of sovereign power, given the rise of transnational corporations. The economy, itself, can become a site of public contestation and action. Thus, scholars have expanded the study of *the* public to studies of publics, counterpublics, and transnational publics.

Counterpublics

A dominant public tends to focus only on the interests and needs of the dominant group, and in the process to subordinate those groups of people who are disempowered. In fourth and fifth century BCE Athens, a civilization often upheld as an ideal of deliberative democracy, the very notion of citizenship was defined by exclusion. Only adult, male, Athenian-born citizens were allowed to participate. Women, slaves, and noncitizens were excluded.[51] The groups excluded had identities, interests, and needs, but they had to find alternative locations and means to articulate them. For example, in 415 BCE, when the boldest Greek military offensive since the Trojan War was launched, statues of the god Hermes were mutilated. Classicist Eva Keuls argues that the act likely was done by the women of Athens to protest yet another war.[52]

To call attention to a multiplicity of publics, and to publics that are alternatives to the dominant public, scholars developed the concept of **counterpublics,** which Fraser defines as "*parallel discursive arenas where members of subordinated social groups invent and circulate counterdiscourse to formulate oppositional interpretations of their identities, interests, and needs.*"[53] Counterpublics expand not only the space for argument, but also what counts in argument. As part of her critique of Habermas, Fraser notes, "these counterpublics emerge in response to exclusions within dominant publics, they help expand discursive space. In principle, assumptions that were previously exempt from contestation will now have to be publicly argued out."[54] New topics are introduced to deliberation; so, too, are new tests for argument. Literary theorist Rita Felski proposes that counterpublics can challenge norms of argument and what is considered useful evidence.[55] Who can speak, what can be spoken about, and how, can all be topics of public discussion. Consequently, some issues not previously considered public can become public as a result of deliberation and argument.

To summarize, counterpublics create safe spaces in which participants: (1) develop alternative norms for public argument and what counts as evidence; (2) regenerate their energy to engage in argument in the political and public spheres; (3) enact identities through new idioms and styles; and (4) formulate oppositional interpretations of identities, interests, and needs through the creation of new language.

Some publics emerge as a counter to a dominant public and can eventually effect change in public policy. Prior to the 1970s, for example, workplace sexual harassment as a concept did not exist, even though the activity did. During slavery, African-American women were sexually used by their white masters. During industrialization, immigrant women were forced by economic necessity to acquiesce to their employers' demands. In contemporary times, women are subjected to work environments where their sex is used as a basis of ridicule, often in the hope of driving them from the workplace; and women and men who violate gender expectations are harassed and ridiculed. Historically, workplaces that were hostile, abusive, and violent to women were attributed to a "bad boss" or explained as further proof that women did not belong in the rough world of the workplace. With the burgeoning of the second wave of women's movements in the 1970s, however, women had both a physical and discursive space in which they could come together to develop ways to make their interests understood. The Women's Center at Cornell University held the first speak-out (a new form and style of public argument) in 1975. Women from around the country came together to name, and refuse to accept, these experiences. Women's experiences began to count as evidence of a public harm. Women would name their experiences "sexual harassment" and articulate the harm in terms of sex discrimination, whether it occurred in the form of hostile environments or *quid pro quo* demands for sex in order to keep a job. Harvard legal scholar Catharine A. MacKinnon describes sexual harassment as "the first legal wrong to be defined by women," believing "it took a women's movement to expose these experiences as systematic and harmful in the first place, a movement that took women's point of view on our own situation as significantly definitive of that situation."[56]

Women as private citizens came together to formulate opinions about a subject of concern, but to do this they had to articulate an understanding of their shared identity, interests, and needs that countered dominant perceptions of women as primarily sexual beings who belonged in the private sphere. In the process, they constituted a counterpublic sphere of discourse, in which they came to understand their identity as workers deserving of rights, their interest in creating harassment-free workplaces, and their needs as human beings. They contested existing norms of argument that only counted men's perspectives as correct. Women's perceptions of harassment came to matter. They developed a vocabulary that enabled them to name an act that previously had been invisible. In 1986, the Supreme Court of the United States recognized sexual harassment as a violation of Title VII of the Civil Rights Act.

A counterpublic sphere *is* a public sphere, even if it is not perceived to be *the* public sphere. To understand the full range of symbolic action happening in contemporary US society, you need to listen to and watch not just the rhetoric occurring in the strong publics of legislatures and in the dominant/hegemonic public sphere, but rhetoric emerging across multiple publics. You can find traces of counterpublic spheres in the discourse of any group resisting what it perceives to be the attitudes, beliefs, and values of the dominant public.

Enclaved and Oscillating Counterpublics. As the last example demonstrates, counterpublics can both focus inward (when attempting to articulate identity, interests, and needs) and oscillate outward (making demands on the state for changes in law). Counterpublics serve two functions: (1) identity formation for those who participate in them and (2) opinion formation in the dominant public about potential state action. Communication scholar Catherine Squires explains a corresponding distinction between enclaved and oscillating counterpublics. **Enclaved publics** are *publics that conceal their "antiestablishment ideas and strategies in order to avoid sanctions, but internally produc[e] lively debate and planning."* By contrast, **oscillating publics** are *publics that exist to "engage in debate with outsiders and to test ideas."*[57] Sometimes counterpublics are internally focused, developing alternative discourses that are relatively independent of the dominant public. Other times, though, a counterpublic oscillates outward, engaging in debate with other publics. This turning outward is most evident when a counterpublic engages with the dominant public.

When they are enclaved, publics create safe spaces for discourse that are necessary to the possibility of oppositional ideas and actions. When counterpublics focus on their own participants and foreground their perspectives, alternative interpretations of identities and needs become possible. A counterpublic sphere provides a location in which rhetoric can empower the group. As groups constitute themselves as counterpublics, they form an understanding of their identity, interests, and needs that symbolically rejects the dominant public's description of them.

Encapsulating the role of the counterpublic and the need for an oppositional discourse, African-American cultural critic bell hooks[58] explains: "The most important of our work—the work of liberation—demands of us that we make a new language, that we create the oppositional discourse, the liberatory voice."[59] Rhetoric plays a central role in counterpublics. People cannot challenge the way things are unless they can see another way to be, and develop a language to articulate that alternative vision. Examples of enclaved counterpublic discourse include the consciousness-raising groups of second-wave feminism, the discussions in black churches about the immanent humanity of all people that fed into the activism of the Civil Rights movement, and the identity formation and needs identification in the farmworkers' organizations founded by Dolores Huerta, Larry Itliong, and César Chávez.

In each case, however, people who had been rendered silent by the dominant public talked back. They demanded recognition of their immanent humanity and opposed dominant perceptions of women as people who should be confined to the domestic arena, black people as second-class citizens who should be segregated from white people, and Hispanics as laborers who deserved atrocious workplace treatment.

If a counterpublic remains enclaved, its participants risk speaking only to each other and failing to make their new language understood by others. Public sphere scholars Robert Asen and Daniel C. Brouwer argue that talking only to others of like mind generates the dangers of "breeding of intolerance for others, difficulty of translating interests, [and] detachment from healthy criticism."[60] Political scientist Jane Mansbridge agrees that if counterpublic participants speak only to each other, "they do not learn how to put what they want to say in words that others can hear and understand."[61] Thus, engaged argument with those with whom they disagree is an essential element of a healthy counterpublic. In terms of the immigration debates, Hasian and Delgado note that people must find and analyze "the bridges as well as the walls that have been built at contested borderlands."[62] Rhetors should search for places of agreement, not just places of difference.

Oscillation also has practical benefits for a counterpublic. In his study of ACT UP and its participation in congressional hearings concerning AIDS, Brouwer identifies a number of benefits. Oscillation can (1) garner national attention for a group and, thus, enhance its credibility; (2) open a forum for the repetition and recognition of the group's message, (3) push for implementation of the group's recommendations that require institutional support (the support of a strong public); and (4) enable the counterpublic to "push for access to strong publics."[63] Historically, counterpublics have used their specialized newspapers both to speak to members and to oscillate outward. For example, the National Association Opposed to Woman Suffrage's newspaper (*The Woman Patriot*) shifted from a single-issue focus against woman suffrage to a broader challenge to what it saw as emerging radical rhetoric.[64] Additional examples of oscillating counterpublic discourse include second-wave feminism's 1968 "No More Miss America" protest against the pageant, including their ten-point brochure outlining their arguments; the Civil Rights movement's 1955 Montgomery Bus Boycott and ensuing legal challenges to segregation; and the United Farm Workers' grape boycott and public education campaign in the late 1960s, as well as their 2010 "Take Our Jobs" campaign,[65] publicized by Stephen Colbert when he actually took a farm worker's job for a segment and then testified to Congress.[66]

Counterpublic theory challenges the idea that a single, universal public sphere is an ideal toward which a diverse society should strive. Although Habermas initially bemoaned the erosion of the public sphere as a multiplicity of publics emerged, Fraser argues this multiplicity is not necessarily a bad thing. For people who are excluded from access to the dominant public sphere, articulation of their needs becomes nearly impossible; a universal public sphere intensifies the subordination of marginal groups' needs. Multiple publics are more likely to promote participation. According to Fraser, forcing all deliberation into the dominant public "will tend to operate to the advantage of dominant groups and to the disadvantage of subordinates" because "members of subordinated groups would have no arenas for deliberation among themselves about their needs, objectives, and strategies. They would have no venues in which to undertake communicative processes that were not . . . under the supervision of dominant groups."[67] Subordinated social groups need a space to develop language to articulate their identities, interests, and needs.

A counterpublic's orientation oscillates; its primary audience shifts. According to Asen and Brouwer, a counterpublic shifts back and forth between the formulation of its identities, interests, and needs within the relative safety of its protected enclaves, where its primary audience is the counterpublic, and its participation in deliberation about administrative state action, where its audience is the strong, dominant public.[68]

Identity as a Public or Counterpublic. Publics engage in deliberative discourse about policy and civic culture—about who they are and what they need. Although identity formation is an element of all public discourse, counterpublic sphere theories clarify the importance of identity creation and self-expression to disempowered peoples and groups. Before people can participate in deliberation over public issues, they need to see themselves as capable of deliberation, their interests and needs as worthy of discussion. The focus on identity in counterpublics, according to Felski, becomes apparent insofar as they are "directed toward an affirmation of specificity in relation to gender, race, ethnicity, age, sexual preference, and so on."[69] According to rhetoric scholar Lisa Flores, the specificity allows people to develop and explore their own identities, and to counter repressive characterizations.[70] For example, immigrant groups seek to define themselves in contrast to dominant public and media depictions of them as diseased masses and an undifferentiated flood overwhelming the United States. Otto Santa Ana, in his book about metaphors used to describe Latinos in contemporary public discourse, notes that countermetaphors emerge. Instead of a flood, immigrants have become a "stream that makes the desert bloom," a flow of workers who could quench the thirst for labor, or the "lifeblood" of the California economy.[71]

Counterpublic discourse that contributes to identity creation is as important as the outward-directed rhetoric that contributes to policy making, as literary critic Michael Warner discusses in his book *Publics and Counterpublics*. To say a group of people is a "public" or "counterpublic" is more than merely descriptive; it also constructs an understanding of who that group is and how to interact with it. When people identify themselves as members of a public or counterpublic and participate in it, their "identities are formed and transformed."[72] Warner's model of the circulation of identities within public discourse is referred to as the circulatory model of counterpublics.

The naming of a public and the construction of identity can be linked to our earlier discussions of language, persona, and audience. Naming can construct social meaning and understanding. How marginalized groups are named affects how, and whether, they participate in the dominant public. In the 1800s, women fought against being named chattel, and asserted their full humanity and right to participate in public discourse. In the 1960s, African Americans fought against racist names, and declared their interests to be public interests. In the 1980s, ACT UP worked with researchers to rename GRID (Gay Related Immune Deficiency) as AIDS (Acquired Immune Deficiency Syndrome), and thus defining it as a public health issue and of general concern. More recently, undocumented workers resist the name "illegal" because it reduces them to a single act and deflects recognition of them as contributing members of the economy.

The power of language is also evident in the naming of "the public." As Warner points out, sometimes *a* public comes to be perceived as *the* public that represents "the people." However, "the people" is a rhetorical construction, an ideograph, that itself seeks to warrant the use of power. "The public" is also an ideograph. In the process of creating identification among members of "the public," divisions are also created, excluding people who are not part of the falsely universal "we." In other words, some publics claim to represent more people than they actually do; their claimed universality is false, not their existence. They create identification that excludes more than includes; just as Burke warned, identification can create division.

Transnational Publics and Counterpublics

Traditionally, public spheres were bounded by nationality; scholars spoke of a British public or a French public or a US public. As globalization proceeds, it forces theorists to consider whether transnational publics are developing. Fraser explains that the development of transnational corporations and institutions, some of which have power equal to that of traditional states, requires a recognition that "states do not fully control their own territories" or the bodies of citizens.[73] Corporations, as much as states, can exert control over people. Nonstate actors and transnational institutions have the same power as the traditional government of a nation-state, given their economic size, ability to set policy, and power over those who work for them. Thus, the state may not be the only target of public discourse.

The transnationalization of the public sphere has affected the who, what, where, when, and how of deliberation. No longer are publics defined by national citizenship; they can now be composed of people dispersed across the globe, such as the international groups who protest Boko Haram's abduction of Nigerian schoolgirls. No longer is common or public interest limited to issues occurring within national boundaries; it can now include global questions, as when international groups seek solutions to global warming, genocide, and species preservation. No longer is public deliberation constrained by whom one can see face-to-face; it now occurs through the Internet, on social networking sites and other online forums. Communication occurs in multiple languages and across a range of media.[74]

Kevin Michael DeLuca and Jennifer Peeples note, in their analysis of the 1999 protests against the World Trade Organization meeting in Seattle, that new conditions call for activists to target more than the state. The anti–World Trade Organization protesters see transnational corporations, rather than governments, as the "dominant powers" in the modern world.[75] As a result of economic globalization, Asen and Brouwer note, "states are not always the primary audience of counterpublic activities"[76] or of public sphere deliberation.

Publics, Counterpublics, and the Economy

In Habermas's formulation, the public sphere is distinct from the state and the economy, which is why many scholars tend to focus on the distinctions between publics and the state, but communication scholar Dana Cloud makes clear that the economy must also be considered.[77] Communication scholars Joshua P. Ewalt, Jessy J. Ohl, and Damien Smith Pfister point out that the 2011 Occupy protests occurred in over fifteen hundred cities around the world. Millions of people organized, gave time and money, and attempted to change the political system.[78] Though the protests originated in Liberty Square in Manhattan's Financial District, they were not just in one country, or directed at one government; they challenged a transnational economic system. Protestors from various countries with distinct identities used common economic interests to counter the dominant economic powers. The Occupy Wall Street movement targeted its criticism on large banks, international corporations, and Wall Street investment practices for creating the "greatest recession in generations."[79]

Cloud argues that because the state, the dominant public sphere, and the economy are intertwined, and the public sphere and state are often in service to the economy, one must challenge all three through identity circulation (for example, by challenging racist, sexist, or class constructions) and through a focus on the state structure as well as on the institutions of the economy (such as the banks and corporations). The state is not a neutral arbiter of class interests.

Given this interweaving of publics, the state, and the economy, two related points emerge about rhetoric in civic life. First, collective economic action can be a form of civic action. Second, civic action cannot be reduced to personal economic choices.

Communication scholar Phaedra Pezzullo argues that "consumer-based advocacy campaigns" such as boycotts ("a concerted refusal to spend money") and buycotts ("a concerted effort to make a point of spending money" to support businesses with which the consumer group is aligned) are "significant tactics worth engaging during a political period in which . . . 'impure politics' have become the norm."[80] Even if people are concerned about how the US culture of consumption contributes to ecological problems, they might need to engage in consumption through buycotts in order to induce a corporation to change its practices. For example, one store began delivering purchases on bicycles rather than with cars as a way to reduce its carbon footprint. Customers supported the store through a buycott as a means of encouraging other stores to follow that example. Particularly if you believe "transnational corporations . . . have become more or equally as powerful as at least some nation-states,"[81] then an economic mechanism becomes a necessary civic mechanism. Pezzullo examines consumer-based advocacy campaigns that address global ecological crises (such as rainforest depletion, mistreatment of agricultural workers, and global warming), and concludes that the collective action of buycotts and boycotts shows "that everyday people can become successful agents of change in the world when they can identify" a specific example of a larger problem, at a specific place, and "mobilize a public to respond."[82] Notice, however, that she is praising *collective* economic action that is announced, organized, publicized, and visually made present through demonstrations or pickets.[83]

In contrast, reducing all political action to individual consumption choices produces a hollow civic life. In the wake of the 9/11 attacks, for example, President George W. Bush, New York Mayor Rudy Giuliani, Senator Tom Daschle, and Senator John Kerry all urged US citizens to go shopping.[84] Citizens were not asked to sacrifice by willingly paying higher taxes, buying war bonds, or enlisting in the military. Political scientists Matthew A. Crenson and Benjamin Ginsberg describe citizens as "demoted to customers" when "the president told Americans the best thing they could do for their country would be to shop more while the government went about the business of fighting terrorism."[85] Good citizenship was consumerism.

The collapse of citizenship into an individual economic exchange is the reason that many theorists are concerned about the health of democracy. English professor Lauren Berlant argues that "downsizing citizenship" to individual acts of volunteering or participating in a nuclear family structure "has radically changed the ways national identity is imagined, experienced, and governed in political and mass-media public spheres and in everyday life."[86] For this reason, she argues, "there is no public sphere in the contemporary United States, no context of communication and debate that makes ordinary citizens feel that they have a common public culture, or influence on a state that holds itself accountable to their opinions."[87] US citizenship has been privatized by "rerouting the critical energies of the emerging political sphere into the sentimental spaces of an amorphous opinion culture, characterized by strong patriotic identification mixed with feelings of practical political powerlessness."[88] No longer is citizen action in the public sphere understood as the formation of public opinion in order to influence the state's governing actions. Instead, "the intimate public sphere of the U.S. . . . renders citizenship as a condition of social membership produced by personal acts and values, especially acts originating in or directed toward the family sphere."[89] Berlant sees the public sphere as privatized, stripped of its public orientation.

This privatization of the public sphere is constructed and maintained through discourse. The claim that the family is the foundation of society is a recent, but now constant, persuasive message that transforms public issues into personal ones. As historian Stephanie Coontz points out, "Ever since the late nineteenth century, when President Theodore Roosevelt warned that the nation's future rested on 'the right kind of home life,' politicians have argued that civic virtue begins at home. As President Ronald Reagan put it in 1984: 'Strong families are the foundation of society.'"[90] Such claims shift public issues to the realm of personal action and responsibility. Social problems can now be blamed on the breakdown of the family, so that to solve them, people must turn inward to their own families.

Our point here is *not* that a rigid distinction between the personal and the public should be maintained. In fact, the second-wave feminist dictum that "the personal is political" is important. What happens in the privacy of the home has implications for the distribution of power; and acts of the state influence what happens in the home. Power dynamics affect even the most apparently personal decisions concerning marriage, children, and sexuality. The personal can, indeed, be political. This does not mean people can only attain political identity in a democracy through their private actions.

In many ways, however, politics has been reduced to the personal (in the form of purchasing decisions and family) and stripped of any concern with power or collective action in the public sphere. Crenson and Ginsberg have noted the same reversal. They argue that "What passes for citizenship today often inverts the feminist dictum that the personal is political. It has transformed the political into the personal. Political activity should feel 'empowering.' It should enhance self-esteem. It should not engender confusion, ambiguity, or frustration."[91]

Relationships among Publics

To understand how publics function, you need to consider not only their relationship to the state and economy, but also to each other. Counterpublics may exist counter to the state or the economy, but they can also replicate some of the more oppressive elements of the state or economy. In other words, counterpublics are not counter to everything for which dominant society stands. Exclusions based on sex, race, class, and sexual orientation can be found in counterpublics, even as they attempt to counter other social problems.

For example, consider the emergence of the environmental movement. Early members of environmental groups came together as individuals to articulate new understandings of humans' relationship to the environment. In the 1800s, arguments were made to preserve nature. In 1864, Lincoln signed a bill granting Yosemite Valley and the Mariposa Grove of Giant Sequoias to California as an inalienable public trust. In 1872, Yellowstone was designated the first national park. Although new understandings of the environment were integrated into the public vocabulary repertoire, they tended to reinforce a notion that the environment was something other than where human beings lived. It was to be visited, preserved, and kept separate from human intervention.

The reality is that *all* human beings live in environments. Not all environments are the same. Some environments are less pristine and have large amounts of pollution. Polluted environments are not equally distributed. People of color and poor people are more likely to live near plants that produce toxic wastes and emissions, and toxic disposal sites tend to be sited closer to where the poor and people of color already live.[92] To describe this phenomenon, African-American civil rights leader Dr. Benjamin Chavis coined the phrase "environmental racism" in the early 1980s.[93] Preservation of pristine parks that socioeconomically privileged people could visit represented an incomplete understanding of humans' relationship to the environment. As a counter to environmental racism, most environmental groups now seek environmental justice and recognize that all of the environment must be valued.

Our point is that just because a counterpublic is *counter* does not mean it is without flaws. Privileges and ideologies weave themselves deeply into people's psyches. The process of testing assumptions is not done easily, nor without the danger of replicating some of the very inequalities people might seek to counter.

PUBLICS IN THE INTERNET AGE

"The public" is a concept central to discussions of US democracy. The tradition of public deliberation is typified by the New England town meeting, where members of a community come together to debate, face-to-face, about issues of common interest. The vitality of such public deliberation has long concerned political and communication theorists in the United States. The issues about which John Dewey wrote in 1927, in his book *The Public and Its Problems*, are issues with which US society continues to grapple. How does a group come to have an identity as a public? What role does public discourse play in democratic politics? How can citizen apathy be lessened? How can experts and the general public interact productively to resolve controversies?[94]

Dewey worried that "increasing social complexity threatened the collective perception and practical judgment of a functioning public of citizens."[95] In particular, he was concerned about the effects that technological change would have on public deliberation (in his time, this meant the emergence of the telephone, cheap reading material, movies, telegraph, railways, and newspapers). He worried that new entertainment technologies would distract people from discussing issues of public concern and change how people interacted.[96] Many people are now exploring this concern in relation to the role of digital technologies, social networking sites, and the Internet.

Although many people now cannot conceive of a world without the Internet and interactive digital communication technologies, they really are relatively recent phenomena. Not until the late 1980s did e-mail become privatized and commercially available. The World Wide Web was created in 1989. Cell phones were not widely used until the early 1990s, when they became small enough to carry in a jacket pocket. The Internet became a common reality in the mid-1990s, when the US government allowed the commercialization of the networking technologies that enabled worldwide participation. At this point, it was primarily used for e-mail (one-to-one communication) or web pages (one-to-many communication). The White House went online in 1994. Google launched its first version in August 1996, revolutionizing how people searched the growing information available on the Internet. Microsoft began marketing FrontPage in 1996 and Macromedia created Dreamweaver in 1997, enabling people without programming skills to create web pages. This was Web 1.0, which simply allowed the early Internet to replicate noninteractive print communications.

Then a variety of new software programs enabled the creation of Web 2.0, supporting interactive many-to-many communication and truly enabling a networking of communication. Wikipedia was launched in 2001. Blogs became popular in 2002 when blogging software became widely available. Myspace was founded in 2003. Facebook was launched in 2004. YouTube was created in 2005. Twitter was created in 2006. Tumblr, a shortform microblogging platform, was launched in 2007, the same year Apple released its first iPhone. In 2008, Apple released its second-generation iPhone and opened its App Store, allowing phone owners to buy and install applications created by third parties. In 2010, Pinterest and Instagram were launched. In July 2011, Snapchat (then called Picaboo) was launched. By 2012, Facebook had one billion active users worldwide per month. By 2013, 56 percent of people in the United States used a smartphone;[97] of online adults, 73 percent used social networking sites, 71 percent used Facebook, 21 percent used Instagram, and 18 percent used Twitter.[98]

The important role interactive digital technology can play in enabling publics to form is evident in the 2011 protests in Tunisia (and then Egypt, Bahrain, Libya, Jordan, and Algeria). When Tunisian President Zine el-Abidine Ben Ali had the police let loose with real bullets, killing hundreds of protestors, the state-controlled media showed no images of the bloodshed. Facebook did. With 20 percent of Tunisians on Facebook, the information spread.[99] Computer and cell phone technology also played a role in the protests in Egypt. The sacrifices of the protesters, who literally put their bodies on the line in public spaces (with hundreds if not thousands losing their lives), were documented and communicated via the Internet and cell phones. On January 28, the government of Egypt, in response to the protesters' reliance on digital communication technologies, cut off all cell phone use and Internet access.

In response to governments' efforts to control protest by controlling communication technology, on February 15, 2011, Secretary of State Hillary Clinton delivered a speech outlining the administration's "Internet Freedom Agenda" at George Washington University. She declared:

> The Internet has become the public space of the 21st century—
> the world's town square, classroom, marketplace, coffeehouse, and
> nightclub. . . . The goal is not to tell people how to use the Internet
> any more than we ought to tell people how to use any public square,
> whether it's Tahrir Square or Times Square. The value of these spaces
> derives from the variety of activities people can pursue in them, from
> holding a rally to selling their vegetables, to having a private conversation.
> These spaces provide an open platform, and so does the Internet.[100]

The Internet is not itself the public sphere, but interactive digital technologies enable the formation of publics. Like the coffeehouses of previous centuries, websites and cell phones enable people to converse about current events and plan public action.

To explore the role of interactive digital technologies on public deliberation, we will now show how the very concept of "public" is made more complicated by interactive communication technologies. Second, we will discuss ways in which digital technologies affect public activism, taking into account inequalities in access. Finally, we explore the possibility of networked publics.

"Publics" in a Digital Age

Reflect on the spaces in which you use the Internet. You get online in your bedroom or kitchen, in a coffee shop, in your car (not while driving, we hope). You access the Web, one of the most open and accessible of forums, from some of the most private and personal physical spaces. You might post on Facebook while lounging on your sofa, send an Instagram selfie taken in your bathroom mirror, or tweet from your bedroom. Your images and statements might be about your most personal events and feelings, yet (depending on the security of your password protocol) they are now potentially accessible to everyone; they are as public as you can get. The Internet presents a conundrum: it offers a medium in which you think you are narrowcasting (to only the friends you admit to your page) the most private of moments (about what you just ate, how you just broke up with a romantic partner, or where you are going to listen to music tonight) yet in reality it is the broadest of broadcast media. If you become angry about a public policy, you can create a Facebook group to protest it. To plan a protest, you can tweet about it. To share images of an event, you can send an Instagram.

Yet, many spaces that used to be considered locations for public discourse have become privatized. The town square, which was once the hub of business, entertainment, and government, is no longer a main gathering place. Instead, people gather in the privately owned mall and its food courts.[101]

So where is public space? The forms of communication on the Internet challenge the understanding of the demarcation between public and private, and may even require a rethinking of what is public and what is private. The concept of a public sphere relied on a spatial metaphor (spheres are a geometric concept), so the concept of networked space becomes relevant. Media theorist Vivian Sobchack notes that the idea of a public sphere is problematic in the electronic age because people's access to others through computers, and now through mobile technology such as tablets and smartphones, has redrawn the boundaries of public and private. She writes that people's notions of public space and private space have "been transformed so that even to pose the notion of a 'public sphere'—as opposed to a 'private sphere'—is problematic in the age of electronic pervasion."[102]

In the process of gaining access to other people's private space through webcams and digital uploads, your own private space may also have been reduced; as much as you can access others' private space, they may be able to access yours. Think about the differences between a generation raised in the world of Web 2.0 and earlier generations. Many people in the Web 2.0 generation think little of posting their most interior thoughts in public, on the Internet. Some people actually write journals on the web and allow others to read them, while people raised before Web 2.0 would find it the most extreme invasion of privacy for others to read their diaries. As another example, consider sexting: According to a 2014 study, "9% of adult cell owners have sent a sext," "20% of cell owners have received a sext of someone else they know on their phone," and "3% of cell owners have forwarded a sext."[103] The strongest predictor of sexting is age, with 26% of people between 18 and 24, and 31% of those between 25 and 34 having received sexts; and 9% of those between 18 and 24, and 14% of those between 25 and 34, having sent sexts.[104]

Although people may think of their cell phone screens and computers as personal space, where only those to whom they send a picture can view it, the image can actually be sent across a range of networks. A sixteen-year-old high school student found that out when an image she and a friend took of themselves ended up being so widely distributed that a print was left in her vice-principal's mailbox. Although she had deleted the image from her own phone, her friend had sent it to another friend, who sent it to a football player, who sent it to the team; then it was sent to the entire senior class.[105]

Public deliberation and civic participation, as well as the development and maintenance of social relationships, take place over the Internet. People are mobilized to support political candidates. Citizens organize themselves to protest government policy. Groups come together to articulate identities, interests, and needs. At the same time, the very boundary between public and private is challenged. Are you really engaging in political action when you "friend" a political candidate on Facebook? Are people's understandings of political participation affected by the format in which it occurs? When is expression on a blog an act of civic culture and identity formation, and when is it just the expression of an individual's interior thoughts on a screen that everyone can see? Scholars and users are just beginning to answer these questions.

Digital Participation and Access

The 2008 election campaign was the first time that more than half (55 percent) of the voting age population went online to get involved in election year politics.[106] The 2012 presidential campaign continued this trend and expanded the use of digital technology from computers to mobile technology. Because 88 percent of registered voters were using cell phones,[107] campaigns had to adapt to mobile technology. The Obama campaign devoted 10 percent of its "advertising budget on outreach through Facebook, Google, and Bing," thus allowing "the campaign to engage in highly targeted outreach and reach people beyond the traditional electorate."[108]

People used the Internet to retrieve information about the candidates and to express their own political opinions. An October 2012 Pew Research Internet Project survey found that 39 percent of adults in the United States "have done at least one of eight civic or political activities with social media."[109] According to that survey, 38 percent of the people who used social media (social networking sites or Twitter) used it to "promote material related to politics or social issues that others have posted" and to encourage others to vote; 34 percent used it "to post their own thoughts or comments on political and social issues"; 33 percent "repost[ed] content related to political or social issues"; 31 percent encouraged others to take political action; 28 percent posted political stories; 21 percent belonged to a site involved in political or social issues; and 20 percent followed politicians.[110] Politics on the web was not a spectator sport, but a form of public discourse in which citizens were actively engaged.

Some of the most memorable moments from the 2012 presidential campaign became memorable as a result of becoming social media phenomena, such as the viral video of Romney's comments that 47 percent of people in the United States are dependent on government, and the Twitter handle of @Romneysbinder in reference to Romney's comment about "binders full of women," in response to a presidential debate question about pay equity and the number of women in his administration when he was governor of Massachusetts.[111] People used Twitter to comment on the candidates and, according to Darrel M. West of the Brookings Institute, "democratize[d] political commentary. During the party conventions, Twitter became a major part of the online conversation. . . . Observers no longer have to wait for professional commentators to judge speech performance or debates. Social media allow ordinary folks to judge performance during the course of actual events."[112] In 2012, all three presidential debates and the vice presidential debate made it to the list of the "Top Ten Social TV Events of All Time."[113] On election day alone, people sent thirty-one million election-related tweets.[114] To get a sense of the interactivity of electoral politics and social media, consider the following statistics from the 2012 nominating convention:

Event	Tweets
Democratic convention week	9.5 million
Republican convention week	7 million
Obama's acceptance speech	52,756 tweets per minute
Michelle Obama	28,000 tweets per minute
Bill Clinton	22,087 tweets per minute
Joe Biden	17,932 tweets per minute
Mitt Romney	14,289 tweets per minute
Marco Rubio	8,937 tweets per minute
Clint Eastwood	7,044 tweets per minute
Paul Ryan	6,669 tweets per minute[115]

The power of social media to interact with electoral politics was evident in the 2012 vice presidential debate between candidates Paul Ryan and Joe Biden at Centre College in Danville, Kentucky. It garnered 4.9 million comments on Twitter and Facebook, according to television analyst Eleanor Dowling. The debate became the eighth most widely discussed on social media television show ever. Over 4,600,000 Tweets discussed it. More than 280,000 Facebook posts offered comments on it. Over 7 percent of the comments on social media focused on Biden's reactions (including his smile and his laugh) to Ryan. A "mock Twitter" account sprang up that night focusing on Biden's reactions.[116] In their analysis of the *Laughing Joe Biden* meme that was generated after this debate, communication scholars Susan Sci and David Dewberry explain:

> Throughout the debate, Biden repeatedly smiled, smirked, laughed, and gestured wildly in disagreement and disbelief at several of Ryan's remarks. This performance—whether an embodiment of frustration, aggravation, or mockery—disturbed the normative standards of appropriate demeanor within vice presidential debates. Biden's behavior became a focal point in social media discourse and, thus, the perfect subject of Internet memes. The iconic moments when Biden grinned and laughed during the debate were commented on, captured, and widely circulated as divisive (and often hilarious) *Laughing Joe Biden* memes.[117]

They also report that, "by the end of the debate, there were approximately 22 hashtags and 53 fake Twitter handles referencing Biden's laughter, smirk, smile, teeth, or dentures. With such attention, mainstream news organizations like *The New York Times* and blogs such as Politico and Buzzfeed soon began to report on the meme itself."[118]

What does this tell us about how people think about political participation? Is it only constituted by attending a rally, or can you experience politics virtually by watching a video of a rally? Is participation limited to going door to door, to brick-and-mortar homes, leaving pamphlets, or can you be a virtual campaigner by forwarding information? Does political participation matter only in relation to campaigns, or does the work of civic identity formation also count? Do you exhibit civic interest only by reading newspapers, or can you participate in opinion formation by responding to a blog?

Historian Mark Poster, in his discussion of cyberdemocracy, describes how the Internet institutes "new social functions" that can only be understood if we are not tied to outdated patterns of interpretation that maintain rigid boundaries among the public and private, forms of political participation, and the government.[119] He explains that the Internet is challenging the ways that society approaches questions of civic participation:

> If one understands politics as the restriction or expansion of the existing
> executive, legislative and judicial branches of government, one will
> not be able even to broach the question of new types of participation in
> government. To ask, then, about the relation of the Internet to democracy
> is to challenge or to risk challenging our existing theoretical approaches
> to these questions.[120]

The relationship of digital networks to counterpublics and publics complicates existing theoretical approaches. For example, in Habermas's ideal of the public, he assumes that people come together in face-to-face interactions to deliberate. Yet, in a digital world, face-to-face interaction is no longer the only means of interaction.

Poster's admonition about an expansive understanding of participation means that activism includes not only participating in institutionalized politics (such as "friending" a presidential candidate) but also broader forms of discursive action on the Internet (such as providing narratives to a state representative to include in a filibuster, tweeting in response to the #YesAllWomen hashtag, or sharing a video that seeks to raise awareness about a social issue).[121] When the political functions of the Internet are discussed, people tend to focus not on its interactive nature, but on its ability to transmit information.[122] Many discussions of the democratic potential of the Internet, even when they recognize its interactive nature, still limit interaction to questions concerning administration and governance, and tend to ignore the role that online publics can play in identity formation.[123]

Some sites and digital activism do challenge the limited uses of the Internet that some theorists describe. In particular, several sites attempt to open space for the formation of publics and counterpublics. For example, the Institute for the Study of Civic Values focuses on neighborhood empowerment. ProtestNet is a location where activists come together to form their own media. For a more whimsical twist, consider The Harry Potter Alliance (HPA), which describes itself as "a 501c3 nonprofit that takes an outside-of-the-box approach to civic engagement by using parallels from the Harry Potter books to educate and mobilize young people across the world toward issues of literacy, equality, and human rights."[124] The HPA tries "to make civic engagement exciting by channeling the entertainment-saturated facets of our culture toward mobilization for deep and lasting social change" among its "worldwide network of enthusiastic fan activists who are connected via the internet and social media."

In many ways, these sites seek to create the space for discussion of ideas, the development of alternative validity claims, and the development of a vocabulary with which subordinated groups can articulate their needs. A dizzying array of issue-specific websites and Facebook pages also exist.

Recent writings about citizen activism on the net include myriad parallels between digital activism, social movements, and counterpublics. Just as social movements can mobilize others of like mind, virtual communities are a way in which "the creative powers of controversy can spread beyond local communities"[125] as people form connections with others who share interests, even people who live in other states or countries.[126]

Two concerns emerge related to digital activism emerge: slacktivism and echo chambers. Slacktivism, a hollow form of activism that does more to make people feel good than to correct a problem, is illustrated by a Facebook "like." Instead of educating others about an issue, donating time or money to a cause, or working to change institutions or laws, a Facebook "like" is simply clicking a button, reducing civic activism to clicktavism.

A 2012 YouTube video brought into relief the question of whether a social media campaign was a substantive, productive form of civic engagement. The video tells the story of Joseph Kony, militant leader of the Lord's Resistance Army (LRA) in Uganda.[127] The goal is to generate enough public outrage among people in the US that they would demand the US government stop Kony. The video seeks to draw connections between the lives of people in the United States and the lives of the more than thirty thousand children Kony abducted for his army. It ends with a call to action: share the video, sign a petition, order an activism kit, and donate.

At one level, the video was a success: it raised awareness. As of June 2014, the video had had 99,473,387 views. It was a "viral phenomenon" targeted at social media users. However, the response to the video also raised concerns about whether awareness was enough and whether the video oversimplified an incredibly complex issue. The problem: Kony was no longer in Uganda, the LRA was tiny, and the militaries of other African countries that the video supported were accused of terrible crimes as well. In simplifying the story, the video offered the feel-good effects of quick action.[128]

In 2013, in response to rising concerns that slacktivism was displacing real activism, UNICEF Sweden launched a campaign urging people to make real monetary contributions rather than merely expressing support through social media.[129] The campaign reminded people that liking or upvoting items on social media leads to no real action; no children will receive polio vaccines because of social media comments. Real action requires money and volunteer efforts.[130] For action to be taken, awareness must be raised; but if social media action is limited to raising awareness, is that enough?

Some analysts fear that the type of participation that occurs on the web will result in increasing fragmentation, as people are able to seek out only that information with which they most agree and to avoid any meaningful interaction with people who have different perspectives. The effect is a kind of echo chamber. Legal scholar Cass R. Sunstein argues most forcibly for this fear, explaining, "If people on the Internet are deliberating mostly with like-minded others, their views will not merely be reinforced; they will instead be shifted to more extreme points. . . . With the Internet, it is exceedingly easy for each of us to find like-minded individuals."[131] It appears the very ability of the Internet to assist in identity formation also enables it to participate in polarization, as differences are identified and then intensified. Instead of being a site where public deliberation can occur despite time and distance constraints, the Internet could result in polarization and lead to an erosion of a sense of common cause.

Not everyone is as pessimistic as Sunstein. People tend to seek reinforcement rather than challenges, and the Internet may contribute to the creation of deliberative enclaves, but it can also be a way to open up those enclaves and allow for the development of community. For example, research indicates that gay and lesbian youths living in rural communities once felt extremely isolated, but the Internet now provides them an opportunity to belong to a virtual community and seek social support outside their own geographic locations.[132] Communication scholar Lincoln Dahlberg claims that "the Internet is being used by many people [to] encounter difference that they would not normally encounter in everyday life."[133] Instead of functioning as an echo chamber, the Internet can provide access to information that people may not be able to access otherwise. When judging the Internet, we should not compare it to some ideal world of civic discourse, but to a non-Internet world. Using the 2004 presidential election as a basis for analysis, the Pew Internet & American Life Project discovered that Internet users were exposed to a wider range of information about the candidates and the political arguments than were nonusers, "including those that challenge their candidate preferences and their positions on some key issues."[134]

Not all people are able to access the Internet, however. Although it is theoretically open to all, material barriers to participation exist. Unfortunately, studies of actual usage indicate those groups most in need of an oppositional interpretation of identity are the very groups who most lack access. The key demographic characteristics that determine access, according to a Pew Research project, are "age, household income, educational attainment, community type, and disability."[135] For example, 87 percent of people with some college education have home broadband or a smartphone; in contrast to only 52 percent of those with no high school diploma; 54 percent of adults with disabilities use the Internet, in contrast to 81 percent of all adults.

In addition, the ways in which people use the Internet is determined by their degree of subordination. According to the National Telecommunications and

Information Administration, for example, "demographic characteristics not only determine *whether* and *where* one uses the Internet. Income, education, race, and gender, among other characteristics, strongly influence what a person does online."[136] People who belong to subordinated demographic groups are more likely to use the Internet to take courses or conduct job searches. They use it as an instrument to enter the economic system of paid labor, not as a means to engage in forming public spheres.

If marginalized groups are not represented on the Internet, then cyberspace cannot expand the discursive arena. Instead, in Fraser's words, it merely replicates the "modes of deliberation that mask domination"[137] as it absorbs the less powerful into a dominant "we." An appearance of deliberation is created on the Internet, but a series of monologues transversing the Web do not substitute for critical engagement. Inequitable Internet access should be troubling, not only because it mirrors other inequalities in society, but also because it masks the existence of those inequalities. It is difficult to recognize the absences of some groups if you cannot even identify who is present.[138]

The digital divide is even worse on a global scale, as only developed countries have the infrastructure and money to provide increased access. As of 2013, 74.8 percent of people in the developing world had mobile-broadband subscriptions, but only 19.8 percent of people in the developing world did, making the global average 29.5 percent.[139] Yet, people around the world have used communication technologies such as cell phones, web pages, and blogs to supplement and sustain civic engagement and political action.

Networked Publics and the Blogosphere

Theories emphasizing multiple publics, as opposed to a unitary public, encourage us to think about how networks of communication constitute civic life.[140] Networks emerge between and among publics, discursive arenas, people, institutions, and organizations. Our use of "networked" in this section reflects both the sense of the multiple publics that make up civic life and the way in which those publics are connected. Internet technology enhances the networked features of publics by allowing the interactive exchange of ideas across multiple media and among multiple rhetors.

Two specific features of networked publics deserve attention. First, digital media technologies enable bidirectional flows of communication. In the pre-Internet, mass-mediated public sphere, in journalist A. J. Liebling's unique phrasing, "freedom of the press" was "guaranteed only to those who own one."[141] Citizens in networked publics can use a variety of means to send messages back and forth. The flow of communication is no longer in only one direction, from professional communicators such as journalists to everyday citizens. Second, the flow of communication has become less vertical (from the powerful few to the less powerful many) and more horizontal (from many to many, regardless of power position). Before the Internet, mass media controlled the agenda: what was discussed and who got to comment on the major stories of the day. In the current Internet era, a range of people find themselves introducing topics for discussion, commenting on stories, and spreading or making news through social networking sites.[142]

The first example to demonstrate the power of the Internet to displace commercial mass media's function as agenda setter and sole informer occurred in December 2002. Then–US Senate Majority Leader Trent Lott toasted Senator Strom Thurmond, a long-time advocate of segregation, on his hundredth birthday by saying: "I want to say this about my state: When Strom Thurmond ran for president, we voted for him. We're proud of it. And if the rest of the country had followed our lead, we wouldn't have had all these problems over all these years either."[143] Initially, as communication scholar Damien Pfister notes in his detailed analysis of this case, the toast celebrating Thurmond's advocacy of segregationist policies was "barely covered by the institutional press. Only after bloggers started connecting the toast to Thurmond's past deeds did the press pick up on the story and eventually generate public pressure for Lott to resign his Senate Majority post."[144] More recently, when commercial media did not cover Wendy Davis's 2013 filibuster, citizens covered it through Twitter.

The emergence of interactive digital communication technologies means that people no longer participate in a "mass-mediated public sphere" where their role is only as information consumers, but in a "networked public sphere" where they perform the roles of producers and consumers.[145] **Networked publics** are *interconnected publics and counterpublics formed or strengthened as a result of the communication practices enabled by the Internet and social media.* The concept of networked publics focuses attention on how digital media technologies change patterns of public participation. Law professor Yochai Benkler says that "the social practices of information and discourse allow a very large number of actors to see themselves as potential contributors to public discourse and as potential actors in political arenas, rather than mostly passive recipients of mediated information who occasionally can vote their preferences."[146] Because everyone is potentially a contributor, creative participatory activities burgeon, including generating memes, blogging, creating parodic video mashups, and culture jamming. As Pfister notes, "The networked public sphere isn't a dour, stale site of elite public deliberation but is in fact a lively, participatory, dynamic arena where creativity thrives (for better or for worse)."[147]

For an example of the speed and power of networked advocacy, consider what happened in June 2014. On June 6, the US Food and Drug Administration (FDA) announced a new rule regarding cheese-making that banned the use of wooden shelves, on which artisan cheeses are aged. The result would have been the end of artisanal cheeses in the United States. Foregoing its usual "comment rule-making" process, the FDA simply announced the new rule.[148] This, however, did not stop comments. Within days, a "We the People" petition on the White House website had thousands of signatures. People e-mailed the FDA directly. Twitter hashtags emerged, including #Savethecheese and #Speakcheesies (referring to the speakeasies of the Prohibition era, in which alcohol was illegal). By June 11, the FDA had backed down from its ruling.[149]

For a less cheesy example, consider the Zapatista movement in Chiapas, Mexico, and its support of pro-democracy reforms.[150] Formed in 1983, the EZLN

(Ejército Zapatista de Liberación Nacional) demanded autonomy for the indigenous people of Chiapas when increasing governmental and economic pressures threatened their communal lands, diverse local cultures, and languages. The movement expanded to the Internet on January 1, 1994, when supporters launched a digital campaign using networks created during an earlier international campaign against the North American Free Trade Agreement (NAFTA). The transition to networked space was not easy. The Zapatistas were transmitting messages from villages that did not have electricity, much less modems. Communiqués were delivered via courier to newspapers in cities within twelve hours of creation and circulated internationally within twenty-four hours. Supporters would translate the messages from Spanish and send them to e-mail list subscribers on networks such as Peacenet, the Internet, and Usenet. The speed with which the world heard about this struggle by a small band of indigenous peoples, and mobilized to support it, was unprecedented.[151] Even though it emerged before Web 2.0, the Zapatistas showed the potential of the Internet to create networks of activism.

The protest was not solely digital. Real bodies were put at risk, even as information was distributed electronically. On the same day the group's demands went digital, material bodies put themselves on the line. Elements of the EZLN seized several towns, with some reports indicating "at least 145 people died in the ensuing battle with state troops."[152] Supporters flocked to Chiapas to document and protest the Mexican government's attempts at military repression. Despite police repression, hundreds of thousands demonstrated in the streets of Mexico City and other cities and towns, eventually forcing the government to shift from overt military attacks on the EZLN to political negotiations and covert repression. Once again, human rights activists from around the world came to Chiapas to observe, report, and constrain government actions.

The Mexican government tried to quash this uprising by limiting the state-controlled television network Televisa's press coverage, but the world heard about it because of messages posted on web sites and sent over the Net. Economics professor Harry Cleaver explains that the pro-Zapatistas' use of electronic and computer communications made it difficult for the government to isolate and silence the movement:

> Despite its initial defeat, a key aspect of the state's war against the Zapatistas (both in Mexico and elsewhere) has been its on-going efforts to isolate them, so that they can be destroyed or forced to accept co-optation. In turn, the Zapatistas and their supporters have fought to maintain and elaborate their political connections throughout the world. This has been a war of words, images, imagination and organization in which the Zapatistas have had surprising success.
>
> Vital to this continuing struggle has been the pro-Zapatista use of computer communications. While the state has all too effectively limited mass media coverage and serious discussion of Zapatista ideas, their supporters have been able, to an astonishing degree, to circumvent and offset this blockage through the use of electronic networks in conjunction with the more familiar tactics of solidarity movements: teach-ins, articles

in the alternative press, demonstrations, the occupation of Mexican government consulates and so on.[153]

Instead of having to rely on traditional commercial or state-controlled media to broadcast their message, the group was able to speak to the world directly through e-mail and then, increasingly, through dozens of transnational supporters' web pages in many languages. A small group of activists supporting indigenous Mayan farmers in Chiapas against repressive policies of the Mexican government were able to take their message global, speaking not just to the "strong public" of the Mexican government or the "weak public" of Mexican citizens, but to a "transnational public" of global citizens. The publics to which the Zapatistas spoke were far larger than those within the nation's borders, and those publics sustained their interest across the years. During periods of renewed military repression in early 1994, and again in early 1995, supporters demonstrated at Mexican embassies and consulates in over forty countries.

The early use of the networked public sphere to communicate with a transnational public was only the first step. The Zapatistas, with the help of supporters, used digital communication technologies to engage in a variety of protests. Early in 1994, Internet-based organizing brought together thousands of prodemocracy advocates in a Zapatista village for a National Democratic Convention to discuss how to get beyond the essentially one-party rule in Mexico. In 1995, the Zapatistas called for, and their supporters organized, a Plebiscite for Peace and Democracy that had over a million attendees. Internet technology enabled international participation. In 1996, Internet connections provided the main vehicle to organize Continental Encounters Against Neoliberalism and For Humanity, as well as an Intercontinental Encounter that brought together thousands of grassroots activists from around the world.

We can trace a direct line from the Intercontinental Encounter in 1996 in Chiapas villages and the rise of the antiglobalization/anti-WTO movement. The 1996 global meeting gave rise to People's Global Action, which organized the 1998 anti-WTO protest in Geneva and participated in the 1999 anti-WTO protest in Seattle. In addition, Indymedia, "a grassroots network committed to using media production and distribution as tools for promoting social and economic justice"[154] that began to emerge during the Zapatista support experience was fully developed "in late November of 1999, to allow participants in the anti-globalization movement to report on the protests against the WTO meeting that took place in Seattle."[155] Ultimately, Zapatistas and their supporters have used "the Internet as a means to build a global grassroots support network" not bound by time or space.[156] Since 1994, using the most basic of digital technologies (cell phones and listservs), you can find discussions of Zapatistas on blogs.[157] The EZLN has a Myspace profile. Zapatistas are on Facebook.

Supporters have sometimes acted autonomously, using digital forms of protest that have generated controversy within the pro-Zapatista movement. In 1998, a small group organized a virtual sit-in against five financial institutions in Mexico. It sent e-mail instructions to supporters, calling on them to connect to the websites and hit "reload" several times during the hour in order to overload the site and stop all business, just as US civil rights sit-ins sought to stop commerce at targeted businesses. These actions were controversial because many in the Zapatista support movement were afraid the state, which was much better equipped, would counterattack and shut down supporters' websites or block their listservs.

Networked publics should be able to fulfill all the functions of counterpublics, even as they face similar challenges. Networked movements can contest existing norms and develop alternative validity claims. Just as counterpublics often renegotiate the distinctions between the public and private, so may Internet activism. Stephen Wray, a member of the Electronic Disturbance Theatre, sees an inherent potential for digital activism to challenge dominant validity claims, but cautions that digital activism should be carefully considered because those engaging in it do not, alone, create the rhetoric about it and are not the only ones who can engage in it. He would like to see his attempts at electronic civil disobedience redefine "infowar" and make it a plausible form of activism, because "We need to seriously question and abandon some of the language that the state uses to demonize genuine political protest and expression."[158] Wray and the EDT have provided software, such as FloodNet, that enables people to stage nonviolent mass protests (virtual sit-ins) in networked space.[159] In many ways, protest in the public sphere is being supplemented and/or replaced by protest on a networked public screen.

In addressing serious social and political issues, digital activism can also be creative, productive, and even joyful. In fact, some scholars argue, "a sense of playfulness [is] common to new media environments."[160] Evolving digital tools have enabled people to generate their own, sometimes hilarious, responses to policies or to influence how public memory is framed. For example, by November 2008, people had created 150 parodies of the bunker scene from the 2004 movie *Downfall* and posted them to YouTube. That scene in the movie shows Hitler in his underground bunker as he learns of the Russian Army's advance into Berlin. The YouTube videos use the emotional affect of the actors (who are speaking in German), but superimpose subtitles onto the scene so that instead of reacting to Berlin's fall, the characters are reacting to Hillary Clinton's loss of the Democratic nomination, Adam Sandler movies, Obama's reelection, Rebecca Black's song "Friday," or the late arrival of pizza. These parodies achieved so much circulation that in February 2010, *The New York Times* offered instructions on how to create one; in October 2010, the German Historical Museum devoted an exhibit section to them; and in 2011, a customized YouTube site offered the "top 24 *Downfall* parodies" for that year.[161] Communication scholar Christopher Gilbert argues that the democratic potential and danger of this "rhetorical play" is "its capacity to manipulate the most grave of cultural texts and open them up to revaluation."[162] These videos may, at their best, enable viewers to see connections between past events with "the predicaments of the present."[163]

THE NETWORKED PUBLIC SCREEN

Historically, public sphere discourse was associated with the type of discussion that happens in a bricks-and-mortar public sphere: the town square or the town hall. Prior to the emergence of electronic mass media, such settings were the only ones in which the discourse that consists of reasoned exchanges of opinion could occur. In such settings, media such as newspapers served a subsidiary role; they provided the information with which (and sometimes the medium in which) members of the public advanced their arguments.

The evolution of media such as television and the Internet challenge such a simple role for media in public discourse. Media no longer transmit information that is primarily verbal. We live in an age in which visuals play a dominant role; people in the United States live in a visual culture. Once you begin to recognize the power of visuals and the places where they appear, you need to consider whether your understanding of participation forms should expand. Instead of talking exclusively about discourse in the public sphere, should critics talk about verbal and visual forms of public interaction?

In the 2006 immigration protests, the rallies not only brought like-minded people together to organize and call for political action, they also functioned as a way to speak to those who were not in attendance. The rallies were planned for the congressional recess so that representatives and senators who had returned to their home states could see the masses of their constituents who attended the demonstrations,[164] but it was not necessary to be present at the rallies to see their size. Television and newspaper reports showed images of the rallies. An Associated Press story posted on MSNBC's website included Lucas Jackson's image for Reuters News Service of a street filled with people.[165] Anti-immigration protests sought to appear on the public screen. Jim Gilchrist, the founder of the Minuteman Project and organizer of the 2006, thirteen-city tour ending in Washington, DC, maintains a website for the group, with a video archive of news stories and member-made videos.[166]

The massive rallies and counterrallies constituted image events that demanded media coverage. Pro-immigration rally organizers thought carefully about the images. Initially, participants waved flags from their countries of origin to demonstrate cultural pride and unity. Italian flags wave during Columbus Day celebrations and Irish flags wave during St. Patrick's Day parades; and rally participants saw flag waving as an expression of pride in the diversity of the United States. When anti-immigration groups responded to the foreign flags as unpatriotic and as proof of immigrants' inability or unwillingness to assimilate, according to rhetoric scholars Richard D. Pineda and Stacey K. Sowards, organizers called for marchers to wave the US flag to "signify their allegiance to US cultural values and principles. Visually, rallies shifted significantly from a profusion of colors and emblems to a more consistent red, white and blue."[167] Such a shift only matters insofar as the image could be distributed and seen.

DeLuca and Peeples offer the concept of the public screen as an alternative way to conceive of public discourse. The **public screen** is composed of *the constant circulation of symbolic action enabled by the relatively new media technologies of television, computers, photography, film, Internet, and smart phones.* DeLuca and Peeples encourage people to recognize "that most, and the most important, public discussions take place via 'screens'—television, computer, and the front page of the newspaper."[168] These scholars recognize that we live in a primarily visual culture. Meaning is shaped and guided by the images people see rather than strictly (or even primarily) by words.[169] Television and the videos people watch on the Internet are prime examples of a discourse grounded in images and the visual. Thus, when we study public communication, the focus should not only be on public speeches, but also on "image events," which are now the primary mode of communication to a public that is characterized by its reliance on commercial, professional communication on public screens.[170]

DeLuca and Peeples's point is not that the visual rhetorics of the public screen are superior to the verbal discourses of the traditional public sphere, nor that everyone should engage in image events instead of public discourse.[171] Instead, they argue that one cannot really understand the complete dynamics of contemporary public controversies unless one accounts for the role of the visual. As they explain, "the public screen is the essential supplement to the public sphere. In comparison to the rationality, embodied conversations, consensus, and civility of the public sphere, the public screen highlights dissemination, images, hypermediacy, spectacular publicity, cacophony, distractions, and dissent."[172] The public screen does not share the ideals of consensus formation and civility that typifies descriptions of the ideal public sphere, but neither does all public communication, as the confrontational rhetoric of British suffrage advocates of the 1800s and the antiwar protests of the 1960s and 1970s demonstrated. Attention to the public screen does emphasizes that public discourse, as it exists, is diffuse, messy, loud, vivid, and immediate. In many cases, it does more to generate controversy than to generate consensus.

Because media technologies are no longer confined to mass media such as television and newspapers, but also include interactive forms of networked media, communication scholars Joshua P. Ewalt, Jessy J. Ohl, and Damien Smith Pfister argue that we need to shift from the concept of the public screen to the concept of *networked* public screens. They explain,

> **"networked public screens"** better captures how *image events, iconic and everyday, are produced and circulated in a networked mediascape.* Images and text hop from screen node to screen node, following the developing logics of social networking and algorithmic culture. Unlike a conventional public address or formal screen presentation . . . with a specific context, internal coherence, and a sequential development, images on networked public screens are often decontextualized, random, and bricolaged.[173]

When thinking about rhetoric in civic life, you need to recognize the following: (1) visual, material, and verbal rhetoric are all involved, so the sphere is also a screen on which rhetoric is viewed and felt as much as heard; (2) with the shift from mass to networked communication, rhetoric, people, organizations, and actions are networked, so circulation across audiences is as important to consider as delivery to the initial audience; and (3) impact needs to be thought of differently, as the effect of circulation in mass media may be less important than the effect of circulation in social media created by individuals.[174] Rhetoric in civic life is not simply a dialogue; it is a messy, vibrant, confounding, sometimes cacophonous multilogue, in which everyone can be involved as a producer and consumer, rhetor and audience, activist and bystander, all at the same time.

CONCLUSION

Defining "public" is a complex process. A group of people that exists prior to a rhetor's message does not come into being as a public until it is constituted through rhetoric. Further, publics are fluid, coming into and out of existence. An understanding of multiple public spheres reveals the multifaceted relationships between the rhetor, audiences, public spheres, power, economy, and state.

Habermas's ideal public sphere is "open to all citizens," addresses "matters of general interest," and is free from coercion.[175] Although everyone should be included in public sphere deliberation, this ideal is not a reality. Not everyone is accorded access to the public sphere; not everyone's words are given the same weight as others. Power differentials matter.

When people perceive that they are outside of the dominant public and that their issues and concerns are not being addressed, they may construct counterpublic spheres in which they offer definitions of their identities and concerns that counter the dominant public sphere perspective. The Internet provides a place in which counterpublic spheres can form, as well as a space for participation in the dominant public sphere and in the strong public of the state.

The concept of the public sphere has been expanded to include networked publics and the networked public screen, as well as visual and verbal messages, because modern media have changed the ways people communicate and obtain messages. Not all public rhetoric achieves the high ideals of reasoned face-to-face communication that theorists such as Habermas and Dewey imagined. Instead, communication on the networked public screen can appear to be emotional, other-than-rational, and disruptive. This is not necessarily a problem. Argument and controversy are signs of a healthy democratic society and central to civic engagement. Disagreement opens space for argument, challenges norms, and urges people to consider which arguments make sense.

Civic engagement occurs whenever a public sphere is brought into being through discourse. People participate in individual and collective action to develop solutions to social, economic, and political challenges in their communities, states, nation, and the world. In any democratic society, change and maintenance of social, political, and economic structures is accomplished through civic engagement, which is accomplished through rhetoric. Civic engagement is not about what people do in the public sphere, but how they interact. It is a process with many different forms, all of which involve rhetoric.

DISCUSSION QUESTIONS

1. In Chapter 1, we defined citizenship not as a single thing you do, but as a process. Identify all the ways you participate in civic life. How many of those forms of participation require collective and coordinated action? How many

are individual and personal? What do your answers tell you about the health of public spheres in contemporary society?

2. Identify publics to which you belong. What identifies you as a member of that public? How has your participation in that public developed your own identity?

3. Is online activism politically productive? Think about the 2012 example of the Kony video. To gather information on the issues that video raises, consider reading the following articles:

> Bailyn, Evan. "The Difference between Slacktivism and Activism: How 'Kony 2012' is Narrowing the Gap." *HuffPost Impact,* March 19, 2012, http://www.huffingtonpost.com/evan-bailyn/kony-2012 -activism_b_1361791.html.

> Watson, Tom. "The #StopKony Backlash: Complexity and the Challenges of Slacktivism." *Forbes,* March 8, 2012, http://www .forbes.com/sites/tomwatson/2012/03/08/the-stopkony-backlash -complexity-and-the-challenges-of-slacktivism.

SUGGESTED READINGS

Asen, Robert, and Daniel C. Brouwer. "Introduction: Reconfigurations of the Public Sphere." In *Counterpublics and the State.* Edited by Robert Asen and Daniel C. Brouwer, 1–32. Albany: State University of New York Press, 2001.

DeLuca, Kevin Michael, and Jennifer Peeples. "From Public Sphere to Public Screen: Democracy, Activism, and the 'Violence' of Seattle." *Critical Studies in Media Communication* 19, no. 2 (June 2002): 125–151.

Fraser, Nancy. "Rethinking the Public Sphere." In *Habermas and the Public Sphere.* Edited by Craig Calhoun, 109–137. Cambridge, MA: MIT Press, 1992.

Mansbridge, Jane. "Using Power/Fighting Power: The Polity." In *Democracy and Difference: Contesting the Boundaries of the Political.* Edited by Seyla Benhabib, 46–66. Princeton, NJ: Princeton University Press, 1996.

Pfister, Damien Smith. *Networked Media, Networked Rhetorics: Attention and Deliberation in the Early Blogosphere.* University Park: Penn State University Press, 2014.

ENDNOTES

[1] The Sensenbrenner Bill, officially known as House Resolution 4377: Border Protection, Antiterrorism, and Illegal Immigration Control Act of 2005, passed in the House in December 2005, catalyzing the Spring 2006 protests. It did not pass in the Senate.

[2] Lindsey Bever, "Protesters in California Block Busloads of Immigrant Children and Families," *Washington Post,* July 2, 2014, http://www.washingtonpost.com/news /morning-mix/wp/2014/07/02/protesters-in-california-block-busloads-of-immigrant -children-and-families.

[3] Ricardo Cano, "Protesters Turn Back Busloads of Immigrants in Murrieta," *Desert Sun* (Palm Springs, CA), July 2, 2014, http://www.desertsun.com/story/news/2014/07/01 /protesters-turn-back-busloads-immigrants-murrieta/11945751.

4 Bever, "Protesters."

5 Anne Demo, "Review Essay: Policy and Media in Immigration Studies," *Rhetoric and Public Affairs* 7, no. 2 (2002): 216.

6 Richard D. Pineda and Stacey K. Sowards, "Flag Waving as Visual Argument: 2006 Immigration Demonstrations and Cultural Citizenship," *Argumentation and Advocacy* 43 (Winter and Spring 2007): 164–174; Kent A. Ono and John M. Sloop, *Shifting Borders: Rhetoric, Immigration, and California's Proposition 187* (Philadelphia: Temple University Press, 2002).

7 Rick Klein, "After the Rallies, a Focus on Momentum; Immigration Rights Leaders Hope for Sustained Effort," *Boston Globe*, April 12, 2006.

8 Nina Bernstein, "In the Streets, Suddenly, an Immigrant Groundswell," *New York Times*, March 27, 2006.

9 Quoted in Rick Klein, "Immigrants' Voice: 'We're in the Fight,'" *Boston Globe*, April 11, 2006, A1.

10 Ralph Ranalli and Yvonne Abraham, "O'Malley Urges Policy Reform Based on Respect: Immigration Backers Stream through Hub," *Boston Globe*, April 11, 2006.

11 Amanda Paulson, "Rallying Immigrants Look Ahead," *Christian Science Monitor*, May 3, 2006.

12 Wes Allison, "When Does a March Become a Movement?" *St. Petersburg Times* (Florida), April 16, 2006.

13 Stephen Dinan, "The Washington Times," *Washington Times,* May 4, 2006.

14 Rachel L. Swarns, "Immigrants Rally in Scores of Cities for Legal Status," *New York Times*, April 11, 2006.

15 Keyonna Summers, "End of Minuteman Tour Marked by Confrontations; Demonstrators Compare Group to Klan," *Washington Times*, May 13, 2006.

16 Richard Sammon, "Immigration Bill Still a Long Shot," *Kiplinger Business Forecasts* 2006, No. 0505, May 1, 2006, LexisNexis.

17 Lou Dobbs, *Lou Dobbs Tonight*, April 1, 2006, http://transcripts.cnn.com /TRANSCRIPTS/0604/01/ldt.01.html.

18 John D. MacKinnon and Sheila V. Kumar, "Obama Vows to Act, Border Protest Goes On," *Wall Street Journal*, July 4, 2014, http://online.wsj.com/articles/obama-vows -immigration-fix-border-protest-goes-on-1404518329.

19 Quoted in Michael Martinez and Holly Yan, "Showdown: California Town Turns Away Buses of Detained Immigrants," CNN.com, July 3, 2014, http://www.cnn .com/2014/07/02/us/california-immigrant-transfers.

20 Gerard A. Hauser, "Features of the Public Sphere," *Critical Studies in Mass Communication* 4, no. 4 (December 1987), 440.

21 James Jasinski, *Sourcebook on Rhetoric* (Thousand Oaks, CA: Sage, 2001), 474. Jürgen Habermas's writings include *The Structural Transformation of the Public Sphere: An Inquiry into a Category of Bourgeois Society,* trans. Thomas Burger (Boston: MIT Press, 1991); *Reason and the Rationalization of Society,* vol. 1, *The Theory of Communicative Action,* trans. Thomas McCarthy (Boston: Beacon, 1984); *Lifeworld and System: A Critique of Functionalist Reason,* vol. 2, *The Theory of Communicative Action,* trans. Thomas McCarthy (Boston: Beacon, 1987).

22 Jürgen Habermas, "The Public Sphere," in *Jürgen Habermas on Society and Politics: A Reader,* ed. S. Seidman, 231–236 (Boston: Beacon, 1989), 230, italics added.

23 Habermas, "The Public Sphere," 232.

24 Habermas, *Structural Transformation*, 32–41.

25 Robert Asen, "The Multiple Mr. Dewey: Multiple Publics and Permeable Borders in John Dewey's Theory of the Public Sphere," *Argument and Advocacy* 39 (Winter

2003): 174–188; Robert Asen, "A Discourse Theory of Citizenship," *Quarterly Journal of Speech* 90, no. 2 (May 2009): 189–211.

26 Nancy Fraser, "Rethinking the Public Sphere," in *Habermas and the Public Sphere,* ed. Craig Calhoun, 109–137 (Cambridge, MA: MIT Press, 1992), 110.

27 Habermas, "The Public Sphere," 231.

28 "Read Gov. Walker's Budget Repair Bill," wisconsinrapidstribune.com, February 24, 2011, http://www.wisconsinrapidstribune.com/article/20110224/WRT0101/110224063/Read-Gov-Walker-s-budget-repair-bill.

29 Judy Keen, "Wisconsin Budget Crisis Has Folks Talking," *USA Today*, February 24, 2011.

30 Although Habermas points to eighteenth- and early nineteenth-century Europe for an example of the emergence of a public sphere, other scholars have noted that his bourgeois public sphere was premised on exclusions based on sex and class. See Mary P. Ryan, "Gender and Public Access: Women's Politics in Nineteenth-Century America," and Geoff Eley, "Nations, Publics, and Political Cultures: Placing Habermas in the Nineteenth Century," in *Habermas and the Public Sphere,* ed. Craig Calhoun, 259–339 (Cambridge: MIT Press, 1992). Habermas recognizes such exclusion. See Jürgen Habermas, "Further Reflections on the Public Sphere," in *Habermas and the Public Sphere,* ed. Craig Calhoun, 421–461 (Cambridge: MIT Press, 1992).

31 Melanie Loehwing and Jeff Motter, "Publics, Counterpublics, and the Promise of Democracy," *Philosophy and Rhetoric* 42, no. 3 (2009): 220–241.

32 Editorial Board, "Putin's Repression Resumes, Now That the Olympics Have Ended" (editorial), *Washington Post,* February 25, 2014, http://www.washingtonpost.com/opinions/putins-repression-resumes-now-that-the-olympics-have-ended/2014/02/25/071f010a-9e5a-11e3-b8d8-94577ff66b28_story.html.

33 Fraser, "Rethinking," 110.

34 Robert Asen and Daniel C. Brouwer, "Introduction: Reconfigurations of the Public Sphere," in *Counterpublics and the State,* ed. Robert Asen and Daniel S. Brouwer, 1–32 (Albany: State University of New York Press) 10. See also John Dewey, *The Public and Its Problems* (1927; repr. Athens, OH: Swallow, 1954).

35 Valeria Fabj and Matthew J. Sobnosky, "AIDS Activism and the Rejuvenation of the Public Sphere," *Argumentation and Advocacy* 31 (Spring 1995): 163–184.

36 The authors thank Robert Asen for his useful distinction between universality and multiplicity.

37 Fraser, "Rethinking," 134, italics added.

38 Fraser, "Rethinking," 134, italics added.

39 Ono and Sloop. See also J. David Cisneros, "Contaminated Communities: The Metaphor of 'Immigrant as Pollutant' in Media Representations of Immigration," *Rhetoric and Public Affairs* 11, no. 4 (2008): 569–602; Otto Santa Anna, *Brown Tide Rising: Metaphors of Latinos in Contemporary American Public Discourse* (Austin: University of Texas Press, 2002).

40 Marouf Hasian, Jr., and Fernando Delgado, "The Trials and Tribulations of Racialized Critical Rhetorical Theory: Understanding the Rhetorical Ambiguities of Proposition 187," *Communication Theory* 8, no. 3 (August 1998): 259.

41 Matthew Webster, "The Border Crossed Us," *Nonviolent Migration,* http://nonviolentmigration.wordpress.com/2007/10/19/the-border-crossed-us; and Rubén Martínez, "Fighting 187: The Different Opposition Strategies," *NACLA: Report of the Americas* 29, no. 3 (November/December 1995): 30.

42 Fraser, "Rethinking," 134.

[43] Fraser, "Rethinking," 134–135.

[44] Hasian and Delgado, "Trials," 254.

[45] Hasian and Delgado, "Trials," 262.

[46] Fraser, "Rethinking," 136.

[47] Hauser, "Features," 439.

[48] Habermas, "Further Reflections," 438.

[49] Michael Warner, *Publics and Counterpublics* (New York: Zone, 2002), 117.

[50] The Black Public Sphere Collective, ed., *The Black Public Sphere* (Chicago: University of Chicago Press, 1995).

[51] George A. Kennedy, *Classical Rhetoric and Its Christian and Secular Tradition from Ancient to Modern Times*, 2nd ed. (Chapel Hill: University of North Carolina Press, 1999): 20.

[52] Eva C. Keuls, *The Reign of the Phallus* (New York: Harper and Row, 1985), 391.

[53] Fraser, "Rethinking," 123, italics added.

[54] Fraser, "Rethinking," 124.

[55] Rita Felski, *Beyond Feminist Aesthetics* (Cambridge, MA: Harvard University Press, 1989), 12.

[56] Catharine A. MacKinnon, *Women's Lives, Men's Laws* (Cambridge, MA: Harvard University Press, 2005), 111.

[57] Catherine Squires, "The Black Press and the State: Attracting Unwanted (?) Attention," in *Counterpublics and the State*, ed. Robert Asen and Daniel C. Brouwer, 111–136 (Albany: State University of New York Press, 2001), 132, n. 1, italics added. In addition to discussing enclaved and oscillating publics, Squires offers two additional levels of distinction: a counterpublic "engages in mass actions to assert its needs . . . utilizing disruptive social movement tactics to make demands on the state," and parallel publics "work in conjunction with other [publics] on equal footing." For our purposes, her discussion of oscillation and enclaved publics is the most useful.

[58] bell hooks does not capitalize her name. Her birth name is Gloria Jean Watkins. She chose the name of bell hooks in remembrance of her lineage (she took her great-grandmother's name), as well as to distinguish her voice from Gloria Watkins's. The pseudonym and the lower-case letters signify the importance of her ideas and writing instead of her socially constructed identity.

[59] bell hooks, *Talking Back: Thinking Feminist, Thinking Black* (Boston: South End, 1989), 29.

[60] Robert Asen and Daniel C. Brouwer, "Reconfigurations," 8.

[61] Jane Mansbridge, "Using Power/Fighting Power: The Polity," in *Democracy and Difference: Contesting the Boundaries of the Political*, ed. Seyla Benhabib, 46–66 (Princeton, NJ: Princeton University Press, 1996), 58.

[62] Hasian and Delgado, "Trials," 259.

[63] Daniel C. Brouwer, "ACT-ing UP in Congressional Hearings," in *Counterpublics and the State*, ed. Robert Asen and Daniel C. Brouwer, 87–110 (Albany: State University of New York Press, 2001), 132, n. 1.

[64] Kristy Maddux, "When Patriots Protest: The Anti-Suffrage Discursive Transformation of 1917," *Rhetoric and Public Affairs* 7, no. 3 (Fall 2004): 283–310.

[65] United Farm Workers, *Take Our Jobs*, 2010, http://www.takeourjobs.org.

[66] United Farm Workers, "Stephen Colbert & Farmworkers Take Fight to Congress," 2010, http://action.ufw.org/page/s/colbert92410.

[67] Fraser, "Rethinking," 99–100.

[68] Asen and Brouwer, "Reconfigurations," 20.

[69] Felski, *Beyond*, 166.

[70] Lisa A. Flores, "Creating Discursive Space through a Rhetoric of Difference: Chicana Feminists Craft a Homeland," *Quarterly Journal of Speech* 82 (1996): 142–156.

[71] Santa Ana, *Brown*, 298–299.

[72] Warner, *Publics*, 57.

[73] Nancy Fraser, "Transnationalizing the Public Sphere: On the Legitimacy and Efficacy of Public Opinion in a Post-Westphalian World," *Theory, Culture and Society* 24, no. 4 (2007): 16.

[74] Fraser, "Transnationalizing," 19.

[75] Kevin Michael DeLuca and Jennifer Peeples, "From Public Sphere to Public Screen: Democracy, Activism, and the 'Violence' of Seattle," *Critical Studies in Media Communication* 19, no. 2 (June 2002): 126.

[76] Asen and Brouwer, "Reconfigurations," 16.

[77] Dana Cloud, presentation at the National Communication Association preconference "Connection and Action in Public Sphere Studies: Conversations about What We Do and Why We Do It," Chicago, November 15, 2006.

[78] Joshua P. Ewalt, Jessy J. Ohl, and Damien Smith Pfister, "Activism, Deliberation, and Networked Public Screens: Rhetorical Scenes from the Occupy Movement in Lincoln, Nebraska (Parts 1 and 2)," *Cultural Studies <=> Critical Methodologies* 13, no. 3 (2013): 173–190, 184.

[79] Occupy Wall Street, "About," http://occupywallst.org/about (accessed July 7, 2014).

[80] Phaedra C. Pezzullo, "Contextualizing Boycotts and Buycotts: The Impure Politics of Consumer-Based Advocacy in an Age of Global Ecological Crises," *Communication and Critical/Cultural Studies* 8, no. 2 (June 2011): 125–126.

[81] Pezzullo, "Contextualizing," 131.

[82] Pezzullo, "Contextualizing," 140.

[83] Pezzullo, "Contextualizing," 129.

[84] Apple, R. W., Jr., "A Nation Challenged: News Analysis: Nature of Foe is Obstacle in Appealing for Sacrifice" (electronic version), *New York Times*, October 15, 2001; Matthew A. Crenson and Benjamin Ginsberg, *Downsizing Democracy: How America Sidelined Its Citizens and Privatized Its Public* (Baltimore: Johns Hopkins University Press, 2002); Liz Kowalczyk, "Patriotic Purchasing Americans Are Being Urged to Spend, But Analysts Doubt the Strategy Will Have an Impact in the Long Run," *Boston Globe*, September 28, 2001.

[85] Crenson and Ginsberg, *Downsizing*, 9, 2.

[86] Lauren Berlant, *The Queen of American Goes to Washington City: Essays on Sex and Citizenship* (Durham, NC: Duke University Press, 1997), 5.

[87] Berlant, *Queen*, 3.

[88] Berlant, *Queen*, 3.

[89] Berlant, *Queen*, 5.

[90] Stephanie Coontz, *The Way We Never Were: American Families and the Nostalgia Trap* (New York: Basic Books, 1992), 94.

[91] Crenson and Ginsberg, *Downsizing*, 7.

[92] Clifford Rechtschaffen, Eileen Gauna, and Catherine O'Neill, *Environmental Justice: Law, Policy & Regulation*, 2nd ed. (Durham, NC: Carolina Academic Press, 2009), esp. excerpt from Vicki Been.

[93] Benjamin Chavis, "Concerning the Historical Evolution of the 'Environmental Justice Movement' and the Definition of the Term: 'Environmental Racism,'" September 4, 2009, http://www.drbenjaminchavis.com/pages/landing?Concerning-the-Historical-Evolution-of-t=1&blockID=73318&feedID=3359.

[94] Asen and Brouwer, "Reconfigurations," 1.

[95] Asen and Brouwer, "Reconfigurations," 1.

[96] Dewey, *The Public*, 30.

[97] For a more extensive timeline, see Pew Research Internet Project, "World Wide Web Timeline," March 11, 2014, http://www.pewinternet.org/2014/03/11/world-wide-web -timeline.

[98] Pew Research Internet Project, "Social Networking Fact Sheet," September 2013, http://www.pewinternet.org/fact-sheets/social-networking-fact-sheet.

[99] Bob Simon, "How a Slap Sparked Tunisia's Revolution," *60 Minutes*, February 20, 2011, http://www.cbsnews.com/stories/2011/02/20/60minutes/main20033404.shtml.

[100] Hillary Clinton, "Internet Rights and Wrongs: Choices and Challenges in a Networked World," February 15, 2011, http://www.state.gov/secretary/rm/2011/02 /156619.htm.

[101] Interestingly, one of the most public places on the University of Northern Iowa's campus, the student union, has a policy prohibiting public speaking. Maucker Union's "Policies and Procedures" clarify: "In an effort to promote a comfortable, student centered, educationally focused community . . . agents of any cause, organization or product are prohibited from active solicitation within Maucker Union. This includes activities such as public speaking . . . ." http://www.uni.edu /maucker/policies/section-0500.shtml.

[102] Vivian Sobchack, "Democratic Franchise and the Electronic Frontier," in *Cyberfutures: Culture and Politics on the Information Superhighway*, ed. Ziauddin Sardar and Jerome R. Ravetz (New York: New York University Press, 1996), 82.

[103] Amanda Lenhart and Maeve Duggan, "Couples, the Internet and Social Media," Pew Research Internet Project, February 11, 2014, http://www.pewinternet.org /2014/02/11/couples-the-internet-and-social-media.

[104] Aaron Smith, "Part V: Cell Phone Usage: Mobile Activities and 'Sexting,'" Pew Research Internet Project, November 30, 2012, http://www.pewinternet.org /2012/11/30/part-v-cell-phone-usage/#fn-99-1.

[105] Chana Joffe-Walt, "'Sexting': A Disturbing New Teen Trend?" *All Things Considered*, March 11, 2009, http://www.npr.org/templates/story/story.php?storyId=101735230.

[106] Aaron Smith, "The Internet's Role in Campaign 2008," Pew Internet & American Life Project, April 15, 2009, http://www.pewinternet.org/Reports/2009/6—The -Internets-Role-in-Campaign-2008.aspx.

[107] Aaron Smith and Maeve Duggan, "The State of the 2012 Election—Mobile Politics," Pew Research Internet Project, October 9, 2012, http://www.pewinternet.org /2012/10/09/the-state-of-the-2012-election-mobile-politics.

[108] Darrell M. West, "Communications Lessons from the 2012 Presidential Election," Brookings.edu, November 6, 2012, http://www.brookings.edu/blogs/up-front/posts /2012/11/06-election-communications-west.

[109] Lee Rainie, Aaron Smith, Kay Lehman Schlozman, Henry Brady, and Sidney Verba, "Social Media and Political Engagement," Pew Research Internet Project, October 19, 2012, http://www.pewinternet.org/2012/10/19/social-media-and -political-engagement.

[110] Rainie, et al., "Social Media."

[111] Juliet Barbara, "5 Unforgettable Social Media Election Moments," *Forbes*, November 6, 2012, http://www.forbes.com/sites/julietbarbara/2012/11/06/5 -unforgettable-social-media-election-moments.

[112] West, "Communications Lessons."

[113] Natan Edelsburg, "Social TV Results from the Third Presidential Debate," LostRemote, October 24, 2012, http://lostremote.com/social-tv-results-from-the -third-presidential-debate_b34678.

114 Adam Sharp, "Election Night 2012," Twitter Blog, November 7, 2012, https://blog
.twitter.com/2012/election-night-2012.

115 West, "Communications Lessons."

116 Eleanor Dowling, "VP Debate Top 10 Social Media Events of All Time," Bluefin
Labs, BostInno, October 14, 2012, http://bostinno.streetwise.co/channels/vp-debate
-tops-10-most-social-tv-events-of-all-time-infographic.

117 Susan A. Sci and David R. Dewberry, "Something Funny? The *Laughing Joe Biden*
Meme as Digital *Topoi* within Political Argumentation," in *Disturbing Argument,*
ed. Catherine Helen Palczewski (New York: Routledge, 2014).

118 Sci and Dewberry, "Something Funny?"

119 Mark Poster, "Cyber Democracy: The Internet and the Public Sphere," in *The
Information Subject: Mark Poster Essays,* ed. Stanley Aronowitz (Amsterdam: G + B
Arts International, 2001), 96.

120 Mark Poster, "The Internet and the Public Sphere," in *Reading Digital Culture,* ed.
David Trend (Malden, MA: Blackwell, 2001), 260.

121 Brenda Chan, "Imagining the Homeland: The Internet and Diasporic Discourse
of Nationalism," *Journal of Communication Inquiry* 29, no. 4 (October 2005):
336–368; Peter Dahlgren, "The Internet, Public Spheres, and Political
Communication: Dispersion and Deliberation," *Political Communication* 22, no. 2
(April/June 2005): 147–162.

122 Wendy M. Grossman, *Net.wars* (New York: New York University Press, 1997).

123 See, for example, Graeme Browning, *Electronic Democracy: Using the Internet
to Influence American Politics* (Wilton, CT: Pemberton, 1996); Lawrence K.
Grossman, *The Electronic Republic: Reshaping Democracy in the Information
Age* (New York: Viking, 1995); Kevin A. Hill and John E. Hughes, *Cyberpolitics:
Citizen Activism in the Age of the Internet* (Lanham, MD: Rowman and Littlefield,
1998); Jay Kinney, "Is There a New Political Paradigm Lurking in Cyberspace?" in
Cyberfutures: Culture and Politics on the Information Superhighway, ed. Ziauddin
Sardar and Jerome R. Ravetz, 138–153 (New York: New York University Press,
1996).

124 Harry Potter Alliance, "What We Do," 2014, http://thehpalliance.org/what-we-do.

125 Patty Riley, James Klumpp, and Thomas Hollihan, "Democratizing the Lifeworld
of the 21st Century: Evaluating New Democratic Sites for Argument," in *Argument
and Values,* ed. Sally Jackson (Annandale, VA: National Communication
Association, 1995), 259.

126 Patty Riley, Thomas Hollihan, and James Klumpp, "The Dark Side of Community
and Democracy: Militias, Patriots and Angry White Guys," in *Argument in a Time of
Change: Definitions, Frameworks, and Critiques,* ed. James F. Klumpp (Annandale,
VA: National Communication Association, 1997), 205.

127 Evan Bailyn, "The Difference between Slacktivism and Activism: How 'Kony 2012' is
Narrowing the Gap," HuffPost Impact, March 19, 2012, http://www.huffingtonpost
.com/evan-bailyn/kony-2012-activism_b_1361791.html.

128 Tom Watson, "The #StopKony Backlash: Complexity and the Challenges of
Slacktivism," *Forbes,* March 8, 2012, http://www.forbes.com/sites/tomwatson
/2012/03/08/the-stopkony-backlash-complexity-and-the-challenges-of-slacktivism.

129 Amar Toor, "UNICEF Says Facebook 'Likes' Won't Save Children's Lives," *Verge,*
May 3, 2013, http://www.theverge.com/2013/5/3/4296194/unicef-facebook
-activism-ad-campaign-likes-dont-save-lives.

130 Brendan Rigby, "Slacktivists Take Note: We Don't Like Your Likes," WhyDev.org,
July 15, 2013, http://www.whydev.org/slacktivists-take-note-we-dont-like-your-likes.

[131] Cass R. Sunstein, *Going to Extremes: How Like Minds Unite and Divide* (New York: Oxford University Press, 2009): 81.

[132] Christopher J. Stapel, *No Longer Alone: A Resource Manual for Rural Sexual Minority Youth and the Adults Who Serve Them* (pamphlet), National Youth Advocacy Coalition, http://www.nyacyouth.org/docs/ruralyouth/NoLongerAlone.pdf.

[133] Lincoln Dahlberg, "Rethinking the Fragmentation of the Cyberpublic: From Consensus to Contestation," *New Media and Society* 9, no. 5 (2007): 830.

[134] John Horrigan, Kelly Garrett, and Paul Resnick, *The Internet and Democratic Debate*, Pew Internet & American Life Project, 2004, http://www.pewinternet.org/Reports /2004/The-Internet-and-Democratic-Debate.aspx.

[135] Lee Rainie, "The State of Digital Divides," Pew Research Internet Project, November 5, 2013, http://www.pewinternet.org/2013/11/05/the-state-of-digital -divides-video-slides.

[136] Commerce Department, *Falling through the Net: Part II: Internet Access and Usage*, http://www.ntia.doc.gov/ntiahome/fttn99/part2.html (accessed January 15, 2007).

[137] Fraser, "Rethinking," 123.

[138] Catherine Helen Palczewski, "Cyber-Movements, New Social Movements, and Counterpublics," in *Counterpublics and the State*, ed. Robert Asen and Daniel C. Brouwer, 161–210 (Albany: State University of New York Press, 2001), 171–172.

[139] "Internet Users per 100 Inhabitants 2006–2013," International Telecommunications Union, Geneva, Switzerland (accessed June 6, 2015).

[140] Asen and Brouwer, "Reconfigurations," 6.

[141] A. J. Liebling, "Do You Belong in Journalism," *New Yorker*, May 14, 1960, 105.

[142] The authors thank Damien Pfister for his assistance in working through this explanation.

[143] Trent Lott, "Toast Delivered at Sen. Strom Thurmond (R-SC) 100th Birthday Celebration," December 5, 2002, transcribed from http://web.archive.org/web /20021207064833/www.c-span.org/politics.

[144] Damien Pfister, "The Logos of the Blogosphere: Flooding the Zone, Invention, and Attention in the Lott Imbroglio," *Argumentation and Advocacy* 47, no. 3 (Winter 2011), 142–3.

[145] Yochai Benkler, *The Wealth of Networks: How Social Production Transforms Markets and Freedom* (New Haven, CT: Yale University Press, 2006), 10, http://www.benkler .org/Benkler_Wealth_Of_Networks.pdf.

[146] Benkler, "Wealth," 220.

[147] Damien Pfister, personal correspondence with Catherine Palczewski, June 2, 2014.

[148] Carly Ledbetter, "Here's Why the FDA's New Cheesemaking Ban is Terrible News for Artisans," *Huffington Post*, June 10, 2014, http://www.huffingtonpost.com /2014/06/10/fda-banning-aging-cheese-_n_5479816.html; Jeanne Carpenter, "Game Changer: FDA Rules No Wooden Boards in Cheese Aging," *Cheese Underground*, June 7, 2014, http://cheeseunderground.blogspot.com/2014/06/game-changer-fda -rules-no-wooden-boards.html.

[149] Ledbetter, "Here's Why."

[150] For more information, see *Zapatistas in Cyberspace*, a website maintained by economics professor Harry M. Cleaver, Jr., http://indigenouspeople.net/zapatist.htm. We are particularly thankful to Professor Cleaver for his expert feedback on this section's discussion of the events in Chiapas.

[151] Harry M. Cleaver, Jr., "The Chiapas Uprising and the Future of Class Struggle in the New World Order," February 14, 1994, la.utexas.edu/users/hcleaver /kcchiapasuprising.html.

[152] Donna Kowal, "Digitizing and Globalizing Indigenous Voices: The Zapatista Movement," in *Critical Perspectives on the Internet*, ed. Greg Elmer, 105–126, (Lanham, MD: Rowman and Littlefield, 2002), 111.

[153] Harry Cleaver, "The Zapatistas and the Electronic Fabric of Struggle," la.utexas.edu /users/hcleaver/zaps.html.

[154] "Mission Statement," indymedia.us, http://indymedia.us/en/static/mission.shtml (accessed January 26, 2011).

[155] Indybay, "Indymedia and Indybay History," http://www.indybay.org/newsitems /2005/03/11/17262451.php.

[156] Jill Lane, "Digital Zapatistas," *Drama Review* 47, no. 2 (2003): 129–144, 135.

[157] Jesus Barraza, "Celebrating 15 years of Zapatista Struggle," January 5, 2009, http:// www.justseeds.org/blog/2009/01/celebrating_15_years_of_zapati.html. Postings also have appeared on the *De Tod@s Para Tod@s* blog (see for instance, http://detodos -paratodos.blogspot.com/2010/05/april-2010-chiapaszapatista-news.html), *the new internationalist* blog (see for instance, http://www.newint.org/blog/majority /2008/06/09/zapatistas-threatened), and *The Frugal Traveler* (see for instance, http:// frugaltraveler.blogs.nytimes.com/2008/12/09/in-the-village-of-the-zapatistas).

[158] Stephen Wray, quoted in B. Paquin, "Hacktivism: Attack of the E-Guerillas!" *Straits Times* (Singapore), December 13, 1998, 32–33, http://www.lexis-nexis.com.

[159] Jill Lane, "Digital Zapatistas," *Drama Review* 47, no. 2 (Summer 2003): 129–144.

[160] Aaron Hess, "Resistance up in Smoke: Analyzing the Limitations of Deliberation on YouTube," *Critical Studies in Media Communication* 25, no. 5 (December 2009): 411–434, 427.

[161] Christopher J. Gilbert, "Playing with Hitler: *Downfall* and its Ludic Uptake," *Critical Studies in Media Communication* 30, no. 5 (December 2013), 407–424, 420.

[162] Gilbert, "Playing," 420.

[163] Gilbert, "Playing," 421.

[164] Pineda and Sowards, "Flag Waving," 164.

[165] Associated Press, "Immigration Issue Draws Thousands into Streets," http://www .msnbc.msn.com/id/11442705/ (accessed October 29, 2009). Image RTR1CZPR on the Reuters website.

[166] http://www.minutemanproject.com/immigration-topics/archive.asp (accessed October 12, 2011).

[167] Pineda and Sowards, "Flag Waving," 172.

[168] DeLuca and Peeples, "From Public," 129, 131, italics added.

[169] DeLuca and Peeples, "From Public," 132.

[170] DeLuca and Peeples, "From Public," 144.

[171] DeLuca and Peeples, "From Public," 147.

[172] DeLuca and Peeples, "From Public," 145.

[173] Joshua P. Ewalt, Jessy J. Ohl, and Damien Smith Pfister, "Activism," 187.

[174] Ewalt, Ohl, and Pfister, "Activism."

[175] Habermas, "The Public Sphere," 231.

Credits and Acknowledgments

308   Credits and Acknowledgments

Excerpts on pages 76 and 95 from Carole Blair, "Contemporary U.S. Memorial Sites as Exemplars of Rhetoric's Materiality," in *Rhetorical Bodies*, ed. Jack Selzer and Sharon Crowley (Madison: University of Wisconsin Press, 1999). Reproduced with permission of University of Wisconsin Press.

Excerpt on pages 88 from Paul Watson, "One Day on the Water with Bob Hunter," Sea Shepherd Conservation Society web site (http://www.seashepherd.org/editorials/editorial_050510_1.html). Reproduced with permission of Sea Shepherd Conservation Society.

Excerpts on pages 99–100, 109 and 113 from Mark Jenkins, "Who Murdered the Virunga Gorillas," *National Geographic* 214, no. 1, July 2008, Mark (Wyoming) Jenkins/National Geographic Creative. Reproduced with permission of National Geographic Creative.

Excerpt on page 100 from Chris Falzon, letter to the editor, *National Geographic* 214, no. 5, November 2008. Reproduced with permission of Chris Falzon.

Excerpt on page 100 from Bryan Berry, letter to the editor, *National Geographic* 214, no. 5, November 2008. Reproduced with permission of Bryan Berry.

Excerpts on page 101 from John Dewey, "Creative Democracy," *1939–1941/Essays, Reviews, and Miscellany*, vol. 14, *John Dewey: The Later Works, 1925–1953* (Carbondale: Southern Illinois University Press, 1988). Reproduced with permission of Southern Illinois University Press.

Definition on page 112 of "Truthiness," Merriam-Webster's Words of the Year 2006. By permission. From *Merriam-Webster Online* © 2011 by Merriam-Webster, Incorporated (www.Merriam-Webster.com).

Excerpt on page 121, from Neil de Grasse Tyson, "Pluto's Honor," From *Natural History* 108, no. 1 (February 1999): 82; copyright © Natural History Magazine, Inc. 1999. Reproduced by permission of Natural History.

"Zach Wahls Speaks about Family" on pages 182–183, delivered January 31, 2011 to Iowa Legislature. Transcribed by Kiran Dhillon, April Larson, and Catherine H. Palczewski. Reproduced with permission of Zach Wahls.

Excerpts on pages 202, 226, 227, 228, 229, 231, 233, and 239 from Lloyd F. Bitzer, "The Rhetorical Situation," *Philosophy and Rhetoric* 1, 1968. Reproduced with permission of Pennsylvania State University Press.

Excerpts on page 214 and 215 from Philip Wander, "The Third Persona: An Ideological Turn in Rhetorical Theory," *Central States Speech Journal* 35 (Winter 1984) copyright © Central States Communication Association (CSCA), reprinted by permission of Taylor & Francis Ltd, http://www.tandfonline.com, on behalf of the Central States Communication Association (CSCA).

Excerpts on pages 239 and 245 from Richard E. Vatz, "The Myth of the Rhetorical Situation," *Philosophy and Rhetoric* 6 (1973). Reproduced with permission of Pennsylvania State University Press.

"Address to the General Audience" on 245–246, John Paul II, September 11, 2002. Reproduced with permission of Libreria Editrice Vaticana.

Excerpts on page 279 from Phaedra C. Pezzullo, "Contextualizing Boycotts and Buycotts: The Impure Politics of Consumer-Based Advocacy in an Age of Global Ecological Crises," *Communication and Critical/Cultural Studies* 8, no. 2, June 2011, copyright © National Communication Association, reprinted by permission of Taylor & Francis Ltd, www.tandfonline.com, on behalf of The National Communication Association.

Excerpts on pages 285 and 286 from Darrell M. West, "Communications Lessons from the 2012 Presidential Election," Brookings.edu, November 6, 2012. Reproduced with permission of The Brookings Institution.

Excerpts on pages 286 and 287 from Susan A. Sci and David R. Dewberry, "Something Funny? The *Laughing Joe Biden* Meme as Digital *Topoi* within Political Argumentation," in *Disturbing Argument*, ed. Catherine Helen Palczewski, Routledge, 2014. Reproduced with permission of Taylor & Francis Group.

Excerpt on page 288 from Harry Potter Alliance, "What We Do," 2014, http://thehpalliance.org/what-we-do. Reproduced with permission of the Harry Potter Alliance.

Excerpt on page 291 from Damien Pfister, personal correspondence with Catherine Palczewski, June 2, 2014. Reproduced with permission of Damien Pfister.

Excerpt on pages 292–293 from Harry Cleaver, "The Zapatistas and the Electronic Fabric of Struggle," la.utexas.edu/users/hcleaver/zaps.html. Reproduced with permission of Harry Cleaver.

Credits for figures appear in the figure captions.

Index

ad hominem fallacy, 116
agency, 10–11, 16
  audience, 201, 211–212, 217, 219
  constraints and, 233
  hegemony and, 29–30
  language and, 49–50, 60
  posthumanist theory of, 11–12
  power and, 27
  rhetor, 175, 191
  rhetorical agency, 211
Ahmadinejad, Mahmoud, 79
Alger, Horatio, 51
Anzaldúa, Gloria, 175, 217–218
arête, 167
argument, 101 (definition)
  audience and, 202
  in *Brown v. Board of Education*,
    199–200
  in civic society, 100–106
  classical conception of, 106–109
  discursive, 55
  fields, 116–117, 117 (definition)
  parts of, 109–116
  in public sphere, 273–274, 276,
    295, 297
  rhetorical proofs, 15
  situation and, 225–226, 245
  spheres of, 119–122
  Toulmin model of, 109–116
  visual, 73, 77–80, 85
argument$_1$, 101
argument$_2$, 101–102
Aristotle, 14–15, 30, 101, 106, 107, 146,
    167–168, 202, 204, 205, 206,
    225–226, 256
artistic proofs, 15
Asen, Robert, 17, 269, 270, 274, 275, 278
attitudes, 23, 203, 208–211,
    209 (definition)
audience, 201
  adapting rhetoric to, 201–211
  adapting to rhetoric, 188–195
  agency, 201, 211–212, 219
  argument and, 202
  artistic proofs and, 12
  consubstantiality, 9 (definition),
    203
  culture and, 24, 208
  eavesdropping, 217, 219

  identification with rhetor, 170, 174,
    176, 180, 203–204, 212, 213,
    214, 219
  particular, 119
  pathos and, 204–206
  persuasive continuum and, 20–23
  power, ideology, and hegemony,
    27–30, 218
  rhetor and, 203–208, 211, 212,
    213, 217
  rhetoric as addressed, 201–203
  rhetorical, 202, 229–231
  rhetorical situation and, 229–231, 232
  symbolic action as component of,
    199–219
  universal, 119
  values and, 202, 203, 208–211
authorial intent, 143–144
authority, 175–179, 190

backing, 104 (definition), 114, 115, 122
Balthrop, V. William, 135–136
Barthes, Roland, 184–185, 186
beliefs, 20–23, 108, 208–211,
    208 (definition)
  audience and, 208–211
  ideology and, 27–30
  myth and, 136
  social truth and, 146
Berger, Peter L., 12
Biden, Joe, 11–12, 286–287
Bieber, Justin, 179–180
Biesecker, Barbara, 212
Bitzer, Lloyd F., 107, 202, 212, 226–233,
    238, 239–240, 252
Black, Edwin, 213
Blair, Carole, 30, 76, 86
Blair, Tony, 53
body rhetoric, 77–80
Boehner, John, 212
Boorstin, Daniel J., 180–181
Booth, Wayne, 165–166
Branham, Robert J., 252, 253, 254, 255
Brock, Bernard L., 28
Brockriede, Wayne, 109
Brouwer, Daniel C., 270, 275
Brown, Michael, 110
Brummett, Barry, 12
Buck, Kenneth, 103

311

burden of proof, 117–118
Burke, Kenneth, 8–9, 16, 29, 45, 47,
  49–50, 56, 90, 150–154, 201,
  203, 214, 254, 278
Bush, George H. W., 70, 84, 143,
  214, 235
Bush, George W., 4, 49, 76, 143,
  153–154, 228–229, 242, 243–245,
  267, 279
  "Address to the Nation,"
    September 11, 2001, 243–245
Butler, Judith, 57, 178, 247

Campbell, Karlyn Kohrs, 10, 16, 20,
  169, 173, 178, 188, 211–212, 232,
  233–236
Caplan, Arthur, 210–211
character development, 142–143, 148
characterization, 49–51
Christie, Chris, 60
Churchill, Winston S., 5–6
Cicero, 167, 168
civic engagement, 16–20,
  16–17 (definition), 23, 31, 219,
  269–270, 285, 299
claim, 101, 104, 105, 109–116,
  109 (definition)
  of definition, 110
  of fact, 110
  of policy, 111
  presumption and, 117–118
  spheres of argument and, 121
  of value, 110
Clinton, Hillary, 116, 177, 283, 294
Clinton, William (Bill) Jefferson, 53, 214,
  216, 235, 286, 294
Cloud, Dana L., 278–279
Colbert, Stephen, 112
collective memory, 24–27, 25 (definition),
  85, 86, 133
Columbus, Christopher, 26, 145
comic frame, 151–154, 151 (definition)
condensation symbols, 55
Condit, Celeste M., 27, 48–49, 50,
  74, 186
conditions for rebuttal, 113
conformity, 253, 256
connotation, 43, 48, 50, 56–57, 74
constitutive rhetoric, 8
constraints, rhetorical, 231–233

consubstantiality, 9, 203, 204
contextual reconstruction, 255–256
Coontz, Stephanie, 280
Cooper, Anderson, 165
Cooper, Martha, 135
Copeland, Gary A., 30
counterpublics, 273–278,
  273 (definition)
  cyberspace and, 255, 259
  economy and, 278–281
  enclaved publics, 274–276,
    275 (definition)
  identity and, 272–273
  oscillating publics, 274–276,
    275 (definition)
  relationship to other publics, 281
  transnational, publics and, 278
Cox, J. Robert, 241
Cram, Dianne Emily, 207
Cramer, Jim, 254–255
Crenshaw, Kimberlé, 171–172
Crenson, Matthew, 279–280, 280–281
Cronkite, Walter, 22
Cruz, Ted, 11–12
culture, 23–24, 23 (definition)
  audiences and, 208, 212
  ideology, power, hegemony, and,
    27–30
  memory and, 24–27, 133–134
  narrative and, 134, 135–137, 140,
    147
  public sphere and, 268, 277, 279
  rhetorical situation and, 251–252
  visual culture, 72–75, 91

Dahlberg, Lincoln, 289
data, 108–116, 111 (definition),
  119–122
Davis, Wendy, 163–165, 189, 291
definition, claim of, 110
Delgado, Fernando, 272, 276
deliberative discourse, 226
DeLuca, Kevin Michael, 13, 76, 78,
  82, 88, 89, 90, 91, 248, 261, 278,
  295–296
Demo, Anne Teresa, 76, 82, 266
denotation, 43 (definition), 50, 54, 74
desecration, 254–255
Dewberry, David, 286
Dewey, John, 101, 282, 297

discourse,
  deliberative, 226
  epideictic, 226
  forensic, 226
discursive symbolism, 53
dominant reading, 74
doublespeak, 58–60, 59 (definition)
Douglas, Stephen A., 251
Douglass, Frederick, 45, 241–242
Dow, Bonnie J., 30
Dowd, Matthew, 229
dramatism, 45
Dworkin, Andrea, 111

eavesdropping audience, 217, 219
Ehninger, Douglas, 109
enactment, 77–78, 77 (definition)
enclaved publics, 274–276,
      275 (definition)
enthymeme, 107–109, 107 (definition)
epideictic discourse, 226
Ernst, Joni, 170, 186, 187
ethos, 15 (definition), 167–168,
      167 (definition), 176, 184, 190
eunoia, 167
euphemism, 59
Evans, Jessica, 72, 74
Ewalt, Joshua P., 278–279, 296
exigence, 221 (definition), 228–229, 232,
      233, 238–239, 240, 250, 256

Fabj, Valeria, 79–80, 270
fact, claim of, 110
Fausto-Sterling, Anne, 45
Felski, Rita, 273, 277
first persona, 213, 215, 217
Fisher, Mary, 77–78
Fisher, Walter, 51, 149
Fiske, John, 186
fitting response, 233–236,
      233 (definition), 239, 250–251,
      252, 256
Flores, Lisa, 277
forensic discourse, 226
Foss, Sonja K., 76
Foucault, Michel, 27–28, 61
fourth persona, 217
frame,
  comic, 151–154, 151 (definition)
  tragic, 151–154, 151(definition)

Franken, Al, 115–116
Franklin, Benjamin, 46
Fraser, Nancy, 268, 270, 271, 272, 273,
      276, 278, 290

Gage, Frances Dana, 189
Gallagher, Victoria J., 85
Geertz, Clifford, 23, 24, 28, 136
genre, 233–235, 233 (definition)
gestalt, 54
Gilbert, Christopher, 294
Ginsberg, Benjamin, 279–281
Giuliani, Rudolph, 279
Goffman, Erving, 166, 169, 178, 208
Goodell, Roger, 185
Goodnight, G. Thomas, 119–120
goodwill, 167
Gorgias, 14
Gramsci, Antonio, 29
Gretzky, Paula, 5
Grimké, Sarah, 44, 62
Grimké Weld, Angelina, 10, 44, 62
Gronbeck, Bruce E., 17, 229, 252

Habermas, Jürgen, 268–270, 271, 272,
      273, 276, 278, 287, 297
Hall, Stuart, 29, 30, 71, 72, 73, 74, 75
Hallenbeck, Sarah, 11
Hamer, Fannie Lou, 226–227
Hariman, Robert, 82–84
Hart, Frederick, 86
Hasian, Marouf, Jr., 272, 276
Hauser, Gerard A., 267
hegemony, 29–30, 29 (definition), 73–74,
      92, 133, 171, 274
Hitler, Adolf, 5, 10, 153
Hollihan, Thomas A., 172
Holmes, Oliver Wendell (Justice), 19
Hope, Diane S., 73, 81, 92
Horwitz, Linda Diane, 79
Howell, Sharon, 28
Huglen, Mark E., 28
Huxman, Susan Schultz, 232
hybrid publics, 272

iconic photographs, 82–83
identification, 8–10, 8 (definition), 16, 17,
      21, 24, 203–204, 203 (definition)
  audience and, 203–204, 212, 213,
      214, 219

language and, 45
publics and, 275, 277–278
rhetor and, 170, 174, 176, 180
visual rhetoric and, 82, 83, 90–91
identity, 9, 25, 27, 169–175, 169
(definition), 176, 177–178, 217
narrative and, 132, 136
as a public or counterpublic, 267,
271, 272, 274, 275, 277–278,
279, 280, 285
as rhetorical, 170–174
strategic essentialism, 174–175
visual rhetoric and, 74, 77, 82, 91
ideograph, 49 (definition), 55, 91, 92,
210, 277
ideology, 27–30, 28 (definition), 49, 74,
75, 208, 215, 253
image (rhetor's), 179–181,
180 (definition)
image event, 88–92, 88 (definition),
181, 295
inflated language, 59–60
intersectionality, 170 (definition),
171, 172
Irwin-Zarecka, Iwona, 25
Isocrates, 14

James, LeBron, 129–130
Jamieson, Kathleen Hall, 138–139,
233–236, 251–252
Jasinski, James, 8
Jenkins, Mark, 99–100, 109, 112, 113
Jeppeson, Marsha S., 86
John Paul II (Pope), 245–247
"Address to the General Audience,"
245–246
Johnson, Davi, 92
Johnson, Lyndon B., 235
Johnson, Mark, 51–52, 105
Jones, John M., 51
Jones, Mary Harris "Mother," 171
Jordan, Barbara, 77

Kennedy, George A., 13, 101
Kennedy, John F., 4, 22, 235
Kerry, John, 50, 279
King, Martin Luther, Jr., 4, 219
Klumpp, James F., 28
Kramarae, Cheris, 27
Krizek, Robert L., 172

Kuusisto, Riikka, 52–53

Lake, Randall, 166
Lakoff, George, 51–52, 105
Langer, Susanne K., 53–54
Lee, Harper, 138, 146
Leff, Michael, 219
Lewis, Stacy, 5
Lincoln, Abraham, 4, 19, 81, 134, 251,
255–256, 281
linguistic relativity, theory of, 43–45
Linkugel, Wil A., 167
logos, 15 (definition), 101
Lott, Trent, 291
Lovell, Terry, 135
Lucaites, John Louis, 23, 27, 49, 50, 82,
83–84
Lutz, William, 59–60

MacIntyre, Alasdair, 51
MacKinnon, Catharine A., 111, 274
Malcolm X, 4
Mandziuk, Roseann M., 189
Mansbridge, Jane, 215–216, 275
Martin, Judith N., 24
McCain, John, 230
McGee, Michael Calvin, 49, 213
memorials, 25, 27, 84–88
memory, 24–27
collective, 24–27, 25 (definition),
85, 132
personal, 131, 140
public, 24–27, 25 (definition), 85, 86,
133–134, 133 (definition), 140
Merkel, Angela, 209
metaphor, 5, 23, 51–53, 51 (definition),
59, 105–106, 122, 277
Michel, Neil, 76
monuments, 25, 27, 73, 84–88
Moraga, Cherríe, 218
Morgan, Piers, 165
Morris, Charles E., III, 217
Morris, Richard, 85, 133
museums, 84–88
myth, 23, 53, 135 (definition), 136,
205, 215

Nakayama, Thomas K., 24, 172
narrative, 49–51, 113 (definition), 166
fidelity, 149–150

form and function, 131–140
  judging, 140–154
  probability, 149–150
  values and, 135–137, 140, 143
negotiated reading, 30, 74 (definition)
networked public screen, 294–297,
    296 (definition)
networked publics, 290–294,
    291 (definition)
Nixon, Richard M., 168
nonparticipation, 253–254
Nothstine, William L., 30

Obama, Barack, 47, 70, 89, 102, 116,
    139, 143, 147, 172, 179, 181,
    202–203, 204, 205, 207, 230,
    232, 250, 251, 267, 286
  "Remarks by the President at 9/11
    Museum Dedication," 248–250
Ohl, Jessy J., 278–279, 296
O'Keefe, Daniel J., 101
Olbrechts-Tyteca, Lucie, 71, 202, 205
Ono, Kent O., 271
oppositional reading, 30, 74 (definition)
Orwell, George, 58–59, 116
oscillating publics, 274–276,
    275 (definition)

Packwood, Joshua, 170
Palin, Sarah, 230
particular audience, 119
pathos, 15 (definition), 101, 201, 203,
    204–206, 204 (definition)
Pearce, W. Barnett, 241, 251, 252, 253,
    254, 255
Peeples, Jennifer, 278, 296
Penelope, Julia, 44, 60
Perelman, Chaïm, 119, 202, 205
performance, 165–167, 166 (definition),
    171, 172, 175, 177–179, 180,
    208, 216
Pericles, 255 (funeral oration)
Perry, Rick, 181
persona, 165–167, 165 (definition)
  facets of, 167–181
  first, 213 (definition), 215, 217
  fourth, 217
  performance of, 165–167, 180
  second, 213–214, 215, 217
  third, 214–216

personal memory, 131
personal sphere of argument, 119
personification, 142
persuasive continuum, 20–23
Pezzullo, Phaedra, 279
Pfister, Damien Smith, 278–279, 291, 296
phronesis, 167
Pierce, Charles Sanders, 42
Pineda, Richard D., 295
Plato, 14, 15, 51
  Gorgias, 14
plot, 142 (definition), 143, 147, 148, 149
policy, claim of, 111
polysemous, 186–187, 186 (definition)
polyvalence, 186–187, 186 (definition)
post hoc ergo propter hoc fallacy, 138
posthumanist theory of agency, 11–12
postmodernism, 184–190, 184 (definition)
Poulakos, John, 14
power, 27 (definition), 28, 31, 106, 134
  audience and, 201, 218
  language and, 49, 61
  publics and, 267, 270, 271, 272,
      277, 278, 280, 297
  rhetor and, 172, 173, 174,
      175–177, 178
  visual rhetoric and, 73–74, 77, 86
practical wisdom, 167
Prelli, Lawrence J., 72
presence, 71 (definition), 79
presentational symbolism, 46 (definition),
    55, 71, 90
presumption, 117–118
public emotion, 206–208, 206 (definition)
public memory, 24–27, 25 (definition),
    85, 86, 133–134, 133 (definition),
    140
public screen, 294–297, 295 (definition)
  networked, 294–297
public sphere, 61–62, 89, 120, 268–272,
    268 (definition), 283, 295, 296, 297
  of argument, 120–122
  counterpublics and, 273–278
  in digital age, 283–285
  public screen, 294–297
  transnational publics and, 278
public vocabulary, 48–53, 49 (definition),
    62, 281
publics, 265–297
  counterpublics, 273–278

in digital age, 283–285
economy and, 278–281
enclaved, 274–276
hybrid, 272
    response to, 235
in Internet age, 281–283
networked, 290–294
oscillating, 274–276, 275 (definition)
relationship among, 281
strong, 271, 274, 276, 293, 297
weak, 271, 293
Pucci, Enrico, Jr., 86
Putin, Vladimir, 254, 270

qualifiers, 113

reading,
dominant, 74
negotiated, 30, 74
oppositional, 30, 74
Reagan, Ronald W., 60, 108, 138–139,
    168–169, 235, 236, 238–239, 240,
    280
"The Space Shuttle *Challenger*
    Tragedy Address," 236–238
rebuttal, conditions of, 113
representative anecdote, 150–151
resignification, 56–58, 56 (definition), 62
rhetor, 6 (definition), 13 (definition), 15,
    163–191
audience and, 203–211
authority and, 175–179
ethos of, 15 (definition), 101, 167–168,
    167 (definition), 190
facets of persona of, 167–181
first persona, 213, 215, 217
fourth persona, 217
identity and, 169–175
image and, 179–181
performance of persona, 165–167, 180
in a postmodern world, 184–190
rhetorical situation and, 225, 226, 228,
    229, 235, 239–240, 241–242,
    245, 250–251, 255
strategic essentialism and, 174–175
rhetoric, 6 (definition), 170
adapting audiences to, 212–219
adapting to audiences, 201–211
as addressed, 16, 201–203
Aristotle's definition of, 15, 225–226
as civic engagement, 13–20

constitutive, 8
constraints on, 20–27, 231–233
of display, 72
public sphere and, 266, 267, 268, 269,
    270, 272, 275, 276, 277
as situational, 226–239
situations as rhetorical, 239–240
as symbolic action, 6–13
synergy with situation, 240–250
visual rhetoric, 12, 30, 69–92, 100,
    211, 296
rhetorical agency, 11, 211
rhetorical audience, 202, 229–231
rhetorical constraints, 231–233
rhetorical situation, 225–257,
    227 (definition)
Aristotle's notion of, 15, 225–226
constraints, 231–233
defining, 241–242, 244, 250, 256
exigence, 227 (definition), 228–229,
    232, 233, 238–239, 240, 250, 256
fitting response, 233–236,
    233 (definition), 239, 250–251,
    252, 256
rhetor and, 225, 226, 228, 229,
    235, 239–240, 241–242, 245,
    205–251, 255
rhetoric as situational, 226–239
situations as rhetorical, 239–240
synergy between rhetoric and situation,
    240–250
visual rhetoric and, 74
Robinson, Jackie, 133–134
Romney, Mitt, 108–109, 142, 285, 286
Roosevelt, Franklin Delano, 148, 214,
    232, 233
Rosenthal, Joe, 83
Rowland, Robert C., 51
Ryan, Paul, 286

Sapir, Edward, 43–44
Sapir-Whorf hypothesis, 43–44
de Saussure, Ferdinand, 42
Schwartz, Barry, 25, 134
Sci, Susan, 286
second persona, 213–214, 215, 217
semiotics, 42–43
Silver, Nate, 141
slacktivism, 288
Sloop, John, 271
Snowden, Edward, 209

Sobnosky, Matthew J., 121, 270
Socrates, 14
social power, 175–177, 175 (definition), 178
social reality, 12–13, 12 (definition), 16, 30, 42, 146, 266, 272
  in definition of rhetoric, 6
  language and the construction of, 42–45
social truth, 136, 146–149, 146 (definition)
sophists, 14, 15, 16
Sowards, Stacey K., 295
spheres of argument 119–122
  personal, 119
  public, 120
  technical, 120
Spivak, Gayatri Chakravorty, 174, 175
Squires, Catherine, 275
Stanton, Elizabeth Cady, 114–115
Stevens, John Paul (Justice), 69
Stewart, Jon, 207–208, 254–255
strategic essentialism, 174–175
strong publics, 271, 274, 276, 293, 297
Sunstein, Cass R., 289
syllogism, 106–107, 106 (definition)
symbolic action, 7–12
  components of
    audiences, 199–219
    publics and counterpublics, 265–297
    rhetorical situation, 225–257
    rhetors, 163–191
  constraints and resources for, 20–30
  forms of,
    argument, 99–123
    language, 41–63
    narrative, 129–154
    visual, 69–92
  social reality, 12–13, 16, 30
symbolism,
  discursive, 53
  presentational, 53 (definition), 55, 71, 90
symbols, 3–7, 6 (definition), 16
  condensation, 55
  social reality and, 6–7
  verbal symbols, 6
  visual symbols, 7

Tanner, Michael, 209–211

technical sphere of argument, 120
terministic screen, 45–48, 47 (definition), 56
third persona, 214–216, 214 (definition)
Todd, Chuck, 202–203
Tonn, Mari Boor, 171
Toomey, Pat, 106–107
Toulmin, Stephen, 109–114, 116–117
tragic frame, 151–154, 151 (definition)
Triechler, Paula A., 27
truncated passive, 58, 60 (definition), 61, 216
Truth, Sojourner, 45, 188–189
Tyson, Neil deGrasse, 104–105, 121

universal audience, 119
Utley, Ebony A., 219

value, claim of, 110
values, 208
  audience and, 202, 203, 208–211
  culture and, 23, 26
  in epideictic discourse (situation), 226
  ideology and, 28–29
  language and, 50, 51, 55
  narrative and, 135–137, 140, 143
  rhetor and, 167, 168–169, 178
  social truth and, 146–149
  visual rhetoric and, 71, 86
Vatz, Richard E., 239–240, 241
verbal symbols, 6
virtue, 13, 167 (definition), 226
visual culture, 72–75, 91
visual rhetoric, 69–92
  analysis of, 76–77
  enactment and, 77–78
  identification and, 82, 83, 90, 91
  types of, 77–92
    bodies, 77–80
    image events, 88–92, 181, 295, 296
    monuments, memorials, and museums, 25, 27, 73, 84–88
    photographs, 80–84
visual symbols, 7
vivacity, 139

Wahls, Zach, 181–184, 188
  "Speaks about Family," 182–183
Walker, Scott, 269
Wander, Philip, 214, 215
Ware, B. L., 167

Warner, Michael, 272, 277
warrant, 109, 112 (definition), 113, 114,
    115, 117, 120
Warren, Earl (Chief Justice), 199–200
Watkins, Carleton, 81, 82
weak publics, 271, 293
Weaver, Richard M., 55
Weld, Angelina Grimké, 10
Wells, Ida B., 21–22
Welter, Barbara, 62
West, Cornell, 177–178

West, Isaac, 9
Whately, Richard, 117
Whedbee, Karen, 117
White, James Boyd, 8
Wiesel, Elie, 139–140
Wilson, Darren, 110
Wing, Adrien Katherine, 170
Wolkowitz, Carol, 135

Yousafzai, Malala, 4

About the Authors

Catherine Helen Palczewski is professor of communication studies, former director of debate, and an affiliate faculty member in Women's and Gender Studies at the University of Northern Iowa. She received her BS, MA, and PhD from Northwestern University. She teaches courses in rhetorical theory, the rhetoric of social protest, rhetorical criticism, argumentation, gender in communication, and political communication. She has served as coeditor of Argumentation and Advocacy and has published essays in that journal, as well as in the Quarterly Journal of Speech, Communication Studies, NWSA Journal, and the Southern Communication Journal. She has also published numerous book chapters. She has served on the editorial boards of the Quarterly Journal of Speech, Argumentation and Advocacy, Women's Studies in Communication, Communication Studies, Controversia, Communication Monographs, and the Southern Communication Journal. She has received the Francine Merritt Award for Outstanding Contributions to the Lives of Women in Communication, the Iowa Regents Award for Faculty Excellence, the University of Northern Iowa College of Humanities and Fine Arts Faculty Excellence Award, the George Ziegelmueller Outstanding Debate Educator Award, and the Rohrer Award for the Outstanding Publication in Argumentation. In 2001, she was the keynote speaker at the AFA/NCA Summer Conference on Argumentation, a conference she directed in 2013. She edited the selected works, Disturbing Argument, from the 2013 conference.

Richard Ice is professor of communication and interim provost at the College of St. Benedict and St. John's University. He received his AB from Wabash College. He received his MA and PhD from the University of Iowa. He teaches courses in rhetorical analysis, classical rhetoric, freedom of speech, public address, group communication, and organizational communication. He has published essays in Management Communication Quarterly and Communication Quarterly, as well as several book chapters. He has received the St. John's University Robert L. Spaeth Teacher of Distinction Award and the College of St. Benedict / St. John's University Academic Advisor Award.

John Fritch is professor of communication studies and dean of the College of Humanities, Arts and Sciences at the University of Northern Iowa. He received his BA from the University of Nebraska–Lincoln. His MA and PhD are from the University of Kansas. He teaches courses in rhetorical theory, language and communication, and ethics. He coedits Argumentation and Advocacy. He has published essays in that journal, as well as in the Southern Journal of Forensics, several editions of the published papers of the biannual NCA/AFA conference on argumentation, and A Century of Transformation: Studies in Honor of the 100th Anniversary of the Eastern Communication Association. Formerly, he was the director of forensics at Southwest Missouri State University. Currently, he is the director of the National Debate Tournament. He has received the Donn W. Parson Young Educator Award, the Outstanding Teaching Award from the College of Arts and Letters at Missouri State University, and the Outstanding Graduate Faculty Member in Communication Studies Award at Missouri State. He was recognized as a Centennial Scholar by the Eastern Communication Association.